OXFORD MONOGRAPHS IN INTERNATIONAL LAW

NECESSITY AND PROPORTIONALITY AND THE RIGHT OF SELF-DEFENCE IN INTERNATIONAL LAW

OXFORD MONOGRAPHS IN INTERNATIONAL LAW

The aim of this series is to publish important and original pieces of research on all aspects of international law. Topics that are given particular prominence are those which, while of interest to the academic lawyer, also have important bearing on issues which touch the actual conduct of international relations. Nonetheless the series is wide in scope and includes monographs on the history and philosophical foundations of international law.

RECENT TITLES IN THE SERIES

The Concept of an International Organization in International Law
Lorenzo Gasbarri

Neutrality in Contemporary International law
James Upcher

Geographical Change and the Law of the Sea
Kate Purcell

Statehood and the State-Like in International Law
Rowan Nicholson

Confronting the Shadow State
Henri Decœur

Irresolvable Norm Conflicts in International Law
The Concept of a Legal Dilemma
Valentin Jeutner

Necessity and Proportionality and the Right of Self-Defence in International Law

CHRIS O'MEARA

OXFORD
UNIVERSITY PRESS

OXFORD
UNIVERSITY PRESS

Great Clarendon Street, Oxford, OX2 6DP,
United Kingdom

Oxford University Press is a department of the University of Oxford.
It furthers the University's objective of excellence in research, scholarship,
and education by publishing worldwide. Oxford is a registered trade mark of
Oxford University Press in the UK and in certain other countries

First Edition published in 2021

Impression: 1

Published in the United States of America by Oxford University Press
198 Madison Avenue, New York, NY 10016, United States of America

British Library Cataloguing in Publication Data

Data available

Library of Congress Control Number: 2020948223

ISBN 978–0–19–886340–3

DOI: 10.1093/oso/9780198863403.001.0001

Printed and bound in the UK by
TJ Books Limited

Series Editors Preface

There can be few more contested topics in international law than the scope and content of the rules regarding the exercise by a state of the right of self-defence. Arguments have persisted over what threshold of force must be reached before a right of self-defence arises, over how the right operates with respect to 'armed attacks' by non-state actors, and over the temporal question of whether there is any right of anticipatory self-defence. But these are not the arguments with which Christopher O'Meara engages in this book. Rather, his focus is on the legal requirements of necessity and proportionality by which the exercise of the right of self-defence is constrained, on which courts and scholars have trodden relatively lightly. Animating his work is the concern that, as long as the scope and content of necessity and proportionality remain normatively undetermined, the potential of international law to regulate when and how states use force is weakened. Accordingly, his focus is on defining in principle and in practice the requirements of necessity and proportionality in order to provide a better understanding of – if not a predictive tool for – how these requirements may be used in future.

With an initial nod to that enduring *locus classicus* on the right of self-defence, the *Caroline* incident of 1837, Dr O'Meara's raw material is an 'audit' of relevant state practice and *opinio juris* during the Charter era, as the foundation for an account of the concepts of and distinctions between necessity and proportionality in the contemporary law of self-defence. An innovative element of his argument is to distinguish between 'general' and 'specific' necessity, a novel contribution to the discourse. He also tackles the thorny question of the exercise of self-defence against non-state actors, shifting from more conventional analysis, which focuses on the problem of determining whether there has been an 'armed attack', to issues of necessity and proportionality. While consistent with, for example, the ILA's recent report on the use of force, this will doubtless fuel further debate, a debate in which Dr O'Meara fights his corner well.

This eloquent, accessible, and well-structured work will appeal to an audience of international legal scholars, adjudicative bodies confronted with these issues, and those in the fields of political science and international relations more generally.

CR, RO'K

Oxford and Milan
February 2021

Acknowledgements

This book began life as a doctoral thesis that I started at University College London in 2014. Writing the thesis and developing it into a monograph has been a transformative process. It has taken me from being a practising lawyer into the world of academia. This could not have happened without the support of an array of noteworthy people who deserve my sincere gratitude.

First and foremost, I owe so much to Professor Kimberley Trapp, my remarkable primary PhD supervisor. Professor Trapp inspired me to be a scholar and an educator, and I am indebted to her for developing and refining my thinking, insisting on precision and for being a source of patient wisdom and friendly encouragement. I thank her for being so generous with her time, for her unfailing good humour, passion for the project and beautifully detailed feedback. I am lucky to have had such a supportive guide and mentor. I thank Professor Roger O'Keefe, my secondary PhD supervisor, for his frank and incisive comments, delivered with his unique style and valuable rigour. Professor James A Green and Professor Phillipe Sands were admirable PhD examiners. They engaged constructively with my work and challenged me to defend and advance my ideas. Professor Green in particular offered wise counsel in developing key aspects of my thesis and I am indebted to him for the time and support that he has offered me ever since. I am also grateful for the backing of friends and colleagues at University College London and to the Faculty of Laws for generously funding my research. Thanks to Dr Steven Vaughan for his guidance regarding structuring my thesis and emphasizing its strengths, as well as his counsel for finding that first precious academic job.

Being a Fellow at the London School of Economics and Political Science gave me the time and space to develop my thesis and turn it into this book. The Law Department was wonderfully supportive of my work and I have been fortunate to have taught gifted students and worked with talented colleagues. Merel Alstein and Jack McNichol of Oxford University Press have been exemplary in guiding me through drafting the initial book proposal, surviving a thorough peer-review process and steering the manuscript to publication. I thank them for making this undertaking such an enjoyable experience.

My research has also benefitted from my time as a Visiting Researcher at the University of Leiden and at Harvard Law School. Throughout the months spent at these marvellous institutions, I spent many hours sharing my work with students, visitors and faculty members, all of whom have aided its progression. Amongst others, I am grateful to Dr Erik Koppe, Professor Jack Goldsmith, Professor Ashley Deeks and Professor Allan Rock.

I am immensely appreciative of the support of my family and friends. They have been stalwarts in trying their hardest to understand a little of 'what I do'. They have wanted the very best for me and have been there to help me along my chosen path. Special mention goes to Dino Fontes, who kindly offered to review sections of this book. I am thankful for his speedy inspection and laser-like attention to detail. Last, but not least, thank you to Piers, my partner, whose care and unflagging encouragement has helped me to navigate some difficult times and to complete this project.

Table of Contents

List of Abbreviations

ANC	African National Congress
ARSIWA	Articles on Responsibility of States for Internationally Wrongful Acts
DPIH	directly participating in hostilities
DRC	Democratic Republic of the Congo
EU	European Union
IAEA	International Atomic Energy Agency
ICJ	International Court of Justice
ICRC	International Committee of the Red Cross
IHL	international humanitarian law
IIFFMCG	Council of the European Union's Independent International Fact-Finding Mission on the Conflict in Georgia
IIS	Iraqi Intelligence Service
ILA	International Law Association
ILC	International Law Commission
NAM	Non-Aligned Movement
NATO	North Atlantic Treaty Organization
NSA	non-state actor
PKK	Kurdistan Workers' Party
PLO	Palestine Liberation Organization
UN	United Nations
UNGA	UN General Assembly
UNSC	UN Security Council
WMD	Weapons of Mass Destruction

1
Introduction

The legal regulation of military force remains at the forefront of international concern and academic debate. States, the International Court of Justice ('ICJ' or the 'Court') and academic commentators have long ruminated over the meaning and scope of the prohibition of the threat or use of force contained in Article 2(4) of the UN Charter and the inherent right of individual and collective self-defence recognized by Article 51.[1] States almost invariably invoke self-defence to justify using force extra-territorially,[2] even in the most dubious of circumstances when their acts are subsequently condemned. Such 'ritual incantation'[3] of the right is nearly universally accompanied, either explicitly or implicitly, by assertions that the purported defensive force is necessary or proportionate, or both.[4] Doubt will always exist regarding the extent to which international law can limit states using force, but the fact that states habitually justify their actions in law points to an acceptance that using force is subject to legal constraints.[5] Consequently, this topic is situated at the heart of preserving international peace and security.

The scope and content of the *jus ad bellum* rules pertaining to the exercise of the right of self-defence remain a controversial and intensely contested topic. In particular, arguments persist over whether a threshold of violence is required before a right of self-defence arises, how the right operates in relation to armed attacks by non-state actors ('NSAs') and temporal issues pertaining to any right of anticipatory self-defence.[6] Yet, within these debates (and as explored further below), it is universally recognized that for defensive force to be lawful, it must be both 'necessary' and 'proportionate'. Although not referenced in the UN Charter itself, these

[1] Charter of the United Nations (adopted 26 June 1945, entered into force 24 October 1945) 892 UNTS 119. Art 2(4) prohibits the threat or use of force against the territorial integrity or political independence of any state, or in any other manner inconsistent with the purposes of the United Nations ('UN'). Art 51 affirms the inherent right of individual or collective self-defence if an armed attack occurs.

[2] Michael N Schmitt, 'Preemptive Strategies in International Law' (2003) 24(2) Mich J Int'l L 513, 543–544; Christine Gray, *International Law and the Use of Force* (4th edn, OUP 2018) 121.

[3] Gray, *Use of Force* (n 2) 125.

[4] James A Green, *The International Court of Justice and Self-Defence in International Law* (Hart Publishing 2009) 108–109, 208. This conclusion will be explored throughout this book. Implicit reference means that a state might not have used the words 'necessary' or 'proportionate' but has nevertheless referred to the content of either or both of these requirements when justifying or responding to claims of self-defence.

[5] Philippe Sands, *Lawless World: America and the Making and Breaking of Global Rules from FDR's Atlantic Charter to George W. Bush's Illegal War* (Viking Penguin 2005) 179–180.

[6] These issues are considered in the following chapters.

Necessity and Proportionality and the Right of Self-Defence in International Law. Chris O'Meara, Oxford University Press (2021). © Chris O'Meara. DOI: 10.1093/oso/9780198863403.003.0001

two requirements are recognized as 'essential components' of the normative framework pertaining to the use of defensive force.[7] They form the core of the contemporary right of self-defence.[8]

Necessity and proportionality are fundamental to the exercise of the right of self-defence but, until now, they have not received the attention they deserve. As Sections 1.1 to 1.3 illustrate, judicial examination of necessity and proportionality has been light and their meaning and importance as legal tools have not been fully explored in the academic literature or by states in their justifications and scrutiny of uses of force. The focus of the ICJ and scholars has instead been on the trigger of the right of self-defence under Article 51 of the UN Charter, being the occurrence of an 'armed attack'. Whereas states place great importance on necessity and proportionality when justifying and reviewing claims of self-defence, they have not reached a consensus regarding what is meant by these terms. The neglect of these core precepts of the *jus ad bellum* might be explained on the basis that the operation of necessity and proportionality is highly contingent on the facts of each case and that they are difficult to apply in practice. Also, proportionality appears in both the *jus ad bellum* and international humanitarian law ('IHL').[9] The relationship between the requirement in each legal regime is complex and states might prefer to rely on the clearer rules of IHL to explain and review putatively defensive actions.[10] These possible explanations do not diminish the importance of *jus ad bellum* necessity and proportionality, however.

That the scope and content of necessity and proportionality remain normatively undetermined weakens the potential of international law to regulate when and how states use force. Such indeterminacy deprives states, courts, international organizations and scholars of effective tools to guide decision-making regarding

[7] Institut de Droit International, Tenth Commission, 'Present Problems of the Use of Armed Force in International Law, Sub-Group on Self-Defence' (27 October 2007) <http://www.idi-iil.org/app/uploads/2017/06/Roucounas.pdf> accessed 5 September 2020, 214, Resolution 2.

[8] The ICJ has confirmed that the UN Charter recognizes a 'natural' or 'inherent' pre-existing customary right of individual and collective self-defence, which has been 'confirmed and influenced by the Charter'. *Military and Paramilitary Activities in and against Nicaragua* (*Nicaragua v US*) (Merits) [1986] ICJ Rep 14 (hereafter '*Nicaragua*') paras 176, 193. The Court recognized that the UN Charter does not regulate all aspects of the right, but operates alongside existing customary international law, including the requirements of necessity and proportionality. *Nicaragua*, paras 176, 194. An argument may be made that the UN Charter and customary rules on the use of force and self-defence are not identical, but the ICJ's approach in *Nicaragua* shows that it considers the two regimes to be largely equivalent. See Claus Kress, 'The International Court of Justice and the "Principle of Non-Use of Force"' in Marc Weller (ed), *The Oxford Handbook on the Use of Force in International Law* (OUP 2015) 561, 568–569. The only difference that the Court has identified is the lack of a customary duty to report the exercise of the right of self-defence to the UN Security Council ('UNSC'). *Nicaragua*, paras 181, 188, 200. Regarding the UN Charter requirements, see n 86. For a contrary judicial position, see *Nicaragua*, diss op Jennings, 529–533. This book proceeds on the basis, as per the prevailing view amongst commentators, that Art 51 excludes any pre-UN Charter customary right that is *incompatible* with the UN Charter.

[9] IHL is also known as the *jus in bello* and the laws of armed conflict. IHL is the term adopted for the purposes of this book.

[10] Judith Gardam, *Necessity, Proportionality and the Use of Force by States* (CUP 2004) 20–24. See further Section 3.4.1.

resorting to force, to review the legality of uses of force and to guard against abuse of the right of self-defence.[11] Necessity and proportionality, more fully understood, can be better employed by such bodies to review and regulate the exercise of a state's right of self-defence. Their application can also help solve some of the long-standing controversies described at the beginning of this chapter that have been traditionally analysed within the ambit of the armed attack trigger of the right of self-defence.

The purpose of this book is to address this legal and normative gap. It seeks to answer two principal questions: (a) what is the meaning in both theory and practice of necessity and proportionality as they pertain to the right of self-defence following the adoption of the UN Charter? and (b) how can a better understanding of these requirements be used in the future?[12] This book provides an up-to-date analytical framework of the current law. It does this by undertaking the most extensive study to date of the applicable jurisprudence, academic commentary and, most importantly, relevant state practice from 1945 to the present day. This enunciation of the *lex lata* encompasses an exploration of the conceptual meanings of necessity and proportionality, explains the distinctions between them, confronts existing preconceptions and clarifies areas of controversy. This book ultimately presents a detailed understanding of each concept that bridges theory and practice.

Sections 1.1 to 1.3 elaborate on how the ICJ, scholars and states have approached necessity and proportionality. These sections situate this book in relation to the current understanding of each requirement and provide context for what follows. Section 1.4 proceeds to examine the provenance of necessity and proportionality and Section 1.5 sets out the approach that this author takes to explore their contemporary meaning. Section 1.6 concludes Chapter 1 by offering some initial observations that frame and underpin the subsequent analysis. Chapter 2 focuses on the meaning and content of necessity. It argues, for the first time, that there are two different types of necessity. In so doing, this author proposes a novel taxonomy to distinguish between them. This distinction addresses, and better explains, the two principal and distinct concerns of necessity that are reflected in state practice, ICJ jurisprudence and scholarship: (a) is military force required at all in the circumstances (an issue of 'general necessity'), and (b) if so, where must such force be directed (an issue of 'specific necessity')? Without general necessity, the applicability of both specific necessity and proportionality is moot. Drawing on core principles

[11] Regarding the benefits of increased normative determinacy, see Ashley Deeks, '"Unwilling or Unable": Toward a Normative Framework for Extra-Territorial Self-Defense' (2012) 52 Va J Int'l L 483.

[12] For an overview of the applicability of necessity and proportionality to collective security and the powers of the UNSC under Chapter VII of the UN Charter, see Gardam, *Necessity, Proportionality* (n 10) 188–229. Absent consent or UNSC authorization, the right of self-defence is the only explicitly recognized basis for the unilateral use of force in international law. This book will not consider the so-called right of humanitarian intervention. For this author's views on that topic, see Chris O'Meara, 'Should International Law Recognize a Right of Humanitarian Intervention?' (2017) 66(2) ICLQ 441.

of IHL, Chapter 2 provides a clearer and more workable understanding of necessity that highlights both the weaknesses in, and opportunities for, its operation.

Chapter 3 proceeds to examine proportionality. As with Chapter 2, it employs primary and secondary sources of international law to provide a more coherent and granular realization of this requirement and how it operates in practice. In particular, it offers a nuanced analysis of the various factors and interests that inform the review of 'how much' force states may use in their defence and whether third parties might view such action as excessive. Chapter 3 draws upon the laws of state responsibility to consider how a diversity of interests are affected by the exercise of self-defence. Applicable rules of IHL are also examined, including how they interact with the *jus ad bellum* on a regime level and might affect a review of *jus ad bellum* proportionality in specific instances. Chapter 4 builds on the analysis of the previous chapters by considering how necessity and proportionality are adapted to apply to defensive action against NSAs. With a particular focus on international terrorism, their utility and limitations are brought to the fore. Chapter 5 completes this book by setting out its conclusions and considerations for the future development of international law.

1.1 ICJ Jurisprudence

The ICJ's jurisprudence on self-defence provides an important, if relatively limited, source of guidance for the present enquiry. The vast majority of disputes regarding self-defence claims do not reach the ICJ on their merits.[13] To date, the Court has dealt directly with the substantive rules of self-defence in only five cases. Three were merits decisions: *Nicaragua*, *Oil Platforms* and *Armed Activities*.[14] Two were advisory opinions: *Nuclear Weapons* and *Wall*.[15] In addition, the Court has touched upon claims pertaining to the use of force in a more limited fashion, the most obvious example being *Corfu Channel*,[16] where the UK claimed to be acting pursuant to a more broadly understood right of 'self-help'.[17]

The five core self-defence cases offer varying degrees of insight. Whereas the majority in *Nicaragua* devoted much of their opinion to the law pertaining to self-defence, the Court in *Wall* dismissed Israel's self-defence claim in a cursory two

[13] See generally Green, *The International Court of Justice* (n 4) 165–206.

[14] *Nicaragua* (n 8); *Case Concerning Oil Platforms (Iran v US)* (Judgment) [2003] ICJ Rep 161 (hereafter '*Oil Platforms*'); *Case Concerning Armed Activities on the Territory of the Congo (Democratic Republic of the Congo v Uganda)* (Judgment) [2007] ICJ Rep 168 (hereafter '*Armed Activities*').

[15] *Legality of the Threat or Use of Nuclear Weapons* (Advisory Opinion) [1996] ICJ Rep 226 (hereafter '*Nuclear Weapons*'); *Legal Consequences of the Construction of a Wall in the Occupied Palestinian Territories* (Advisory Opinion) [2004] ICJ Rep 136 (hereafter '*Wall*').

[16] *Corfu Channel (United Kingdom v Albania)* (Merits) [1949] ICJ Rep 4 (hereafter '*Corfu Channel*').

[17] *Corfu Channel*, ibid, Reply Submitted, Under the Order of the Court of 26 March, 1948, by the Government of the United Kingdom of Great Britain and Northern Ireland, 30 July 1948, para 82(g).

paragraphs.[18] As noted, the cases have also tended to focus on the 'armed attack', which the ICJ has viewed as the most important element of the right.[19] The Court has, however, emphasized the importance of necessity and proportionality in four of the five self-defence cases[20] and confirmed that they are requirements of customary international law in three.[21] The Court has also been clear that it expects rigid and objective adherence to these requirements. Whereas a state might form its own initial view, the Court has strongly rejected the notion that the determination of necessity lies within a state's discretion, even where acting in good faith. Instead, it has stipulated that the test of necessity is 'strict and objective, leaving no room for any "measure of discretion"'.[22] The Court presumably adopts the same approach for proportionality.

Nevertheless, the ICJ has treated necessity and proportionality as subsidiary or accessory criteria. This is demonstrated by the limited amount of space it has devoted to them in its judgments.[23] Furthermore, the Court has not sought to define necessity or proportionality in general or abstract terms, or to place them within a wider conceptual framework. Therefore, it has been steadfast in affirming their application to claims of self-defence, but has offered only minimal insight into their scope and content. This is perhaps understandable, given that no case has been determined on the basis of necessity and proportionality. Other than *Nuclear Weapons*, the legality of avowed acts of self-defence was decided on the basis that none of the respondent states was able to establish that it had been the victim of an armed attack.[24]

This fact has not prevented the Court from making *obiter dicta* pronouncements that have often been confusing. For example, it has rightly confirmed an armed attack as the condition *sine qua non* of the right of self-defence.[25] Yet, it has also noted that in the absence of an armed attack, strict compliance with the canons of necessity and proportionality will not render any purported defensive action lawful, and any breach of these additional prerequisites will constitute additional grounds of wrongfulness.[26] It is difficult to fathom, however, how these latter comments have

[18] Paras 138–139.

[19] See further Green, *The International Court of Justice* (n 4) 7, 23–62.

[20] *Nicaragua* (n 8) paras 176, 194, 237; *Nuclear Weapons* (n 15) paras 30, 41, 48; *Oil Platforms* (n 14) paras 43, 51, 73–77; *Armed Activities* (n 14) paras 147, 304.

[21] *Nicaragua* (n 8) para 176; *Nuclear Weapons* (n 15) para 41; *Oil Platforms* (n 14) paras 73–77.

[22] *Oil Platforms* (n 14) para 73.

[23] This is particularly noticeable in the contentious cases involving specific claims of self-defence. In *Nicaragua* (n 8) the Court devoted only one paragraph (para 237) to considering necessity and proportionality. Its approach in *Oil Platforms* (n 14) (see paras 74–77) and *Armed Activities* (n 14) (see paras 147, 304) was likewise cursory. In the latter case, this was despite the fact that both parties claimed a right of self-defence.

[24] For an overview of the ICJ's jurisprudence on the use of force, see Green, *The International Court of Justice* (n 4); Christine Gray, 'The International Court of Justice and the Use of Force' in Christian J Tams and James Sloan (eds), *The Development of International Law by the International Court of Justice* (Oxford Scholarship Online 2014) 237; Kress, 'The International Court of Justice' (n 8) 561–604.

[25] *Nicaragua* (n 8) para 237.

[26] Ibid.

meaning. Absent an armed attack, the right of self-defence is not triggered, and any use of force not consented to or sanctioned by the UNSC will be unlawful. In these circumstances, necessity and proportionality are inapplicable and cannot be complied with, nor breached. In addition, like states, the Court has sometimes been inattentive in identifying whether its observations on necessity and proportionality relate to the *jus ad bellum* or to IHL.[27] Certain judges might even be accused of conflating the two. For example, in the course of his review of IHL proportionality in *Nuclear Weapons*, Judge Schwebel refers to the UK's oral arguments.[28] However, in the passage that Judge Schwebel cites in support of his opinion, the UK Attorney General is clearly presenting his views on *jus ad bellum* proportionality, not IHL proportionality.[29]

Such judicial comments obscure the meaning and operation of necessity and proportionality. As an armed attack was not established in any of the cases referred to above, the question of both necessity and proportionality was moot. It is unclear, therefore, why the Court has chosen to comment on them in the manner referred to in this and subsequent sections. The circumstances of the cases might have incentivized the Court to speak out on these issues, but the need for clarity in the *jus ad bellum* requires that when it takes these opportunities, the Court does so diligently and with meaningful sufficiency.[30] Its approach to necessity and proportionality appears particularly remiss given the overriding importance that states place on them. As will be made clear, there is sufficient state practice for the Court to draw upon for it to clarify the content and operation of these requirements, but it has so far avoided doing so. Accordingly, it is both what the Court has said on necessity and proportionality and what it has not said that is problematic.[31]

The Court has offered some guidance, however, regarding how it approaches necessity and proportionality. In *Nicaragua*, it clearly dealt with the two requirements separately, first opining on the necessity of the USA's actions, before going on to assess whether they were proportionate.[32] In *Oil Platforms*, the Court also treated the two concepts independently, and considered them in the same order.[33] In *Armed Activities*, however, its approach was less structured.[34] In line with *Nicaragua* and *Oil Platforms*, this book contends that necessity must be applied and assessed before proportionality. This order is crucial so that the true meaning and practical application of each requirement can be fully understood and realized in practice.[35]

[27] See Sections 1.3 and 3.4.2.

[28] *Nuclear Weapons* (n 15) diss op Schwebel, 321.

[29] *Nuclear Weapons* (n 15) Oral Proceedings, Verbatim Record, 15 November 1995, CR 95/34, 34.

[30] *Oil Platforms* (n 14) sep op Simma, para 6; *Armed Activities* (n 14) sep op Simma, paras 8–9.

[31] *Armed Activities* (n 14) sep op Simma, paras 8–9. Green suggests that, for the most part, it is what the Court has not said that is the problem. Green, *The International Court of Justice* (n 4) 106.

[32] *Nicaragua* (n 8) para 237.

[33] *Oil Platforms* (n 14) paras 76–77.

[34] *Armed Activities* (n 14) para 147.

[35] This approach also finds support in the literature. For example, Gardam, *Necessity, Proportionality* (n 10) 138–139; Green, *The International Court of Justice* (n 4) 89.

On this basis, if a declared act of self-defence is unnecessary, it cannot be disproportionate or proportionate. It will simply be an unlawful use of force. If necessity is satisfied, however, an exercise of self-defence might be proportionate or disproportionate. The importance of the order of consideration and application of necessity and proportionality will be considered further in Chapters 2 and 3.

Finally, on the ICJ's jurisprudence, as a general matter the Court's examination of necessity and proportionality must be viewed with a degree of circumspection. This book recognizes the general importance of ICJ judgments and examines the relevant aspects of the aforementioned cases in some detail, but it does so critically. We should not draw conclusions that are too wide ranging. The small number of propositions made by the Court must be read in light of, and confined to, the particular facts of the case before it. We should also bear in mind the time that has passed since each judgment was rendered. The principal self-defence case, *Nicaragua*, is approximately 35 years old. The most recent, *Armed Activities*, was delivered over 15 years ago. This does not diminish the importance of these judgments, but rather sets their enduring legacy into context. These cases represent the law as understood by the majority of the ICJ at the relevant time and within the confines of the facts presented to the Court. As Green notes, we must be cautious when assessing the jurisprudence and bear in mind these considerations and the fact that any judgment represents, at best, a 'freeze frame' of international law at a particular juncture.[36]

1.2 Scholarship

Academic commentary to date on necessity and proportionality has also been relatively light. Instead, the focus has been on the controversies surrounding the *ratione materiae*, *ratione temporis* and *ratione personae* elements of the armed attack trigger.[37] Scholarship acknowledges the importance of necessity and proportionality to the theory and operation of the right of self-defence, but a comprehensive analytical framework has not been forthcoming. With limited notable exceptions,[38] to the extent that necessity and proportionality have been considered, commentators have been fairly selective with their analysis. They have tended to focus on individual incidents of self-defence and whether, typically as a matter of

[36] Green, *The International Court of Justice* (n 4) 24–25.

[37] The debates are well known, and the associated literature is vast. For an overview, see Tom Ruys, *'Armed Attack' and Article 51 of the UN Charter: Evolutions in Customary Law and Practice* (CUP 2010).

[38] For example, Gardam, *Necessity, Proportionality* (n 10); Christian J Tams, 'The Necessity and Proportionality of Anti-Terrorist Self-Defence' in Larissa van den Herik and Nico Schrijver (eds), *Counter-Terrorism Strategies in a Fragmented International Legal Order: Meeting the Challenges* (CUP 2013) 373; David Kretzmer, 'The Inherent Right to Self-Defence and Proportionality in *Jus Ad Bellum*' (2013) 24(1) EJIL 235; Sina Etezazian, 'The Nature of the Self-Defence Proportionality Requirement' (2016) 3(2) JUFIL 260.

fact, they satisfy the two criteria. Consideration of necessity and proportionality is often cursory, with a brief overview of their content, or remarks that are limited to noting the lack of academic examination of these requirements, their indeterminate nature, or that they require further analysis.[39]

The paucity of scholarship on necessity and proportionality is perhaps a natural and understandable consequence of their complex nature and the ICJ's focus on 'armed attack'. Proportionality has posed particular problems for scholars. Gardam noted this phenomenon back in 2004, in her book that has generally been regarded as the most extensive review of necessity and proportionality so far.[40] This author references a number of commentators who have since contributed to a better understanding of necessity and proportionality, but there remains a lack of academic consensus regarding their meaning and application. It is hoped, therefore, that this book brings the scholarship up to date and offers a novel contribution to this topic.

1.3 State Practice

As noted, states invariably invoke necessity and proportionality when seeking to justify claims of self-defence. Whilst occasionally recognizing that the concepts require further clarification and study,[41] states almost universally accept that necessity and proportionality regulate their defensive actions.[42] Whether in compliance or breach, state practice reveals that necessity and proportionality occupy a central, and often decisive, role in how states justify their own uses of force and assess the military actions of other states.[43] We will see that states often resort to necessity and proportionality as the main, or only, factors to determine the legality of a particular action. In contrast to the position taken by the ICJ and scholars, states tend to avoid doctrinal debates over whether or not there has been

[39] For example, Ian Brownlie, *International Law and the Use of Force by States* (Clarendon Press 1963) 261; Kress, 'The International Court of Justice' (n 8) 586; Gray, *Use of Force* (n 2) 159. See also Gardam, *Necessity, Proportionality* (n 10) 20.

[40] Gardam, *Necessity, Proportionality* (n 10) 155. Gardam's work makes an important contribution to the field, including to this book, but it takes us only so far. Gardam devotes only one chapter of her book to necessity and proportionality as they pertain to the right of self-defence and her analysis is in need of updating, particularly in light of more recent state practice.

[41] See, for example, UNGA 'Special Committee on the Question of Defining Aggression', 3rd Session, Volume 2, Summary Records of the 67th to 68th Meetings (19 October 1970) UN Doc A/AC.134/SR.67–78, 83 (Iraq).

[42] This is not without exception. During the negotiations of UNGA Res 3314 (XXIX) (14 December 1974) (hereafter 'Definition of Aggression'), for example, the representative of Ghana argued that the principle of proportionality, as it applied to self-defence, had 'no basis in modern jurisprudence'. Ibid, 86. The Syrian delegate was equally dismissive. Ibid, 87–88.

[43] Examples where states have expressly asserted that their actions are necessary and proportionate, as well as incidents where such criteria form the basis of reactions of other states and international organizations, are referenced throughout this book.

an armed attack and instead turn to these requirements to regulate the exercise of self-defence.[44]

That states focus on necessity and proportionality is the principal reason why a better understanding of these terms is so important. Concentrating our attention on these customary international law requirements reflects how states approach the operation of the right of self-defence. A more coherent and determinate conception of necessity and proportionality speaks directly to this fact. Greater clarity can assist states to form policies and reach decisions regarding resorting to military force, as well as enabling them to justify claims of self-defence to the rest of the international community with increased precision. Moreover, other states, international organizations, courts and academics will have more effective tools with which to appraise such claims and review avowed uses of defensive force.

1.4 Provenance of Necessity and Proportionality

Necessity and proportionality have been associated with the use of force long before the adoption of the UN Charter in 1945. They formed part of the just war tradition, stretching back centuries.[45] However, the contemporary understanding of these requirements is typically derived from the *Caroline* incident of 1837. More specifically, their provenance is the ensuing correspondence between Mr Webster, the American Secretary of State, and Lord Ashburton, the British representative in Washington.[46] The incident stemmed from the rebellion against British rule in Canada. The steamboat *Caroline* was being used to ship reinforcements and supplies from the USA to the rebels on Navy Island located in British controlled Canada. To stop this, a British force entered American territory, boarded the

[44] Green, *The International Court of Justice* (n 4) 9, 108–109; Gray, *Use of Force* (n 2) 163–164; Christian Henderson, *The Use of Force and International Law* (CUP 2018) 228–229. For example, in relation to necessity, the current debates regarding the legality of particular defensive action against NSAs centre on the controversial unwilling or unable doctrine and the notion of 'imminence'. See respectively Sections 4.2.2 and 2.5.1.2. Proportionality is often central in determining legality. Notable examples include Israel's (disproportionate) intervention into Lebanon 2006 and Turkey's (proportionate) Operation Sun in 2008. See in particular Section 3.3.5. Other examples are examined in the following chapters.

[45] For an overview of necessity and proportionality in just war theory and more generally prior to the adoption of the UN Charter, see Gardam, *Necessity, Proportionality* (n 10) 28–58.

[46] See *British and Foreign State Papers*, 1841–1842, Vol. XXX, 193. On this incident generally, see Robert Y Jennings, 'The *Caroline* and McLeod Cases' (1938) 32(1) AJIL 82; Timothy Kearley, 'Raising the *Caroline*' (1999) 17 Wisconsin Int'l L J 325; James A Green, 'Docking the *Caroline*: Understanding the Relevance of the Formula in Contemporary Customary International Law Concerning Self-Defense' (2006) 14(2) Cardozo J Int'l & Comp L 429; Michael Wood, 'The *Caroline* Incident–1837' in Tom Ruys and Olivier Corten (eds) with Alexandra Hofer, *The Use of Force in International Law: A Case-Based Approach* (OUP 2018) 5; Craig Forcese, *Destroying the Caroline: The Frontier Raid that Reshaped the Right to War* (Irwin Law Inc 2018).

Caroline, set it on fire and sent it over Niagara Falls. At least one American citizen was killed in the process.[47]

A number of defences were raised by the British to justify their actions. It is Webster's response to such justifications, and to the incident more generally, that informs the present study. Regarding the necessity of a state's ability to act in self-defence, Webster famously proclaimed that it was limited to cases in which the 'necessity of that self-defense is instant, overwhelming, and leaving no choice of means and no moment for deliberation'.[48] Supposing the necessity of the moment required action, Webster asserted that it would also be incumbent on a government purportedly acting in self-defence to show that it 'did nothing unreasonable or excessive; since the act, justified by the necessity of self-defence, must be limited by that necessity, and kept clearly within it'.[49] These pronouncements are commonly referred to as the 'Webster formula' or the '*Caroline* formula'. In response, whilst Lord Ashburton disagreed on the facts at issue, in justifying the British action he agreed with Webster's characterization of self-defence and the applicable international law.[50]

The precedential value of the *Caroline* incident is questionable. Well-known debates persist regarding the extent to which Webster's formula informs the application of necessity and proportionality to a modern, post-UN Charter, right of self-defence. On the one hand, it is said that the *Caroline* incident changed self-defence from a political excuse to a legal doctrine.[51] After all, the correspondence between Webster and the British ministers consistently refers to self-defence in legal terms. Ashburton described it as 'the first law of nature' and the 'great law of self-defence'.[52] Along these lines, certain commentators continue to emphasize the *Caroline* incident's influence on the contemporary *jus ad bellum*.[53]

Others are more measured in their views. Gray notes how the episode 'has attained an authority far beyond what can be legally justified'.[54] Indeed, the particular factual matrix might be said to narrow its precedential application. For instance, some scholars understand the British action to be pre-emptive, suggesting that

[47] Forcese, *Destroying the Caroline* (n 46) 31–47. Jennings notes that two people lost their lives. Jennings, 'The *Caroline* and McLeod Cases' (n 46) 84.

[48] Letter from Mr Webster to Lord Ashburton (6 August 1842) *British and Foreign State Papers*, 1841–1842, Vol. XXX, 201. Webster was referring to earlier correspondence between him and Lord Ashburton's predecessor, Mr Fox. See Letter from Mr Webster to Mr Fox (24 April 1841) *British and Foreign State Papers*, 1840–1841, Vol. XXIX, 1129–1139, especially 1137–1138.

[49] *British and Foreign State Papers*, 1840–1841, Vol. XXIX (n 48) 1138.

[50] Letter from Lord Ashburton to Mr Webster (28 July 1842) *British and Foreign State Papers*, 1841–1842, Vol. XXX, 195.

[51] Jennings, 'The *Caroline* and McLeod Cases' (n 46) 82.

[52] *British and Foreign State Papers*, 1841–1842, Vol. XXX (n 50) 196, 201.

[53] For example, Gardam, *Necessity, Proportionality* (n 10) 31; Terry D Gill, 'The Temporal Dimension of Self-Defence: Anticipation, Pre-emption, Prevention and Immediacy' (2006) 11(3) JC&SL 361, 366–368; Elizabeth Wilmshurst, 'The Chatham House Principles of International Law on the Use of Force in Self-Defence' (2006) 55(4) ICLQ 963 (hereafter 'The Chatham House Principles') 965.

[54] Gray, *Use of Force* (n 2) 158.

its purview might be limited to anticipatory self-defence.[55] There is a strong case, however, for viewing the British action as a response to an ongoing armed attack.[56] Other commentators focus on the fact that the British were targeting NSA rebels operating from American territory, in circumstances where Britain and the USA were not themselves in conflict. As a result, the Webster formula is potentially limited to self-defence against NSAs operating from the territory of another state that is unable or unwilling to suppress them.[57] Combining these two factors might further limit the *Caroline* precedent to a right of anticipatory action of an extra-territorial nature against NSAs.[58]

Moreover, the episode occurred in 1837, when international law did not outlaw the use of force. Any invocation of self-defence at that time had little substantive legal meaning. The incident might, therefore, be described as one of a state of necessity rather than self-defence.[59] The correspondence further justifies a characterization of the wider right of self-preservation, or self-help.[60] As a result, there is doubt whether the Webster formula represented at the time it was expressed state practice pertaining to the right of self-defence.[61] It is also questionable whether it properly depicts custom today.[62] Whilst the ICJ has consistently confirmed necessity and proportionality as customary requirements,[63] at no point has the majority referenced the *Caroline* incident or Webster's formula.[64]

However, we should not simply dismiss the *Caroline* incident as an outdated distraction.[65] Following the Second World War, the Nuremberg Tribunal cited Webster's formula with approval in the context of the necessity of anticipatory

[55] See Derek W Bowett, *Self-Defence in International Law* (Manchester University Press 1958) 188–189. Gill emphasizes *Caroline*'s particular relevance to such debate. Gill, 'The Temporal Dimension of Self-Defence' (n 53) 366. Judge Schwebel in his dissent in *Nicaragua* (n 8) para 200, also explicitly limits the *Caroline* formula in this manner. Cf Yoram Dinstein, *War, Aggression and Self-Defence* (6th edn, CUP 2017) 225, asserting that there was nothing anticipatory about the British action against the *Caroline*. See also Gardam, *Necessity, Proportionality* (n 10) 149; Michael Schmitt (ed), *Tallinn Manual on the International Law Applicable to Cyber Warfare* (CUP 2013) 64.

[56] See Forcese, *Destroying the Caroline* (n 46), especially 227–229.

[57] Kearley, 'Raising the *Caroline*' (n 46) 325, notes that this was the position taken by writers in the pre-UN Charter era and describes this as the proper context in which to apply the *Caroline* formula. He concludes, however, that the formula is commonly, though not universally, accepted as applying to all forms of self-defence. See Section 4.2.2 regarding the unwilling or unable doctrine.

[58] Green, 'Docking the *Caroline*' (n 46) 444.

[59] Bowett, *Self-Defence in International Law* (n 55) 59–60, although he affirms that Webster's principles apply to both necessity and self-defence. The International Law Commission ('ILC') also characterizes the incident in this way. See ILC, Draft Articles on Responsibility of States for Internationally Wrongful Acts, with Commentaries (2001) UN Doc A/56/10 ('ARSIWA') para 5 of commentary to Art 25. For a critique of this characterization, and a conclusion that the incident is best regarded as an example of self-defence, see Federica Paddeu, *Justification and Excuse in International Law* (CUP 2018) 351–357.

[60] See Jennings, 'The *Caroline* and McLeod Cases' (n 46) 91–92.

[61] Gardam, *Necessity, Proportionality* (n 10) 42–44.

[62] See generally Green, 'Docking the *Caroline*' (n 46).

[63] See Section 1.1.

[64] The only reference is found in *Nicaragua* (n 8) diss op Schwebel, para 200.

[65] Green, 'Docking the *Caroline*' (n 46) 449.

self-defence.[66] In the post-UN Charter era, states have occasionally referred to the *Caroline* incident as a precedent during the discussion, justification and condemnation of particular claims of self-defence, as well as when considering the genesis and nature of the right.[67] States have also relied on the incident generally, and Webster's formula in particular, to establish the conditions of necessity and proportionality in pleadings before the ICJ.[68] Furthermore, even if the *Caroline* incident has not been referenced explicitly, states have employed Webster's words during deliberations of the UNSC.[69]

These state practice examples are not all that common, but the *Caroline* incident endures as the *locus classicus* of international law pertaining to the right of self-defence.[70] Its impact on the interpretation of the UN Charter and the development of customary international law, including necessity and proportionality, persists to this day.[71] The *lex lata* and the Webster formula are not synonymous, but they have much in common. As Jennings and Watts conclude, the 'basic elements of the right of self-defence were aptly set out in connection with the *Caroline* incident'.[72]

[66] *Judgment of the International Military Tribunal for the Trial of the German Major War Criminals, Nuremberg* 1946 (1947) Vol I, 205, referring to 'preventative' action in foreign territory.

[67] See, for example, UNSC Verbatim Record (9 July 1976) UN Doc S/PV.1939, para 115 (Israel); UNSC Verbatim Record (15 October 1980) UN Doc S/PV.2250, para 40 (Iraq); UNSC Verbatim Record (15 June 1981) UN Doc S/PV.2282, paras 14–15 (Uganda); UNSC Verbatim Record (19 June 1981) UN Doc S/PV.2288, para 80 (Israel); Joint Committee on Human Rights, *The Government's Policy on the Use of Drones for Targeted Killing* (2015-16, HL 141, HC 574) 45; Brian Egan, Legal Adviser, U.S. Department of State, 'International Law, Legal Diplomacy, and the Counter-ISIL Campaign: Some Observations', Speech to the 110th Annual Meeting of the American Society of International Law (1 April 2016) (2016) 92 Int'l L Stud. 235, 239; UK Attorney General's Speech at the International Institute for Strategic Studies, 'The Modern Law of Self-Defence' (11 January 2017) <https://www.gov.uk/government/uploads/system/uploads/attachment_data/file/583171/170111_Imminence_Speech_.pdf> accessed 5 September 2020, 2, 7, 8, 14; Australian Attorney-General, Senator the Hon. George Brandis QC, 'The Right of Self-Defence Against Imminent Armed Attack in International Law', Public Lecture at the T C Beirne School of Law, University of Queensland (11 April 2017) <https://www.ejiltalk.org/the-right-of-self-defence-against-imminent-armed-attack-in-international-law/> accessed 5 September 2020 (hereafter 'Australian Attorney-General Speech 2017').

[68] For example, *Nicaragua* (n 8) Memorial of Nicaragua, 30 April 1985, paras 297–298; *Nuclear Weapons* (n 15) Note Verbale from the Embassy of Mexico, together with Written Statement of the Government of Mexico, 19 June 1995, para 63; *Nuclear Weapons* (n 15) Note Verbale from the Embassy of New Zealand, together with Written Statement of the Government of New Zealand, 20 June 1995, para 56; *Oil Platforms* (n 14) Memorial Submitted by the Islamic Republic of Iran, 8 June 1993, para 4.18; *Oil Platforms. Oil Platforms* (n 14) Rejoinder Submitted by the United States of America, 23 March 2001, para 5.35; *Armed Activities* (n 14) Reply of the Democratic Republic of the Congo, 29 May 2002, para 3.159.

[69] For example, UNSC Verbatim Record (24 October 1962) S/PV.1024, para 110 (Ghana); UNSC Verbatim Record (14 June 1979) S/PV.2148, para 10 (Egypt); UNSC Verbatim Record (15 June 1981) S/PV.2283, para 148 (Sierra Leone); UNSC Verbatim Record (21 July 1981) S/PV.2293, para 69 (Egypt); UNSC Verbatim Record (15 April 1996) S/PV.3653, 15 (Egypt).

[70] Jennings, 'The *Caroline* and McLeod Cases' (n 46) 92; Bowett, *Self-Defence in International Law* (n 55) 58.

[71] As noted, this book focuses on necessity and proportionality post adoption of the UN Charter. For a review of how these requirements were perceived following the *Caroline* incident and up until 1945, see Gardam, *Necessity, Proportionality* (n 10) 42–49.

[72] Robert Jennings and Arthur Watts (eds), *Oppenheim's International Law: Volume I, Peace* (9th edn, Longman 1996) 420.

Gardam agrees that the *Caroline* incident 'encapsulates' the contemporary position[73] and Dinstein notes that the modern requirements may be 'distilled' from the yardsticks set by Webster.[74] This author agrees with these observations. Even if dissociated from the original factual circumstances of the *Caroline* incident, the Webster formula is rightly regarded as shorthand in international relations for when force may be used by states in self-defence.[75] The formula is the starting point for our examination of the modern requirements of necessity and proportionality.

1.5 Approach of the Current Study

Regarding the contemporary picture, this book undertakes an audit of relevant state practice and *opinio juris* since the signing of the UN Charter in 1945 in order to determine how we should understand necessity and proportionality today.[76] Given that state practice and *opinio juris* are the key to mapping out an understanding of this topic, this review is intended to be as thorough and as comprehensive as possible. The 'quest for custom' is not an exact science, however,[77] and controversies abound regarding the identification of customary international law.[78] Eschewing a binary choice between an 'extensive' or 'restrictive' approach to determining custom,[79] a balanced methodology is adopted herein that accords with the ICJ's

[73] Gardam, *Necessity, Proportionality* (n 10) 148.

[74] Dinstein, *War, Aggression and Self-Defence* (n 55) 249. Green takes a similar view. Green, 'Docking the *Caroline*' (n 46) 450.

[75] Forcese, *Destroying the Caroline* (n 47) xix.

[76] As a doctrinal matter, state practice and *opinio juris* determine the existence and content of rules of customary international law. Statute of the International Court of Justice, 26 June 1945, 15 UNCIO 355, Art 38(1)(b); *North Sea Continental Shelf Cases* (*Federal Republic of Germany/Denmark; Federal Republic of Germany/Netherlands*) (Judgment) [1969] ICJ Rep 3, para 77; *Nicaragua* (n 8) paras 184, 186. General consistency of state practice is sufficient. *Nicaragua* (n 8) para 186. Regarding the requisite amount, uniformity, representativity and duration of state practice, as well as the position of 'specially affected states', in each case regarding the *jus ad bellum*, see Ruys, *'Armed Attack'* (n 37) 44–51. See further the ILC's draft conclusions regarding the identification of customary international law. UNGA, 'Report of the International Law Commission, Sixty-Eighth Session' (2 May–10 June and 4 July–12 August 2016) UN Doc A/71/10, Chapter V.

[77] Ruys, *'Armed Attack'* (n 37) 30.

[78] The identification of customary *jus ad bellum* is a relatively under-theorized topic. For an overview of relevant issues, representing a range of opinion, see Enzo Cannizzaro and Paolo Palchetti (eds), *Customary International Law on the Use of Force: A Methodological Approach* (Martinus Nijhoff 2005); Olivier Corten, *The Law Against War: The Prohibition on the Use of Force in Contemporary International Law* (Hart Publishing 2010) 4–49; Ruys, *'Armed Attack'* (n 37) 29–52; Raphaël van Steenberghe, 'State Practice and the Evolution of the Law of Self-Defence: Clarifying the Methodological Debate' (2015) 2(1) JUFIL 81; Stefan Talmon, 'Determining Customary International Law: The ICJ's Methodology between Induction, Deduction and Assertion' (2015) 26(2) EJIL 417; Gray, *Use of Force* (n 2) 9–26. See further the ILC's draft conclusions regarding the identification of customary international law (n 76).

[79] See Corten, *The Law Against War* (n 78) 5–27; Ruys, *'Armed Attack'* (n 37) 31–44. The so-called 'extensive approach', *inter alia*, prioritizes state practice (meaning the physical conduct of states in this instance), in particular that of powerful states. The so-called 'restrictive approach' focuses on *opinio juris*. This means that states must be convinced that their acts accord with a legal rule. It posits that all states equally contribute to customary formation. Whereas the former approach gives rise to accounts of the

jurisprudence on the identification of rules of customary international law.[80] This approach examines both the words and deeds of states,[81] with a focus on specific incidents where states have claimed a right of self-defence, or can be taken to have used force in self-defence.[82] Such incidents have a central practical importance in the formation of customary international law, including in relation to the right of self-defence.[83] This is because they give rise to a form of dialogue comprising claims of self-defence made by states to justify using force and counter-claims by other states in response. Any legal justifications embodied in these claims, together with any legal positions advanced in counterclaims, are capable of contributing to the affirmation or modification of the applicable rules of customary international law.[84] Accordingly, incidents stand as important precedents for its development.[85]

The following chapters seek to establish the particular facts relating to the relevant incidents, the action taken by the states involved, any legal claims advanced, and the corresponding reactions of other states. Where available, letters sent to or put before the UNSC by states invoking the right of self-defence (in accordance with the reporting obligation contained in Article 51 of the UN Charter) are the starting point in attempting to identify a legal justification for a particular use of force.[86] Thereafter, the focus is on state practice and *opinio juris* in respect of

law that admit of uses of force in a wide range of circumstances, the latter adheres strictly to a broad prohibition on the use of force.

[80] See further Ruys, *'Armed Attack'* (n 37) 51–52; Corten, *The Law Against War* (n 78) 27–49.

[81] A distinction between words and deeds is semantically convenient, but ontologically untenable. Both are acts of states. See Conclusion 6 and related commentary of the ILC's draft conclusions regarding the identification of customary international law (n 76). See further n 89.

[82] The right of self-defence might be explicitly claimed by a state, but equally it might not be. Where it is claimed, the veracity of the facts and/or the legality of military action might be in doubt or contested. Yet, any invocations of the right and subsequent reactions by other states provide state practice and *opinio juris*. Whether or not a state's right of self-defence has lawfully been triggered, that state's enunciation of the international legal restraints to which it considers itself subject when exercising that right, together with other states' reactions, constitute state practice and *opinio juris* relevant to the content of the applicable customary rules. There is also value in examining cases where the facts speak to a claim of self-defence that could have been advanced but was not. The lack of an express legal justification means that a state's *opinio juris* might be absent but ensuing reactions from other states can be elucidating. Therefore, the approach adopted examines concrete examples where the right of self-defence is at issue and states have made their views known on the lawfulness of the purported exercise of that right.

[83] The importance of the incident-based approach to the examination of state practice and *opinio juris* has been emphasized by a number of scholars. For example, Michael Reisman, 'International Incidents: Introduction to a New Genre in the Study of International Law' (1984) 10 Yale J Int'l L 1; Ruth Wedgwood, 'The ICJ Advisory Opinion on the Israeli Security Fence and the Limits of Self-Defense' (2005) 99 AJIL 52, 52; Green, *The International Court of Justice* (n 4) 7–9; Ruys, *'Armed Attack'* (n 37) 34, 41.

[84] *South West Africa Cases* (*Ethiopia v South Africa; Liberia v South Africa*) (Judgment) [1966] ICJ Rep 6, para 49. Where a state using force has advanced no explicit legal claim to justify its actions, a legal justification might nevertheless be implicit in official statements and from the particular context. Ruys, *'Armed Attack'* (n 37) 36–37.

[85] Tom Ruys, Olivier Corten, and Alexandra Hofer, 'Introduction: The *Jus Contra Bellum* and the Power of Precedent' in Ruys and Corten, *The Use of Force in International Law* (n 46) 1.

[86] Art 51 of the UN Charter requires measures taken by states in the exercise of the right of self-defence to be reported immediately to the UNSC.

specific incidents and the consideration by states of legal issues before the UNSC and the UN General Assembly ('UNGA').[87] Official statements made by,[88] and to, other international bodies (such as NATO, the European Union and the Arab League) are also cited, as are statements made elsewhere (such as to the media, or before national parliaments). In addition, pleadings by states before international courts and tribunals have been a valuable source of *opinio juris* and state practice.[89] These pleadings tend to contain more clearly articulated legal positions on the part of states than might be provided to political organs such as the UNSC and in other diplomatic fora, where politics and law tend to be intermingled.[90] With every declaration regarding an incident, great care has been taken to distinguish, where possible, legal from political or moral justifications advanced by the relevant state.[91]

Potential incidents run into the hundreds, however, and are varied in nature.[92] They comprise uses of force by states accompanied by explicit claims of

[87] Statements made by states to the UNSC regarding particular incidents are important to the identification of state practice and *opinio juris* in the *jus ad bellum*. In respect of the UNSC's role itself in developing custom, '[i]n certain cases, the practice of international organizations also contributes to the formation, or expression, of rules of customary international law.' See Conclusion 4, para 2, and related commentary of the ILC's draft conclusions regarding the identification of customary international law (n 76). A particular UNSC Resolution might constitute *prima facie* evidence of legality or illegality, but caution is needed. Statements made by members of the Council concerning the adoption of a Resolution, as well as the reactions of other states outside of its fifteen members, must also be accounted for when considering the customary position. See Ruys, *'Armed Attack'* (n 37) 39–41, 49. See further Gray, *Use of Force* (n 2) 16–26, regarding the relative importance of the UNSC and the UNGA in developing the *jus ad bellum*. Insight is also gained by statements made in fora, such as the UNGA, that do not relate to particular incidents of self-defence, but rather engage in the abstract with legal issues relevant to the present study. Examples include statements made during the drafting of the Definition of Aggression (n 42). UNGA Resolutions, in particular state votes that relate to their adoption or otherwise, may also be used to establish state practice and *opinio juris*. See *Nicaragua* (n 8) para 188.

[88] As with the role of the UNSC and UNGA in developing custom, caution must be had regarding whether statements made by such organizations reflect the state practice and *opinio juris* of states. See n 87.

[89] That such pleadings are generally regarded as state practice, see International Law Association, 'Statement of Principles Applicable to the Formation of General Customary International Law', Report of the Committee on Formation of Customary (General) International Law (2000) 14. See also James Crawford, Alain Pellet and Catherine Redgwell, 'Anglo-American and Continental Traditions in Advocacy before International Courts and Tribunals' (2013) 2(4) CJICL 715, 724. The ILC, whilst recognizing that verbal conduct (whether written or oral) may constitute state practice, notes that assertions made in written and oral pleadings before courts and tribunals might also evidence *opinio juris*. See ILC's draft conclusions regarding the identification of customary international law (n 76) para 2 of the commentary to Conclusion 6 and para 4 of the commentary to Conclusion 10.

[90] Federica Paddeu, 'Self-Defence as a Circumstance Precluding Wrongfulness: Understanding Article 21 of the Articles on State Responsibility' (2015) 85 BYIL 90, 118–119.

[91] As such, although the UNSC is relied upon for the present analysis, caution has been taken to discern from debates and UNSC Resolutions any legal statements. This author is mindful of the need not to ascribe legal views to states that they themselves do not advance (per *Nicaragua* (n 8) para 207). As noted, however, such views might be implicit in statements made or from the particular context.

[92] See, for example, Green, *The International Court of Justice* (n 4) 3. This author's own research has identified hundreds of potential incidents and recognizes that many more exist. For a catalogue of over 400 potential claims of self-defence, see Dustin A Lewis, Naz K Modirzadeh and Gabriella Blum, 'Quantum Of Silence: Inaction and *Jus Ad Bellum*', The Harvard Law School Program on International Law and Armed Conflict (2019) <https://pilac.law.harvard.edu/quantum-of-silence> accessed 5 September 2020, Annex.

self-defence, as well as where the right of self-defence is relied on implicitly or is arguable on the facts. It is simply not possible to identify each and every invocation of the right of self-defence advanced since the signing of the UN Charter, let alone appraise them all, within the word limits of this book. States do not always comply with the Article 51 reporting obligation[93] and there is no official or definitive log of claims of self-defence that might facilitate this review. Furthermore, not all incidents provide insight into the law. This is particularly so where claims of self-defence illicit no response from other states and are not debated in the UNSC or other public fora.[94]

It is impossible to be exhaustive, but this author has identified as many examples as is feasible of actual or putative exercises of self-defence since 1945 in order to provide a picture of the *lex lata* that is as comprehensive as possible. The focus is on those incidents particularly pertinent to and instructive for this task. Examples that have generated the most discussion between states, particularly within the UNSC, have proved the most useful in establishing state positions on the customary restraints of necessity and proportionality. In seeking to avoid the inherent deficiencies that selecting some incidents over others necessarily entails,[95] the incidents cited are intended to be representative of a breadth and diversity of practice. They have been selected from over the entire period from 1945 to the present. Collectively, they constitute the practice of states from all continents and represent a spectrum of political, economic and legal systems, of levels of economic development, and so on. Such practice also covers the full range of types of self-defence claims, including traditional state-to-state violence, uses of force against NSAs and anticipatory action.

In the course of this review, legal significance must be inferred from primary materials and factual context, which necessarily involves a degree of personal judgement.[96] Identifying relevant state practice and discerning *opinio juris* requires a measure of subjectivity.[97] To avoid arbitrariness, this subjective element must be grounded in legal doctrine and theory and must take account of assessments of the evidence by systemically recognized bodies and individuals. Our exploration of necessity and proportionality must, therefore, include a review of the jurisprudence of the ICJ and of the writings of academic commentators. These constitute subsidiary sources for determining rules of international law, with the

[93] For further details of this phenomenon, and on reporting more generally, see James A Green, 'The Article 51 Reporting Requirement for Self-Defense Actions' (2015) 55 Va J Int'l L 563.

[94] Gray notes, for example, that it used to be common for minor incidents to be referred to the UNSC and debated, but that this is no longer the case. Gray, *Use of Force* (n 2) 16.

[95] This includes any selection bias of the author. See Reisman, 'International Incidents' (n 83) 13–15.

[96] For example, states do not always invoke necessity and proportionality explicitly, instead alluding in more general terms to the content of these requirements. Where this is the case, it is indicated. As noted in Chapter 3, states may also invoke 'proportionality' without further explanation, not making it clear whether the reference is to *jus ad bellum* or to IHL (where the term is also used to different ends).

[97] Corten, *The Law Against War* (n 78) 17–20; Talmon, 'Determining Customary International Law' (n 78).

former carrying particular authority.[98] Both not only help to establish an analytical framework that informs this author's review of the evidence, but also provide standards against which the cogency of the author's assessments of this evidence can be measured.

1.6 Initial Observations

Before moving to the detail of Chapters 2 to 4, the following sections set out some initial observations to frame the ensuing analysis. Substantive content is touched upon but, at this stage, the primary intent is to offer an introductory guide for the reader to understand the fundamentals of necessity and proportionality and their place in regulating the right of self-defence in international law. This first foray into the subject is developed in the subsequent chapters.

1.6.1 The Nature and Function of Necessity and Proportionality

Necessity and proportionality condition the exercise of the right of self-defence.[99] Necessity determines *whether* defensive force may be used to respond to an actual or imminent armed attack and *where* it must be directed. Proportionality governs *how much* force is permissible. Once the availability of the right is triggered in response to an armed attack, these two requirements operate to restrain the scope of defensive action and ensure that it remains defensive. As Ago notes, 'the objective to be achieved by [self-defence], its *raison d'être*, is necessarily that of repelling an attack and preventing it from succeeding, and nothing else'.[100] Therefore, compliance with necessity and proportionality indicates that the purposes of self-defence are achieved, and nothing beyond that.[101] As guardians of the parameters of the right of self-defence, they are the 'touchstones' that ground such action in the principle of legality.[102]

Necessity and proportionality seek to strike a balance between the rights and interests of three different groups of actors. First, we must consider the right of defending states to respond effectively to actual (or potentially imminent) armed attacks.[103] For the purposes of this book, a 'defending state' is a state that is, *or*

[98] Statute of the International Court of Justice (n 76) Art 38(1)(d). See further Section 1.1.

[99] *Nuclear Weapons* (n 15) para 41.

[100] International Law Commission, 'Addendum—Eighth Report on State Responsibility by Mr. Roberto Ago, Special Rapporteur—The Internationally Wrongful Act of the State, Source of International Responsibility (Part 1)' (1980) UN Doc A/CN.4/318/Add.5-7 (hereafter 'Ago, "Addendum—Eighth Report on State Responsibility"') para 119.

[101] The purposes of self-defence are examined in Section 1.6.2.

[102] Australian Attorney-General Speech 2017 (n 67).

[103] See Section 2.5.1 regarding the timing of an armed attack, including armed attacks that are 'imminent'.

claims to be, the victim of an armed attack by another state or by NSAs. Second, the right of an attacker to be protected from excessive defensive responses must be accounted for. An 'attacker' might be a state or NSAs, in each case, that have launched, or intend to launch, armed attacks against a defending state.[104] Third, are the interests of other states and the wider international community. These latter interests include concern for civilian harm and the environment, as well as the operation of the collective security system. In this latter respect, necessity and proportionality function to contain the risk of escalating violence and instability. They thereby contribute to international peace and security, whilst reserving to the UNSC the primary responsibility for its long-term maintenance. These three groups of actors with their attendant rights and interests are examined in the following chapters.

As will be made clear, necessity and proportionality apply on an ongoing basis, throughout the duration of an armed conflict prompted by self-defence, and not just at its commencement.[105] This enduring obligation is often overlooked in the literature, yet it is crucial to appreciating the potential of necessity and proportionality to restrain military action. The *jus ad bellum* regulates the use of force by states as a whole and its rules must be continually monitored and reviewed by states. Put simply, if the recourse to force is, or the continuing use of force becomes, unnecessary or disproportionate, it is not lawful self-defence and will breach Article 2(4) of the UN Charter. Therefore, either force must not be employed in the first place or it must cease.[106]

Necessity and proportionality have been described as two sides of the same coin.[107] This characterization emphasizes that they are closely linked conceptually. In recognizing this relationship, Gray has suggested that an unnecessary use of force cannot be proportionate and if it is not proportionate, it is difficult to see how it can be necessary.[108] This statement oversimplifies the relationship yet exemplifies how the two requirements are sometimes referred to without due distinction. Their close connection means that academics and states have sometimes used the term interchangeably or questioned their distinctiveness.[109] This book confronts this

[104] See Chapter 4 regarding armed attacks by NSAs.

[105] Christopher Greenwood 'The Relationship Between *Jus ad Bellum* and *Jus in Bello*' (1983) 9 Rev Int'l Stud 221, 222–225; Gardam, *Necessity, Proportionality* (n 10) 155–156; Tarcisio Gazzini, *The Changing Rules on the Use of Force in International Law* (Manchester University Press 2005) 146–147; Ruys, *'Armed Attack'* (n 37) 124. See Sections 3.4.1 and 3.5.

[106] A distinction should be drawn between applying these rules and assessing compliance with them. Necessity and proportionality apply to a defending state's actions on an enduring basis and the state must continually monitor its own compliance with them. However, their review is likely to occur on a *post facto* basis. The full picture of putative defensive conduct is only likely to be available once over and the facts regarding its scope are made known, for example, in debates before the UNSC or arising out of an official fact-finding process. Therefore, unless such deliberations occur during the course of a lengthy ongoing conflict, or in the context of an enduring threat, an assessment of necessity and proportionality will typically take place as a retrospective exercise. See further Section 3.5.

[107] Ago, 'Addendum—Eighth Report on State Responsibility' (n 100) para 121.

[108] Gray, *Use of Force* (n 2) 159.

[109] For example, during discussions regarding the Definition of Aggression (n 42), the USSR maintained that 'the word "necessary" contained the idea of proportionality.' UN Doc A/AC.134/SR.67–78

approach. As will be made clear in Chapters 2 and 3, necessity and proportionality are distinct and separate requirements of customary international law and must be applied as such.[110]

Given their close relationship, occasional conflation of the two concepts is perhaps inevitable. Yet, differentiating between them, and challenging assertions that seek to equate them, is important and not simply a question of semantics: 'Failure to distinguish between necessity and proportionality would seem to be one of the key factors contributing to the uncertainty surrounding both concepts.'[111] The greater the determinacy of these rules, therefore, the greater the potential for states to comply with them.[112] This compels us to consider specifically what it is about a use of force that is 'necessary' or 'unnecessary', 'proportionate' or 'disproportionate' and, as a result, lawful or unlawful. It is not enough to say that necessity amounts to the same thing as proportionality without further justification or explanation. Neither is it sufficient to conclude that an act satisfies or breaches either or both criteria without considering first how the criteria apply and, crucially, in what order.[113] This book seeks a clearer normative structure of each requirement, marking these distinctions to the fullest extent possible and applying them in the correct order. Only with such clarity can necessity and proportionality have proper meaning and be applied effectively in practice.

An investigation of necessity and proportionality has its limitations, however. They are essentially abstract and flexible concepts that, as the following chapters reveal, often incorporate equally indeterminate ideas of 'excessiveness' and 'reasonableness'.[114] Their nature is also such that their potential to curb state action is very much context-dependent. This means that establishing general rules for their application is challenging. Further, they are creatures of custom that, by its nature, will always be less precise and detailed than conventional law.[115] These factors, together with competing views on the scope and purpose of self-defence, make them difficult to apply to an increasing diversity of situations in which the right of self-defence has been invoked.[116]

(n 41) 91. Gray questions how far the two concepts can operate separately. Gray, *Use of Force* (n 2) 159. See also Noam Lubell and Amichai Cohen, 'Strategic Proportionality: Limitations on the Use of Force in Modern Armed Conflicts' (2020) 96 Int'l L Stud 159, 170.

110 Reaching the same conclusion, see Christopher Greenwood, 'Self-Defence' in *Max Planck Encyclopaedia of Public International Law* (OUP 2011) para 26.

111 Tams, 'Necessity and Proportionality' (n 38) 377.

112 Thomas M Franck, 'Legitimacy in the International System' (1988) 82 AJIL 705 713–725.

113 As noted in Section 1.1, this author contends that necessity must be considered and applied before proportionality.

114 James A Green 'The *Ratione Temporis* Elements of Self-Defence' (2015) 2(1) JUFIL 97, 101.

115 This might be no bad thing. The flexibility that this allows will also be discussed in the following chapters.

116 Georg Nolte and Albrecht Randelzhofer, 'Ch.VII Action with Respect to Threats to the Peace, Breaches of the Peace, and Acts of Aggression, Article 51' in Bruno Simma and others (eds), *The Charter of the United Nations: A Commentary, Volume II* (3rd edn, OUP 2012) 1397, 1426.

Despite these challenges, a thorough review of state practice, whilst demonstrating that the two requirements are applied flexibly, reveals their core content and outer limits. In addition, a better theoretical grasp of necessity and proportionality helps us to understand and interpret that state practice and provides guidance on identifying potential objective characteristics. Compliance with necessity and proportionality is essentially contextual, but this book provides tools for states, international organizations, courts and scholars to adopt a more coherent approach to appraising defensive action and mitigating its abuse. This strengthens the potential for international law to regulate when and how states resort to using force.

1.6.2 The Purposes of the Right of Self-Defence

1.6.2.1 Halting, Repelling or Preventing an Armed Attack

Compliance with necessity and proportionality guarantees that the purposes of self-defence are achieved, and nothing more.[117] The result is a lawful use of force. Such compliance in turn depends on establishing the purposes of self-defence. These purposes provide the benchmark against which adherence to the requirements of necessity and proportionality is gauged.[118] This benchmark defines their content and scope. It answers the two questions that govern the present analysis: 'necessary to do what?' and 'proportionate to what?' There can be no meaningful deliberation of necessity and proportionality without concomitant consideration of these purposes. Whether a narrow or expansive view is adopted on this issue delineates the conceptual boundaries of these requirements.

The legitimate purposes of the right of self-defence remain highly controversial, however.[119] Disagreements regarding how far a state may go to defend itself risk making an assessment of necessity and proportionality an overly subjective exercise, beholden to the position of the reviewer, be it a state, international organization, court or scholar. Even if subject to a later, objective review by a court (which is rare), continuing controversies mean that it might be very difficult to identify when the defensive purpose is fulfilled and, as a result, the right to exercise self-defence ceases. Many of these controversies are discussed in the following chapters. One of the most notable is whether states possess a right of some form of anticipatory self-defence. The ability to counter potential future threats

[117] Proportionality also ensures that third-party interests are not unduly disrupted. See Chapter 3.

[118] See Greenwood, 'Self-Defence' (n 110) para 27.

[119] See, for example, Kress, 'The International Court of Justice' (n 8) 586–587. Tams speaks of a 'normative drift' of the legitimate aims of self-defence in the context of combatting terrorism. He notes that, in this context, states are subsuming far-reaching military goals under a broadly defined concept of self-defence. Tams, 'Necessity and Proportionality' (n 38) 399–401, 419. See further Chapter 4.

that have not yet materialized is widely rejected by scholars and states alike, although a right to respond to 'imminent' armed attacks occupies a much less clear position in international law.[120] If one does accept the existence of a limited right of anticipatory self-defence against imminent armed attacks, then the purposes of the right of self-defence are to halt, repel or prevent an armed attack. However, such purposes, and the attendant analysis of both necessity and proportionality, change if one rejects this possibility. For commentators and states that deny any right of anticipatory self-defence, necessity and proportionality become much narrower concepts. This is because the purposes of self-defence are reduced to halting and repelling, and not preventing, an armed attack. As explored further below, the more limited the view of self-defence the more circumscribing these requirements become.

Although the outer parameters of self-defence may be debated along these lines, the core purpose is not. A use of force in self-defence must be defensive in nature. Force going beyond halting, repelling or preventing an armed attack will be either unnecessary or disproportionate and, *ipso facto*, unlawful.[121] Yet, the reality beyond the pages of an academic text, or courtroom judgment, might not be so clear-cut. States do not confine themselves to the neat argot of 'halting, repelling or preventing' when discussing defence and their national security. They may employ other terms, including 'deterring' or 'discouraging' armed attacks.[122] This language appears to take action beyond an immediate defensive purpose and into a more uncertain and distant future of possibilities. 'Deterrence', it can be argued, is an inherent part of punitive measures and cannot, therefore, be recognized as a legitimate motive for using force.[123] Yet, an element of deterrence might in fact be considered by states to be an integral part of a defensive response. Instead of focusing on the label that might be employed to describe a particular act, the key factor that will determine the legality of a putatively defensive response is whether there is a continuing threat to a defending state and its actions are necessary and proportionate to counter that threat.[124] This points to the existence of a legitimate defensive purpose.

1.6.2.2 An Overriding Defensive Purpose

The existence of additional and even decisive motives, over and above self-defence, does not deprive a state of the right to resort to self-defence, provided the conditions

[120] See Section 2.5.1.2 for detailed consideration of this issue.

[121] Defensive force can be necessary and proportionate or necessary and disproportionate, but it cannot be unnecessary and proportionate or unnecessary and disproportionate. See Section 3.4.2.

[122] See further Section 2.5.2.2.

[123] See Keiichiro Okimoto, 'The Cumulative Requirements of *Jus ad Bellum* and *Jus in Bello* in the Context of Self-Defense' (2012) 11 Chinese JIL 45, 64; Kretzmer, 'Proportionality in *Jus Ad Bellum*' (n 38) 268.

[124] See Section 2.5.2.2.

for an armed attack are met.[125] Particular motives for taking military action, and the outcomes of such action do, however, relate to the issue of whether a purported defensive act is necessary and proportionate. For example, the appropriation of resources, changing a border, destroying state infrastructure, occupation and regime change are all possible results of purported defensive action. Whether these outcomes are a result of coincidence or design, the question is whether they are necessary and proportionate to achieving a defensive purpose (*viz* halting, repelling or preventing an armed attack), not whether they are additional legitimate purposes of the right of self-defence itself.

Simma maintains that as long as defensive action 'visibly and credibly preserve[s] a primary repelling character it is immaterial if [a defending state] simultaneously harbours additional, but subordinate deterrent, retributive or even punitive motives when conducting them'.[126] Reference here to retribution and punishment is potentially troubling. Such terms are at odds with the notion of defence. Yet, as Dinstein notes, 'the motives driving States to action are usually multifaceted, and a tinge of retribution can probably be traced in every instance of response to force'.[127] This issue goes to the question of how far a state may go to protect itself. Ultimately, any motive or purpose beyond defence risks rendering ostensibly defensive action an unlawful armed reprisal.[128]

Corten argues that it is better to think of the 'main' or 'ultimate aim' of defensive action. Subordinate aims, such as overthrowing a government, are permitted, provided they are necessary to put an end to an armed attack. Such approach, Corten argues, best accords with Ago's reference to the *raison d'être* of self-defence.[129] This account is logical. It recognizes that a state might pursue other subsidiary aims in exercising its right of self-defence but requires such aims to be necessary and proportionate to halting, repelling or preventing an armed attack. It might not be easy to establish clear lines of distinction on this point, but adding a potentially open-ended list of extra possible defensive aims risks rendering self-defence meaningless. The analytical framework set out in this book aims to assist with assessing adherence to an overriding defensive purpose.

1.6.2.3 Fulfilling the Defensive Purpose

It is also important to consider what sort of action a defending state might be permitted to take to fulfil a defensive purpose that complies with the requirements of necessity and proportionality. As an example, it is logical to conclude that an armed attack that has succeeded in capturing territory can only be successfully defended

[125] *Nicaragua* (n 8) para 127.
[126] Nolte and Randelzhofer, 'Ch.VII Action' (n 116) 1426–1427.
[127] Yoram Dinstein, *War, Aggression and Self-Defence* (3rd edn, CUP 2001) 199.
[128] See Section 2.5.2.
[129] Corten, *The Law Against War* (n 78) 484–485. See n 78.

against by repulsing the attacker and restoring that territory. A return to the territorial *status quo ante bellum* is the minimum legitimate defensive goal in such circumstances. However, it is clear that states can do more than this, whilst remaining within the bounds of necessity and proportionality.[130] As Green notes, it might not be enough simply to expel the attacker from captured territory. A defending state's troops are not required to stop at the border and idly watch the attacker regroup and prepare a fresh attack. Steps may be taken to ensure there is no repeat occurrence.[131] An example is Operation Desert Storm, being the coalition response in 1991 to Iraq's invasion of Kuwait. Forcing Iraq's withdrawal from Kuwait meant that the response was not restricted to the latter's territory.[132]

In terms of how much further a state may go beyond re-establishing the *status quo ante bellum*, it seems sensible to suggest that action taken that 'reasonably secures the state following an armed attack will be acceptable'.[133] An example is the maritime exclusion zone maintained by the British for five years around the Falkland Islands following the end of active hostilities arising out of Argentina's 1982 invasion. Given that Argentina had refused to proclaim a formal end to hostilities, excluding Argentine military aircraft and vessels from this area was probably a lawful defensive measure.[134] This ability to re-establish and guarantee the security of the defending state can be sensibly interpreted as part of, or attendant to, halting, repelling or preventing an armed attack. Without this ability, these purposes might not be achieved effectively and the threat to the defending state might subsist.

States are not permitted to protect 'perceived security interests', however.[135] Any defensive action taken by a defending state must relate to a distinct and identifiable threat. Furthermore, temporal considerations limit the extent to which states may claim a defensive necessity. This reflects the fact that self-defence is a temporary emergency right. To be considered necessary, such acts must be aimed at provisionally guaranteeing the legitimate and immediate security of defending states. Once the threat has been successfully countered, the necessity of self-defence falls away.[136] Beyond the immediate security needs of the defending state, 'the creation

[130] Green, 'The *Ratione Temporis* Elements of Self-Defence' (n 114) 113. See also Gardam, *Necessity, Proportionality* (n 10) 156.

[131] Green, 'The *Ratione Temporis* Elements of Self-Defence' (n 114) 114. See further Section 2.5.

[132] See generally Christopher Greenwood 'New World Order or Old—The Invasion of Kuwait and the Rule of Law' (1992) 55 MLR 153; Erika de Wet, 'The Gulf War—1990–91' in Ruys and Corten, *The Use of Force in International Law* (n 46) 456.

[133] Green, 'The *Ratione Temporis* Elements of Self-Defence' (n 114) 114. Gardam, *Necessity, Proportionality* (n 10) 157, likewise acknowledges a right to 'restore the security of the State after an armed attack', suggesting the international response to 9/11 as an example.

[134] Christopher Greenwood, 'Self-Defence and the Conduct of International Armed Conflict' in Yoram Dinstein (ed), *International Law at a Time of Perplexity: Essays in Honour of Shabtai Rosenne* (Martinus Nijhoff Publishers 1989) 273, 276; Green, 'The *Ratione Temporis* Elements of Self-Defence' (n 114) 114. See further Section 3.3.6.2.

[135] *Armed Activities* (n 14) para 148. See also Section 2.5.1.2 regarding preventive self-defence.

[136] See further Sections 2.5.1, 3.3.2 and 4.2.4.

of permanent conditions of security seem to have been reserved by the international community as tasks to be performed collectively'.[137] An enduring solution to the situation is to be provided by the collective security mechanisms of the UN Charter, with the UNSC at its head. These considerations are explored further in the following chapters.

[137] Enzo Cannizzaro, 'Contextualizing Proportionality: *Jus ad Bellum* and *Jus in Bello* in the Lebanese War' (2006) 88 International Review of the Red Cross 779, 782.

2
Necessity

2.1 Introduction

In the *jus ad bellum*, necessity acts as an immediate limitation on the use of defensive force. It is the first international law requirement that operates to condition a state's exercise of its right of self-defence.[1] In response to an actual or imminent armed attack,[2] necessity determines if defensive force is required at all by way of a response or whether peaceful alternatives will suffice. If defensive force is required, necessity further restricts where such force may be directed. If these two elements of necessity are satisfied, the proportionality of defensive action may then be considered.

Necessity has been described as more straightforward, or at least less problematic, than proportionality.[3] Certainly, whether or not necessity is satisfied might be readily apparent when states justify acts of self-defence and review uses of force by other states. This will not always be so, however. As Green has rightly noted, necessity is a notoriously indeterminate concept.[4] Indeed, on a conceptual level, necessity raises challenging questions that go to the heart of the right of self-defence and its exercise. These issues are rarely explored in the literature in a systematic and comprehensive manner. As such, it is a mistake to dismiss necessity as uncomplicated. There is much more to be said regarding its conceptual scope and its practical content. A clear exposition of these elements enables a delimitation of its parameters and its potential to limit or bar the use of military force.

In this chapter, a distinction will first be made between necessity in the *jus ad bellum* and necessity in the laws of state responsibility and international humanitarian law ('IHL'). Highlighting the differences in the operation of necessity within these three regimes of international law helps to explain *jus ad bellum* necessity. It will be seen that, conceptually, there are in fact two types of *jus ad bellum* necessity.

[1] In respect of the distinction between an armed attack (as a trigger of the right of self-defence) and necessity (as rule that conditions is exercise), see Section 2.3.3.

[2] Regarding imminent armed attacks, see Section 2.5.1.2. This chapter proceeds on the basis that a right of pre-emptive self-defence might exist as a matter of *lex lata*. If not, such right has the potential to exist as *lex ferenda*.

[3] Judith Gardam, *Necessity Proportionality and the Use of Force by States* (CUP 2004) 26; Dapo Akande and Thomas Liefländer, 'Clarifying Necessity, Imminence, and Proportionality in the Law of Self-Defence' (2013) 107 AJIL 563, 564.

[4] James A Green, 'Docking the *Caroline*: Understanding the Relevance of the Formula in Contemporary Customary International Law Concerning Self-Defense' (2006) 14(2) Cardozo J Int'l & Comp L. 429, 450–451.

Necessity and Proportionality and the Right of Self-Defence in International Law. Chris O'Meara, Oxford University Press (2021). © Chris O'Meara. DOI: 10.1093/oso/9780198863403.003.0002

A novel taxonomy is, therefore, proposed to capture this separation, before moving on to parse Webster's formula in detail. This investigation encompasses consideration of whether peaceful alternatives are open to a defending state when faced with an actual or imminent armed attack. Temporal questions inherent in the concept of necessity are then reviewed, in particular whether a state has time to consider such alternatives. The issue of targeting completes the analysis.

2.2 Necessity in Other Areas of International Law

Necessity is only relevant where a state has first been the victim of an armed attack. In this respect, it may be contrasted with a plea of necessity under the laws of state responsibility that does not require any prior act (wrongful or otherwise) on the part of the state against which the act of necessity is taken.[5] Instead, pursuant to Article 25 of the ARSIWA, states may invoke necessity to preclude the wrongfulness of an act if it 'is the only way for the state to safeguard an essential interest against a grave and imminent peril'.[6] Some scholars have suggested, therefore, that a plea of necessity might justify a use of defensive force on its own terms. They argue that, in certain circumstances, it might be elevated to an independent legal basis to use military force, akin to self-defence.[7]

Relying solely on a plea of necessity to excuse an otherwise illegal use of force faces significant problems, however. Article 25 is drafted in the negative, thereby restricting its invocation and emphasizing that states may only invoke it in

[5] As a point of doctrine, this book adopts the position that self-defence is an independent right under the UN Charter. This means that the right is triggered on the terms of Art 51 of the UN Charter by an armed attack. It is not a responsive right that requires a prior breach of Art 2(4). A state exercising its right of self-defence recognized by Art 51 is not, 'even potentially', in breach of Art 2(4). International Law Commission ('ILC'), 'Second Report on State Responsibility, by Mr. James Crawford, Special Rapporteur' (1999) UN Doc A/CN.4/498 and Add.1–4 (hereafter 'Crawford, "Second Report on State Responsibility"') para 298; ILC, Draft Articles on Responsibility of States for Internationally Wrongful Acts, with Commentaries (2001) UN Doc A/56/10 ('ARSIWA') para 1 of commentary to Art 21. Therefore, the Art 2(4) prohibition on the use of force must be read as incorporating the self-defence exception within its terms. Kimberley N Trapp, 'Actor-Pluralism, the "Turn to Responsibility" and the *Jus ad Bellum*: "Unwilling or Unable" in Context' (2015) 2(2) JUFIL 199, 214–220. See also Federica Paddeu, 'Self-Defence as a Circumstance Precluding Wrongfulness: Understanding Article 21 of the Articles on State Responsibility' (2015) 85 BYIL 90. Cf ILC, 'Addendum—Eighth Report on State Responsibility by Mr. Roberto Ago, Special Rapporteur—The Internationally Wrongful Act of the State, Source of International Responsibility (Part 1)' (1980) UN Doc A/CN.4/318/Add.5–7 (hereafter 'Ago, "Addendum—Eighth Report on State Responsibility"') paras 87–89. See further n 18 and Chapter 4 regarding the ability of NSAs to carry out armed attacks that are not attributable to a state.

[6] ARSIWA (n 5) Art 25(1) and related commentary. For further discussion of the distinction between necessity and self-defence, see Ago, 'Addendum—Eighth Report on State Responsibility' (n 5) paras 82–124.

[7] See, for example, Andreas Laursen, 'The Use of Force and (the State of) Necessity' (2004) 37 Vand J Transnat'l L 485; Jure Vidmar, 'The Use of Force as a Plea of Necessity' (2017) 111 AJIL Unbound 302. For a general discussion (and rejection) of this argument, see Olivier Corten, 'Necessity' in Marc Weller (ed), *The Oxford Handbook on the Use of Force in International Law* (OUP 2015) 861, 863–867; Nicholas Tsagourias, 'Necessity and the Use of Force: A Special Regime' (2010) 41 NYIL 11.

exceptional circumstances.[8] Although the existence of an armed attack might be said to satisfy this requirement, resorting to a plea of necessity is disbarred if the international obligation in question (being Article 2(4) of the UN Charter in this instance) excludes the possibility of its invocation.[9] Accepting that Article 2(4) constitutes an absolute prohibition on the use of force, subject only to the explicit exceptions set out in the UN Charter, on its own terms Article 2(4) likely prevents wrongfulness preclusion on the basis of a separate plea of necessity. *A fortiori* if the Article 2(4) prohibition is *jus cogens*.[10]

Accordingly, a plea of necessity should not be viewed as an independent justification that allows for the circumvention of the prohibition of the use of force. *Jus ad bellum* necessity is a customary requirement that, whilst related to, is distinct from the laws of state responsibility. On this basis, a 'state of necessity' is a constituent element of the primary rule, being the right of self-defence recognized by Article 51 of the UN Charter. Such right accounts for the necessity criterion and, by implication, excludes the possibility of invoking a general 'state of necessity' as a circumstance precluding wrongfulness.[11] As part of an existing primary rule of international law, therefore, there is no need to rely on a secondary rule of international law as a general excuse to use force.[12]

It could be argued, however, that a plea of necessity and the right of self-defence affirmed by Article 51 of the UN Charter are not precisely co-extensive in respect of their relationship with the prohibition of the use of force. Situations

[8] *Gabčíkovo-Nagymaros Project (Hungary/Slovakia)* (Judgment) [1997] ICJ Rep 7 (hereafter '*Gabčíkovo-Nagymaros*') para 51; James Crawford, *State Responsibility: The General Part* (CUP 2013) 306–307.

[9] ARSIWA (n 5) Art 25(2)(a).

[10] ARSIWA (n 5) Art 26 denies a preclusion of wrongfulness where a *jus cogens* norm is violated. The Art 2(4) prohibition is often regarded by scholars as *jus cogens* (see, for example, Bruno Simma, 'NATO, the UN and the Use of Force: Legal Aspects' (1999) 10 EJIL 1, 3), although such characterization is contested. In *Military and Paramilitary Activities in and against Nicaragua (Nicaragua v US)* (Merits) [1986] ICJ Rep 14 (hereafter '*Nicaragua*') para 190, the ICJ noted that the ILC and the USA (in its Memorial on the Merits in the case) characterized the prohibition on the use of force as *jus cogens*, but the Court has never ruled on this point. Questioning its peremptory status, see James A Green, 'Questioning the Peremptory Status of the Prohibition of the Use of Force' (2011) 32 Mich J Int'l L 215.

[11] Para 21 of the commentary to the ARSIWA (n 5) Art 25 states that 'the plea of necessity is not intended to cover conduct which is in principle regulated by the primary obligations'. It gives the example of the doctrine of 'military necessity' in IHL as one that already takes into account the concept of necessity. Adopting this approach, Section 2.3 of the UK Ministry of Defence, *The Manual of the Law of Armed Conflict* (OUP 2005) (hereafter 'UK Military Manual') concludes that necessity cannot be used to justify actions prohibited by law. This reasoning directly translates to the primary rules of the *jus ad bellum*. Note also that Art 55 of the ARSIWA expressly recognizes the rule of *lex specialis* by disapplying the ARSIWA 'where and to the extent that the conditions for the existence of an internationally wrongful act or the content or implementation of the international responsibility of a state are governed by special rules of international law'. This is also the case with the *jus ad bellum* rules governing the right of self-defence. See further Crawford, *State Responsibility* (n 8) 308.

[12] See further Nicholas Tsagourias, 'Self-Defence Against Non-State Actors: The Interaction Between Self-Defence as a Primary Rule and Self-Defence as a Secondary Rule' (2016) 29(3) LJIL 801, 813–819; Federica Paddeu, 'Use of Force against Non-state Actors and the Circumstance Precluding Wrongfulness of Self-Defence' (2017) 30 LJIL 93.

might be said to exist where the right of self-defence is not triggered, but a plea of necessity may nevertheless excuse a use of force.[13] Examples include the controversial right to employ defensive force against non-state actors ('NSAs') on foreign territory and anticipatory action to counter future armed attacks.[14] On this logic, Article 25 of the ARSIWA has the potential to operate beyond the boundaries of self-defence and UN Security Council ('UNSC') authorization as an independent basis for using force. This argument faces a significant hurdle, however. Necessity may not be invoked where the actions taken 'seriously impair an essential interest of the State or States towards which the obligation exists, or of the international community as a whole.'[15] The interest relied on (being the right to take defensive action) must outweigh all other considerations, both individual and collective.[16]

The essential interests of sovereignty and territorial integrity would appear to preclude the operation of a plea of necessity in this context. Absent an established right of self-defence, these essential interests (which are legally protected by Article 2(4) of the UN Charter) will be violated by a use of force that is deployed in or against the territory of an aggressor state or,[17] in the case of armed attacks by NSAs, a host state.[18] Using force beyond the parameters of Article 51 also has

[13] See Vidmar, 'The Use of Force as a Plea of Necessity' (n 7) 305.

[14] Ibid.

[15] ARSIWA (n 5) Art 25(1)(b).

[16] Para 17 of the commentary to the ARSIWA (n 5) Art 25.

[17] In an interstate context, these essential interests are not a barrier to a lawful exercise of self-defence covered by Art 51 of the UN Charter. An exercise of lawful self-defence against an aggressor state does not violate Art 2(4) of the UN Charter (see n 5) and the incidental breaches of an aggressor state's sovereignty and territorial integrity (resulting from a lawful act of self-defence) are excused by operation of the ARSIWA (n 5) Art 21. See Crawford, 'Second Report on State Responsibility' (n 5) paras 298–299; para 2 of the commentary to the ARSIWA, Art 21; Crawford, *State Responsibility* (n 8) 290; Paddeu, 'Use of Force against Non-state Actors' (n 12) 100–105. In such cases, self-defence has two functions. First, it operates as a primary right and as an exception to Art 2(4) of the UN Charter. Second, in respect of incidental breaches of certain other obligations, it operates as a secondary rule, precluding responsibility for an internationally wrongful act. See generally Crawford, *State Responsibility* (n 8) 290–292; Paddeu, 'Use of Force against Non-state Actors' (n 12).

[18] A 'host state' is a state from whose territory NSAs operate (including launching armed attacks) and in whose territory a defending state uses force to respond to armed attacks. In respect of an exercise of self-defence against NSAs on the territory of a host state, the position of these essential interests of the host state is more complicated and controversial. Absent attribution of the armed attack to the host state there are various potential justifications that might be argued to excuse the temporary breach of a host state's sovereignty and territorial integrity. Albeit disputed, these potential justifications rely on the lawful exercise of self-defence, rather than on a plea of necessity. They include the argument that lawful self-defence operates in the same way as the circumstance precluding wrongfulness of necessity, thereby excusing any breach of these Art 2(4) protected rights (*viz* sovereignty and territorial integrity). This is so even if the breach affects innocent third-party states. Trapp, 'Actor-Pluralism' (n 5) 216–219. Another potential justification is where the host state is either unwilling to prevent its territory from being used as a base for NSAs or is unable to do so and is unwilling to co-operate with other states by accepting assistance (thereby acquiescing to the NSA activities). This host state conduct is itself a breach of Art 2(4), meaning that the host state cannot claim the protection of Art 2(4). Trapp, 'Actor-Pluralism' (n 5) 219–20, in the context of a responsive reading of Art 51 that requires a prior breach of Art 2(4) (although, as

wider negative implications for international peace and security, which is an essential interest of the international community as a whole. As such, a plea of necessity should not be regarded as precluding wrongfulness vis-à-vis the prohibition on the use of force contained in Article 2(4). The use of defensive force forms part of that primary obligation and it operates solely under the auspices of the 'inherent' right recognized by Article 51 UN Charter.[19]

In addition to necessity under the laws of state responsibility, a distinction must also be drawn between *jus ad bellum* necessity and IHL necessity. In IHL, necessity is referred to as 'military necessity', which:

> permits a state engaged in an armed conflict to use only that degree and kind of force, not otherwise prohibited by the law of armed conflict, that is required in order to achieve the legitimate purpose of the conflict, namely the complete or partial submission of the enemy at the earliest possible moment with the minimum expenditure of life and resources.[20]

Throughout the rules of IHL, military necessity operates in conjunction with, and is balanced by, the principle of humanity.[21] The function of necessity within this relationship is to permit the attainment of military objectives and simultaneously to curb the potential excesses of war in the name of humanitarianism. The underlying purpose of military necessity is not, therefore, dissimilar to the operation of *jus ad bellum* necessity and proportionality. Both sets of rules seek to contain the use of military force. However, IHL and the *jus ad bellum* are separate and distinct regimes, with the former operating principally at the micro level, and the latter at the macro level. These distinctions and overlaps are explored in detail below and in Chapter 3.[22]

explained in n 5, this author does not adopt such a responsive reading). A third argument is that the incidental breaches of a host state's sovereignty and territorial integrity (resulting from a lawful act of self-defence) are also excused by operation of the ARSIWA (n 5) Art 21. Tsagourias, 'Self-Defence against Non-State Actors' (n 12) 819–824; Paddeu, 'Use of Force against Non-state Actors' (n 12) 110–114. It is notable that the ILC explicitly leaves open the question of the effects of defensive force on other states. Para 5 of the commentary to the ARSIWA (n 5) Art 21. 'Lawful' self-defence requires compliance with the primary rules of Art 51 and customary international law, including the existence of an armed attack and adherence to the requirements of necessity and proportionality. It also implies compliance with obligations of 'total restraint', such as non-derogable human rights and 'intransgressible' rules of IHL, breaches of which may not be justified by operation of Art 21. See paras 3–4 and 6 of the commentary to the ARSIWA, Art 21; Crawford, *State Responsibility* (n 8) 291–292; Paddeu, 'Use of Force against Non-state Actors' (n 12) 104. See further Section 3.3.6 and Chapter 4.

[19] Crawford, *State Responsibility* (n 8) 290.

[20] UK Military Manual (n 11) Section 2.2.

[21] 'Humanity forbids the infliction of suffering, injury, or destruction not actually necessary for the accomplishment of legitimate military purposes.' UK Military Manual (n 11) Section 2.4.

[22] See in particular Sections 2.6 and 3.4.

2.3 General and Specific Necessity

2.3.1 A Novel Taxonomy

It was noted in Chapter 1 that necessity and proportionality are sometimes conflated by states and academics, and/or used interchangeably in a way that does not distinguish between them. Gray, for example, has questioned how far the two concepts can operate separately.[23] Likewise, Corten argues that necessity depends on a 'criterion of exclusive purpose', being self-defence. This, Corten maintains, 'amounts to the same thing' as saying that a response is proportionate.[24] Other examples are referenced in subsequent sections. The challenge, therefore, is to see whether it is in fact possible, or even desirable, to distinguish clearly between necessity and proportionality, rather than employing them jointly or alternatively as a general description of illegality.

In exploring how far a state may go to defend itself, this author believes that there is much to be gained by conceptual clarity that distinguishes between necessity and proportionality. Separating them, and identifying their particular characteristics, render these requirements easier to apply in both principle and in practice. To approach this task, this author proposes a novel taxonomy to describe necessity. This taxonomy is set out in the following paragraphs. Its purpose is to assist in constructing an analytical framework of necessity and to demonstrate how such concept may be compared to, and contrasted with, both proportionality and an armed attack.[25] It draws a clearer division between these concepts. Furthermore, the proposed taxonomy constitutes a tool to analyse and interpret state practice and expressions of *opinio juris*, as well as academic commentary and the jurisprudence of the International Court of Justice ('ICJ' or the 'Court').[26] This author uses it to capture and clarify what already exists in these primary and secondary sources of international law. The taxonomy is derived from such sources. It reflects how states, courts and scholars refer to two distinct aspects of necessity, even if they do not articulate these aspects in the terms set out below. It is submitted that this new approach to necessity is a lens through which we can better view the *lex lata* and *lex ferenda*.

The proposed taxonomy distinguishes between two 'types' of necessity. In response to an actual or imminent armed attack, the first type governs whether there is a necessity of *some form* of defensive response. In conditioning the exercise of

[23] Christine Gray, *International Law and the Use of Force* (4th edn, OUP 2018) 159.

[24] Olivier Corten, *The Law Against War: The Prohibition on the Use of Force in Contemporary International Law* (Hart Publishing 2010) 484. In so doing, it is notable that Corten refers to Gardam's analysis of proportionality, not necessity. See Gardam, *Necessity, Proportionality* (n 3) 156.

[25] On the distinction between necessity and armed attack, see Section 2.3.3.

[26] Regarding this taxonomy and the ICJ's jurisprudence, see Section 2.3.2.

the right of self-defence, once triggered, it requires that (i) there are no reasonable alternatives available to halt, repel or prevent an armed attack (meaning that force is the *only* reasonable way to resolve the particular situation); and/or (ii) there is no time to pursue such alternatives.[27] In these circumstances, we may conclude that there is a 'general necessity' of employing defensive force. Such conclusion is irrespective, at this point in time, of the means and methods of effecting that defensive response. Importantly, general necessity cannot be confused or conflated with proportionality. The two are conceptually distinct.[28]

In response to an actual or imminent armed attack, therefore, general necessity is the first barrier that must be passed before a state may respond lawfully with force. Its absence means that there is no necessity of self-defence (at all) and any ensuing use of force will be unlawful. If, and only if, general necessity is established, the next question to be answered is whether the requirements of the second 'type' of necessity are also satisfied. This separate and distinct category of necessity relates to the specific acts that effect the right of self-defence. This concept of 'specific necessity' requires a rational connection between the force used and a defensive purpose. The nature of the targets chosen to fulfil such defensive purpose is determinative of this test.[29]

An example of specific necessity's operation is evident when considering deliberately targeting civilians. As non-military targets, they can have no connection with the armed attack. Their neutralization or destruction can achieve no defensive purpose and suggests instead that a use of force has a punitive and, therefore, unlawful goal.[30] Specific necessity perhaps explains references that, at first sight, sound like comments on proportionality. For example, it has been suggested that the size, duration and *the target* of the response are all relevant to proportionality.[31] Specific necessity is most closely related to proportionality, as it acts to constrain the defensive response to what is necessary to halt, repel or prevent an armed attack.[32] In contrast, general necessity conditions the *prima facie* right to exercise defensive force, once that right has been triggered by an actual or imminent armed attack. As such, these two forms of necessity capture the two distinct questions that arise in state practice, scholarship and ICJ jurisprudence that are considered under the generic umbrella of 'necessity': (i) can a state use force at all in the circumstances, and (ii) if so, where must such force be directed?

[27] These requirements are examined in Sections 2.4 and 2.5.

[28] See Section 3.4.2.

[29] See Section 2.6.

[30] See Section 2.6. The fact that such targeting would breach IHL is a separate, albeit closely connected, issue.

[31] Gray, *Use of Force* (n 23) 159.

[32] Okimoto notes that this understanding of necessity is effectively identical to proportionality. Keiichiro Okimoto, 'The Cumulative Requirements of *Jus ad Bellum* and *Jus in Bello* in the Context of Self-Defense' (2012) 11 Chinese JIL 4565. See further Section 3.4.2.

2.3.2 General and Specific Necessity and ICJ Jurisprudence

The distinction between two types of necessity, although novel, is reflected in the ICJ's jurisprudence[33] and can be employed to analyse its reasoning more fully. *Oil Platforms* provides a clear example. In this case, the USA claimed a right of self-defence in respect of attacks on two vessels, which it attributed to Iran. The Court rejected this argument. It determined that neither the missile attack on the *Sea Isle City* nor the mining of the *USS Samuel B. Roberts* constituted armed attacks imputable to Iran. These attacks did not, therefore, give rise to a right of self-defence on the part of the USA.[34] Despite the absence of an armed attack, the Court nevertheless went on to consider necessity, concluding that the American response to both incidents was unnecessary.[35] The distinctions clarified by the taxonomy proposed in Section 2.3.1 clearly appear in the majority's reasoning.

First, the Court did not opine explicitly on the prior question of the general necessity of the USA acting in self-defence in the particular circumstances. It did not say that the right of self-defence was, or was not, exercisable in general terms. It simply concluded that it could not be exercised *against Iran*. The issue of general necessity is nevertheless implicit in the judgment. In respect of its consideration of the mining of the *USS Samuel B. Roberts*, the Court recognized that the mining might be sufficient to 'bring into play' the right of self-defence, or at least it could not exclude that possibility.[36] The basis for this conclusion appears to be that the act of mining might constitute an armed attack, which triggers the right of self-defence. However, also implicit in this statement is that general necessity, which conditions the exercise of the right once triggered, might also be satisfied. This is because, without general necessity, the right cannot be 'brought into play'.

The proposed taxonomy helps to draw out this factor of general necessity from the judgment and to highlight the contrast between it and specific necessity. It was specific necessity that was determinative of the Court's finding of a lack of 'necessity'. The Court concluded that, in the circumstances, the American response *against Iran* was not justifiable in response to an armed attack on the USA that could not conclusively be attributed *to Iran*.[37] Moreover, the Court made it clear that it did not believe that the oil platforms were military targets.[38] These are issues of specific necessity. The target of the defensive response is clearly distinct from whether there has there been an armed attack and, if so, whether *prima facie* there

[33] Although, as noted, it is not expressed in these terms.

[34] *Case Concerning Oil Platforms* (*Iran v US*) (Judgment) [2003] ICJ Rep 161 (hereafter '*Oil Platforms*') paras 61, 64, 72.

[35] Ibid, para 76. The Court also considered proportionality. See Section 3.2.1.6.

[36] Ibid, para 72.

[37] Ibid (emphasis added). See further Section 2.6.

[38] Ibid, para 76.

is a need to resort to force under the circumstances. Albeit not expressed in these terms, these distinctions are reflected in the Court's judgment.

This conceptual separation of the two constituent elements of necessity provides greater clarity regarding the Court's reasoning and conclusions. It sheds light on why the Court deemed the exercise of self-defence to be 'unnecessary' and what it requires for it to be necessary. It also helps us to interpret and critique the Court's analysis of whether or not the USA had first been the victim of an armed attack. The Court's analysis of the armed attack requirement on the one hand (being the trigger of the right) and necessity on the other (being the requirement that conditions its exercise) appears somewhat conflated. The Court's approach to the legality of the missile attack on the *Sea Isle City* was that the USA had to prove that it was the victim of an armed attack *by Iran*, such as to justify it using armed force in self-defence[39] and that the burden of proof had not been discharged.[40] It took the same approach to determining the legality of the mining of the *USS Samuel B. Roberts*.[41]

As such, for the majority, the identity of the attacker was an intrinsic part of establishing the existence of an armed attack. This approach is illogical, however. The fact of whether or not a state has been the victim of an armed attack is quite different from, and separate to, the question of identifying the attacker. The former does not require the latter to be confirmed for it to have factually occurred.[42] For the purposes of a defensive response, it is submitted that the identity of the attacker is a significant factor, but it relates to necessity. With respect to general necessity, the identity of the attacker informs whether any sort of military response is required, or whether the defending state can resolve the issue peacefully with the attacker, without resorting to force.[43] For specific necessity, the identity of the attacker goes to the question of to what/whom any defensive force is to be directed. Following an armed attack, it is simply unnecessary for a state to defend itself against anything/anyone other than the attacker.

That the attack and the identity of the attacker are two separate factors is apparent in the Court's reasoning in *Oil Platforms*. In respect of the missile attack on the *Sea Isle City*, the Court insisted that when considering whether the missile attack was grave enough (for the purposes of the *Nicaragua* gravity threshold test) it was setting aside the question of attribution to Iran of the attack.[44] This was also

[39] Ibid, para 57 (emphasis added).

[40] Ibid, para 61.

[41] Ibid, paras 71–72.

[42] This author adopts the position that the existence of an armed attack is essentially a factual rather than a normative question. Although potentially subject to a *de minimis* gravity threshold (*Nicaragua* (n 10) para 191), the identity of the attacker, whether it be a state or group of NSAs, is a separate question. See further n 60 and accompanying text. Regarding the timing of an armed attack, see Section 2.5.1. See further Chapter 4 regarding armed attacks by NSAs.

[43] For example, diplomatic resolution. See Section 2.4.

[44] *Oil Platforms* (n 34) para 64. Regarding the *Nicaragua* gravity threshold test, see Section 2.3.3.

the case for the related incidents to which the USA alleged it was responding.[45] In respect of the mining of the *USS Samuel B. Roberts*, the Court did not exclude the possibility that the mining of a single military vessel might be sufficient to give rise to the right of self-defence, but concluded, principally relying on the 'inconclusiveness of the evidence of Iran's responsibility', that there had not been an armed attack.[46]

In principle, therefore, the Court has recognized the distinction between the attack and its attribution to the perpetrator. However, it has treated both as separate parts of the armed attack trigger. It is submitted that the better view is that in response to an actual or imminent armed attack (complying with any gravity threshold), the next question is whether there is the necessity of some form of defensive response (which is an issue of general necessity). Only if general necessity is satisfied does the question of where the defensive force should be directed arise (being an issue of specific necessity). Conceptually separating out the stages in this manner leads to a more accurate description of the factual and legal position.

Had the Court followed this approach, it might have determined that the USA had been the victim of an armed attack. This conclusion reflects the particular facts of the incident, being the physical damage incurred and the Court's comments regarding the mining of the *USS Samuel B. Roberts*. It could then have addressed the issue of attribution of the attacks to Iran and considered the availability of reasonable alternatives to force to resolve the dispute. Finally, absent such alternatives, it was in a position to consider whether the USA had properly directed its military response. Without attribution of the armed attacks to Iran, a decision based on specific necessity leads to the same result reached by the Court. However, the process described here would have led to a better reasoned and more transparent judgment. It would have enabled an appreciation of what elements of an armed attack and/or necessity were operative in, and determinative of, the Court's reasoning. It could have avoided much of the confusion that persists to this day regarding issues like the gravity threshold, attribution, and belligerent intent,[47] and if and how they

[45] Part of the American case was that it had been the victim of a number of related attacks, of which the attack on the *Sea Isle City* had been the latest. *Oil Platforms* (n 34) paras 61–64.

[46] Ibid, para 72.

[47] The Court also appeared to require belligerent intent on the part of Iran when considering the existence of an armed attack. Ibid, para 64. Previously in *Nicaragua* (n 10) para 231, the Court referred to 'possible motivations' relating to trans-border incursions allegedly carried out by Nicaragua. The Court did not go into any detail in either case or provide any support for this requirement in international law. Requiring aggressive intent to establish an armed attack is controversial. See, for example, William H Taft, 'Self-Defense and the *Oil Platforms* Decision' (2004) 29 Yale J Int'l L 295, 302–303; James A Green, 'Self-Defence: A State of Mind for States?' (2008) 55 NILR 181, 201–206; Gray, *Use of Force* (n 23) 152; Christian Henderson, *The Use of Force and International Law* (CUP 2018) 214–216. Belligerent intent does, however, relate to the issue of the need to respond to unintended attacks, such as accidental incursions into territory, munitions going astray, or military personnel acting in error or beyond the scope of their orders. Requiring a hostile motive for an armed attack to have occurred might help to exclude forcible responses to such incidents of error or accident. However, this concern would be better addressed by considering intent as part of the general necessity calculus, rather than as a constituent part of an armed attack. This to ask whether there is *prima facie* a need to resort to force in response to an attack

all relate to an armed attack. Moreover, following this process would have provided a clear and predictable framework to be adopted for deciding future judgments. Such framework could also have served as a decision-making tool for states when considering whether or not to resort to defensive force, how they explain their decisions, and how they review the actions of other states.

2.3.3 General Necessity, Specific Necessity and Armed Attack

As the above example and analysis highlights, distinguishing between specific and general necessity also helps to draw a line between both types of necessity and the prior armed attack trigger. This distinction requires further elaboration. Green suggests that, in the vast majority of situations, the requirements of an armed attack and of necessity are likely to condition a use of force in the same manner. This is because, it is argued, if one applies the *Nicaragua* standard of 'armed attack as a grave use of force',[48] only in extreme cases (being grave uses of force) may self-defence be exercised. The situation is the same on an understanding of necessity that limits defensive force to extreme cases, where such action is a last resort. Therefore, these two requirements are performing a similar function, which raises the question: 'if an armed attack is established, does this automatically prove necessity?'[49] Green's response is that establishing an armed attack (amounting to a 'grave' use of force) is tantamount to establishing necessity in virtually all cases.[50]

It might be true that a state faced with a grave use of force easily establishes the defensive necessity that permits a forcible response. However, as Green notes, the Court has clearly recognized that 'armed attack' and 'necessity' are distinct concepts.[51] It has set out a two-stage test for assessing the lawfulness of self-defence, even if confusion may arise from the jurisprudence regarding how they are applied. First is the requirement of the armed attack. If (and only if) that triggering element is present may we proceed to the *additional requirements* that the defensive response be necessary and proportionate.[52] Yet, Green rightly highlights that this distinction may not be so clear in state practice. States do not always employ this two-stage evaluation and may instead present the two concepts as part of the same legal claim.[53]

that appears to be accidental or made in error, or whether peaceful alternative means would suffice to resolve the situation.

[48] See *Nicaragua* (n 10) para 191.

[49] James A Green, *The International Court of Justice and Self-Defence in International Law* (Hart Publishing 2009) 135.

[50] Ibid, 135, 138.

[51] Ibid, 138.

[52] *Nicaragua* (n 10) para 194; *Oil Platforms* (n 34) para 51.

[53] Green, *The International Court of Justice* (n 49) 135–136.

Applying the concepts of general and specific necessity to this issue of coextensive operation of armed attack and necessity helps to draw a brighter line between them. This approach demonstrates that it is not just a conceptual possibility that an armed attack might not, in all cases, establish the necessity of responding to a 'grave use of force'.[54] The answer, therefore, to the question of whether an established armed attack automatically proves necessity, is that it does not.[55] First, we should not over-emphasize the 'most grave uses of force' description of an armed attack. The *Nicaragua* gravity threshold, to the extent it is accepted, is not generally regarded as being particularly high. Ruys concludes that '[e]ven small-scale attacks involving the use of (possibly) lethal force may trigger Article 51'.[56] As noted, the ICJ has suggested that the mining of a single military vessel might be enough to engage the right of self-defence.[57] Regardless, whilst gravity might be a factor that determines the existence of an armed attack, it does not inevitably establish general necessity.

As addressed in detail in Section 2.4, general necessity evaluates whether other reasonable options are open to the defending state to respond to an armed attack, before resorting to defensive force as a last resort. This assessment is context-dependent and draws upon a number of factors, which may or may not include the gravity of the armed attack. Accordingly, even if an armed attack is established (because a particular, undefined, threshold of violence has been surpassed), this does not automatically mean that there are no peaceful alternatives available to resolve the situation. An unintentional armed attack provides a cogent example. Factually, although this could surpass any gravity threshold, a peaceful resolution might suffice to resolve the issue, such as negotiations leading to reparations.

Therefore, considerations other than the gravity of an armed attack might determine whether there is a general necessary to resort to defensive force. One of the principal factors is timing. With fully completed armed attacks, for example, because they are factually over, there might be no need to rely on force where the situation can be resolved reasonably by other means.[58] The gravity of the attack could be irrelevant to this determination of general necessity. In situations where a state is facing an imminent armed attack, whether it has time to pursue peaceful alternatives is likely to govern the general necessity question. Addressing this timing issue is required in every case of an imminent armed attack, regardless of its gravity.[59]

The foregoing evaluation offers a clearer conceptual division between armed attack and general necessity. The gravity of an armed attack might factor in

[54] Ibid, 138.
[55] For possible conflation of general necessity and imminence, however, see Section 2.5.1.2.
[56] Tom Ruys, *'Armed Attack' and Article 51 of the UN Charter: Evolutions in Customary Law and Practice* (CUP 2010) 155.
[57] *Oil Platforms* (n 34) para 72.
[58] See Section 2.5.1.3.
[59] See Section 2.5.1.2.

considering general necessity, but this calculation goes beyond questions relating purely to the level of force directed at a state and addresses concerns that are clearly distinct from the armed attack trigger that precedes it. If the *Nicaragua* gravity threshold is accepted, however, the result is that the magnitude of force potentially features in both the armed attack trigger and considerations of general necessity. This is redundant. If the right of self-defence is not triggered until a particular level of force is surpassed, it is questionable whether a threshold requirement can also condition its exercise. It is doing no additional legal work in regulating the use of defensive force.

It is submitted that an armed attack is better conceived of as a baseline factual trigger of a use, or threatened use, of military force that *prima facie* engages the right of self-defence. This would equate 'armed attack' in Article 51 UN Charter with 'use of force' in Article 2(4).[60] If accepted, issues of gravity are confined to conditioning the exercise of the right. Gravity features in determining whether the exercise of self-defence is necessary and proportionate.[61] Rather than gravity factoring in an ill-defined manner as part of the preceding armed attack trigger, it fits more naturally into the overall contextual assessment of both of these requirements. Drawing a clear line between armed attack and general necessity emphasizes this fact.

A further distinction may be drawn between an armed attack and specific necessity. Clearly, specific necessity does not perform the same function as either the armed attack trigger or general necessity. It is not limiting force to cases where it is a last resort. Rather, once the right of self-defence is triggered and its exercise is established to be *prima facie* necessary, specific necessity limits defensive force to legitimate targets that enable the defending state to pursue a defensive purpose. It confines action to the pursuit of that aim. Therefore, parsing the concepts of armed attack and the two types of necessity helps to understand the function and content of these distinct and separate requirements. Even if the ICJ has not been clear in applying these criteria, it is entirely correct from a conceptual perspective for the Court to have affirmed a two-stage test that distinguishes between armed attack and necessity.

In sum, following an armed attack, or in response to one that is imminent, general necessity determines whether using force is the only reasonable way to resolve

[60] This author has written elsewhere regarding the gravity threshold controversy, whether there exists a gap between Arts 2(4) and 51, and how this might affect the rights of individual military personnel and their units to defend themselves. Chris O'Meara, 'The Relationship Between National, Unit and Personal Self-Defence in International Law: Bridging the Disconnect' (2017) 4(2) JUFIL 273, 289–298. On the gravity threshold issue more generally, see Green, *The International Court of Justice* (n 49) 111–146, 148–163; Ruys, *'Armed Attack'* (n 56) 139–157; Henderson, *The Use of Force and International Law* (n 47) 222–223; International Law Association ('ILA') Committee on the Use of Force, 'Final Report on Aggression and the Use of Force', Sydney Conference (2018) 5–7. See also Chapter 3 regarding how the gravity of the armed attack informs the proportionality of the defensive response.

[61] Regarding the relationship between the gravity of the armed attack and proportionality, see Section 3.3.4.1.

the situation. If it is, any application of force that goes beyond what is required to halt, repel or prevent that armed attack is either an issue regarding specific necessity (because of the nature of the target) or an issue of proportionality (because the overall defensive response is excessive).[62] This proposed distinction between two types of necessity identifies what is meant by references to 'necessity'. It may be used as a tool to analyse the literature, judicial pronouncements, state practice and expressions of *opinio juris*. It also helps us to tease out the conceptual differences between armed attack, necessity and proportionality and to draw a clearer dividing line between them. This novel terminology and associated analytical approach are adopted throughout this book.

2.4 General Necessity—Other Options Open to a State

2.4.1 General Principles

In response to an actual or imminent armed attack, Webster's formula suggests that self-defence is only available to a defending state if there is 'no choice of means'. Today, the common understanding amongst scholars of this element of necessity is that resorting to defensive force is exceptional. It is a measure of last resort,[63] where the particular situation compelled a certain course of conduct.[64] This means that there must not be any non-military alternative to using force.[65] If a state can counter an actual or imminent armed attack by measures not involving armed force, it has no justification for using it.[66] Under our novel taxonomy, this conclusion equates to the requirement of general necessity.

The general academic consensus is that necessity does not require a defending state to consider all peaceful alternatives open to it, and to pursue and exhaust them before acting with force to end or avert an armed attack. This is despite the general obligation under international law requiring peaceful settlement of disputes

[62] See, respectively, Sections 2.6 and Chapter 3.

[63] The *Caroline* incident occurred in a period where emerging state practice already contained the notion that war was a means of last resort. Ian Brownlie, *International Law and the Use of Force by States* (Clarendon Press 1963) 21–22. Regarding necessity as a principle of last resort in the just war tradition, see Jens David Ohlin and Larry May, *Necessity in International Law* (OUP 2016) 15–37.

[64] Christian J Tams, 'The Necessity and Proportionality of Anti-Terrorist Self-Defence' in Larissa van den Herik and Nico Schrijver (eds), *Counter-Terrorism Strategies in a Fragmented International Legal Order: Meeting the Challenges* (CUP 2013) 373, 380.

[65] Ago, 'Addendum—Eighth Report on State Responsibility' (n 5) para 120; Oscar Schachter, 'The Right of States to Use Armed Force' (1984) 82 Mich L Rev 1620, 1635–1637; Elizabeth Wilmshurst, 'The Chatham House Principles of International Law on the Use of Force in Self-Defence' (2006) 55(4) ICLQ 963 (hereafter 'The Chatham House Principles') 967; Yoram Dinstein, *War, Aggression and Self-Defence* (6th edn, CUP 2017) 250–251; Gray, *Use of Force* (n 23) 159. See also *Nicaragua* (n 10) diss op Schwebel, 201, 204.

[66] Ago, 'Addendum—Eighth Report on State Responsibility' (n 5) para 120.

between nations.[67] Terminology varies amongst scholars, but there is widespread agreement that the essence of necessity (to be understood as general necessity) is that states are only required to consider peaceable options that are practical and which are likely to be effective in averting a threat or bringing an attack to an end, or have a reasonable chance of so doing.[68] This focus on the lack of effective alternatives recalls the writings of just war theorists such as Vattel, who believed that force only becomes necessary when every other option 'proves ineffectual'.[69] It also echoes Webster's insistence that '[i]t must be shown that that admonition or remonstrance to the persons on board the *Caroline* was impracticable, or would have been unavailing'.[70]

An alternative to relying on 'effectiveness' is a belief that general necessity 'merely requires that non-forceful measures be *insufficient* to address the situation'.[71] The UK has explicitly referenced this standard of sufficiency, whilst The Netherlands has stated that there must be no 'viable' alternatives.[72] Notions of the feasibility and effectiveness of alternative measures are echoed by others who maintain that, where peaceful means have been found wanting, or when they clearly would be futile, then force should be considered necessary.[73] Green, noting this variant

[67] UN Charter, Arts 1(1), 2(3), 33. See also the preamble to UNGA Res 2625 (XXV) (24 October 1970) (hereafter 'Friendly Relations Declaration').

[68] The Chatham House Principles (n 65) 967. That alternative measures must be effective, see Christopher Greenwood, 'International Law and the United States' Air Operation Against Libya' (1987) 89 W Va L Rev 933, 945; Noam Lubell, *Extraterritorial Use of Force Against Non-State Actors* (OUP 2010) 45; Christian J Tams and James Devaney, 'Applying Necessity and Proportionality to Anti-Terrorist Self-Defence' (2012) 45(1) Israel L Rev 91, 96; Daniel Bethlehem, 'Self-Defense Against an Imminent or Actual Armed Attack by Nonstate Actors' (2012) 106 AJIL 770, 775; Tams, 'Necessity and Proportionality' (n 64) 380; Henderson, *The Use of Force and International Law* (n 47) 230; ILA, 'Final Report on Aggression and the Use of Force' (n 60) 12.

[69] Emer de Vattel, *The Law of Nations, Or, Principles of the Law of Nature, Applied to the Conduct and Affairs of Nations and Sovereigns* (1797, reprinted Indianapolis: Liberty Fund 2011) Book III, Chapter III, para 25.

[70] Letter from Mr Webster to Mr Fox (24 April 1841) *British and Foreign State Papers*, 1840–1841, Vol. XXIX, 1138.

[71] Michael Schmitt (ed), *Tallinn Manual on the International Law Applicable to Cyber Warfare* (CUP 2013) 62 (emphasis added). Elsewhere, Schmitt has argued that necessity requires the absence of 'adequate' non-forceful options. Michael Schmitt, '"Change Direction" 2006: Israeli Operations in Lebanon and the International Law of Self-Defense' (2008) 29(2) Mich J Int'l L 127, 151.

[72] UK Attorney General's Speech at the International Institute for Strategic Studies, 'The Modern Law of Self-Defence' (11 January 2017) <https://www.gov.uk/government/uploads/system/uploads/attachment_data/file/583171/170111_Imminence_Speech_.pdf> accessed 5 September 2020 (hereafter 'UK Attorney General Speech 2017') 10; The Netherlands, Ministry of Foreign Affairs, 'Appendix: International Law in Cyberspace' to 'Letter of 5 July 2019 from the Minister of Foreign Affairs to the President of the House of Representatives on the International Legal Order in Cyberspace' (26 September 2019) <https://www.government.nl/ministries/ministry-of-foreign-affairs/documents/parliamentary-documents/2019/09/26/letter-to-the-parliament-on-the-international-legal-order-in-cyberspace> accessed 5 September 2020, 9.

[73] Oscar Schachter, *International Law in Theory and Practice* (Martinus Nijhoff Publishers 1991) 152; Dinstein, *War, Aggression and Self-Defence* (n 65) 250–251, citing Schachter and asserting that alternative means of redress must be 'practicable'. Gill acknowledges that necessity usually refers to the lack of 'feasible alternatives'. Terry D Gill, 'When Does Self-Defence End?' in Weller (ed), *The Oxford Handbook* (n 7) 737, 743–744.

terminology, concludes that the contemporary *Caroline* requirement of last resort will be met where it would have been unreasonable to expect the defending state to attempt to deploy means other than force to resolve the situation. There must, therefore, be no *reasonable* choice of means available to the defending state in the particular circumstances.[74] This view has been expressed explicitly by Australia.[75] It is also reflected, in general terms, in state practice relating to specific incidents of self-defence.[76]

A conception of general necessity that maintains force as a last resort, and where it is the only reasonable choice of means, is further reflected in the wider operation of the collective security system. Under Article 42 of the UN Charter, the UNSC may take forcible measures to maintain or restore international peace and security if it considers that non-forcible Article 41 measures 'would be inadequate or have proved to be inadequate'.[77] For the right of self-defence, this premise requires that peaceful options are actually available to the defending state. Availability might be determined by the temporal considerations examined in Section 2.5, as well as more practical considerations. The latter include whether diplomatic channels are open between an attacker and the defending state.

In cases of armed attacks by states, diplomacy (whether by the defending state or other members of the international community) will constitute the primary alternative means of resolution.[78] If the attackers are NSAs, however, the option of communicating with them in order to pursue a peaceful resolution takes on additional complications. This is particularly difficult if states consider the NSAs to be terrorists.[79] In terms of the availability of dispute resolution, this assumes consent by both parties. In any event, recourse to an international court or tribunal is unlikely, on its own, to be effective in halting, repelling or preventing an armed attack. It is doubtful whether dispute resolution is a viable and reasonable alternative to defensive force, particularly in response to an ongoing armed attack.

[74] Green, 'Docking the *Caroline*' (n 4) 453, 455–456 (emphasis added). Focusing on the absence of a reasonable alternative such that force is the *only* reasonable option of addressing an armed attack is supported by other scholars. See David Rodin, *War and Self-Defense* (OUP 2002) 111; Taft, '*Oil Platforms* Decision' (n 47) 304; Gardam, *Necessity, Proportionality* (n 3) 26; Schmitt, '"Change Direction" 2006' (n 71) 151; The Chatham House Principles (n 65) 967; Ruys, '*Armed Attack*' (n 56) 95; Tams and Devaney, 'Necessity and Proportionality' (n 68) 96; Henderson, *The Use of Force and International Law* (n 47) 230.

[75] Australian Attorney-General, Senator the Hon. George Brandis QC, 'The Right of Self-Defence Against Imminent Armed Attack in International Law', Public Lecture at the T C Beirne School of Law, University of Queensland (11 April 2017) <https://www.ejiltalk.org/the-right-of-self-defence-against-imminent-armed-attack-in-international-law/> accessed 5 September 2020 (hereafter 'Australian Attorney-General Speech 2017').

[76] See Section 2.4.2.

[77] It is debatable whether necessity in this context is legally justiciable. Gardam, *Necessity, Proportionality* (n 3) 7, 206. Analogies with the operation of the collective security system are not straightforward, and more general consideration of the application necessity and proportionality to Chapter VII of the UN Charter is beyond the scope of the present work. See Gardam, *Necessity, Proportionality* (n 3) 188–229.

[78] Lubell, *Non-State Actors* (n 68) 45.

[79] See Chapter 4.

Alternatively, states can look to the UNSC for resolution. Under Article 51 of the UN Charter, the right of self-defence remains unimpaired until the UNSC has taken 'necessary measures' to restore international peace and security. As and when this happens, the necessity of self-defence is removed, and any continuing use of force by a defending state thereafter risks being characterized as punitive and unlawful. 'Necessary measures' are not defined in the UN Charter, although it is generally understood that the UNSC has the final say on this point.[80] This Charter mechanism recognizes that self-defence is an exceptional emergency action, pending resolution via the collective security framework with the UNSC at its head. For the right of self-defence to be terminated by reason of lack of necessity, however, the UNSC must take adequate and effective action to restore international peace and security.[81] Where the UNSC fails to act, or where states fail to abide by its resolutions, the necessity of a response *prima facie* persists.[82]

If the availability of reasonable alternatives is established, then the summation of scholastic opinion places emphasis on whether non-military responses are, or will be, feasible and effective to address the situation. On this academic evaluation, general necessity requires that a defending state shows that *either* (i) it has resorted to peaceful measures before using defensive force (and they have failed), *or* (ii) peaceful measures are unfeasible and/or, *on their own*, they will be ineffective to halt, repel or prevent an armed attack. In relation to the latter point, it should be stressed that general necessity requires that force be needed as a response, but it does not demand that force be the only response. Military action may be combined with non-forceful measures such as diplomacy, economic sanctions, or law

[80] Gill, 'When Does Self-Defence End?' (n 73) 746–749; Gray, *Use of Force* (n 23) 131–132. It is clear that not all measures taken by the UNSC will interfere with self-defence. UNSC action may be complimentary to its exercise, and the UNSC may also choose to affirm the right. This happened, for example, after Iraq's invasion of Kuwait in 1990 (UNSC Res 661 (6 August 1990)) UN Doc S/RES/661) and the 9/11 attacks in 2001 (UNSC Res 1368 (12 September 2001) UN Doc S/RES/1368; UNSC Res 1373 (28 September 2001) UN Doc S/RES/1373).

[81] Malvina Halberstam, 'The Right to Self-Defence Once the Security Council Takes Action' (1996) 17(2) Mich J Int'l L 229; Gill, 'When Does Self-Defence End?' (n 73) 746–749; ILA, 'Final Report on Aggression and the Use of Force' (n 60) 10. The UNSC might, for example, order a ceasefire, a withdrawal of forces, a cessation of hostilities and so forth. Such binding decrees remove the necessity of self-defence where they succeed in restoring international peace and security. Dinstein, *War, Aggression and Self-Defence* (n 65) 255–258. That the UNSC must take adequate and effective action to restore international peace and security before the right of self-defence is terminated is confirmed by the drafting history of the UN Charter. Halbertsam, 'The Right to Self-Defence Once the Security Council Takes Action', 240–248.

[82] For example, the UK explained the necessity of self-defence against Argentina's invasion of the Falkland Islands by reference to Argentina's refusal to comply with UNSC Res 502 (3 April 1982) UN Doc S/RES/502. The Resolution had demanded an immediate cessation of hostilities and an immediate withdrawal of all Argentine forces from the Islands. Therefore, the UK justified its enduring and unimpaired right of self-defence by the fact that the Resolution had failed to be effective in maintaining international peace and security. Letter dated 1 May 1982 from the Permanent Representative of the United Kingdom of Great Britain and Northern Ireland to the United Nations addressed to the President of the Security Council (1 May 1982) UN Doc S/15025. See further Geoffrey Marston (ed), 'United Kingdom Materials on International Law 1982' (1983) 53(1) BYIL 337, 543, 548, 551–552.

enforcement.[83] The point is that force may only be used either on its own, or in combination with non-forceful measures, if the latter are unfeasible and/or will be ineffective if used exclusively. The focus is on the availability of real alternatives.

The existing literature sets out the broad premise of general necessity and alternative measures, but not the complete picture. For example, there is no consensus, or much discussion, amongst scholars of *how* unlikely to succeed alternative courses of action need to be before defensive armed force becomes a permissible option. More fundamentally, the summation set out in the preceding paragraphs does not fully explain the nuances of the role of alternatives to force in state practice. The review in the next section shows that the importance of peaceful alternatives in determining the legality or otherwise of purported defensive force is highly contextual. Indeed, they may not factor at all in either the justification for, or review of, military action.

2.4.2 State Practice

State practice affirms the aforementioned presumption that self-defence, by virtue of general necessity, is a measure of last resort. However, states have yet to agree what this means beyond a general proposition. The following analysis shows that there is no consistent practice regarding what role alternative measures play in respect of particular incidents involving claims of self-defence. Such practice is varied and highly context specific. Neither is there consensus amongst states regarding what they require by way of alternatives. What measures might constitute reasonable substitutes to force is left open. The availability of peaceful measures is viewed by states as evidence of whether the resort to force is reasonable in the circumstances (*viz* that general necessity is satisfied). Yet, whether or not such measures are pursued or adopted does not appear to be determinative of their view of the legality of military action. Therefore, there is no requirement on states to *prove* general necessity.[84]

2.4.2.1 Defending States

States that are the objects of purported defensive force might highlight by way of protest that alternatives to force were open to the defending state. The Democratic Republic of the Congo ('DRC') adopted this approach when it argued its case in *Armed Activities*.[85] Likewise, in respect of the 1981 Osiraq incident discussed in

[83] Schmitt, *Tallinn Manual* (n 71) 62.

[84] Along these lines, Corten argues that an attacked state is not obliged to prove that it has exhausted all peaceful means before reacting in self-defence. Olivier Corten, 'Necessity' in Weller (ed), *The Oxford Handbook* (n 7) 861, 872.

[85] *Case Concerning Armed Activities on the Territory of the Congo (Democratic Republic of the Congo v Uganda)* (Judgment) [2007] ICJ Rep 168 (hereafter '*Armed Activities*') Memorial of the Democratic Republic of the Congo, 6 July 2000, para 5.29.

detail below, Iraq argued that Israel had effective multilateral and bilateral recourses available to it in order to avoid any perceived threat.[86] Yet, such states have a natural self-interest in highlighting the existence of alternatives to the force directed against them. In contrast to references to alternatives made by defending states (which are self-limiting and consequently carry particular evidentiary weight), such protestations have much less probative value in determining what states require as a matter of law when seeking to establish general necessity.

Defending states might vigorously assert their right of self-defence, yet they accept that the exercise of such right is conditioned. In seeking to justify their defensive acts, they will often refer to peaceful alternatives being unavailable or futile. In the early post-UN Charter period, for example, Tunisia claimed a right of self-defence against France and attempted to expel French troops stationed on its territory.[87] It stressed before the UNSC that it did everything in its power to avoid aggravating the situation and tried every method of reaching an amicable agreement, before resorting to self-defence.[88] Tunisia's efforts included repeatedly requesting the French government over a period of two years to settle the issue of their troops, direct negotiation and the use of good offices.[89] Similarly, during the Six Day War in 1967, Israel emphasized how it had waited for a peaceful settlement before resorting to force, claiming it only used military means at the point at which there was no alternative.[90]

In 1986, South Africa faced criticism for its armed intervention in Zambia, Zimbabwe and Botswana, ostensibly aimed at the African National Congress ('ANC') targets operating in those countries.[91] South Africa claimed a right of self-defence,[92] emphasizing not only that it had repeatedly warned Zambia, Zimbabwe and Botswana that the continued 'harbouring of terrorists' would result in a response against the threat emanating from their territory, but also that such states had rejected a South African offer to set up a 'joint mechanism' to negotiate an

[86] UNGA Verbatim Record (11 November 1981) UN Doc A/36/PV.52, para 24.

[87] Letter dated 13 February 1958 from the Permanent Representative of Tunisia addressed to the President of the Security Council (13 February 1958) UN Doc S/3951. France also claimed a right of self-defence in respect of alleged Algerian NSA attacks against it originating from Tunisian territory. Letter dated 14 February 1958 from the Permanent Representative of France to the President of the Security Council (14 February 1958) UN Doc S/3954. See further 'Political and Security Questions: Questions Concerning Africa' (1958) UNYB 77, 77–79. This is an example of both states claiming a right of self-defence on the basis of disputed facts. What is instructive is Tunisia's recourse to the language of alternative measures to justify its defensive action as a 'no choice of means' measure of last resort.

[88] UNSC Verbatim Record (2 June 1958) UN Doc S/PV.819, paras 22, 65.

[89] Ibid, paras 58, 65.

[90] UNSC Verbatim Record (6 June 1967) UN Doc S/PV.1348, paras 176–178. On this incident generally, see John Quigley, 'The Six Day War–1967' in Tom Ruys and Olivier Corten (eds) with Alexandra Hofer, *The Use of Force in International Law: A Case-Based Approach* (OUP 2018) 131.

[91] See generally Edward Kwakwa, 'South Africa's May 1986 Military Incursions into Neighboring African States' (1987) 12 Yale J Int'l L 421.

[92] UNSC Verbatim Record (22 May 1986) UN Doc S/PV.2684, 27–30.

end to the ANC's cross-border incursions.[93] Its justification in this incident echoed previous action against the ANC operating in foreign territory.[94] The military action was broadly condemned, however.[95] It was deemed to be particularly objectionable because it took place at the same time that mechanisms were available and being used to resolve peacefully the issues at hand.[96] These included efforts by the Commonwealth at mediations and negotiations between the four states involved.[97] Therefore, for all sides, the potential for peaceful resolution was a focal point for assessing the necessity of self-defence, even though there was general disagreement that defensive force was genuinely being used as a last resort.

When the USA invaded Panama in 1989, it justified its actions, *inter alia*, by claiming to act in self-defence following aggression against American forces.[98] In so doing, it referred to repeated prior attempts to deal with the Noriega government, including diplomacy and negotiations, all of which it had exhausted.[99] In 1993, the USA maintained this approach when it claimed a right of self-defence to justify its strikes against the headquarters of the Iraqi Intelligence Service ('IIS') in Baghdad in response to the failed attempt to assassinate former President George HW Bush and Iraq's 'continuing threat to United States nationals'.[100] In so doing, the USA emphasized that there was no reasonable prospect that diplomatic initiatives or economic measures would suffice to counter the threat. Consequently, as a last resort, it used force to respond to the attempted attack and the threat of further attacks.[101]

[93] Ibid, 22, 24–26. Warnings by defending states to other states supposedly harbouring terrorists is a common theme where self-defence is invoked to justify force against NSAs operating in foreign territory. See Chapter 4.

[94] In action taken the previous year against the ANC in Angola, South Africa pointed to previous failed attempts at peaceful resolution and to Angola's persistent harbouring of terrorists on its territory. This, it said, justified the necessity of its actions. UN Doc S/PV.2597 (1985) paras 58–60.

[95] Kwakwa, 'South Africa's May 1986 Military Incursions' (n 91) 429–432.

[96] Ibid, 432.

[97] See UNSC Verbatim Record (23 May 1986) UN Doc S/PV.2685, 5 (Australia); 7 (USA).

[98] Letter dated 20 December 1989 from the Permanent Representative of the United States of America to the United Nations addressed to the President of the Security Council (20 December 1989) UN Doc S/21035; UNSC Verbatim Record (20 December 1989) UN Doc S/PV.2899, 31–32. On this incident generally, see Louis Henkin, 'The Invasion of Panama Under International Law: A Gross Violation' (1991) 29 Colum J Transnat'l L 293; Nicholas Tsagourias, 'The US Intervention in Panama–1989' in Ruys and Corten, *The Use of Force in International Law* (n 90) 426.

[99] UN Doc S/PV.2899 (n 98) 31, 36. The American action was widely condemned, however, and its claim of self-defence is controversial. See generally UN Doc S/PV.2899 (n 98); UNSC Verbatim Record (21 December 1989) UN Doc S/PV.2900. See further Henkin, 'The Invasion of Panama' (n 98) 306; Tsagourias, 'The US Intervention in Panama' (n 98) 429–432.

[100] Letter dated 26 June 1993 from the Permanent Representative of the United States of America to the United Nations addressed to the President of the Security Council (26 June 1993) UN Doc S/26003. On this incident generally, see Dino Kritsiotis, 'The Legality of the 1993 US Missile Strike on Iraq and the Right of Self-Defence in International Law' (1996) 45(1) ICLQ 162; Paulina Starski, 'The US Airstrike Against the Iraqi Intelligence Headquarters–1993' in Ruys and Corten, *The Use of Force in International Law* (n 90) 504.

[101] UN Doc S/26003 (n 100).

The USA also referred to the exhaustion of diplomatic efforts when it carried out strikes against Iraq in 1998[102] and argued that there were no peaceful diplomatic alternatives to using force when justifying the necessity of its actions before the ICJ in *Oil Platforms*.[103] These are but a few examples of practice. References to a prior failure or unavailability of diplomacy or negotiation are fairly common in justifications of self-defence.[104] They are often included explicitly in reports to the UNSC.[105] More recently, in the context of combatting NSAs, the USA has publicly affirmed that the necessity of resorting to self-defence only arises when 'measures short of force have been exhausted or are inadequate to address the threat'.[106] In the same context, the UK has likewise confirmed that resort to forces is always a last resort, to be used where alternatives are insufficient or unavailable.[107] Australia has concurred, noting that necessity is satisfied where force is the only reasonable option.[108]

The aforementioned incidents and public statements exemplify how defending states may refer to alternatives to force when seeking to establish the general necessity of resorting to self-defence (even if not expressed in those precise terms). Such states justify their actions as a genuine need to use force as a last resort. Albeit not

[102] Letter dated 16 December 1998 from the Chargé D'Affaires A.I. of the United States Mission to the United Nations addressed to the President of the Security Council (16 December 1998) UN Doc S/1998/1181.

[103] *Oil Platforms* (n 34) Counter-Memorial and Counter-Claim Submitted by the United States of America, 23 June 1997, paras 4.23–4.26.

[104] Green, 'Docking the *Caroline*' (n 4) 454.

[105] See, for example, Letter dated 27 February 1987 from the Permanent Representative of the Islamic Republic of Iran to the United Nations addressed to the Security-General (27 February 1987) UN Doc S/18728; Letter dated 3 September 1987 from the Chargé D'Affaires A.I. of the Permanent Mission of the Libyan Arab Jamahiriya to the United Nations addressed to the President of the Security Council (4 September 1987) UN Doc S/19106; Letter dated 28 January 1995 from the Permanent Representative of Ecuador to the United Nations addressed to the President of the Security Council (28 January 1995) UN Doc S/1995/87; Letter dated 30 July 1997 from the Chargé D'Affaires A.I. of the Permanent Mission of Israel to the United Nations addressed to the Secretary-General (1 August 1997) UN Doc S/1997/603; Letter dated 31 August 1998 from the Permanent Representative of the Democratic Republic of the Congo to the United Nations addressed to the President of the Security Council (2 September 1998) UN Doc S/1998/827; Letter dated 10 February 1999 from the Permanent Representative of Ethiopia to the United Nations addressed to the President of the Security Council (10 February 1999) UN Doc S/1999/134; Letter dated 22 March 1999 from the Permanent Representative of Eritrea to the United Nations addressed to the President of the Security Council (24 March 1999) UN Doc S/1999/304; Letter dated 11 May 2001 from the Permanent Representative of Burundi to the United Nations addressed to the President of the Security Council (11 May 2001) UN Doc S/2001/472; Letter dated 15 January 2008 from the Permanent Representative of Chad to the United Nations addressed to the President of the Security Council (15 January 2008) UN Doc S/2008/21; Letter dated 23 April 2012 from the Permanent Representative of the Sudan to the United Nations addressed to the President of the Security Council (23 April 2012) UN Doc S/2012/252.

[106] Brian Egan, Legal Adviser, U.S. Department of State, 'International Law, Legal Diplomacy, and the Counter-ISIL Campaign: Some Observations', Speech to the 110th Annual Meeting of the American Society of International Law (1 April 2016) (2016) 92 Int'l L Stud 235 (hereafter 'USA State Department Legal Adviser Speech 2016') 241. The USA regards this view as an application of the unwilling or unable doctrine. See Section 4.2.2.

[107] UK Attorney General Speech 2017 (n 72) 1, 10, 13.

[108] Australian Attorney-General Speech 2017 (n 75).

always explicit, it seems inherent in these justifications that the states concerned viewed military responses as the only reasonable option in the circumstances. In the incidents referred to, alternatives such as diplomacy or negotiation were expressed to be exhausted or insufficient to address the situation at hand. These assertions were made in the course of legal claims of self-defence. As such, it might be concluded that states consider themselves *legally* bound to contemplate or explore these alternatives before using force, rather than making such pronouncements out of political or moral expediency.[109]

However, defending states do not always consider alternatives before resorting to force. Context is key. When faced with an ongoing armed attack, for example, it would be unreasonable for states to employ peaceful options by way of a response, instead of using defensive force. The timing of the armed attack is determinative of general necessity in such cases.[110] Furthermore, state practice, in particular since 9/11, indicates that defending states are much less likely to consider or have recourse to peaceful alternatives before resorting to force against NSA armed attacks in the context of transnational terrorism.[111] The importance of the particular circumstances is also highlighted by the reactions of other states to claims of self-defence.

2.4.2.2 Reactions of Other States

Other states, in criticizing or condemning a purported use of defensive force by defending states, often employ the medium of peaceful alternatives to comment upon the legality of self-defence. This might be in ambiguous or general terms, however, without detailed engagement with the facts or legal justifications advanced by defending states. For example, in response to the American strikes in 1993 against the IIS headquarters in Baghdad, China simply maintained that disputes between countries should be settled through 'peaceful means of dialogue and consultation', and that they did not endorse action that might intensify tension in the region, including the use of force.[112] Moreover, references to alternatives to force are typically only one of a number of reasons for negative reactions by other

[109] Gardam maintains that states regard themselves as under a 'continuing obligation' to endeavour to settle their differences by peaceful means. Therefore, '[d]epending on the circumstances, a failure to acknowledge peaceful overtures could transform a legitimate response in self-defence into an aggressive use of force'. Gardam, *Necessity, Proportionality* (n 3) 155. See also Tarcisio Gazzini, *The Changing Rules on the Use of Force in International Law* (Manchester University Press 2005) 147. Whether or not Gardam considers this to be a legal, as opposed to a moral, obligation based on state practice is unclear. However, if such overtures constitute an option to resolve the situation in an effective manner then, as a matter of general principle, it would be difficult to maintain that a use of force continues to be necessary.

[110] See further Sections 2.4.4 and 2.5.1.

[111] Peaceful alternatives vis-à-vis the NSAs themselves and the role of the host state are explored in Section 4.2.1.

[112] UNSC Verbatim Record (27 June 1993) UN Doc S/PV.3245, 21. See the equally ambiguous statement presented on behalf of the Non-Aligned Movement members of the UNSC relating to the same incident. UN Doc S/PV.3245, 16–17 (Cape Verde).

states. The context of the particular incident usually provides additional grounds for such responses.

During the 1956 Suez crisis, for instance, Yugoslavia maintained that rather than using military force in Egyptian territory, Israel should have availed itself of the 'armistice machinery' to deal with the fedayeen raids against it.[113] This comment was made, however, in the context of general concern for peace in the Middle East and Israel's pattern of behaviour. This pattern consisted of 'a policy of largescale armed reprisals against its neighbours', as well as the view that Israel had flouted UNSC Resolutions and ignored its UN Charter obligations.[114] Wider factual and political factors, beyond recourse to peaceful alternatives, clearly informed the response to Israel's action.

This trend continues. In respect of the 1967 Six Day War, Zambia proclaimed before the UN General Assembly ('UNGA') that Israel should have had recourse to the UN before resorting to what it labelled as aggressive action against Egypt.[115] The factual and legal analysis relating to this incident is debated, however, and concern over preventive military action and accusations of Israeli aggression dominated the reactions of other states.[116] When Israel claimed a right of self-defence against terrorist armed attacks in 1972, resulting in incursions into Lebanon,[117] Argentina asserted that, as a general matter, the principle of 'need' meant that there must be no alternative to using force and Israel had breached this requirement.[118] Argentina's negative reaction was also based, however, on the disproportionality of the Israeli response, the view that it was punitive, and concerns regarding stability in the Middle East.[119]

Israel was further criticized for acting during ongoing, and increasingly productive, negotiations before its raid into Uganda over the Entebbe hostage crisis of 1976.[120] Yet, these concerns regarding recourse to alternatives were again comingled with doubts regarding whether Israel had been the subject of an armed attack, controversy over the right to protect nationals abroad and unease over how best to respond to international terrorism and hijacking.[121] When it launched air

[113] UNSC Verbatim Record (30 October 1956) UN Doc S/PV.748, para 22.

[114] Ibid, para 21.

[115] UNGA Verbatim Record (27 June 1967) UN Doc A/PV.1538, para 84.

[116] See Quigley, 'The Six Day War' (n 90).

[117] Letter dated 25 February 1972 from the Acting Permanent Representative of Israel to the United Nations addressed to the President of the Security Council (25 February 1972) UN Doc S/10550.

[118] UNSC Verbatim Record (27/28 February 1972) UN Doc S/PV.1644, paras 25, 28. The reference to 'need' is understood as referring to general necessity.

[119] Ibid, paras 28–31. Regarding proportionality, see Section 3.2.1.2.

[120] On this incident generally, see Claus Kress and Benjamin K Nussberger, 'The Entebbe Raid–1976' in Ruys and Corten, *The Use of Force in International Law* (n 90) 220.

[121] See UNSC Verbatim Record (12 July 1976) UN Doc S/PV.1940, para 35 (Guinea); para 120 (Sweden); UNSC Verbatim Record (12 July 1976) UN Doc S/PV.1941, para 102 (Tanzania); UNSC Verbatim Record (13 July 1976) UN Doc S/PV.1942, paras 144–146 (India); UNSC Verbatim Record (14 July 1976) UN Doc S/PV.1943, paras 18, 22 (Libya). See further 'Other Political and Security Questions: Complaint of Aggression by Israel Against Uganda' (1976) UNYB 315, 315–320.

strikes on the Palestine Liberation Organization ('PLO') headquarters in Tunis in 1985, Israel again faced criticism for not pursuing peaceful settlement.[122] Although Israel insisted that no other remedies were available to combat the PLO, the perpetrators of the terrorist attacks that had prompted the raid had in fact been arrested.[123] Furthermore, states were generally scathing of Israel's actions, which were condemned by the UNSC as an act of 'armed aggression'.[124]

Perhaps the best-known example involving Israel was its airstrike on an Iraqi nuclear facility in Osiraq in 1981.[125] Israel justified its actions as an act of self-defence in response to a threat of 'nuclear obliteration'. It claimed that the facility was designed to produce atomic bombs that Iraq would use to target Israel.[126] Israel argued that that they were required to strike the nuclear reactor before it went 'hot'.[127] In terms of the necessity of that action and peaceful alternatives, Israel asserted that it had tried unsuccessfully to have the threat removed by diplomacy, which left it with no choice but to remove the 'mortal danger' using force.[128] It highlighted that Iraq had rejected UN efforts at peaceful settlement and had ignored relevant UNSC Resolutions.[129] Therefore, Israel had acted only after 'the usual international procedures and avenues had proved futile' and 'the diplomatic clock had run out'.[130]

States, at least implicitly, universally rejected this no choice of means justification. All states intervening in the UNSC debates explicitly condemned Israel's attack, with many characterizing is at as act of aggression.[131] Japan noted the recent International Atomic Energy Agency ('IAEA') inspection of the facility and the assurance regarding applicable safeguards given by the IAEA. In its view, '[i]f, in spite of that assurance, Israel suspected that Iraq intended to produce atomic bombs, it should […] have sought to settle the matter by peaceful means, for example by submitting it to IAEA for consideration'.[132] The Philippines also highlighted the availability to Israel of recourse to 'appropriate international bodies'.[133] Sierra Leone agreed with the need to resort to peaceful alternatives, in particular by Israel seeking protection from the UNSC.[134]

[122] See UNSC Verbatim Record (2 October 1985) UN Doc S/PV.2611, 38 (Turkey).

[123] Ibid, para 40 (Turkey); para 69 (Israel).

[124] UNSC Res 573 (4 October 1985) UN Doc S/RES/573, para 1.

[125] On this incident generally, see Tom Ruys, 'Israel's Airstrike Against Iraq's Osiraq Nuclear Reactor–1981' in Ruys and Corten, *The Use of Force in International Law* (n 90) 329.

[126] Letter dated 8 June 1981 from the Permanent Representative of Israel to the United Nations addressed to the President of the Security Council (8 June 1981) UN Doc S/14510; UNSC Verbatim Record (12 June 1981) UN Doc S/PV.2280, paras 58–59.

[127] UN Doc S/PV.2280 (n 126) para 95.

[128] Ibid, para 59.

[129] Ibid, para 67.

[130] Ibid, para 102.

[131] UN Docs S/PV.2280, ibid–UNSC Verbatim Record (19 June 1981) UN Doc S/PV.2288.

[132] UNSC Verbatim Record (15 June 1981) UN Doc S/PV.2282, 95.

[133] UNSC Verbatim Record (16 June 1981) UN Doc S/PV.2284, para 26.

[134] UNSC Verbatim Record (15 June 1981) UN Doc S/PV.2283, para 149. See also UNSC Verbatim Record (13 June 1981) UN Doc S/PV.2281, para 70 (Pakistan).

Significantly, the USA stood with those states condemning the Israeli airstrikes.[135] Its judgement that such acts had violated the UN Charter was 'based solely on the conviction that Israel had failed to exhaust peaceful means'.[136] Given the usually close relationship between Israel and the USA, the negative American reaction to its staunch ally is exceptionally strong evidence of illegality.[137] That Israel's actions were unlawful is also reflected in the UN's reaction. In UNSC Resolution 487, the UNSC unanimously condemned Israel's military action as a clear violation of the UN Charter.[138] The UNGA followed suit by condemning Israel's aggression.[139]

The Osiraq incident suggests that alternative measures might be placed at the forefront of the debate regarding the legality of purported defensive action. Their importance must be viewed in light of the particular context, however. It is clear from the UNSC debates that states were concerned by a number of factors, *inter alia*, the general impact of Israel's action on regional instability, the Middle East peace process, the issue of non-proliferation of nuclear weapons and the right to develop nuclear technology for peaceful purposes. Of central importance was Israel's attempt to justify its actions on the basis of preventive self-defence in response to a *non*-imminent threat, rather than by way of a response to an actual or imminent armed attack.[140] State concern over such 'pre-emptive' or 'preventive' action (both terms were employed) was readily apparent during the UNSC consideration of the incident and it formed an integral part of the censure of Israel.[141] As such, the focus on peaceful alternatives and the issue of 'no choice of means' should be viewed in the light of the broader discussion concerning the existence of a right of anticipatory self-defence and the dangers surrounding the potential

[135] UN Doc S/PV.2288 (n 131) para 27.

[136] 'Political and Security Questions: Middle East' (1981) UNYB 255, 276.

[137] Gray, *Use of Force* (n 23) 22.

[138] UNSC Res 487 (19 June 1981) UN Doc S/RES/487.

[139] UNGA Res 36/27 (13 November 1981) UN Doc A/RES/36/27.

[140] Although pointing to the threat of 'mortal danger' posed by Iraq's nuclear programme, Israel did not explicitly rely on a legal right to respond to an imminent armed attack (*viz* a specifically identified impending nuclear strike) and it is clear on the facts that Israel did not actually face an imminent armed attack. See Ruys, 'Israel's Airstrike' (n 125), especially 336. The reaction of states to Israel's self-defence claim reflects the dismissal of the existence of an imminent threat. Even on a broad interpretation of imminence (see Section 2.5.1.2), it is difficult to argue that Israel was truly facing an imminent armed attack. The nuclear facility was not yet operational at the time of the airstrikes and peaceful alternatives were clearly available to Israel to deal with any perceived threat, including recourse to the UN Security Council. This is so despite Israel's assertion that it had to act when it did or lose its opportunity to respond to the perceived threat. See UN Docs S/14510 (n 126); S/PV.2280 (n 126) 92–96; S/PV.2288 (n 131) 60. For the contrary view that Israel considered itself to be subject to an imminent threat on the basis that if it had not destroyed the Osiraq facility when it did, it would have been impossible to destroy it at all, see Green, *The International Court of Justice* (n 49) 97. Franck likewise interprets Israel's actions as responding to an imminent armed attack. Thomas M Franck, *Recourse to Force: State Action Against Threats and Armed Attacks* (CUP 2002) 103.

[141] UN Docs S/PV.2280 (n 126)–S/PV.2288 (n 131).

for its abuse. This context strongly influenced states' assessment of this particular incident.[142]

Israel should not be singled out for special criticism, however. Its allies have also been censured for not pursing alternatives to force. For example, during discussions in the UNSC that followed the USA's claim of self-defence to justify its airstrikes against Libya in 1986,[143] Ghana was trenchant in its criticism of the American action, noting that it 'did not bother to exhaust the provisions and arrangements set forth in the Charter for settling disputes'.[144] Yet, this came after the delegate had first expressed doubt regarding whether the USA had been the victim of an armed attack and over its attribution to Libya.[145] Therefore, the need to settle disputes peacefully was part of the Ghanaian denunciation, but the failure to pursue alternatives was not itself determinative. It was instead part of a package of a number of arguably more important rationales.

2.4.2.3 Proving General Necessity?

A review of state practice provides a mixed account. States might justify their acts by reference, in whole or in part, to the absence of reasonable alternatives to force, but this is not always the case. Peaceful resolution is not invariably sought and a failure to negotiate does not automatically lead to an act being condemned as unnecessary.[146] The American-led action against the Taliban in response to 9/11 and Global Coalition action against Daesh in Syria stand as clear examples.[147] Other states may also reference alternative measures when responding negatively to acts of putative self-defence, but this is not a consistent or uniform response.

Where they are referred to, alternatives to force are often remarked upon in abstract terms. Whereas defending states' justificatory statements might implicitly allude to force being the only reasonable option, other states tend not to touch upon how effective or reasonable such alternatives might be. Rather, general concern is expressed that defending states should, or could, have tried peaceful alternatives.

142 See Ruys, *'Armed Attack'* (n 56) 97, 280–287. The impact of the timing of an armed attack on the importance of alterative measures is explored further in Section 2.5.1. For discussion of a right of anticipatory self-defence (including 'pre-emptive' and 'preventive' self-defence) see Section 2.5.1.2.

143 Letter dated 25 March 1986 from the Permanent Representative of the United States of America to the United Nations addressed to the President of the Security Council (25 March 1986) UN Doc S/17938; Letter dated 14 April 1986 from the Acting Representative of the United States of America to the United Nations addressed to the President of the Security Council (14 April 1986) UN Doc S/17990. For commentary on this controversial and widely condemned incident, see Greenwood, 'United States' Air Operation Against Libya' (n 68); Maurice Kamto, 'The US Strikes Against Libya–1986' in Ruys and Corten, *The Use of Force in International Law* (n 90) 408.

144 UNSC Verbatim Record (18 April 1986) UN Doc S/PV.2680, 33–35.

145 Ibid, 32–35.

146 Green, *The International Court of Justice* (n 49) 81.

147 See Section 4.2.1.

Moreover, the previous section highlights that the role and importance of alternatives is highly contextual. If they are mentioned by other states, a lack of recourse to them tends to be one of a number of (potentially more important) reasons for criticism or condemnation. It is difficult to identify a case where there is a general consensus amongst states that the *sole* reason for condemnation was that the necessity of using force was absent because reasonable alternatives to force were available to resolve a situation. The American statement in respect of the Osiraq incident is a rare exception.

Furthermore, in those cases where alternatives are adduced, either by way of justification (by defending states) or critique (by other states), there is no indication by such states that the need to consider or pursue them stems from a legal obligation. An exercise of good faith, political expediency, or a combination of all these things could likewise account for such comments. The firmest conclusion that may be drawn regarding state practice is that the resort, or otherwise, to peaceful alternatives is not determinative of the legality of a purported use of defensive force. Defending states are not required to prove that general necessity is established because of an absence of a reasonable alternative. Instead, states view the resort to peaceful alternatives as desirable and as constituting *evidence* of whether or not there was a true necessity to employ force defensively and to continue to do so. Failing to pursue reasonable alternatives to force might point to a lack of general necessity but, *on its own*, such failure is unlikely to abrogate a determination of necessity.

Ultimately, general necessity will be established where there is a reasonable need to respond with force.[148] How much other states will credit a defending state's subjective evaluation of the necessity of resorting to force is contingent on the surrounding circumstances. An assessment of the legality of a claim of self-defence will also depend on what other *jus ad bellum* considerations pertain to the particular facts. Although peaceful alternatives are likely to be the focus of greater scrutiny when states claim a right of anticipatory self-defence, the more fundamental matter that is likely to be determinative of the legality in such cases is whether such right exists and/or what are its content and parameters. The Osiraq incident serves as a good example. Conversely, alternatives will be of less importance in respect of ongoing armed attacks, where there is no time to consider other options and where the necessity of self-defence is likely to be established per se.[149] In respect of action against NSAs in the context of international terrorism, recourse to alternative means plays a different role. As will be seen in Section 4.2, rather than negotiation or other peaceful dispute resolution mechanisms, the focus is instead on the primacy of host state action to combat the terrorist threat.

[148] See Green, 'Docking the *Caroline*' (n 4) 456.
[149] See Sections 2.4.4 and 2.5.1.1.

2.4.3 ICJ Jurisprudence and Alternative Measures

The ICJ's consideration of necessity and proportionality has been cursory, yet guidance may be found in its jurisprudence regarding the need for defending states to pursue alternative measures. Starting with *Nicaragua*, it is notable that the Court did not require the USA to have exhausted all peaceful means of resolution before resorting to military force. Nor did it censure the USA for this omission. Instead, as discussed in Section 2.5.2, the Court went directly to the issue of the timing (or 'immediacy') of the USA's putative defensive acts in order to reach its decision on necessity. The fact that the majority preferred to focus on temporal considerations and avoid consideration of alternative measures is notable. It accords with the state practice set out in the preceding section that the option of alternative measures is not necessarily the determinant of legality, particularly where temporal issues are the focal point of the incident.

In contrast, Judge Schwebel did spend time in his dissent ruminating over whether the USA should have pursued peaceful alternatives. His comments represent the most extensive judicial review of the topic by an ICJ judge and raise some interesting issues regarding the interplay between forceful and non-forceful responses. For Judge Schwebel, the necessity of the USA's actions against Nicaragua turned on whether there were available to the USA 'peaceful means of realizing the ends which it has sought to achieve by forceful measures'.[150] He began his analysis with the position of the victim state, El Salvador. He quickly accepted the necessity of El Salvador's recourse to defensive force, rather than limiting itself to peaceful negotiations, given that it faced an ongoing large-scale insurgency.[151]

Judge Schwebel proceeded to explain why the American response in the purported collective self-defence of El Salvador was also necessary. In so doing, he highlighted how the USA had mounted serious bilateral efforts to settle its dispute with Nicaragua peacefully and only when they had failed had the USA resorted to armed force.[152] He noted that, before employing such force, an argument might be maintained that the USA should have first exhausted the multilateral means of peaceful settlement open to it, notably those of the Organization of American States and the UN.[153] Interestingly, however, Judge Schwebel did not conclude that failure to exhaust these multilateral alternatives abrogated the necessity of the American action. Implicitly, this was because the failure was mitigated by the peaceful measures taken by the USA on both a bilateral and multilateral basis to try and resolve the situation, whilst it was also involved in its armed activities.[154] He

[150] *Nicaragua* (n 10) diss op Schwebel, para 201.
[151] Ibid, para 202. See further Section 2.5.1.1.
[152] Ibid, paras 203, 209.
[153] Ibid, para 204.
[154] These included maintaining diplomatic relations with Nicaragua and showing a readiness to negotiate a resolution whilst its support for the *contras* was underway. Ibid, para 205.

thereby explicitly recognized that the USA was employing both forceful and non-forceful means at the same time.

We must exercise caution regarding how much weight we give to Judge Schwebel's observations on recourse to peaceful measure of resolution, but there are number of observations to be made.[155] His approach reflects the general premise stated in Sections 2.4.1 and 2.4.2 that where they constitute a reasonable alternative to force, states are expected to pursue peaceful means of resolution before resorting to force. This is subject to a number of caveats, however. First, his comments might be confined to states acting in collective self-defence of an ally that is the direct victim of an armed attack. For the victims of an ongoing armed attack, he waives this expectation completely and the necessity for them to act in self-defence appears to be established per se. Arguably, the determinative factor is timing, being the immediate need of the direct victim of an armed attack to respond to force with force. Such need is not shared by the other state acting in collective self-defence.[156]

Second, for Judge Schwebel, resorting to force does not require the *exhaustion* of peaceful alternatives. He clearly recognizes that defensive force may be employed at the same time that peaceful resolution is sought. Therefore, attempting negotiation or seizing the UNSC of the matter do not *ipso facto* deny the necessity of exercising self-defence. This approach accords with the notion that peaceful alternatives and action taken by the UNSC must provide an effective resolution (so that force is not the *only* reasonable option in such circumstances).[157] Ultimately, necessity may 'turn on' the availability of reasonable alternatives to the USA to achieve its goals, but there is no suggestion in Judge Schwebel's opinion that positive international law requires the pursuit or exhaustion of peaceful means *to the exclusion of exercising self-defence*. The implication is that both individual and collective self-defence are necessary in the face of an ongoing armed attack until such time as the (concomitant) resort to alternatives, on their own, are effective to resolve the situation. On this basis, his judgment essentially boils down to what action is reasonable in the circumstances.[158] This is both logical and accords with the conclusions set out in Sections 2.4.1 and 2.4.2.

[155] His conclusions regarding alternatives are part of a dissenting opinion. They are also tightly tied up with his response to the particular facts and his view of the justifiability of necessity per se. See ibid, para 206. Judge Schwebel denied that the necessity of the USA's actions was justiciable but felt bound to express a judgment. Ibid, paras 69–77, 201.

[156] See Section 2.5.1.1. In addition, Judge Schwebel is responding here to the majority's judgment that the actions of the USA were unnecessary. As such, it is perhaps understandable that he goes into much greater detail regarding the American response, given that he is attempting to justify that their actions were necessary.

[157] It is clear from Judge Schwebel's dissent that such alternatives would need to be effective in resolving the situation. Ibid, paras 203–204.

[158] 'In circumstances where an aggressor State cannot be persuaded to cease its aggressive intervention, it is not *unreasonable* to seek to force the aggressor State to cease its aggressive intervention.' Ibid, para 203 (emphasis added).

In *Oil Platforms*, the ICJ considered in some detail the issue of necessity. Significantly, however, it did not expressly refer to peaceful alternatives. Instead, rather than focusing on this issue of general necessity, the Court devoted its scrutiny to specific necessity. This comprised consideration of the nature of the targets chosen by the USA in the course of their military responses, being a number of Iranian oil platforms. The Court did not view these platforms as legitimate military targets, which rendered using force against them unnecessary.[159] The Court followed this approach in *Armed Activities*. In this case, the DRC argued that Uganda's defensive action was unnecessary because Uganda had used force without first resorting to peaceful means of resolution, even though it had time to do so.[160] The Court did not address this fact, however. Instead, as with *Oil Platforms*, it focused on specific necessity. It based its finding that the defensive force was unnecessary (and disproportionate) on the nature of the targets selected by Uganda.[161]

These three cases are the only examples where the ICJ has condemned a state for an unnecessary use of force that it attempted to justify by reference to self-defence.[162] Although not indisputable, the Court's approach to general necessity suggests that it will not require states to prove that they have pursued or exhausted alternatives to force in order to establish such claim.[163] This conclusion corresponds with the state practice examined in Section 2.4.2. The Court's examination of necessity has been contingent on the facts surrounding the particular use of force, however. The context has determined if the Court focuses on whether the resort to any form of force was reasonable in the circumstances (*viz Nicaragua*, in particular, regarding the timing of the USA's actions), or whether such force was appropriately directed (*viz Oil Platforms* and *Armed Activities*). Although not a picture of clarity, these approaches broadly accord with the taxonomy adopted in this book of, respectively, general and specific necessity. This book argues that necessity should be considered strictly in this order, but the context of the

[159] *Oil Platforms* (n 34) paras 74–76. Targeting is covered in Sections 2.6 and 3.4.

[160] *Armed Activities* (n 85) Memorial of The Democratic Republic of the Congo, 6 July 2000, para 5.28; *Armed Activities* (n 85) Oral Proceedings, Verbatim Record, 12 April 2005, CR 2005/3, 47–48 (para 4), 50–52 (paras 9–16); *Armed Activities* (n 85) Reply of The Democratic Republic of the Congo, 29 May 2002, 230 (para 3.159).

[161] *Armed Activities* (n 85) para 147. See further Section 2.6.

[162] The Court did not raise the issue in *Corfu Channel* (*United Kingdom v Albania*) (Merits) [1949] ICJ Rep 4 (hereafter '*Corfu Channel*'). In *Legality of the Threat or Use of Nuclear Weapons* (Advisory Opinion) [1996] ICJ Rep 226 (hereafter '*Nuclear Weapons*'), the Court made general pronouncements regarding the use of force, but necessity and alternative measures were not part of its reasoning. In *Legal Consequences of the Construction of a Wall in the Occupied Palestinian Territories* (Advisory Opinion) [2004] ICJ Rep 136 (hereafter '*Wall*'), the ICJ limited its pronouncements on the right of self-defence to one paragraph (para 139). At no point did it refer to alternative measures.

[163] The issue of pursuing or exhausting alternatives has not been necessary to determine any ICJ case to date and this conclusion is not explicit in the judgments referred to. However, this conclusion is a logical implication of the fact that the majorities have never addressed this issue when considering other aspects of necessity. The conclusion is also implicit in Judge Schwebel's dissent in *Nicaragua*, which did consider alternatives.

case appears to have led the Court to focus on one type of necessity or the other, depending on the most obvious or pertinent facts.

2.4.4 A Temporal Distinction—Ongoing, Imminent and Completed Armed Attacks

Temporal considerations are central to the question of whether it is reasonable for a defending state to resort to other options not involving the use of force. Timing appears determinative to Webster's assertion that a state must in fact have 'no choice of means'. He maintained that:

> [i]t must be shown that admonition or remonstrance to the persons on board the *Caroline* was impracticable, or would have been unavailing [. . .] that it would not have been enough to seize and detain the vessel; but that there was a necessity, *present and inevitable*, for attacking her in the darkness of the night.[164]

Therefore, Webster's assertion that peaceful means must first be explored is based on elements of (i) reasonableness (*viz* availability and effectiveness of alternative means) and (ii) considerations of timing (*viz* a 'present and inevitable' necessity). This relationship between reasonableness and timing is best explored by distinguishing between ongoing, imminent and completed armed attacks. This distinction, as a determinant of general necessity, will be discussed in the next section, together with general considerations of how timing relates to the exercise of self-defence.

2.5 General Necessity—Imminence, Immediacy and Duration

Modern weaponry and delivery systems, coupled with the rise of international terrorism and attacks by NSAs, have increasingly highlighted the complexities surrounding the temporal element of the right of self-defence.[165] Timing is pivotal to whether or not a defensive riposte is necessary. It is the chronology of events that establishes if there is a genuine situation of emergency and a pressing need for a state to resort to force at the expense of nonviolent means of settlement. This is a question of general necessity.

[164] *British and Foreign State Papers*, 1840–1841, Vol. XXIX, 1138 (emphasis added).

[165] For a general discussion of these issues and the *ratione temporis* element of the right of self-defence, see Ruys, *'Armed Attack'* (n 56) 250–367; James A Green 'The *Ratione Temporis* Elements of Self-Defence' (2015) 2(1) JUFIL 97.

The genesis of some form of temporal limitation on the right of self-defence is also typically derived from Webster's assertion that the necessity of self-defence must be 'instant, overwhelming, and leaving [...] no moment for deliberation'.[166] The timing elements of Webster's formula elicit much debate amongst scholars. This is understandable, given that Webster's statement can be read as pertaining to the timing of the armed attack, or the defensive response, or both. In addition, temporal considerations are often mooted in very broad terms. References to 'instancy', 'immediacy' and 'imminence' are sometimes used without distinction and/or conflated with other considerations that mean a clear view of the timing element is lost.[167] Some even question whether necessity places any temporal restraints on the use of defensive force at all.[168]

Temporal issues should be considered in relation to two aspects of the right of self-defence. The first is the armed attack and whether it is ongoing, completed, or might occur at some point in the future. Although the timing of the armed attack is typically examined in terms of when the right of self-defence is triggered, it also plays a central role in the factual context that determines whether the right of self-defence is exercisable. As explored in Section 2.5.1, this is an issue of general necessity, which responds to the timing of the armed attack. Most controversially, the prospect of future armed attacks engages the issue of anticipatory self-defence and considerations of 'imminence'.

The second aspect is the timing of the defending state's response to an armed attack. This factors in the general necessity calculus by considering how long it takes a defending state to respond in self-defence. It engages the notion of 'immediacy'. Immediacy is sometimes stipulated as a third precondition, in addition to the requirements of necessity and proportionality.[169] However, as will be made clear in Section 2.5.2, immediacy is most naturally analysed as part of general necessity. The ICJ has adopted this approach, rather than recognizing it as a distinct and separate criterion.[170] Many of the leading *jus ad bellum* scholars also contemplate necessity along these lines.[171] As such, the issue of the timing of both the armed attack and the defensive response is essential to our understanding of general necessity.

[166] Letter from Mr Webster to Lord Ashburton (6 August 1842) *British and Foreign State Papers*, 1841–1842, Vol. XXX, 201.

[167] See, for example, Gardam, *Necessity, Proportionality* (n 3) 148–155. See further below in this section.

[168] See, for example, Claus Kress, 'The International Court of Justice and the "Principle of Non-Use of Force"' in Weller (ed), *The Oxford Handbook* (n 7) 561, 587. Gardam in contrast maintains that, arguably, 'instancy' (or immediacy) is the only element of the *Caroline* formula that needs to be satisfied. Gardam, ibid, 149.

[169] See Ago, 'Addendum—Eighth Report on State Responsibility' (n 5) para 122; Dinstein, *War, Aggression and Self-Defence* (n 65) 252, 287–288; Gill, 'When Does Self-Defence End?' (n 73) 743–745.

[170] *Nicaragua* (n 10) para 237. The ICJ adopted the same approach in the context of necessity as a circumstance precluding wrongfulness. *Gabčíkovo-Nagymaros* (n 8) para 54. See further Section 2.5.1.2.

[171] For example, The Chatham House Principles (n 65) 967; Ruys, *'Armed Attack'* (n 56) 99–108; Green, 'The *Ratione Temporis* Elements of Self-Defence' (n 165) 108.

2.5.1 The Timing of the Armed Attack

As noted in the preceding section, the timing of an armed attack bears heavily on whether it is reasonable for a defending state to pursue other options not involving the use of force. In order to explain this relationship, and how it alters with the time available, the following analysis distinguishes between ongoing, imminent and completed armed attacks.

2.5.1.1 Ongoing Armed Attacks

Ongoing armed attacks pose few conceptual complexities regarding recourse to alternative measures. This author adopts Schachter's contention that where a state is under current armed attack the necessity (understood as general necessity) of self-defence is established per se, irrespective of probabilities as to the effectiveness of peaceful settlement.[172] This conclusion assumes that any gravity threshold is met. Along similar lines, other authors maintain that necessity will usually be satisfied in such circumstances, or there exists a strong presumption of necessity.[173] That the general necessity of using armed force to repel an ongoing attack is automatically established is reflected in state practice. Examples include the UK's response to the Argentinian invasion of the Falklands Islands in 1982[174] and Israel's intervention in Lebanon in 2006.[175] A more recent case, in the context of combatting NSAs, is the ongoing Global Coalition action in Syria.[176]

The presumption in favour of general necessity being established in the case of ongoing armed attacks is logical. In such instances, there exists a present and exigent need for a state to protect its territory and citizens by using force, without time to consider other options. It is unreasonable to expect a state to forego its right of forcible response in favour of a peaceful alternative, and there is nothing in the UN Charter or state practice to suggest otherwise.[177] International law does not oblige a state to turn the other cheek when it is faced with continuing military violence. Until the UNSC acts effectively, or a peaceful resolution is otherwise found,

[172] Schachter, *International Law* (n 73) 152. See further Section 2.4.3 and consideration of Judge Schwebel's dissent in *Nicaragua*.

[173] For example, Yoram Dinstein, *War, Aggression and Self-Defence* (4th edn, CUP 2005) 237; Green, 'Docking the *Caroline*' (n 4) 455; Lubell, *Non-State Actors* (n 68) 43, 45; Akande and Liefländer, 'Clarifying Necessity, Imminence, and Proportionality' (n 3) 564; Tams, 'Necessity and Proportionality' (n 64) 417; Henderson, *The Use of Force and International Law* (n 47) 230. For further consideration by this author of this issue and related academic opinion, see O'Meara, 'The Relationship Between National, Unit and Personal Self-Defence' (n 60), in particular 301–304.

[174] See Section 2.5.2.2.

[175] See in particular Section 3.3.5.

[176] This latter example is more controversial, however. See Section 4.2.

[177] This conclusion mirrors the operation of the collective security system. The UN Charter does not require the UNSC to exhaust peaceful means before relying on force to maintain or restore international peace and security. Art 42 allows the UNSC to deploy force where non-forcible Art 41 measures *would be inadequate* or have proved to be inadequate. Therefore, Art 42 explicitly recognizes that force might be the appropriate response, even if viewed as a measure of last resort.

defending states retain the option to respond to current force with force. Whether or not the defending state chooses to exercise that option is a separate question. Yet, to require a state to attempt peaceful methods of resolution, *instead* of using defensive force, is to abrogate the right of self-defence.[178]

2.5.1.2 Imminent Armed Attacks

Whether states possess a right of some form of anticipatory self-defence in response to threats of future armed attacks remains a disputed topic of international law.[179] Terminology varies,[180] but the ability for states to counter potential unmaterialized threats (what this book calls 'preventive self-defence') has been almost universally denounced by scholars and is broadly rejected by states. With the exception of the USA and Israel, state practice in support of such right is virtually non-existent.[181] In contrast, whether states currently possess the right to respond to imminent armed attacks (what this book calls 'pre-emptive self-defence') occupies a much less clear position in the *lex lata*. State practice is mixed, and credible arguments can be made either way. This diverse body of state practice led Ruys in 2010 to conclude rightly that *opinio juris* in favour of a right of pre-emptive self-defence against imminent armed attacks had increasingly been more widespread and explicit in recent years, but consistent opposition to such a right by a considerable group of states meant that there was no widespread acceptance of it. As such, it was impossible to identify as *lex lata* a legal right of pre-emptive self-defence.[182] In 2018, the ILA noted the increasing academic support for the right of pre-emptive self-defence, concluding that '[a]lthough the matter remains unsettled, there may be reason to accept that when faced with a specific imminent armed attack based on objectively verifiable indicators, States may engage in measures to defend themselves in order to prevent the attack'.[183]

The most contemporary state practice has largely taken place in the context of state responses to international terrorism. Notable examples include the UK's use of an RAF drone to carry out a targeted killing of a British citizen, Reyaad Khan,

[178] There is nothing to prevent a defending state pursuing peaceful means of settlement in addition to using force to respond to an ongoing armed attack. See generally Ruys, *'Armed Attack'* (n 56) 250–367.

[179] See Terry D Gill, 'The Temporal Dimension of Self-Defence: Anticipation, Pre-emption, Prevention and Immediacy' (2006) 11(3) JC&SL 361; Ruys, *'Armed Attack'* (n 56) 250–367; Green, 'The *Ratione Temporis* Elements of Self-Defence' (n 165); Henderson, *The Use of Force and International Law* (n 47) 274–307.

[180] For present purposes, anticipatory self-defence refers to any defensive response to the threat of a future armed attack. This term is then sub-divided into two 'types' of anticipatory self-defence, being preventive and pre-emptive self-defence. See Ruys, *'Armed Attack'* (n 56) 250–254 for a general discussion of the terminology that this book adopts.

[181] For an overview of academic opinion and state practice pertaining to preventive self-defence, see Corten, *The Law Against War* (n 24) 406–443; Ruys, *'Armed Attack'* (n 56) 322–324; Green, 'The *Ratione Temporis* Elements of Self-Defence' (n 165) 106–107; Gray, *Use of Force* (n 23) 248–261; Henderson, *The Use of Force and International Law* (n 47) 285–296.

[182] Ruys, *'Armed Attack'* (n 56) 341–342. More recent state practice is discussed in this section.

[183] ILA, 'Final Report on Aggression and the Use of Force' (n 60) 13–14.

in Syria in August 2015.[184] The UK justified its action as self-defence on the basis that the target was 'actively engaged in planning and directing imminent armed attacks against the United Kingdom'.[185] The UK has since reaffirmed its claim to a right of self-defence against imminent armed attacks and set out in some detail its understanding of imminence.[186] Allies of the UK have followed suit. In 2016, the U.S. Department of State Legal Adviser delivered a speech on international law and America's ongoing armed conflict against Daesh. In it, he confirmed the USA's long held view that the *jus ad bellum* permits a state to exercise its right of self-defence against imminent armed attacks and detailed how the Americans interpret imminence.[187] The USA most recently invoked this right of pre-emptive self-defence to justify its targeted killing by drone strike of Iran's General Qassem Soleimani in 2020.[188]

Likewise in the context of the ongoing military action against Daesh, Australia has explicitly asserted this ability, as well expressing their views on imminence.[189] The remaining two 'Five Eyes' nations *might* also agree with this position, although this is currently speculative.[190] Other states that have recently asserted and/or recognized a right of pre-emptive self-defence include Japan,[191] India,[192] Israel and

[184] 'Cardiff Jihadist Reyaad Khan, 21, Killed by RAF Drone', *BBC News* (7 September 2015) <https://www.bbc.co.uk/news/uk-wales-34176790> accessed 5 September 2020.

[185] Letter dated 7 September 2015 from the Permanent Representative of the United Kingdom of Great Britain and Northern Ireland to the United Nations addressed to the President of the Security Council (8 September 2015) UN Doc S/2015/688. The UK also claimed to have acted against Daesh in Syria in the collective self-defence of Iraq. See further Christine Gray, 'Targeted Killing Outside Armed Conflict: A New Departure for the UK?' (2016) 3(2) JUFIL 198.

[186] UK Attorney General Speech 2017 (n 72) 7–8, 12–20.

[187] USA State Department Legal Adviser Speech 2016 (n 106) 239. The USA's position is also reflected in their current Department of Defense Law of War Manual. Department of Defense, Law of War Manual (June 2015) (updated December 2016) <https://dod.defense.gov/Portals/1/Documents/pubs/DoD%20Law%20of%20War%20Manual%20-%20June%202015%20Updated%20Dec%202016.pdf?ver=2016-12-13-172036-190> accessed 5 September 2020, para 1.11.5.1.

[188] The Trump administration's initial justifications for this action centred on self-defence against an imminent armed attack, although the rationale for the killing shifted over time. See Mehrnusch Anssari and Benjamin Nussberger, 'Compilation of States' Reactions to U.S. and Iranian Uses of Force in Iraq in January 2020' (*Just Security*, 22 January 2020) <https://www.justsecurity.org/68173/compilation-of-states-reactions-to-u-s-and-iranian-uses-of-force-in-iraq-in-january-2020/> accessed 5 September 2020. Imminence was also a central feature of the ensuing analysis by legal commentators, journalists and the Special Rapporteur on Extrajudicial, Summary or Arbitrary Executions that considered the legality of the strike. See Human Rights Council, 'Report of the Special Rapporteur on Extrajudicial, Summary or Arbitrary Executions' (29 June 2020) UN Doc A/HRC/44/38, paras 52–57, 61(b), 67–68, 92(a). See in particular the Annex to the report, especially paras 10(a), 54, 58, 61–62, 64, 82.

[189] Australian Attorney-General Speech 2017 (n 75).

[190] Although not explicit, in his speech the UK Attorney General implied that Canada and New Zealand might also adopt the UK's interpretation of imminence. These countries have not publicly affirmed this, however. UK Attorney General Speech 2017 (n 72) 18.

[191] See Japan, Ministry of Defence, 'Defense of Japan 2019' (2019) <https://www.mod.go.jp/e/publ/w_paper/wp2019/pdf/DOJ2019_Full.pdf> accessed 5 September 2020, 198–199, 248.

[192] In 2019, India justified a pre-emptive airstrike against a terrorist training camp in Pakistan in response to what it called an 'imminent danger' comprised of anticipated future terrorist attacks. Indian Ministry of External Affairs, 'Statement by Foreign Secretary on 26 February 2019 on the Strike on JeM training camp at Balakot' (26 February 2019) <https://www.mea.gov.in/press-releases.htm?dtl/31091/Statement_by_Foreign_Secretary_on_26_February_2019_on_the_Strike_on_JeM_training_camp_at_Balakot> accessed 5 September 2020.

Iran in 2019.[193] Following the Soleimani targeted killing in 2020, Lithuania and South Africa explicitly recognized the ability of states to respond to 'imminent threats', whilst Liechtenstein offered implicit support for a right of pre-emptive self-defence.[194] These latter assertions lack elaboration regarding how these states interpret imminence, however. Therefore, it is because of the detailed nature of the positions set forth by the UK, USA and Australia that these examples of state practice are examined in detail below.

Whether or not international law currently recognizes a right of pre-emptive self-defence, or might do in the future, undoubtedly states have had, and continue to have, recourse to a right of pre-emptive action to justify using force. In these circumstances, general necessity takes on additional significance.[195] The fact that such armed attacks, by definition, occur in the future places emphasis on peaceful alternatives to force and whether resorting to them is reasonable in the circumstances. As the Chatham House Principles explain it: '[n]ecessity is a threshold and the criterion of imminence can be seen to be an aspect of it, inasmuch as it requires that there be no time to pursue non-forcible measures with a reasonable chance of averting or stopping the attack'.[196] The analysis set out in Section 2.4.2 and in this section suggests that states will consider peaceful ways to resolve a situation up until the point that the opportunity to defend themselves effectively is lost. Ultimately, general necessity will be determined by whether, in the particular circumstances, self-defence was a reasonable choice to counter the future threat. This raises the further question of whether the trigger for the right of self-defence (being armed attacks that are 'imminent') and the conditioning of its exercise (being general necessity) are equated in this context. This potential is explored further below.

The difficulty with considering whether states have the time to consider and/or resort to alternatives to force when faced with the threat of imminent armed attacks is the lack of consensus regarding the meaning of imminence. There is no authoritative legal definition of this term as it relates to an armed attack.[197] The ICJ has not expressed its view on this issue[198] and there is a relative paucity of consideration by

[193] Israeli Defense Forces justified intervening militarily in Syria in 2019 to prevent 'an imminent, large-scale terror attack by multiple killer drones targeting northern Israel'. Israel blamed Iran for the anticipated attack. Iran denounced the violation of Syrian territory, expressly recognizing a right of self-defence against any 'imminent or attempted attack' from Israel. See Patrick M Butchard (ed), 'Digest of State Practice: 1 July–31 December 2019' (2020) 7(1) JUFIL 156, 184–187.

[194] UNSC Verbatim Record (9 January 2020) UN Doc S/PV.8699, 11 (South Africa); 37 (Liechtenstein). Lithuania's Ministry of Foreign Affairs tweeted its affirmation of such right. See <https://twitter.com/LinkeviciusL/status/1213125016465891328> accessed 5 September 2020.

[195] Ago, 'Addendum—Eighth Report on State Responsibility' (n 5) para 120. Ago's reference to 'preventative' self-defence is expressed by him to include self-defence in relation to imminent attacks.

[196] The Chatham House Principles (n 65) 967. This statement is understood as a reference to general necessity.

[197] Noam Lubell, 'The Problem of Imminence in an Uncertain World' in Weller (ed), *The Oxford Handbook* (n 7) 697, 702; Dinstein, *War, Aggression and Self-Defence* (n 65) 233.

[198] In *Nicaragua* (n 10) para 194, as the parties did not raise the issue of 'the imminent threat of an armed attack', the Court declined to express a view on the issue. It took the same approach in *Armed Activities* (n 85) para 143.

scholars.[199] That said, the starting point for considering imminence is traditionally Webster's assertion that the necessity of self-defence must be 'instant, overwhelming, and leaving no choice of means and no moment for deliberation'.[200] This formulation is typically understood as encapsulating the meaning of imminence, even if the facts of the *Caroline* incident do not necessarily comprise a response to an anticipated future armed attack.[201]

Understood along the lines of the *Caroline* formula, imminence is conceptualized on the basis of the temporal proximity of the threatened armed attack. This approach reflects a common understanding of the word that something is impending. Following the 2015 drone strike on Reyaad Khan, for example, the UK's All Party Parliamentary Group on Drones Inquiry Report noted that the ordinary meaning of imminence 'requires an *assessment of temporal factors only* and translates to an attempt to answer the question: is the attack about to happen?'[202] Lubell, in one of the few wide-ranging academic attempts to explore the meaning of imminence, emphasizes that an imminent armed attack 'must be an impending attack over which there is a reasonable level of certainty that it will occur in the foreseeable future' and the threat must be 'specific and identifiable'.[203]

That a state must identify a specific armed attack before being able to respond militarily rightly draws a line between (potentially lawful) pre-emptive self-defence and (almost certainly) unlawful preventive self-defence. It is uncontroversial that imminence, as it relates to pre-emptive self-defence, must refer to an 'objectively verifiable, concretely imminent attack',[204] rather than to unmaterialized

[199] Notable exceptions include Bethlehem, 'Self-Defense Against an Imminent or Actual Armed Attack by Nonstate Actors' (n 68); Lubell, 'The Problem of Imminence' (n 197). See also Akande and Liefländer, 'Clarifying Necessity, Imminence, and Proportionality' (n 3) 564–565; Green, 'The *Ratione Temporis* Elements of Self-Defence' (n 165); Dennis R Schmidt and Luca Trenta, 'Changes in the Law of Self-Defence? Drones, Imminence, and International Norm Dynamics' (2018) 5(2) JUFIL 201.

[200] *British and Foreign State Papers*, 1841–1842, Vol. XXX, 201 (n 166).

[201] The *Caroline* incident is frequently cited in the context of a right of anticipatory self-defence (see, for example, *Nicaragua* (n 10), diss op Schwebel, para 200), but the facts of the British raid and the wider context of the incident are often misunderstood and/or misrepresented. Rather than pertaining to the anticipation of a future armed attack, the incident might be better characterized as a response to an ongoing armed attack. For a comprehensive and compelling review of the *Caroline* incident that supports such a conclusion, see Craig Forcese, *Destroying the Caroline: The Frontier Raid that Reshaped the Right to War* (Irwin Law Inc 2018), especially 225–231. Nevertheless, and despite the precise factual matrix, the *Caroline* formula persists as the benchmark for any discussion of the right of pre-emptive self-defence and, particularly for present purposes, considering 'imminence'.

[202] The UK's All Party Parliamentary Group on Drones Inquiry Report, 'The UK's Use of Armed Drones: Working with Partners' (July 2018) <http://appgdrones.org.uk/wp-content/uploads/2014/08/INH_PG_Drones_AllInOne_v25.pdf> accessed 5 September 2020, 36 (emphasis added).

[203] Lubell, 'The Problem of Imminence' (n 197) 702–705, 718. Although offering one of the few extensive reviews of imminence, Lubell describes it as a separate, third customary requirement for measuring defensive action, in addition to necessity and proportionality. This minority position is not generally shared by scholars, nor in the state practice referred to herein from the USA, UK and Australia. As explored in this book, imminence is better understood as relating to the requirement of necessity.

[204] The Council of the European Union's Independent International Fact-Finding Mission on the Conflict in Georgia, Report, Vol II (September 2009) <http://www.mpil.de/files/pdf4/IIFFMCG_Volume_II1.pdf> accessed 5 September 2020 (hereafter 'IIFFMCG Report') 254. See also Lubell, 'The

and speculative threats that are the domain of preventive self-defence. On the temporal aspect, however, Lubell notes that an armed attack might be imminent, but self-defence is not necessary where non-forcible alternatives are available, or where the action by the UNSC precludes the need for defensive action.[205] This logic, like that of the UK's All Party Parliamentary Group on Drones Inquiry Report, reduces imminence solely to a question of the timing of a specifically identified future armed attack. Yet, imminence is also understood by scholars to include additional non-temporal components. The authors of The Chatham House Principles, for example, assert that '[i]n the context of contemporary threats imminence cannot be construed by reference to a temporal criterion only, but must reflect the wider circumstances of the threat'.[206]

Recent state practice has reflected the latter approach that imminence goes beyond consideration of solely the temporal proximity of a future armed attack. Notable case studies are the explanations put forward by the USA, the UK and Australia regarding how they construe imminence.[207] In so doing, each state has explicitly adopted Bethlehem's 'Principle 8' amongst a number of factors that they take into account:

> Whether an armed attack may be regarded as 'imminent' will fall to be assessed by reference to all relevant circumstances, including (a) the nature and immediacy of the threat, (b) the probability of an attack, (c) whether the anticipated attack is part of a concerted pattern of continuing armed activity, (d) the likely scale of the attack and the injury, loss, or damage likely to result therefrom in the absence of mitigating action, and (e) the likelihood that there will be other opportunities to undertake effective action in self-defense that may be expected to cause less serious collateral injury, loss, or damage.[208]

In considering this formulation, we should note that the Bethlehem Principles are controversial and do not necessarily reflect the *lex lata* in whole or in part. Indeed, they have been the object of understandable criticism.[209] Moreover, the positions

Problem of Imminence' (n 197) 703–704; Green, 'The *Ratione Temporis* Elements of Self-Defence' (n 165) 105.

[205] Lubell, 'The Problem of Imminence' (n 197) 699–700.

[206] The Chatham House Principles (n 65) 967.

[207] See USA State Department Legal Adviser Speech 2016 (n 106); UK Attorney General Speech 2017 (n 72); Australian Attorney-General Speech 2017 (n 75).

[208] Bethlehem, 'Self-Defense Against an Imminent or Actual Armed Attack by Nonstate Actors' (n 68) 775–776. Bethlehem's Principle 8 is one of sixteen Principles relating to self-defence against actual or imminent armed attacks by NSAs. Bethlehem states that the Principles were formed from detailed discussions with a number of state representatives with relevant operational experience. He describes these factors as indicative, rather than exhaustive, of imminence.

[209] See, for example, Elizabeth Wilmshurst and Michael Wood, 'Self-Defense Against Nonstate Actors: Reflections on the "Bethlehem Principles"' (2013) 107 AJIL 390.

of these three states vis-à-vis Bethlehem's appreciation of imminence remain open to varying interpretations and have raised as many questions as answers.[210] It is not clear, for example, how these various factor relate to each other, or whether they carry equal or differing weights.[211]

Nevertheless, even if not representative of contemporary international law, and despite the criticisms and controversies, Bethlehem's formulation and its adoption by the three states concerned are highly instructive for our examination of imminence and its relationship with general necessity. First, such public pronouncements indicate how these particular states construe imminence and might act upon that understanding in exercising their right of self-defence, either on their own or in concert with allies and coalition partners. States seldom make such statements about their interpretation of international law, as it potentially limits their right of action. Therefore, these rare and explicit examples of state practice are extremely valuable (if not entirely coherent) in terms of the detail that they provide for contemplation of the subject at hand. Second, as the ILC reminds us, the practice of a relatively small number of states *might* be sufficient to create custom 'if such practice, as well as other States' inaction in response, is generally accepted as law (*opinio juris*)'.[212] Other states' silence in response to the UK, USA and Australia's respective articulations of imminence does not necessarily equate to acquiescence,[213] but

[210] For commentary representing a variety of views on these examples of state practice, see Marty Lederman, 'ASIL Speech by State Legal Adviser Egan on International Law and the Use of Force against ISIL' (*Just Security*, 4 April 2016) <https://www.justsecurity.org/30377/asil-speech-state-legal-adviser-international-law-basis-for-limits-on-force-isil> accessed 5 September 2020; Ashley Deeks, '"Imminence" in the Legal Adviser's Speech' (*Lawfare*, 6 April 2016) <https://www.lawfareblog.com/imminence-legal-advisers-speech> accessed 5 September 2020; Marty Lederman, 'The Egan Speech and the Bush Doctrine: Imminence, Necessity, and "First Use" in the *Jus ad Bellum*' (*Just Security*, 11 April 2016) <https://www.justsecurity.org/30522/egan-speech-bush-doctrine-imminence-necessity-first-use-jus-ad-bellum/> accessed 5 September 2020; Monica Hakimi, 'The UK's Most Recent Volley on Defensive Force' (*EJIL:Talk!*, 12 January 2017) <https://www.ejiltalk.org/the-uks-most-recent-volley-on-defensive-force/> accessed 5 September 2020; Adil Haque, 'The United Kingdom's "Modern Law of Self-Defence"—Part I' (*Just Security*, 12 January 2017) <https://www.justsecurity.org/36235/united-kingdoms-modern-law-self-defence-part/> accessed 5 September 2020; Marko Milanovic, 'What is an Imminent Armed Attack? A Hopefully Helpful Hypo', (*EJIL:Talk!*, 12 January 2017) <https://www.ejiltalk.org/what-is-an-imminent-armed-attack-a-hopefully-helpful-hypo/> accessed 5 September 2020; James A Green, 'Initial Thoughts on the UK Attorney General's Self-Defence Speech' (*EJIL:Talk!*, 13 January 2017) <https://www.ejiltalk.org/initial-thoughts-on-the-uk-attorney-generals-self-defence-speech/> accessed 5 September 2020; Adil Haque, 'Imminence and Self-Defense Against Non-State Actors: Australia Weighs In' (*Just Security*, 30 May 2017) <https://www.justsecurity.org/41500/imminence-self-defense-non-state-actors-australia-weighs/> accessed 5 September 2020; Henderson, *The Use of Force and International Law* (n 47) 297–307.

[211] Monica Hakimi, 'The UK's Most Recent Volley on Defensive Force' (n 210).

[212] UNGA, 'Report of the International Law Commission, Sixty-Eighth Session' (2 May–10 June and 4 July–12 August 2016) UN Doc A/71/10, 95, footnote 296.

[213] The issue of interpreting silence when attempting to divine normative change (whether by way of customary development or treaty interpretation) is a complex and controversial issue. Conclusions are difficult to draw from silence, in particular as to whether it should be construed as acquiescence or supportive of a course of action or a particular legal proposition. The ICJ has recognized in principle that '[t]he absence of reaction may well amount to acquiescence […] That is to say, silence may also speak, but only if the conduct of the other State calls for a response'. *Sovereignty over Pedra Branca/Pulau Batu Puteh, Middle Rocks and South Ledge (Malaysia/Singapore)* (Judgment) [2008] ICJ Rep 12, para 121. On the issue of silence/inaction and custom, with particular reference to the *jus ad bellum*,

there is potential for such standard to be sufficiently widespread so as to become normatively constitutive. This is perhaps most likely if allies and coalition partners act together on the same understanding. As such, these case studies are not the end of matter, and do not necessarily represent the *lex lata*, but they might constitute the seeds for future legal development.

The stated positions of the USA, the UK and Australia (including Bethlehem's Principle 8) reflect the commonly held understanding that a temporal element is inherent in imminence. This is encapsulated by reference to the 'immediacy of the threat' and the 'other opportunities to undertake effective action'. Although the timing of the armed attack is clearly important under the Bethlehem formulation, determining imminence also depends on other non-temporal factors that relate to the wider circumstances of the threat. Justifications regarding ongoing military action against Daesh (discussed in particular in Section 4.2.4) also point in this direction. These recent examples of state practice reflect earlier academic attempts such as The Chatham House Principles of 2006 and the 2010 Leiden Policy Recommendations that sought to define whether or not an armed attack is imminent. Both scholarly projects include a set of contextual indicators that speak more generally to the threat. These factors include the timing of the armed attack, its nature and its gravity. The Chatham House Principles also include the capability of the relevant attacker, the geographical situation of the defending state and the past record of attacks.[214] Ago also noted the need to examine the wider circumstances pertaining to the future threat, stating that 'a State acting in self-defence [. . .] acts in response to an imminent danger—which must [. . .] be serious, immediate and incapable of being countered by other means'.[215] Henderson appropriately refers to such conception as 'contextual imminence'.[216]

On the account of imminence endorsed by these scholars and states, the temporal proximity of the anticipated attack is highly relevant, but the nature of the threat and the prospect of peaceful alternatives to counter it also feature. If this account is accepted, contrary to Lubell's position, where alternative measures are available and on their own are effective to prevent the attack from happening then,

see further, Etienne Henry, 'Alleged Acquiescence of the International Community to Revisionist Claims of International Customary Law (With Special Reference to the *Jus Contra Bellum* Regime)' (2017) 18 Melbourne Journal of International Law 260; Paulina Starski, 'Silence Within the Process of Normative Change and Evolution of the Prohibition on the Use of Force: Normative Volatility and Legislative Responsibility' (2017) 4(1) JUFIL 14; Dustin A Lewis, Naz K Modirzadeh, Gabriella Blum, 'Quantum Of Silence: Inaction and *Jus Ad Bellum*', The Harvard Law School Program on International Law and Armed Conflict (2019) <https://pilac.law.harvard.edu/quantum-of-silence> accessed 5 September 2020.

[214] The Chatham House Principles (n 65) 967–968; Nico Schrijver and Larissa van den Herik, 'Leiden Policy Recommendations on Counter-Terrorism and International Law' (2010) 57(3) NILR 531 (hereafter 'Leiden Policy Recommendations') para 46.

[215] Ago, 'Addendum—Eighth Report on State Responsibility' (n 5) 88.

[216] Henderson, *The Use of Force and International Law* (n 47) 297–307.

ipso facto, such attack is not truly imminent. The general necessity of self-defence will also be absent, as force is not the only reasonable option in the circumstances. To develop this proposition further, Akande and Liefländer likewise suggest that imminence 'describes a certain pressing quality that a threat must have for anticipatory self-defense to be lawful'. This involves an assessment of the type of attack threatened, its likelihood of occurring, its gravity and timing.[217] Most noteworthy, is the fact that these authors deny that imminence encompasses an *independent* temporal requirement, meaning that the temporal remoteness of a threat does not, on its own, constitute a bar to an exercise of self-defence where that action is necessary and proportionate.[218]

Positing that the temporal aspect of imminence might act on its own to deny defensive action is potentially to deny a right of self-defence in the face of a highly probable and severe threat, the realization of which might be temporally remote, but where there will be no future opportunity to eliminate the threat.[219] The ICJ adopted this approach to timing in the context of necessity as a circumstance precluding wrongfulness. The Court stated that imminence is traditionally understood as temporal immediacy or proximity, but it does not establish an independent temporal requirement. Following this reasoning, a '"peril" appearing in the long term might be held to be "imminent" as soon as it is established, at the relevant point in time, that the realization of that peril, however far off it might be, is not thereby any less certain and inevitable'.[220] Consequently, imminence so conceived relates not only to timing, but also to the likelihood of the relevant threat occurring. Although potentially *prima facie* supportive of the foregoing analysis, it must be noted that in making these comments the ICJ was not concerned with a situation of self-defence. Indeed, Lubell cautions against transposing this precedent from the laws of state responsibility into the *jus ad bellum* and delinking immediacy from imminence.[221] Yet, the analysis set out in this section suggests that the contemporary *jus ad bellum* position might not be so different.

The description of imminence contained in the preceding paragraphs accords with the idea, presented by a number of scholars, of a last 'window of opportunity' to respond effectively to an anticipated armed attack. It also reflects imminence

[217] Akande and Liefländer, 'Clarifying Necessity, Imminence, and Proportionality' (n 3) 564–565. The authors highlight, however, that it is unclear how these four elements of imminence interrelate or whether they are independent. For example, is a low probability of threat permissible where the gravity of the threat is severe? Conversely, where a threat is mild, is there a requirement of a higher probability that the attack will occur? The position is unsettled. See further the Leiden Policy Recommendations (n 214) 543. Milanovic concludes that imminence in the *jus ad bellum* is not really a temporal criterion, but a certainty/likelihood criterion. Milanovic, 'What is an Imminent Armed Attack? A Hopefully Helpful Hypo' (n 210).

[218] Akande and Liefländer, 'Clarifying Necessity, Imminence, and Proportionality' (n 3) 565. See also Schmitt, *Tallinn Manual* (n 71) 64; Lederman, 'The Egan Speech and the Bush Doctrine' (n 210).

[219] Akande and Liefländer, 'Clarifying Necessity, Imminence, and Proportionality' (n 3) 565.

[220] *Gabčíkovo-Nagymaros* (n 8) para 54.

[221] Lubell, 'The Problem of Imminence' (n 197) 703.

as espoused in Bethlehem's Principle 8 and the positions of the USA, the UK and Australia. By this standard:

> a State may act in anticipatory self-defence against an armed attack [...] when the attacker is clearly committed to launching an armed attack and the victim State will lose its opportunity to effectively defend itself unless it acts. In other words, it may act anticipatorily only during the last window of opportunity to defend itself against an armed attack that is forthcoming.[222]

On this construction of imminence, temporal considerations are clearly significant for the decision-making process, but they do not act as an independent injunction against defensive action.[223]

When we conceive of imminence along these lines, the timing of the threatened armed attack does not, by itself, determine whether the defending state may lawfully exercise its right of self-defence. Rather, the temporal question is when the last possible window of opportunity to act will close, such that the ability to avert an attack will be lost.[224] The timing of the armed attack interacts with other factors (including the likelihood of whether that future armed attack will be launched, its nature and gravity and the availability of reasonable alternatives to force) to determine how long a state has to respond in order to defend itself effectively, before it is too late.

It is suggested that the window of opportunity might present itself immediately before the attack in question or, in some cases, long before it occurs.[225] The latter prospect is clearly controversial. It raises the prospect of states being able to respond defensively to a latent threat on the basis that it is perceived to be extremely grave, such as a future armed attack using weapons of mass destruction. When considering the nature and gravity of an armed attack, however, the timing element is not to be ignored. Temporal considerations have a heavy impact on the possibility of making accurate predictions pertaining to future threats.[226] In addition to ascertaining the probability of the anticipated armed attack, the issue of its temporal proximity is essential to determining the necessity of a defensive response. States cannot act lawfully using force on the basis of mere speculation. The

[222] Schmitt, *Tallinn Manual* (n 71) 64–65. See also Vaughan Lowe, '"Clear and Present Danger": Responses to Terrorism' (2005) 54 ICLQ 185, 192; The Chatham House Principles (n 65) 967–968; Leiden Policy Recommendations (n 214) 543; Lubell, 'The Problem of Imminence' (n 197) 710–713. Albeit in the context of a discussion on interceptive self-defence, Ruys agrees that '[s]elf-defence can only be exercised during the last window of opportunity to ward off an attack.' Ruys, *'Armed Attack'* (n 56) 355.

[223] Akande and Liefländer, 'Clarifying Necessity, Imminence, and Proportionality' (n 3) 565.

[224] Michael N Schmitt, 'State-Sponsored Assassination in International and Domestic Law' (1992) 17 Yale J Int'l L 609, 648.

[225] Ibid.

[226] Akande and Liefländer, 'Clarifying Necessity, Imminence, and Proportionality' (n 3) 565; Lederman, 'The Egan Speech and the Bush Doctrine' (n 210).

further into the future the timeline goes, and the less impending the armed attack is, the harder it will be for a state to justify that an attack is in fact identifiable and/or probable and that there exists a genuine state of irreversible emergency that necessitates the resort to defensive military force at a particular point in time.[227] This is true regardless of the nature and gravity of the threat.

Although it is illogical and impossible to require absolute certainty of the impending armed attack, as we can never be certain about something that has not yet happened, the degree of uncertainty can only increase the more temporally distant a threat to a state is deemed to be.[228] This temporal hurdle tempers the risk of abuse, as assessing the probability of an armed attack becomes harder with time. More time means that more variables will need to factor into a defending state's decision-making process. These variables include the possibility of the attacker reversing its course of action (such as delaying the attack or not launching it at all), alternative peaceful measures being effective to resolve the dispute, or the UNSC taking effective action so as to render the resort to defensive force unnecessary. Therefore, the longer the period between the anticipated armed attack and the response, the more pressure there will be on the potential victim state to resolve the matter peacefully, rather than resorting to military force.[229]

As such, the window of opportunity is not thrown wide open to permit countering non-specific anticipated threats, regardless of how deadly they are thought to be. As noted at the beginning of this section, states and scholars have roundly rejected the idea of preventive self-defence and the ICJ has confirmed that Article 51 of the UN Charter 'does not allow the use of force by a state to protect perceived security interests'.[230] Belligerent rhetoric or the possible future acquisition of nuclear weapons will not, therefore, be sufficient to trigger a right of self-defence. The UK Attorney General made this point abundantly clear in 2017, stating that the UK's position on imminence requires an identified and direct threat to the UK and does not countenance a right to respond to remote threats that have not yet materialized.[231] He likewise accepted in respect of each exercise of self-defence that the UK must ask whether there is anything else it can credibly do to prevent an attack.[232]

These elements (*viz* a concrete anticipated armed attack and no choice of means to combat it) were also clearly apparent when the UK Prime Minister

[227] The Chatham House Principles (n 65) 967–968, state that there 'must exist a circumstance of irreversible emergency' to be able to respond to an armed attack that is imminent.

[228] Green, 'The *Ratione Temporis* Elements of Self-Defence' (n 165) 105. Regarding the level of certainty that should be required before states may respond to imminent armed attacks, Lubell concludes that a reasonable level of certainty is required. Lubell, 'The Problem of Imminence' (n 197) 713–716, 718.

[229] Gardam, *Necessity, Proportionality* (n 3) 150–151. See also The Chatham House Principles (n 65) 967; Dinstein, *War, Aggression and Self-Defence* (n 65) 252.

[230] *Armed Activities* (n 85) para 148.

[231] UK Attorney General Speech 2017 (n 72) 13, 19.

[232] Ibid, 16.

David Cameron justified the UK's targeted killing of Reyaad Khan in 2015.[233] He asserted that:

> [t]here was clear evidence of these individuals planning and directing armed attacks against the UK. These were part of a series of actual and foiled attempts to attack the UK and our allies, and given the prevailing circumstances in Syria, the airstrike was the only feasible means of effectively disrupting the attacks that had been planned and directed. It was therefore necessary and proportionate for the individual self-defence of the United Kingdom [...] it was a targeted strike to deal with a clear, credible and specific terrorist threat to our country at home.[234]

The UK Government Response to the Joint Committee's Drones Report elaborated on the 'no choice of means' justification, asserting that the targeted killing was:

> the only feasible means of effectively disrupting the attacks planned and directed by Reyaad Khan due to the prevailing circumstances in Syria. There was no realistic prospect that Khan would travel outside Syria so that other means of disruption could be attempted. Nor was there any prospect of the Syrian Government being willing or able to deal with the imminent threat he posed.[235]

In 2017, the Australian Attorney-General explicitly concurred with the UK's position regarding the need for a specifically identified future armed attack and no choice of means to combat it.[236]

When considering the relationship between general necessity and imminence as described in the preceding paragraphs, a conundrum arises. In 2006, the authors of The Chatham House Principles queried 'whether "imminence" is a separate criterion in its own right, or simply part of the criterion of "necessity" properly understood.'[237] For this author, if the preceding analysis rightly characterizes how certain states and scholars understand imminence (*viz* that it is contextual), then a conflation of imminence and necessity is revealed. A summation of the UK's position on

[233] See nn 184–185 and accompanying text.

[234] HC Deb 7 September 2015, vol 599, col 26. Such threat was specifically said to include 'plots to attack high-profile public commemorations, including those taking place this summer'. See col 25.

[235] UK Government, 'The Government's Policy on the Use of Drones For Targeted Killing: Government Response to the Committee's Second Report of Session 2015-16' (18 October 2016) <https://publications.parliament.uk/pa/jt201617/jtselect/jtrights/747/74705.htm#_idTextAnchor032> accessed 5 September 2020.

[236] As well as generally agreeing with the UK Attorney General's 2017 speech and adopting Bethlehem's Principle 8, the Australian Attorney-General stated that, 'Australia regards the use of force always as a last resort. Where a threat is not an actual or imminent 'armed attack', as that term is understood in international law, Australia responds in a variety of other ways.' Australian Attorney-General Speech 2017 (n 75).

[237] The Chatham House Principles (n 65) 968.

imminence demonstrates this conflation:[238] is action against an identifiable threat necessary now,[239] before the last clear opportunity to take action disappears,[240] or are effective alternatives to force available?[241] In this analysis, imminence stands as a proxy for general necessity.

As such, adopting a contextual (rather than purely temporal) approach to imminence does not simply refine or redefine an understanding of an 'armed attack'. Rather, this conflation of imminence and general necessity blurs the conceptual demarcation between the trigger for the right of self-defence (being armed attacks, in this case that that are imminent) and the conditioning of its exercise (being necessity). This is because a contextual analysis of the armed attack to determine whether or not it is 'imminent' and a contextual analysis of necessity is duplicative in answering the single governing question: can a state act defensively now to prevent an attack in the future? General necessity represents the legal litmus test for whether defensive action is exercisable in response to any form of armed attack. As such, it already speaks to this question. Imminence (as associated with the armed attack) does no additional legal work in answering it. This convergence of two previously distinct concepts might be regarded as unhelpful or even misguided, but it is clearly a feature of certain scholarship and state practice referred to in this section. Therefore, it must be examined further.

On the one hand, the aforementioned conflation emphasizes the ambiguities of Bethlehem's Principle 8 and the UK's, USA's and Australia's respective accounts of necessity, imminent armed attacks and self-defence more broadly. The dangers associated generally with ambiguity and the legal regulation of the use of force are clear. The *jus ad bellum* will always contain a degree of indeterminacy, but the possibility that different states are potentially acting militarily on the basis of varying understandings of the applicable legal rules raises real concerns, not least over the potential for abuse and *post facto* accountability. For allies and coalition partners, practical operational difficulties might also arise regarding coordinating defensive military action when states interpret imminence differently.[242]

On the other hand, the conflation of imminence and general necessity essentially renders the former term nugatory (at least as it applies to an armed attack), but the forgoing account of imminence does capture the substance of how these states conceive of the general necessity of responding anticipatorily to future armed attacks. The very fact of conflation, whilst potentially misguided, should

[238] Noting this conflation and reaching the same conclusion, see Haque 'The United Kingdom's "Modern Law of Self-Defence"—Part I' Force' (n 210); UK's All Party Parliamentary Group on Drones Inquiry Report (n 202) 36–37. See also Abraham D Sofaer, 'On the Necessity of Pre-emption' (2003) 14(2) EJIL 209, 220.

[239] UK Attorney General Speech 2017 (n 72) 7.

[240] Ibid, 16.

[241] Ibid, 10, 13, 16, 20.

[242] For further discussion by this author of this possibility, see O'Meara, 'The Relationship Between National, Unit and Personal Self-Defence' (n 60) 21–23.

help to assuage (to some degree at least) concerns regarding an overly flexible right to exercise self-defence. This is because whether there is a genuine situation of emergency giving rise to a pressing need to resort to self-defence will be determined by the particular context. Accordingly, it is not that the armed attack must be 'imminent' in any legally significant and independent sense. Rather, to quote Webster once more, it is the *necessity of using force in self-defence*, that must be 'instant, overwhelming, and leaving no choice of means and no moment for deliberation' (not the armed attack). The bottom line of imminence is that: '[w]hat is really at stake is whether some sort of self-defence action is demonstrably necessary'.[243] For those states that have adopted this contextual understanding, the term 'imminence' simply describes the type of (positively identified) future armed attack that triggers a lawful defensive response today.[244]

Any right of pre-emptive self-defence, whether as a matter of *lex lata* or *lex ferenda*, will always depend on a case-by-case contextual assessment of necessity. In response to the threat of specifically identified future armed attacks, Bethlehem's Principle 8 and the idea of a last window of opportunity to act allow for defensive force to meet offensive force based on the facts of the situation at hand. It is this understanding of general necessity (and/or imminence if we are using that term interchangeably) that provides defending states with a degree of flexibility and the means to protect themselves, rather than having to sit idly by and suffer an attack. Yet, at the same time, general necessity requires that the defending state is suffering a situation of genuine irreversible emergency. This means that the pursuit of peaceful alternatives to force was not reasonable in the circumstances and the recourse to force at a particular time was the only reasonable option. If a defending state can demonstrate that it used force when it did, because failure to do so would have deprived it of the ability to defend itself effectively, on the preceding analysis, the general necessity of self-defence will be established.

Alternatively, if force is not the only reasonable option in the circumstances, then imminence will not, *ipso facto*, be established and an exercise of self-defence will be unnecessary. As with the Osiraq incident, there will be no instant or overwhelming necessity of self-defence.[245] Indeed, this incident of state practice is highly elucidating regarding how states may potentially conflate imminence and

[243] Akande and Liefländer, 'Clarifying Necessity, Imminence, and Proportionality' (n 3) 565.

[244] See Milanovic, 'What is an Imminent Armed Attack? A Hopefully Helpful Hypo' (n 210), concluding that the approach to imminence described here looks very much like necessity. Following the Soleimani strike, Milanovic further elaborated on his view of how the USA and its allies construe imminence and necessity: 'an armed attack will be regarded as imminent if *responding* to the attack is *necessary now*, regardless of when and how exactly the attack will take place […] An imminent attack is thus one where the attacker has committed to particular aggressive course of action which they will not desist from absent some kind of intervention in the causal chain, such as a use of force in self-defence'. Marko Milanovic, 'The Soleimani Strike and Self-Defence Against an Imminent Armed Attack' (*EJIL:Talk!*, 7 January 2020) <https://www.ejiltalk.org/the-soleimani-strike-and-self-defence-against-an-imminent-armed-attack/> accessed 5 September 2020.

[245] As noted in the UK's condemnation of the Israeli airstrikes. UN Doc S/PV 2282 (n 132) para 106.

necessity or use the former as a proxy for the latter. Although state responses to Israel's actions were mixed, a review of the UNSC debates and the reasons given by states for condemning the airstrikes show that, for certain states, there is little to no distinction between imminence and necessity. The bottom line for such states appeared to be that Israel was not facing a situation of emergency that meant that force was the only reasonable option at the time that Israel resorted to it.[246] Similarly, and conversely, the UK's justification for the UK's targeted killing of Reyaad Khan in 2015 appeared to rest largely on the lack of any reasonable alternatives to defensive force at the time he was killed by the British drone.[247]

2.5.1.3 Completed Armed Attacks

Completed armed attacks raise their own complexities, not least factually determining if and when an armed attack has ended. Conceptually, it helps to make a distinction between three types of completed armed attacks: (i) fully completed armed attacks; (ii) completed armed attacks resulting in occupation and (iii) self-contained armed attacks where further armed attacks are imminent. In the first case, where the attack is a one-off, the lack of emergency negates the 'present and inevitable' necessity of using defensive force that Webster required. There is no pressing need to halt, repel or prevent an armed attack, meaning there is no general necessity of self-defence. Rather, the emphasis switches to non-forcible options to resolve the issue and seek redress. Any force used to respond to such armed attacks that are fully complete risks being characterized as an unlawful armed reprisal.[248]

Where completed armed attacks result in the occupation of territory, the legal analysis is more nuanced. Arguably, occupation equates to an ongoing armed attack, thereby retaining the general necessity of defensive force to recapture it.[249] It would be unrealistic in such circumstances for a defending state faced with continuing hostility (as evidenced by the factor of occupation) to forego its right of self-defence in favour of negotiation. The threat to it subsists. In *Oil Platforms*, Iran emphasized this distinction between fully completed armed attacks, and those that continue by virtue of occupation.[250] On this understanding, a use of force by the defending state amounts to repelling an armed attack and is thereby in keeping with the purposes of self-defence.[251]

[246] See nn 125–139 and accompanying text.

[247] See nn 234–235 and accompanying text.

[248] See Section 2.5.2.

[249] Gill, 'When Does Self-Defence End?' (n 73) 745; Corten, *The Law Against War* (n 24) 486. Aust agrees that using force to retake unlawfully captured territory is a lawful exercise of self-defence. Anthony Aust, *Handbook of International Law* (CUP 2005) 229. See also Dinstein, *War, Aggression and Self-Defence* (n 65) 230; David Kretzmer, 'The Inherent Right to Self-Defence and Proportionality in *Jus Ad Bellum*' (2013) 24(1) EJIL 235, 250.

[250] 'In the case of the invasion of another State's territory, in principle an attack still exists as long as the occupation continues. But in cases of single armed attacks (as distinguished from a general situation of armed conflict), the attack is terminated when the incident is over.' *Oil Platforms* (n 34) Reply and Defence to Counter-Claim Submitted by the Islamic Republic of Iran, 10 March 1999, para 7.47.

[251] See further Section 2.5.2.2.

Finally, there are armed attacks that might appear completed and self-contained but are in fact part of a series of armed attacks. In such instances, the defending state also faces a current threat.[252] The general necessity analysis is largely one of anticipatory self-defence in these circumstances, as explored in Section 2.5.1.2. The operative question is whether or not a new attack is imminent. If not, the armed attack is fully completed. Where the current threat (comprising past and imminent armed attacks) is no more, the *prima facie* general necessity of self-defence is also absent. The focus must then switch to peaceful options of resolution.

2.5.2 The Timing of the Defending State's Response to an Armed Attack

2.5.2.1 An Immediate Need to Respond

General necessity not only takes account of the timing of the armed attack, but also the timing of the defensive response to such attack. Like imminence, this element of necessity is traditionally derived from Webster's insistence that defensive force must be shown to be 'instant, overwhelming, leaving […] no moment for deliberation'.[253] As such, this temporal element is often referred to as the 'immediacy' requirement. Before we look at 'how immediate' a response must be, it is important to appreciate the function of a temporal link between attack and defence in determining the legality of the latter. Understanding the theory informs how we view the relevant state practice and jurisprudence on this point.

Establishing a temporal limitation on a state's defensive reaction retains the principle that self-defence is an emergency response. Any act of self-defence should, in principle, be temporally proximate to the peril faced. As with imminence, if there is no genuine irreversible emergency, there may be a 'moment for deliberation' and no 'instant' and 'overwhelming' need for a response. Absent a new *casus belli*, an undue delay in responding to an armed attack indicates that, in the circumstances, there was no general necessity of self-defence. Therefore, a temporal link avoids the right of self-defence being used to respond to attacks long passed. It seeks to counter concerns that the response was in fact in retaliation or punishment. Accordingly, this timing element is crucial to distinguish lawful acts of self-defence from unlawful armed reprisals.

Armed reprisals are punitive rather than protective in nature. '[T]hey seek to impose reparation for the harm done, or to compel a satisfactory settlement of the dispute created by the initial illegal act, or to compel the delinquent state to abide by the law in the future'.[254] The ICJ has confirmed that international law prohibits

[252] Ibid.

[253] *British and Foreign State Papers*, 1841–1842, Vol. XXX, 201 (n 166).

[254] Derek W Bowett, 'Reprisals Involving Recourse to Armed Force' (1972) 66 AJIL 1, 3. For further analysis of the timing of defensive action and the controversies that surround the distinction between

armed reprisals.[255] The prohibition is also reflected in the Friendly Relations Declaration.[256] A defining feature of reprisals is that they take place after the armed attack. Those commentators that reject their legality rely on this fact to highlight that, by their nature, they can only ever be punitive, rather than defensive or protective.[257] However, depending on the particular facts and timing of the response, the dividing line between acts that seek to protect and those that punish may be hard to draw. Defending states may be faced with a real challenge to satisfy the demands of such distinction.

Nevertheless, the need for a defending state to respond within a certain timeframe is clearly reflected in the ICJ's jurisprudence. In *Nicaragua*, the Court's determination that purported defensive measures taken by the USA were unnecessary was primarily determined by the fact that such measures were taken several months after the major offensive of the armed opposition against the Government of El Salvador had been completely repulsed.[258] The extent of the time lag between the purported armed attack and the claimed act of self-defence was determinative of the majority's opinion. Possible permissible time limits for defensive responses were not indicated in the judgment, however. Where the Court draws the line between lawful self-defence and unlawful reprisal remains unclear.

Returning to Webster's formula for possible answers, on one interpretation it appears to require that military resistance to an armed attack should take place immediately, while the attack is still in process and not after it has ended.[259] Such a strict view of immediacy does find limited support in state practice. For example, in responding to Israel's claimed acts of self-defence against terrorists acting from Lebanese territory in 1972,[260] Argentina was forthright in stating:

> It is necessary that such [defensive] measures be indispensable and immediate; there must be no alternative and no time must pass in deliberating or reflecting on the desirability of a reaction. This means that the reaction must immediately follow the illegal attack.[261]

defensive acts and reprisals, see Schachter, 'The Right of States to Use Armed Force' (n 65) 1638; Dinstein, *War, Aggression and Self-Defence* (n 65) 264–275; Corten, *The Law Against War* (n 24) 485–487; Gardam, *Necessity, Proportionality* (n 3) 148–155; Shane Darcy, 'Retaliation and Reprisal' in Weller (ed), *The Oxford Handbook* (n 7) 879; Henderson, *The Use of Force and International Law* (n 47) 240–247.

255 *Corfu Channel* (n 162) para 38; *Nuclear Weapons* (n 162) para 46.
256 Friendly Relations Declaration (n 67) para 1.
257 Bowett, 'Reprisals' (n 254) 3.
258 *Nicaragua* (n 10) para 237.
259 Ago, 'Addendum—Eighth Report on State Responsibility' (n 5) para 122.
260 UN Doc S/10550 (n 117).
261 UN Doc S/PV.1644 (n 118) para 25.

'Immediacy' might be a convenient label, yet taking this as a literal requirement for a defending state's response seems too narrow and inflexible. General necessity requires that the defensive response be made close in time to the armed attack, but this temporal link is to be interpreted reasonably. No precise limit can be fixed.[262] The best contemporary understanding amongst academics of immediacy is that a state acting in self-defence must do so within a reasonable timeframe, without unduly postponing the taking of measures.[263]

This understanding of immediacy is reflected in state practice. Such practice reveals that the particular context will determine how quickly a defending state is in a position to respond. Relevant factors include the need to gather intelligence, the geographical locale of an attack, the level of military preparedness of the defending state, the need for internal constitutional permissions to use force and to consult and engage allies, and so forth. Many of these elements are necessary to ensure an adequate defence may be mounted and may accordingly militate against an instantaneous response. States may need to prepare, before taking defensive action.

In response to the UK raid on the Harib Fort in 1964, for example, Iraq condemned the UK's acts based, in part, on the fact that a day had passed before the UK responded to the alleged attacks against the Federation of South Arabia.[264] The UK justified its actions, *inter alia*, on the basis that its attack on Harib Fort was carefully planned and required approved at a high level by the British Government. Such approval and planning ensured that only those responsible for the alleged terror campaign were involved in the attack and that civilians were not affected.[265] Iraq's criticism was but one of a number of reasons for the widespread negative reaction to the British raid,[266] but the UK's stance exemplifies the fact that states might assert that they are not in a position to respond 'immediately' in any strict sense of the word and may assert justifiable reasons for the delay (even if these justifications are not always accepted by other states).

Further state practice more clearly demonstrates that the immediacy requirement must be viewed flexibly. In 1993, America took over two months to respond to the attempted assassination of former President George HW Bush and what it described as an enduring threat to the USA.[267] It justified such delay by pointing to the need to confirm responsibility for the assassination attempt before a response was made. This included a meticulous and exhaustive investigation of the incident

[262] Ruys, *'Armed Attack'* (n 56) 99.

[263] Oscar Schachter, 'The Lawful Resort to Unilateral Use of Force' (1985) 10 Yale J Int'l L 291, 292; Gardam, *Necessity, Proportionality* (n 3) 150; Dinstein, *War, Aggression and Self-Defence* (n 65) 252; Schmitt, *Tallinn Manual* (n 71) 65; Gill, 'When Does Self-Defence End?' (n 73) 745. Franck argues that '[t]he assertion that self-defense requires "immediate" action comes from a misunderstanding of the *Caroline* decision, which deals only with *anticipatory* self-defense'. Thomas M Franck, 'Terrorism and the Right of Self-Defense' (2001) 95 AJIL 839, 840.

[264] UNSC Verbatim Record (3 April 1964) UN Doc S/PV.1107, 17.

[265] UNSC Verbatim Record (7 April 1964) UN Doc S/PV.1109, paras 23–24.

[266] See Sections 2.6.2, 3.2.1.3 and 3.2.1.4.

[267] See Section 2.4.2.1.

to establish the facts, thereby ensuring that there was no rush to judgement before action was taken.[268] The delay was not noted by any state during consideration of the incident by the UNSC. Indeed, the American action, justified as a lawful act of self-defence, was broadly supported.[269] New Zealand went so far as expressing its appreciation for the fact that the USA promptly informed the Security Council of the action it had taken.[270] Likewise, a delay of two weeks between attack and defence was not a factor in the review by states of the USA's strikes against Afghanistan and Sudan in response to the 1998 African embassy bombings, attributed by the USA to Al-Qaeda.[271]

The insistence that states have a right to reflect, investigate and confirm both that they have been attacked and by whom before responding against carefully selected targets, was reiterated again by the USA before the ICJ in *Oil Platforms*.[272] It saw the need to take care over ensuring an appropriate response (rather than using force instantly and without reflection) to be paramount, because requiring an 'instantaneous response could dramatically increase the risk of disproportionate damage'.[273] Given the analysis set out in the rest of this book, including the purposes of self-defence and the requirements related to targeting and proportionality generally, this conclusion and approach to immediacy is entirely proper. Rash defensive action risks breaching both necessity and proportionality.

In his dissent in *Nicaragua*, Judge Schwebel appeared to take judicial note of this fact. He emphasized the efforts that the USA had made for more than a year in assisting El Salvador to suppress the insurgency within its own borders and by diplomatic representations to the government of Nicaragua, both of which had proved to be insufficient to quell the insurgency. Under these circumstances, Judge Schwebel concluded that it was not unreasonable for the USA to decide that the exertion of armed force was necessary.[274] Although the majority in *Nicaragua* decided the case on a different appreciation of the facts, Judge Schwebel's views highlight the importance of assessing the temporal element of immediacy in conjunction with other relevant factors. Together, they will determine whether the purpose of the

[268] UN Doc S/PV.3245 (n 112) 3.

[269] Ibid, 13 (France); 16 (Japan); 18 (Hungary); 19–20 (UK); 21–22 (Russia); 23 (New Zealand); 24 (Spain). This incident comprised a completed armed attack that was unlikely to be repeated. Therefore, the claim of self-defence is questionable. It might be better characterized as a reprisal, being punitive rather than defensive in nature. See Kritsiotis, 'The Legality of the 1993 US Missile Strike' (n 100) 175; Ruys, *'Armed Attack'* (n 56) 107–108; Gray, *Use of Force* (n 23) 205; Starski, 'The US Airstrike' (n 100) 523–526.

[270] UN Doc S/PV.3245 (n 112) 23.

[271] Letter dated 20 August 1998 from the Permanent Representative of the United States of America to the United Nations addressed to the President of the Security Council (20 August 1998) UN Doc S/1998/780. On this incident generally, see Enzo Cannizzaro and Aurora Rasi, 'The US Strikes in Sudan and Afghanistan–1998' in Ruys and Corten, *The Use of Force in International Law* (n 90) 541.

[272] *Oil Platforms* (n 34) Counter-Memorial and Counter-Claim Submitted by the United States of America, 23 June 1997, paras 4.37–4.39.

[273] Ibid, paras 4.37, 4.39.

[274] *Nicaragua* (n 10) diss op Schwebel, para 203.

response is indeed defensive. His dissent also exemplifies how alternative measures to force factor into an appreciation of reasonableness. The longer the period between attack and response, the greater the pressure there will be on the defending state to resolve the issue by peaceful means,[275] but pursuing such means should not, *ipso facto*, defeat the right of self-defence. If a defending state makes genuine attempts to settle the dispute amicably, but such attempts prove unproductive, it should not be faulted for losing time unduly before employing its armed forces in a defensive response.[276]

Therefore, as a general proposition, the greater the time-lapse between the armed attack and the defensive riposte, the higher the likelihood that the latter will be characterized as an unlawful reprisal. However, assessing the reasonableness of the time period and determining where to draw the line between necessary and unnecessary defensive responses is not governed solely by how many days or months have elapsed since the attack. Establishing what is a sufficiently proximate timeframe in the circumstances is highly contextual. A reasonable conclusion on the basis of the preceding analysis and state practice is that so long as the defending state takes action to defend itself in a reasonable timeframe and without undue delay, the right of self-defence will not be forfeited.[277] Immediacy is a flexible concept such that there must be an immediate *need* to respond, but not that there must necessarily be an immediate *response*.[278] Such an approach to self-defence is particularly persuasive when we consider whether a state is facing an ongoing threat when it responds to an armed attack militarily.

2.5.2.2 An Ongoing Threat

Whether general necessity is satisfied is ultimately determined by whether a defending state is facing an ongoing threat when it resorts to self-defence. This is best explained if we again consider the distinction between ongoing, completed and imminent armed attacks referred to in Section 2.5.1. The risk that a response might be characterized as an unlawful armed reprisal principally arises in respect of armed attacks that appear to be fully complete.[279] In such cases, even if a response might be viewed as 'immediate', it is likely to be unnecessary, given the absence of a current threat. Completed armed attacks resulting in occupation or the

[275] Gardam, *Necessity, Proportionality* (n 3) 150–151.

[276] Dinstein, *War, Aggression and Self-Defence* (n 65) 252. See also Ruys, *'Armed Attack'* (n 56) 100.

[277] Gill, 'When Does Self-Defence End?' (n 73) 745.

[278] Green, 'Docking the *Caroline*' (n 4) 471. See also Ruys, *'Armed Attack'* (n 56) 100. This conclusion was also reflected, for example, by Mexico in its pleadings before the ICJ in *Nuclear Weapons*: 'The right of self-defense is actualized only when *the need for defense* is immediate and overwhelming' (emphasis added). *Nuclear Weapons* (n 162) Note Verbale from the Embassy of Mexico, together with Written Statement of the Government of Mexico, 19 June 1995, para 57.

[279] For imminent armed attacks, as they have not yet happened, the question of immediacy and the fear of armed reprisals are not relevant. Unless imminent armed attacks form part of a series of armed attacks, it is difficult to see how a response to a future attack could be characterized as a reprisal. The timing of the response to imminent armed attacks instead forms part of the last window of opportunity analysis discussed in Section 2.5.1.2.

capture of territory are different, however. In this instance, as explained in Section 2.5.2.1, it might not always possible for a defending state to take immediate action to defend itself and recover that territory. Where a state is not in a position promptly to resist invasion, provided that it does act to repel it as soon as it is able, or as soon as all attempts to secure a peaceful withdrawal have failed, such action will still be considered lawful self-defence.[280] This is because the factor of occupied territory allows a state to treat such situation as an ongoing armed attack, which maintains the general necessity of defensive action.[281]

The most obvious example is the 1982 Falkland Islands conflict. In this incident, a delay of approximately three weeks between the Argentine invasion and the commencement of active military operations by the UK against Argentina was widely seen as an acceptable time delay.[282] For some, the factor of continuing occupation of the Islands by Argentina accounts for the UK's continuing right of self-defence.[283] Also relevant to when the response could be mounted was the geographical location of the Islands and the time needed to assemble and put in place an adequate military force to mount an effective campaign.[284] That the British Cabinet met on the same day as the invasion to agree to dispatch a task force to regain the Islands might, by itself, constitute an immediate response.[285]

Whatever the particular reason, a lack of 'immediate' action was not raised during the UNSC debates and it was relatively uncontroversial that the UK retained its right of self-defence for some time after the initial attack and occupation.[286] Also notable from this incident is that the British did not consider themselves under a *legal obligation* to pursue peaceable alternatives during this period, even if attempts for a peaceful settlement were in fact made. Instead, they felt their right to act in self-defence would have justified a 'purely military policy'.[287] The fact of continuing occupation might account for this belief. The British state practice and widespread acceptance of it indicates that where there is an ongoing armed attack, aiming for peaceful settlement might be desirable as an additional policy option, but it does

[280] Rosalyn Higgins, *Problems and Process: International Law and How We Use It* (OUP 1994) 241.

[281] See Section 2.5.1.3.

[282] Michael J Levitin, 'The Law of Force and the Force of Law: Grenada, the Falklands, and Humanitarian Intervention' 27 (1986) Harv Int'l LJ 621, 638; Ruys, *'Armed Attack'* (n 56) 102; Green, 'The *Ratione Temporis* Elements of Self-Defence' (n 165) 109; Henderson, *The Use of Force and International Law* (n 47) 231. For an overview of the conflict, including timing and the reactions of the international community, see 'Trusteeship and Decolonization: Other Colonial Territories' (1982) UNYB 1319, 1320–1347; Etienne Henry, 'The Falklands/Malvinas War–1982' in Ruys and Corten, *The Use of Force in International Law* (n 90) 361.

[283] Eric PJ Myjer and Nigel D White 'The Twin Towers Attack: An Unlimited Right to Self-Defence' (2002) 7(1) JC&SL 5, 8. See also Section 2.5.1.3.

[284] Higgins, *Problems and Process* (n 280) 241; Green, 'The *Ratione Temporis* Elements of Self-Defence' (n 165) 109; Henderson, *The Use of Force and International Law* (n 47) 231.

[285] Levitin, 'The Law of Force and the Force of Law' (n 282) 638.

[286] Gardam, *Necessity, Proportionality* (n 3) 151.

[287] Foreign and Commonwealth Office, 'Falkland Islands: Negotiations for a Peaceful Settlement', Paper for Parliament (20 May 1982) <https://c59574e9047e61130f13-3f71d0fe2b653c4f00f32175760e96e7.ssl.cf1.rackcdn.com/CC465EA9FF1E4DD2A9024D630CCAD7E5.pdf> accessed 5 September 2020, para 3.

not deny a military response. The 1990–1991 Gulf War might also point to the acceptability of a delayed response to an armed attack. A period of approximately five months elapsed between the invasion by Iraq of Kuwait in August 1990 and the commencement of Operation Desert Storm in January 1991.[288]

Turning to self-contained armed attacks where further armed attacks are imminent, different considerations apply. Where a defending state is subjected to a series of armed attacks, Ago argues that the immediacy of a response should be judged against the threat considered as a whole.[289] It would be inimical to the purpose of self-defence to require that a state waits for the next armed attack before reacting,[290] or to require that it react immediately to each armed attack.[291] Ultimately, immediacy requires that the defensive riposte be aimed at behaviour that is still current, even if the material effects of its latest manifestation have already disappeared.[292] This logic encompasses the prospective element of general necessity, whilst at the same time recognizing that a state may go no further than responding to an immediate protective need.

Self-defence is only permissible to prevent further armed attacks on this basis when a state has good reason to expect a series of armed attacks from the same source and retaliation serves as a deterrent or protective action against those armed attacks.[293] References to an ongoing or persisting 'threat' should be understood accordingly. In such cases, however, the purpose of self-defence must remain clearly apparent at all times. In terms of looking at events cumulatively, the need to respond to the prospect of imminent armed attacks makes the purpose preventative. Force against a new attack is permissible, however, provided that it remains defensive rather than punitive in nature and is not a reprisal for revenge or as a penalty or a 'lesson'.[294]

[288] This incident might be cited in support of the flexibility of the immediacy criterion in the case of self-defence against ongoing armed attacks constituted by the occupation of territory (Kuwait was continually occupied during this period). However, its precedential value is obscured. This is because of the controversy over whether the incident stands as an example of self-defence and/or UNSC authorization to use force. See Section 3.2.1.4.

[289] Ago, 'Addendum—Eighth Report on State Responsibility' (n 5) para 122.

[290] Argued by the USA in *Oil Platforms*. *Oil Platforms* (n 34) Rejoinder Submitted by the United States of America, 23 March 2001, para 5.33.

[291] Corten, *The Law Against War* (n 24) 486. See also Gardam, *Necessity, Proportionality* (n 3) 148–155.

[292] Corten, *The Law Against War* (n 24) 487.

[293] Schachter, *International Law* (n 73) 154. Greenwood likewise recognizes that necessary and proportionate force extends to preventing the reoccurrence of a threat. Christopher Greenwood, 'Memorandum: The Legality of Using Force Against Iraq' (24 October 2002) Select Committee on Foreign Affairs Minutes of Evidence <http://www.publications.parliament.uk/pa/cm200203/cmselect/cmfaff/196/2102406.htm> accessed 5 September 2020, para 26. Taft, '*Oil Platforms* Decision' (n 47) 295, argues that the right of self-defence 'allows States to deter armed attacks that would otherwise occur and to discourage further armed attacks.' Ruys, '*Armed Attack*' (n 56) 123, argues that in 'exceptional circumstances' necessity and proportionality allow for the halting and repelling of 'successive and interlinked armed attacks' and the prevention of their reoccurrence.

[294] Schachter, *International Law* (n 73) 154. See also Corten, 'Necessity' (n 84) 873.

For Ruys, there must be 'convincing proof' of further attacks, after the last attack has factually ended. Only in such cases may self-defence be relied upon to 'impede' further attacks.[295] Where this conclusion regarding a campaign or series of attacks is not reasonable, however, in light of the circumstances prevailing at the time, any further use of force is liable to be characterized as mere retaliation rather than self-defence.[296] In addition, such a right should not be understood as stretching to counter unspecified possible future attacks. This would indicate an unlawful exercise of preventive self-defence.[297]

Looking at a series of attacks from the same source as a whole and combining completed armed attacks with imminent armed attacks so as to collectively amount to an ongoing threat is conceptually interesting. It is sometimes referred to as the 'accumulation of events' or 'pin-prick' theory of self-defence and may be equated to an ongoing armed attack.[298] Ago's view that the immediacy of a response should be judged against the 'threat considered as a whole' is based on the assumption that an armed attack has already occurred. As such, it has been argued that it should be distinguished from a purely pre-emptive or preventive justification of action.[299] Claims of 'pure' anticipatory self-defence are, in any event, rare. In practice, states tend to invoke the need to respond to future armed attacks when they have already been the victim of a previous one.[300] This point is also reflected in Bethlehem's Principle 8, which considers whether the anticipated imminent armed attack is part of a 'concerted pattern of continuing armed activity'.[301]

In such circumstances, absent ongoing hostilities, it is only the prospect of an imminent armed attack that keeps the threat current, thereby maintaining the general necessity of self-defence. This is logically assumed, given the widespread rejection of any right of preventive self-defence.[302] Without the threat of an imminent armed attack, any prior armed attack would simply be complete and the general necessity of self-defence would come to an end. The UN Special Rapporteur on Extrajudicial, Summary or Arbitrary Executions recently adopted this approaching when considering the legality of the targeted killing of General Qassem

295 Ruys, *'Armed Attack'* (n 56) 102.

296 Schmitt, *Tallinn Manual* (n 71) 66.

297 See Section 2.5.1.2.

298 See Kress, 'The International Court of Justice' (n 168) 588; Gray, *Use of Force* (n 23) 164–165. The ICJ has, in principle, accepted that a number of small-scale uses off force, individually falling below the level of an armed attack, may be accrued such that, collectively, they amount to an armed attack. This is most clearly seen in *Oil Platforms* (n 34) para 64. See also the implicit acceptance of this principle in *Nicaragua* (n 10) para 231; *Armed Activities* (n 85) para 146. For further analysis and examples of state practice, see Green, *The International Court of Justice* (n 49) 42–44; Ruys, *'Armed Attack'* (n 56) 168–175; Henderson, *The Use of Force and International Law* (n 47) 224–226.

299 Ruys, *'Armed Attack'* (n 56) 102.

300 See ibid, 342–343; Lederman, 'The Egan Speech and the Bush Doctrine' (n 210); Lederman, 'ASIL Speech' (n 210); Milanovic, 'What is an Imminent Armed Attack? A Hopefully Helpful Hypo' (n 210).

301 See Section 2.5.1.2.

302 See Section 2.5.1.2. See also Greenwood, 'United States' Air Operation Against Libya' (n 68) 946.

Soleimani in 2020: '[i]f an "attack" is clearly over, then the legal "clock" resets. If no further attack is imminent, then there is nothing to lawfully defend against'.[303] With a series of armed attacks, therefore, the self-defence analysis largely depends on that related to imminent armed attacks. This fact should help to assuage the fear that adoption of the accumulation of events theory does away with the immediacy requirement and risks becoming an open-ended licence to use force.[304] In such cases, the real relevance of the prior armed attack is that it might be strongly indicative of further attacks. Imminence is thereby linked to immediacy, which returns us to the last window of opportunity analysis referred to in Section 2.5.1.2.

This analysis is reflected, for example, in Iran's arguments before the ICJ in *Oil Platforms*. Iran recognized that self-defence may be required in response to previous armed attacks where 'the victim State has experienced a series of attacks, and apprehends further attacks, so that the measures taken, although taken after the last actual attack are designed to protect the State against future attacks'.[305] It went on to stress that such a view of self-defence had been rightly rejected in the UNSC, because:

> the apprehended future attacks, if not imminent, are hypothetical; and in any event the measures tend to be designed to 'teach a lesson', to inflict retribution and to deter only by demonstrating that aggression does not pay.[306]

The ICJ determined that the American attacks were unnecessary,[307] but did not offer a view on the issue of immediacy, or the right to respond to a continuing threat. Rather, the Court's verdict was based largely on the lack of a proven armed attack and the nature of the USA's choice of targets.[308] However, Iran's stance on the right to respond to a series of attacks is interesting.[309] First, it encapsulates the belief that future threats must be imminent, which accords with this author's analysis above. In addition, Iran's view is consistent with the proposition that a clear defensive purpose must be apparent in the response. This reflects the aforementioned position that retributive acts will be viewed as unlawful acts of reprisal.

303 UN Doc A/HRC/44/38 (n 188) Annex, para 61.

304 Christian J Tams, 'The Use of Force against Terrorists' (2009) 20(2) EJIL 359, 389–390.

305 *Oil Platforms* (n 34) Memorial Submitted by the Islamic Republic of Iran, 8 June 1993, para 4.33.

306 Ibid. It should also be noted that Iran took a strict review on the question of immediacy in relation to completed armed attacks: 'But in cases of single armed attacks [. . .] the attack is terminated when the incident is over. In such a case the subsequent use of counter-force constitutes a reprisal and not an exercise of self-defence.' *Oil Platforms* (n 34) Reply and Defence to Counter-Claim Submitted by the Islamic Republic of Iran, 10 March 1999, para 7.47. The USA, in response, argued that this position rendered the right of self-defence 'illusory' and insisted that it had the right to respond to remove continuing threats to its security. *Oil Platforms* (n 34) Counter-Memorial and Counter-Claim Submitted by the United States of America, 23 June 1997, paras 4.27–4.29.

307 *Oil Platforms* (n 34) para 76.

308 Ruys, *'Armed Attack'* (n 56) 106. See Section 2.6.

309 As the object of force, however, Iran's views on self-defence have less probative value and should be approached with caution. See Section 2.4.2.1.

Other state practice provides support for the notion that, once an armed attack has occurred, further anticipated attacks may be prevented. During the Gulf of Tonkin incident in 1964, the USA claimed a right of self-defence to 'deter future aggression' by North Vietnam against its naval units following previous alleged attacks whilst operating in international waters.[310] In support of the American action, the UK stated that the repeated nature of the attacks, and their mounting scale, permitted the USA to take action to prevent their recurrence.[311] Preventive action, in these circumstances, was viewed by the UK as being essential to the right of self-defence.[312] The general principle that self-defence was allowed to 'discourage and prevent further violence' was repeated by the UK in supporting the USA's claim of self-defence against an 'ongoing pattern' of Libyan-sponsored terrorist attacks in 1986.[313] Similar support was given to the USA when it targeted the IIS headquarters in 1993, with the stated aim of deterring further acts of aggression.[314]

Therefore, the right to prevent and/or deter the continuation of further attacks has often been claimed by states. Other examples include Israel's action in Lebanon in 1975,[315] South Africa' incursions into Lesotho in 1982,[316] and Iran's claim of self-defence against terrorists operating from Iraq in 1999.[317] As Ruys notes, although several of these cited interventions received criticism or even condemnation by states, 'negative reactions were generally related to factual circumstances and other aspects of the incidents concerned and should therefore not be read as a principled rejection of *post facto* defensive measures'.[318]

More recent state practice, most notably in the context of the response to transnational terrorism, points to an increased willingness of states to accept more expansive defensive action to counter further threats from the same source. Israel, in defending its action against Hezbollah in Lebanon in 2006, referred to the necessity of removing the 'overall threat' faced by a state, meaning that 'the right of self-defense includes not only acts taken to prevent the immediate threat, but also

[310] UNSC Verbatim Record (5 August 1964) UN Doc S/PV.1140, 44–5. On this incident generally, see Douglas Guilfoyle, 'The Gulf of Tonkin Incident–1964' in Ruys and Corten, *The Use of Force in International Law* (n 90) 108.

[311] UN Doc S/PV.1140 (n 310) para 78.

[312] Ibid.

[313] UN Doc S/17990 (n 143).

[314] See UN Doc S/PV.3245 (n 112) 6; 17 (Brazil); 19–20 (Hungary); 21–22 (UK). The USA repeated this aim following the 1998 African embassy bombings. UN Doc S/1998/780 (n 271).

[315] UNSC Verbatim Record (4 December 1975) UN Doc S/PV.1859, para 119.

[316] UNSC Verbatim Record (16 December 1982) UN Doc S/PV.2409, paras 146–147. On this incident generally, see Theresa Reinold, 'South African Incursions into Lesotho–1982' in Ruys and Corten, *The Use of Force in International Law* (n 90) 379.

[317] Letter dated 12 July 1999 from the Permanent Representative of the Islamic Republic of Iran to the United Nations addressed to the President of the Security Council (12 July 1999) UN Doc S/1999/781, 2.

[318] Ruys, *'Armed Attack'* (n 56) 103–104.

to prevent subsequent attacks'.[319] In 2008, in response to repeated violence from the Kurdistan Workers' Party ('PKK'), the Turkish military explained that their resulting Operation Sun was to 'prevent the region from being a permanent and safe base for the terrorists'.[320] A clearer example occurred after 9/11.[321] In justifying its actions, the USA referred to the 'ongoing threat' against it. It maintained that their actions, which were designed to prevent and deter further attacks, were in accordance with the inherent right of individual and collective self-defence.[322] The USA also adopted this approach in justifying its targeted killing by drone strike of Iran's General Qassem Soleimani in 2020.[323]

The UK, along similar lines to the USA, asserted that their defensive response to 9/11 was designed 'to avert the continuing threat of attacks from the same source'.[324] It is noteworthy that the British opinion regarding this incident is that the combination of past attacks, current capabilities and ongoing and future aims amounted to a current threat that gave rise to a right of self-defence. That the 9/11 attacks were factually complete, and the defensive response did not occur until several weeks afterwards, appeared irrelevant to this determination. It also seemed to play no part in the wider assessment of the general necessity of the response. The UNSC recognized and reaffirmed the right to self-defence in the circumstances,[325] and the characterization of lawful self-defence was not generally

[319] Israel Ministry of Foreign Affairs, 'Responding to Hezbollah Attacks From Lebanon: Issues of Proportionality' (25 July 2006) <http://www.mfa.gov.il/MFA/AboutIsrael/State/Law/Pages/Responding%20to%20Hizbullah%20attacks%20from%20Lebanon-%20Issues%20of%20proportionality%20July%202006.aspx> accessed 5 September 2020. Israel's actions were nevertheless deemed to be disproportionate. See Section 3.3.5.

[320] Sabrina Tavernise and Sebnem Arsu, 'Turkey Says It Has Sent Ground Troops Into Iraq' *The New York Times* (22 February 2008) <http://www.nytimes.com/2008/02/22/world/middleeast/22iraq.html> accessed 5 September 2020. On this incident generally, see Tom Ruys, '*Quo Vadit Jus ad Bellum*?: A Legal Analysis of Turkey's Military Operations Against the PKK in Northern Iraq' (2008) 9 Melbourne Journal of International Law 334; Kimberley N Trapp, 'The Turkish Intervention Against the PKK in Northern Iraq–2007-08' in Ruys and Corten, *The Use of Force in International Law* (n 90) 689. Turkey did not report its actions to the UNSC as self-defence under Art 51 of the UN Charter, but Prime Minister Erdogan publicly justified Turkish action on this basis. Sebnem Arsu, 'Iraq Moves to Dissuade Turkey from Raids' *The New York Times* (17 October 2007) <www.nytimes.com/2007/10/17/world/europe/17turkey.html> access 5 September 2020.

[321] On this incident generally, see Michael Byers, 'The Intervention in Afghanistan–2001-' in Ruys and Corten, *The Use of Force in International Law* (n 90) 625. See further Section 4.2.3.1.

[322] Letter dated 7 October 2001 from the Permanent Representative of the United State of America to the United Nations addressed to the President of the Security Council (7 October 2001) UN Doc S/2001/946.

[323] The USA justified its actions to the UNSC as a response to 'an escalating series of armed attacks' by Iran and Iran-supported militias and the need to deter Iran from conducting or supporting further attacks against the USA and to degrade their ability to do so. Letter dated 8 January 2020 from the Permanent Representative of the United States of America to the United Nations addressed to the President of the Security Council (9 January 2020) UN Doc S/2020/20.

[324] Letter dated 7 October 2001 from the Chargé D'Affaires A.I. of the Permanent Mission of the United Kingdom of Great Britain and Northern Ireland to the United Nations addressed to the President of the Security Council (7 October 2001) UN Doc S/2001/947.

[325] UN Doc S/RES/1368 (n 80); UNSC Res 1373 (n 80).

questioned by states. To the contrary, the ensuing Operation Enduring Freedom received almost universal support from the international community.[326]

Ruys concludes on the basis of state practice up to 2010 that if a state has been subject to a series of armed attacks, and if there is a considerable likelihood that more attacks will imminently follow, then self-defence is not automatically excluded. This, he argues, is logical, since otherwise states 'would have little defence against consecutive pin-prick attacks whereby opposing forces withdraw immediately after having carried out an attack'.[327] This logic is inescapable and remains applicable today, especially in the context of armed attacks by NSAs deemed to be terrorists (see Chapter 4). Sporadic, but often devastating, attacks, possibly across a number of geographical locales, might occur under the umbrella of a continuing threat comprising past and imminent armed attacks. The most recent state practice relating to the international community's response to Daesh reinforces the proposition that states have a lawful right to respond to such a continuing threat.[328] The issue, however, in this context is the risk of states abusing the right of self-defence. Section 4.2.4.2 examines the worrying prospect of an enduring defensive response

[326] The reports to the UNSC from the USA and the UK of their actions in self-defence were followed by others. See Letter dated 24 October 2001 from the Chargé D'Affaires A.I. of the Permanent Mission of Canada to the United Nations addressed to the President of the Security Council (24 October 2001) UN Doc S/2001/1005; Letter dated 23 November 2001 from the Permanent Representative of France to the United Nations addressed to the President of the Security Council (23 November 2001) UN Doc S/2001/1103; Letter dated 23 November 2001 from the Permanent Representative of Australia to the United Nations addressed to the President of the Security Council (23 November 2001) UN Doc S/2001/1104; Letter dated 29 November 2001 from the Permanent Representative of Germany to the United Nations addressed to the President of the Security Council (29 November 2001) UN Doc S/2001/1127; Letter dated 6 December 2001 from the Permanent Representative of The Netherlands to the United Nations addressed to the President of the Security Council (6 December 2001) UN Doc S/2001/1171; Letter dated 17 December 2001 from the Permanent Representative of New Zealand to the United Nations addressed to the President of the Security Council (18 December 2001) UN Doc S/2001/1193; Letter dated 15 March 2002 from the Permanent Representative of Poland to the United Nations addressed to the President of the Security Council (15 March 2002) UN Doc S/2002/275. The European Union declared 'its full solidarity with the United States of America and its wholehearted support for the action that is being taken in self-defence and in conformity with the Charter of the United Nations'. Letter dated 8 October 2001 from the Permanent Representative of Belgium to the United Nations addressed to the Secretary-General (15 October 2001) UN Doc S/2001/967. NATO also offered its full support, invoking the right of collective self-defence pursuant to Art 5 of the Washington Treaty for the first time in its history. 'Statement by NATO Secretary General, Lord Robertson' (2001) 40 ILM 1268. The Organization of American States followed suit, also invoking collective self-defence. Organization of American States, 'Terrorist Threat to the Americas', Resolution of the Twenty-Fourth Meeting of Consultation of Ministers of Foreign Affairs, OAS Doc OEA/Ser.F/II.24, RC.24/RES.1/01 (21 September 2001) <http://www.oas.org/OASpage/crisis/RC.24e.htm> accessed 5 September 2020. Support was furthermore expressed by Russia, China, Norway, Mexico, Egypt and others. See Sean D Murphy (ed), 'Contemporary Practice of the United States Relating to International Law' (2002) 96 AJIL 237, 244–248; Ruys, *'Armed Attack'* (n 56) 436–437; Byers, 'The Intervention in Afghanistan' (n 321) 628–634.

[327] Ruys, *'Armed Attack'* (n 56) 106.

[328] Daesh is known by a number of names, including 'the so-called Islamic State', 'ISIL' and 'ISIS'. This book adopts the former nomenclature.

based on a notion of 'permanent imminence', which keeps the general necessity of self-defence rolling on indefinitely.[329]

2.6 Specific Necessity—Targeting

Necessity also relates to the target of defensive action. In the review that follows, it will be seen that states, scholars and the ICJ typically treat targeting as a distinct element of the necessity calculus. This issue of where defensive force must be directed is considered separately to the prior general necessity question of whether there is a *prima facie* need for a defending state to resort to force at all. To reflect this distinction, this book refers to targeting as an issue of specific necessity.[330] However, it is also true that states, scholars and the ICJ sometimes consider targeting alternatively, or cumulatively, within the rubric of proportionality.[331] This inconsistent narrative provides a mixed doctrinal picture. The following analysis seeks to provide greater conceptual clarity to avoid a catch-all depiction of unlawfulness. Further analytical work distinguishes between general necessity, specific necessity and proportionality, and explains where the issue of targeting is best situated.

2.6.1 A *Jus ad Bellum* Military Target

The ICJ's most explicit deliberations regarding the application of necessity and proportionality to the issue of targeting are to be found in *Oil Platforms*.[332] In this case, the Court asserted that the USA 'must also show that its actions were necessary and proportional to the armed attack made on it, *and* that the platforms were a *legitimate military target* open to attack in the exercise of self-defence'.[333] This statement might suggest that the Court considers the nature of the target to stand alongside necessity and proportionality as an additional determinant of legality. Later in its judgment, however, the Court rejected the USA's assertions that the oil platforms they attacked in purported acts of self-defence performed a military function. On the basis of that determination, the Court concluded that the American attacks were not necessary to respond to either the missile attack on the *Sea Isle City* or the

[329] See also Tams, 'Necessity and Proportionality' (n 64) 399–401, suggesting that state practice might point to a right of states to respond to *non*-imminent attacks, in cases where the 'fear of future attacks' seems genuine.

[330] See Section 2.3.

[331] In the context of the Iran/Iraq War 1980–88, for example, Iraq appeared to link not targeting civilians to the requirements of proportionality. UNSC Verbatim Record (15 October 1980) UN Doc S/PV.2250, para 40. Other examples are referenced in this section.

[332] See further Sections 3.2.1.6 and 3.4.2.2.

[333] *Oil Platforms* (n 34) para 51 (emphasis added).

mining of the *USS Samuel B. Roberts*.[334] As such, the Court's view that the nature of the target must be military appears to form part of the necessity analysis, rather than constituting an independent requirement.

The Court has been less explicit on this point in its other relevant jurisprudence. In *Nicaragua*, it concluded that the American attacks on Nicaraguan ports and oil installations were not proportionate.[335] This statement might implicitly refer to the nature of the target, or not. The Court does not go into any details, and its account of proportionality is unclear.[336] In *Nuclear Weapons*, the Court held that 'States must take environmental considerations into account when assessing what is necessary and proportionate in the pursuit of legitimate military objectives'.[337] The reference to 'legitimate military objectives' could be interpreted as an IHL issue, yet the Court is clearly referring here to the right of self-defence and *jus ad bellum* necessity and proportionality. However, no further detail was provided. In *Armed Activities*, the Court simply observed that the taking of airports and towns many hundreds of kilometres from Uganda's border was not necessary or proportionate.[338] It provided no explanation for this conclusion.

Other than in *Oil Platforms*, the ICJ did not clarify in any of these cases how or why the issue of targeting was relevant to either necessity or proportionality, or both. Perhaps the *Nuclear Weapons* and *Armed Activities* recourse to 'necessity and/or proportionality' is the ICJ's own 'ritual incantation'[339] that generally denotes illegality. States and scholars sometimes follow this approach of referring to the two requirements cumulatively, or in the alternative, as a nebulous catch-all description of behaviour. Under the taxonomy adopted in this book, it is submitted that targeting is better understood as an element of specific necessity rather than proportionality.

The logic of this conclusion can be explained as follows. First, as noted in Section 1.1, necessity must be addressed before proportionality can be considered. Second, it is difficult to argue from the position of principle or state practice that deliberately targeting a non-military target can be necessary to halt, repel or prevent an armed attack.[340] Using force against a civilian target might *also* be regarded

[334] Ibid, paras 74–77.
[335] *Nicaragua* (n 10) para 237.
[336] See Section 3.2.1.6.
[337] *Nuclear Weapons* (n 162) para 30. Regarding proportionality, see Section 3.3.7.
[338] *Armed Activities* (n 85) para 147.
[339] Gray, *Use of Force* (n 23) 125.
[340] In terms of state practice in support, see Section 2.6.2 and the concern regarding civilian harm reflected in state practice in Section 3.3.5. This assumes that civilians are not directly participating in hostilities ('DPIH') for the purposes of IHL and that civilian objects are not being used for military purposes. Where a civilian is DPIH and/or where a civilian object is being used for military purposes, they are potentially targetable under the rules of IHL. Where, in each case, there is also a connection with the armed attack, it would be also potentially possible to establish the *jus ad bellum* specific necessity of targeting them. See further Sections 2.6.2 and 3.4.2.2.

as excessive (*viz* disproportionate).[341] However, this conclusion is inconsequential. This is because the necessity hurdle must be overcome before proportionality can be considered and specific necessity incorporates the issue of targeting (as per *Oil Platforms* and the state practice referred to below). As such, also considering targeting within a proportionality assessment serves no additional legal function. Third, as explored in Chapter 3, the approach of the ICJ, scholars and states to proportionality reveals that proportionality is concerned with a defending state's *overall* defensive response and whether such response is excessive. Proportionality looks at outcomes. These outcomes comprise the cumulative effects of self-defence, not individual targeting decisions.[342] Therefore, proportionality plays a very different role to specific necessity and the two are conceptually distinct.

The consequence of this analysis is that where specific necessity is not satisfied, an act of targeting will be unlawful. It cannot also be disproportionate. Where targeting does satisfy specific necessity, it may nevertheless breach *jus ad bellum* proportionality.[343] This latter conclusion is not due to the nature of the target, however, but the consequential effects of the defensive conduct. An example that helps to reveal this distinction between specific necessity and proportionality as regards targeting is the sinking of the Argentine cruiser *General Belgrano* by a British submarine during the 1982 Falklands War. Gardam suggests it as an instance of state practice that supports the notion that proportionally may act to limit attacks on military targets.[344] Her analysis can also be read, however, as referring to specific necessity.[345] The key factor to note in this incident was the loss of life: over three hundred men were killed, far exceeding the total casualties on both sides up to that date.[346] The act resulted in much international criticism and reasonable arguments may be presented on either side regarding its proportionality.[347] Crucially, however, the review of the *proportionality* of this episode is framed in terms of whether

[341] Green and Waters, for example, suggest that it is unlikely that a direct attack on a civilian target will be anything other than excessive when measured against a defensive need. James A Green and Christopher PM Waters, 'Military Targeting in the Context of Self-Defence Actions' 84 (2015) Nord J Int'l L 3, 12

[342] See in particular Sections 3.4.1 and 3.4.2.

[343] This may be the case even if such acts are IHL compliant. See Section 3.4.1.

[344] Gardam, *Necessity, Proportionality* (n 3) 171–172.

[345] 'At the time of the attack, the *General Belgrano* was outside of the total exclusion zone declared by the UK and appeared to pose no immediate threat.' Ibid, 171. This suggests a lack of connection with the ongoing armed attack, meaning an absence of a defensive purpose in targeting it. See further Section 2.6.2.

[346] See Christopher Greenwood, 'Self-Defence and the Conduct of International Armed Conflict' in Dinstein, Y (ed), *International Law at a Time of Perplexity: Essays in Honour of Shabtai Rosenne* (Martinus Nijhoff Publishers 1989) 273, 279.

[347] Greenwood concludes: 'On balance, it is thought that the sinking was lawful, but the terms in which it is debated, and the intensity of that debate, show that the concept of self-defence may impose serious restrictions upon the right of a State to attack what, in terms of the *jus in bello*, is a legitimate military target.' Ibid, 279. Gardam notes that the international criticism was not so much based on legal criteria, but rather that the British attack was somehow dishonourable. Gardam, *Necessity, Proportionality* (n 3) 172.

the British action was an unjustifiable escalation of the conflict.[348] It is tied to the effect on the wider context and the overall defensive response.[349] Therefore, it is submitted that the issue for proportionality is whether damaging or destroying a legitimate military target (for the purposes of both IHL and *jus ad bellum* specific necessity) takes a defending state's conduct, to be viewed as a whole, beyond a defensive purpose. Is it 'excessive' (to quote Webster)?[350]

Distinguishing between necessity and proportionality when considering targeting, including the need to apply the former first, is *prima facie* reflected in *Oil Platforms*. The Court began by considering whether targeting the oil platforms was a necessary act of self-defence. Focusing on the non-military nature of the oil platforms, the Court concluded that it was not necessary.[351] The judgment thereby expressly connects the nature of target to the *necessity* of the response. The Court then considered proportionality as a subsequent and separate issue.[352] In so doing, it stated that the American response to the attack on *Sea Isle City* might, '*had the Court found that it was necessary* in response to [. . .] an armed attack committed by Iran, have been considered proportionate'.[353] This approach reflects the logic that a finding of proportionality (and disproportionality) can only flow from a conclusion that a use of defensive force is first necessary. It confirms that the operation of both requirements relies on the existence of a defensive purpose. Without necessity, there is no defensive purpose against which proportionality can be gauged. There is only an unlawful use of force.

The Court proceeded to muddy the conceptual waters, however. Despite, and contrary to, the aforementioned logic and its approach to the attack on *Sea Isle City*, the Court adopted a different approach to proportionality and the mining of the *USS Samuel B. Roberts*. The Court concluded that the American response in this context, despite being unnecessary, was also disproportionate.[354] Given the foregoing analysis, in the absence of necessity, it is not clear why the Court chose to opine on proportionality. The propriety of such comments is questionable. Moreover, it is uncertain why the Court held that proportionality might have been satisfied in the former case and not the latter. However, its finding of disproportionality of the response to the mining of the *USS Samuel B. Roberts* does provide some clues regarding how the Court distinguishes between necessity and proportionality. Its view is clearly coloured by the effects of the totality of the American

348 Greenwood, 'Self-Defence and the Conduct of International Armed Conflict' (n 346) 279. Gardam (n 3) 171, also recognizes the issue of escalation in her commentary on proportionality.

349 Escalation may affect other interests that factor in whether self-defence is proportionate, such as international peace and security, the rights of other states, the environment, and so forth. See Section 3.3.

350 See generally Chapter 3.

351 *Oil Platforms* (n 34) para 76.

352 Ibid, paras 76–77.

353 Ibid, para 77 (emphasis added).

354 Ibid.

military operation, which consisted of a wider campaign that went beyond the reaction to the mining alone.[355] This focus on the overall response reflects the analysis referred to above regarding how proportionality operates by examining the outcomes of defensive action, in contrast to specific necessity, which regulates the selection of the targets of that action.

The general rule that self-defence is limited to military targets finds support in state practice, where claims of self-defence and responses thereto have focused on this issue.[356] An example includes the Israeli strike on the Osiraq reactor in 1981. In justifying its claim of self-defence, Israel insisted that the nuclear reactor was a legitimate military target. This characterization was greeted with scepticism in the UNSC, however. The fact that other states instead regarded the reactor as civilian in nature provided one of the reasons for the widespread condemnation of the Israeli action.[357] Another instance is South Africa's justification of its purported defensive action in Zambia, Zimbabwe and Botswana in 1986 on the basis that it was limited to ANC targets, with great care taken not to involve local civilians.[358] Similar claims appear consistently in the context of fighting international terrorism.[359] One of the bases for condemnation of this particular action, however, was that the targets chosen were not connected to hostile acts, despite South Africa's assertions to the contrary.[360] Tanzania specifically referred to this fact in rejecting the claim of self-defence.[361] Under this book's proposed taxonomy, this is interpreted as a lack of *jus ad bellum* specific necessity.[362] The following section develops this analysis.

2.6.2 IHL and a *Jus ad Bellum* Connection with the Armed Attack

In IHL, it has long been established that targeting in armed conflict is limited to 'military objectives', with the corollary being that civilians and civilian objects must not be the object of attack.[363] These targeting rules impose a continuous obligation

[355] Ibid. For further details of the response and the ensuing proportionality analysis, see Section 3.2.1.6.

[356] Section 2.6.2 provides examples of state practice that both confirm and go beyond this general premise, suggesting a need for a connection between a military target and an armed attack.

[357] See UN Doc S/PV.2280 (n 126) paras 71–92 (Israel); para 147 (Algeria); UN Doc S/PV.2284 (n 133) 77 (Syria); UNSC Verbatim Record (16 June 1981) UN Doc S/PV.2285, para 29 (Cuba). See further Section 2.4.2.2.

[358] UN Doc S/PV.2684 (n 92) 26–27.

[359] See Sections 2.6.2, 4.2 and 4.3.3.

[360] See Kwakwa, 'South Africa's May 1986 Military Incursions' (n 91) 440.

[361] UN Doc S/PV.2684 (n 92) 44–45. Green describes the military target issue as determinative of Tanzania's conclusion. Green, 'Docking the *Caroline*' (n 4) 478.

[362] Green and Waters interpret Tanzania's words as a lack of necessity and proportionality under the *jus ad bellum*. Green and Waters, 'Military Targeting' (n 341) 13.

[363] Arts 48, 51(2) and 52(2) of the Protocol Additional to the Geneva Conventions, 12 August 1949, and Relating to the Protection of Victims of International Armed Conflicts, 8 June 1977, 1125 UNTS 3 ('API'). This prohibition is an uncontroversial principle of customary international law. See Rule 1 of

on those who plan or decide upon an attack to evaluate whether or not something is a military objective. Attacks must be cancelled or suspended if it becomes apparent that the objective is not military, if it is protected, or it would violate the IHL rules of proportionality.[364] Therefore, how and to what extent IHL and the *jus ad bellum* interrelate on this topic is directly relevant to the present enquiry.

Green and Waters rightly note that IHL has primacy in the area of targeting and will generally be the 'first point of call' in relation to such decisions. They argue, however, that limitations on targeting also form part of the customary rules of necessity and proportionality in the *jus ad bellum*. In their view, IHL and the *jus ad bellum* impose broadly equivalent parallel but cumulative obligations.[365] The ensuing review reflects this general premise. There is also wider academic support for the idea that non-military targeting will fall foul of *jus ad bellum* necessity, in addition to IHL.[366] The Council of the European Union's Independent International Fact-Finding Mission on the Conflict in Georgia likewise adopted this position.[367] This point also seems to have been recognized, at least to a degree, by Webster who took the view that it is necessary to show that there had been an attempt to discriminate between the innocent and the guilty.[368]

The coextensive governance of targeting by IHL and the *jus ad bellum* raises the question of whether a 'military target' under the *jus ad bellum* is identical to a 'military objective' under IHL. For the present consideration of *jus ad bellum* necessity, there are clear distinctions to be drawn. As noted, the generalities of the *jus ad bellum*, based on the principles set out in this section, should not be directly equated with the specific provisions of IHL. Yet, drawing on the principles of IHL

The International Committee of the Red Cross's Customary IHL Database <https://ihl-databases.icrc.org/customary-ihl/eng/docs/v1_rul_rule1> accessed 5 September 2020.

364 Arts 52(2) and 57(2)(b) of API (n 363).

365 Green and Waters, 'Military Targeting' (n 341) 6–7, 9–11, 13–25. In so doing, Green and Waters do not argue that custom contains specific stand-alone targeting limitations, but that the restrictions inherent in *jus ad bellum* necessity and proportionality regulate the choice of targets. They accept that in the majority of cases the targeting rules will apply in tandem and will be substantively identical, with certain limited exceptions. Such concurrent application principle is in line with the ICJ's decision in *Nuclear Weapons* (n 162), which is discussed in Section 3.4.1. See generally Section 3.4 for further discussion of proportionality and targeting.

366 Greenwood, 'Self-Defence and the Conduct of International Armed Conflict' (n 346) 278–279; Gardam, *Necessity, Proportionality* (n 3) 171–172; Corten, *The Law Against War* (n 24) 488; Ruys, *'Armed Attack'* (n 56) 108–110, 121–123. These commentators also maintain that targeting is limited by proportionality.

367 IIFFMCG Report (n 204) 272. The Report's adopted methodology vis-à-vis the *jus ad bellum* has been criticized, however. See Christian Henderson and James A Green, 'The *Jus ad Bellum* and Entities Short of Statehood in the Report on the Conflict in Georgia' (2010) ICLQ 129. On this incident generally, see Christine Gray, 'The Conflict in Georgia–2008' in Ruys and Corten, *The Use of Force in International Law* (n 90) 712.

368 Letter from Mr Webster to Mr Fox (24 April 1841) *British and Foreign State Papers*, 1840–1841, Vol. XXIX, 1138. Although, Green and Waters note that Webster did not go so far as to claim that actions taken in self-defence must always be directed against military targets. Green and Waters, 'Military Targeting' (n 341) 10.

helps to explore what the ICJ and states (for which, see further below) consider is targetable under the *jus ad bellum*. Under IHL, to constitute a targetable 'military objective', objects by their nature, location, purpose or use must make an effective contribution to military action. In addition, their total or partial destruction, capture or neutralization in the circumstances ruling at the time must offer a definite 'military advantage'.[369] This definition provides a logical starting point regarding how we might conceive of the military activities that the Court in *Oil Platforms* considered necessary for targeting purposes.[370] Like the IHL position on targeting, this *jus ad bellum* approach requires a connection with hostile activities.

Whereas compliance (in broad terms at least) with this IHL definition of 'military objective' might be necessary to constitute a 'military target' for the purposes of the *jus ad bellum*, it is not sufficient to establish legality under the latter regime. There is an obvious additional *jus ad bellum* requirement for targeting in the context of defensive action. The target of self-defence must have some military connection, whether or not precisely equating to an IHL 'military objective', but not any military target will suffice. There must be a defensive purpose to the act. This means that a target's destruction, capture or neutralization must also be connected with the force to be halted, repelled or prevented. For the *jus ad bellum*, therefore, defensive force should in principle be directed against the source of the armed attack(s).[371]

A general *jus ad bellum* targeting precept that requires a connection between attack and defence is entirely logical and is in keeping with the approach taken by the ICJ in *Oil Platforms*.[372] Destroying, capturing or neutralizing military objectives (for the purposes of IHL) connected with the armed attack (making them *jus ad bellum* military targets) clearly points to a *prima facie* defensive purpose. Conversely, other states may rightly question the *jus ad bellum* necessity of a defending state targeting IHL-compliant military objectives of the attacker that are not related directly to the current threat that it faces. Depending on the circumstances, it would be difficult for a defending state to establish that destroying or neutralizing such military objectives carries with it a defensive purpose.[373]

369 API (n 363) Art 52(2). See generally Stefan Oeter, 'Methods and Means of Combat' in Dieter Fleck (ed), *The Handbook of International Humanitarian Law* (3rd edn, OUP 2013) 115, 166–187.

370 *Oil Platforms* (n 34) para 76.

371 Ruys, *'Armed Attack'* (n 56) 108–109. Cannizzaro notes along similar lines that necessity secures the existence of a 'functional link' between military action and defensive purpose. Enzo Cannizzaro, 'Proportionality in the Law of Armed Conflict' in Andrew Clapham and Paola Gaeta (eds), *The Oxford Handbook of International Law in Armed Conflict* (OUP 2014) 332, 346.

372 Specific necessity requires that the defending state only targets the attacker. See Section 2.3. The analysis in this section takes that general proposition one step further. The Court in *Oil Platforms* (n 34) para 77, also criticized the USA for attacking a 'target of opportunity', which might suggest that it requires a connection between the target and the purported threat to the state taking military action against it.

373 From an IHL perspective, destroying, capturing or neutralizing a military objective during a defensive operation that is not connected with an armed attack is unlikely to offer a 'military advantage'. Although the application of IHL does not rely on the lawfulness under the *jus ad bellum* of a state resorting to armed force (thereby ensuring equal application of IHL to belligerents), it is influenced by its

In this respect, we should recall that self-defence is a temporary right that enables a defending state to counter a situation of emergency and address its immediate defensive needs. It is not designed to address longer-term security concerns, which are reserved for the collective security mechanisms of the UN Charter.[374] Therefore, the *jus ad bellum* overlays an additional and concurrent obligation on defending states when selecting targets. IHL and the *jus ad bellum* operate separately, but in tandem, to regulate targeting. The rules of both regimes must be complied with on a continuous basis to ensure that defensive action is lawful.[375]

State practice ostensibly reflects this coextensive application of IHL and the *jus ad bellum*. The difficulty, however, in assessing this practice is that states do not tend to refer to the source of the targeting obligations incumbent upon them. For instance, Iran argued before the ICJ in *Oil Platforms* that 'self-defence must be addressed to the right target—to the source of the threat'.[376] Whether or not Iran clearly identified such requirement as forming part of the proportionality or necessity requirement (or both) is not clear, however.[377] What is clear, is that it viewed force used against targets that had no direct connection with the armed attacks as being punitive or retaliatory acts, thereby constituting reprisals.[378] This logic is compelling and Iran's comments clearly relate to the *jus ad bellum*. In 2020, Iran reported to the UNSC that it had acted in self-defence in response to the targeted killing by the USA of General Qassem Soleimani. Iran's letter stressed that the target of its military response was an American air base in Iraq from which the attack had been launched.[379] This letter appears to confirm Iran's approach to targeting when exercising its right of self-defence.

The following incidents of practice likewise comprise claims of self-defence and also indicate that targeting obligations fall under the purview of the *jus ad bellum*. For example, the UK defended its targeting of the Harib Fort in 1964 by reference

reasons for doing so. Therefore, the overall (defensive) purpose of the action may be taken as defining the military advantage. Absent such advantage, a military objective is not targetable under IHL. See further Oeter, 'Methods and Means of Combat' (n 369) 175–177; Section 3.4.1.

374 See Section 1.6.2.3 and also Section 2.5.2 regarding deterring future threats.

375 The joint and separate application of the *jus ad bellum* and IHL is discussed further in Sections 3.4 and 3.5.

376 *Oil Platforms* (n 34) Memorial Submitted by the Islamic Republic of Iran, 8 June 1993, para 4.25.

377 Iran purported to argue this point under the rubric of proportionality, making reference to the ICJ's dictum in *Nicaragua* (n 10) regarding the American mining of the Nicaraguan ports and the attacks on ports, oil installations, etc. Ibid, paras 4.22–4.25. However, its reasoning also reflects an appreciation of specific necessity and/or conflates the two. This is apparent in Iran's statement that '[t]he Court [in *Nicaragua*] regarded such attacks as unable to meet the criterion of necessity because they could not be proportionate to the aid provided to the armed opposition inside El Salvador by Nicaragua. In other words, the mining, attacks on ports and selected installations were the wrong target. The measures could not therefore be proportionate and limited to the necessities of the case'. Ibid, para 4.25.

378 Ibid, para 4.38.

379 Letter dated 8 January 2020 from the Permanent Representative of the Islamic Republic of Iran to the United Nations addressed to the Secretary-General and the President of the Security Council (8 January 2020) UN Doc S/2020/19.

to its military nature and the fact that it was a centre for subversion and aggression against the South Arabian Federation.[380] Czechoslovakia rejected the British claim of self-defence. Yet, by pointing to the object of the response having no connection with the alleged raids to which the UK claimed to be responding, Czechoslovakia appeared nevertheless to confirm the requirement of a nexus between the armed attack and (claimed) acts of self-defence.[381] Iraq also adopted this position. It noted that the destruction of the Harib Fort, which was a military barracks for ground forces, provided no protection against the aerial attacks that had prompted the British raid.[382] The UK's position is more recently reflected in the UK Military Manual, which not only recognizes that the *jus ad bellum* may limit the choice of targets, but also suggests that such target must have a connection to the armed attack, or risk unjustifiably escalating the conflict.[383]

Similarly, in 1964 the USA defended its actions against North Vietnamese torpedo boats and support facilities in the Gulf of Tonkin on the basis that such action was limited to targets against which they had been forced to defend themselves.[384] The USA provided a similar justification for it acts during the Vietnam War in 1972,[385] and when it bombed Libya in 1986.[386] In 1993, the USA also justified its targeting of the IIS headquarters in Baghdad on the basis that it was 'a target directly linked to the operation against President Bush'.[387] When targeting NSAs operating in foreign territory, defending states, in justifying claims of self-defence, will typically assert that their action is limited to the terrorists responsible for the armed attacks and to military targets. At the same time, they maintain that they are not targeting civilians or the host state. This was the case for Operation Sun in 2008,[388] Operation Enduring Freedom in 9/11,[389] the ongoing Global Coalition action in Syria,[390] as well as Turkey's Operation Olive Branch in 2018 and Operation

[380] UNSC Verbatim Record (2 April 1964) UN Doc S/PV.1106, paras 54–55; UNSC Verbatim Record (6 April 1964) UN Doc S/PV.1108, para 112; UN Doc S/PV.1109 (n 265) para 30.

[381] UNSC Verbatim Record (8 April 1964) UN Doc S/PV.1110, para 24.

[382] UN Doc S/PV.1109 (n 265) para 57.

[383] UK Military Manual (n 11) Section 2.8.1. It is interesting that the UK's position that self-defence might limit the choice of targets and weaponry is linked with the risk of conflict escalation. It is, perhaps, for this reason that the UK's position on these issues is placed in a section dealing with *jus ad bellum* proportionality, rather than necessity. See further Section 3.4.2.

[384] UN Doc S/PV.1140 (n 310) para 44.

[385] Office of the Legal Adviser, Department of State, 'Rights and Duties of States' (1972) 66 AJIL 836, 837.

[386] UNSC Verbatim Record (15 April 1986) UN Doc S/PV.2674, 13–15.

[387] UN Doc S/PV.3245 (n 112) 6. As noted, this claim of self-defence is contestable, but the fact that the defending state felt bound to justify it actions by pointing to the nexus between attack and defence is instructive.

[388] Note Verbale dated 26 March 2008 from the Permanent Mission of Turkey to the United Nations Office at Geneva addressed to the Secretariat of the Human Rights Council (28 March 2008) UN Doc A/HRC/7/G/15.

[389] See UNGA Verbatim Record (10 November 2001) A/56/PV.44, 9 (USA); 11 (South Africa); 27 (Chile).

[390] See Sections 4.2.3.2 and 4.3.3.2.

Peace Spring in 2019.[391] It is also a general theme within state practice pertaining to the so-called 'unwilling or unable' debate.[392]

Other state reactions to purported acts of self-defence support the premise that targets should be military and connected with the armed attack. For example, in respect of Turkey's Operation Sun in 2008, states emphasized the need for Turkey to limit its action to PKK targets.[393] Israeli interventions in and against Lebanon over the years are similarly expositive. In 1968 the UNSC's condemnation of Israel's attack on Beirut airport was largely based on the lack of any connection between the airport and the prior attack on an Israeli aircraft.[394] In 1972, the UNSC condemned 'the repeated attacks of Israeli forces on Lebanese territory and population'.[395] In 1982, it condemned 'Israeli incursions into Beirut', reaffirming 'the rights of the civilian populations' and repudiating 'all acts of violence against those populations'.[396] Israel's operation against Hezbollah in Lebanon in 2006 is also elucidating on this point. Israel attempted to vindicate its action on the basis that it was concentrating its response on Hezbollah strongholds, positions and infrastructure.[397] Although this assertion was regarded with general scepticism, it is another example of a state attempting to justify its targeting decisions within a claim of self-defence by reference to a connection with the armed attacks.[398]

2.6.3 Prior Complaints and the Effectiveness of the Defensive Measures

To conclude our consideration of specific necessity and targeting, it is worth noting two additional points. The first relates to a comment that the ICJ made in *Oil Platforms* on the American military response:

> there is no evidence that the United States complained to Iran of the military activities of the platforms, in the same way as it complained repeatedly of minelaying

[391] See Section 4.2.3.2.

[392] See Section 4.2.2.

[393] See, for example, EU Presidency Statement on the Military Action Undertaken by Turkey in Iraqi Territory (25 February 2008) <www.eu2008.si/en/News_and_Documents/CFSP_Statements/February/0225MZZturkey.html> accessed 5 September 2020; Ruys, '*Quo Vadit Jus ad Bellum*?' (n 320) 362–363.

[394] UNSC Res 262 (31 December 1968) UN Doc S/RES/262; 'Political and Security Questions: The Situation in the Middle East' (1968) UNYB 190, 228–232. See further Gray, *Use of Force* (n 23) 203.

[395] UNSC Res 316 (26 June 1972) UN Doc S/RES/316.

[396] UNSC Res 520 (17 September 1982) UN Doc S/RES/520.

[397] UNSC Verbatim Record (14 July 2006) UN Doc S/PV.5489, 6.

[398] The principle source of state criticism and condemnation of this action was not based on explicit pronouncements that might be regarded as pertaining to specific necessity. Although great concern was expressed by states and international organizations regarding the nature of Israel's targeting of civilian infrastructure, states focused on the cumulative consequences of such actions. It was the overall effect of the Israeli response that led to a general consensus that it was disproportionate. See Section 3.3.5.

> and attacks on neutral shipping, which does not suggest that the targeting of the platforms was seen as a necessary act.[399]

This statement might be read as suggesting that self-defence must be directed only against targets that have been the subject of specific prior complaints by the defending state, and it has been criticized on this basis.[400]

The better view is that the Court was not laying down a new requirement of prior complaint. Rather, it was simply considering whether the American attacks on the Iranian oil platforms were necessary.[401] The Court was drawing a distinction between the American action in response to the mine laying (in respect of which the USA made repeated complaints) and their response to the military activities of the oil platforms (for which no complaints were made). This distinction formed part of the Court's general scepticism that the platforms were genuine military targets. This conclusion is supported by the Court's observation that the attack on the R-4 platform was a '"target of opportunity", not one previously identified as an appropriate military target'.[402] Consequently, the Court's statement should be understood in light of its focus on the (non-military) nature of the American targets. It constitutes an observation of fact that contributed to the Court's conclusion that targeting the oil platforms was not justified by self-defence.[403]

Finally, for some scholars, targeting also raises the issue of the adequacy or effectiveness of a state's defensive response. Corten, for example, argues that 'utterly ineffective' measures of self-defence cannot be characterized as necessary.[404] Although he caveats this assertion by stating that only 'obvious inefficacy' will be sanctioned in practice, this seems to be a rather ambiguous general limitation to impose on a state's exercise of self-defence. In support of his argument, Corten draws on the ICJ's requirement in *Oil Platforms* (and, he argues, *Armed Activities*) that targets must be of a military nature. As such, Corten's statement should be confined to that context, rather than extrapolated to place a specific duty on the defending state to mount an effective response. Nevertheless, Corten is not alone in making such comments on effectiveness. Gray also questions, in the context of combatting terrorism post-9/11, whether an ineffective response can be considered necessary.[405]

Whether actions in self-defence are effective or adequate are not straightforward issues. It is unclear on what basis these questions are to be assessed, when that

[399] *Oil Platforms* (n 34) para 76.

[400] Taft, for example, argues that a requirement of prior complaint has no basis in international law and would undermine the right of self-defence. Taft, '*Oil Platforms* Decision' (n 47) 304.

[401] Christine Gray, 'The International Court of Justice and the Use of Force' in Christian J Tams and James Sloan (eds), *The Development of International Law by the International Court of Justice* (Oxford Scholarship Online 2014) 255.

[402] *Oil Platforms* (n 34) para 76.

[403] Ibid.

[404] Corten, *The Law Against War* (n 24) 488.

[405] Gray, *Use of Force* (n 23) 233.

assessment can be made determinatively, and by whom. Ultimately, as Corten concedes, determinations of effectiveness or adequacy are issues of military strategy. Such issues are also tied up with the respective military resources and capabilities of the defending state and the attackers.[406] If there is indeed an obligation that state actions in self-defence must be effective or adequate, the state practice and associated analysis set out in Sections 2.6.1 and 2.6.2 suggest that such obligation should be understood as requiring that the defending state's response must be *capable* of being effective. This is to say that the response must have the potential of halting, repelling or preventing an armed attack because (i) the targets of self-defence are of a military nature, and (ii) the targets are connected with an actual or imminent armed attack.[407]

2.7 Conclusions

Albeit not expressed using the taxonomy proposed in this chapter, general and specific necessity are clearly reflected in state practice, ICJ jurisprudence and scholarship. A review of these sources reveals that necessity relates to two distinct questions. The first is whether, following an armed attack, any form of military force is required to resolve the issue, or peaceful alternatives suffice (general necessity). If force is the only reasonable response in the circumstances, the subsequent question is where such force must be aimed so as to be capable of achieving a defensive purpose (specific necessity). Proportionality assesses the overall outcomes of the decision to use force in self-defence.

States undoubtedly consider an exercise of self-defence to be a measure of last resort. Yet, general necessity is revealed to be highly contextually sensitive. A defending state might seek to justify a claim of self-defence by pointing to the lack of reasonable alternatives to force to establish general necessity. However, the specific facts of the case will ultimately determine whether other states deem the resort to self-defence to be reasonable in the circumstances. The availability and pursuit of peaceful alternatives might feature in this review and count as evidence of general necessity. However, they might not appear at all in either the justification or review of claims of self-defence. Where they are noted, the issue of

[406] The Chatham House Principles state that '[i]n applying the test of necessity, reference may be made to the means available to the state under attack; the kinds of forces and the level of armament to hand will be relevant to the nature and intensity of response that it would be reasonable to expect, as well as the realistic possibilities of resorting to non-military means in the circumstances'. The Chatham House Principles (n 65) 967. The meaning of this statement is not entirely clear, but the authors of the Principles seem to imply that the resources and capabilities of (at least) the defending state are viewed as being part of the necessity calculus.

[407] See Ruys, *'Armed Attack'* (n 56) 108, reaching the same conclusion. See also *Wall* (n 162) Written Statement Submitted by the Government of the Republic of Indonesia, 30 January 2004, para 6, whereby Indonesia ties necessity and effectiveness with the achievement of a defensive purpose.

peaceful alternatives is unlikely to be the sole determinant of legality. Other factors will tend to govern the final conclusion, such as the timing of the armed attack, its likelihood and gravity, the nature of the relationship between the defending state and the aggressor, the relevant history between the two and whether the threat is current and likely to persist. Additional factors pertain to armed attacks by terrorist NSAs.[408]

State practice, ICJ jurisprudence and scholarship suggest that a review of the legality of self-defence will ultimately rest on whether it was reasonable for a state to resort to self-defence in the circumstances. This raises questions over the ability of general necessity to restrain the use of defensive force, especially in the context of armed attacks against terrorist NSAs. In such cases in particular, general necessity is revealed to be a weak limitation on state action. In contrast, specific necessity operates as a clear restriction on the exercise of the right of self-defence. By requiring that force is limited to military targets connected with the actual or imminent armed attack, specific necessity ensures that their capture, neutralization or destruction is confined to a defensive purpose. A lack of this nexus suggests that a use of force is punitive and, therefore, unlawful. In this way, the *jus ad bellum* overlays onto IHL additional targeting rules that determine whether the exercise of self-defence is lawful.

[408] See Chapter 4.

3
Proportionality

3.1 Introduction

At its core, *jus ad bellum* proportionality is a relatively straightforward concept: it is a prohibition against excess.[1] Its role is to limit permitted harm done to others.[2] Yet, identifying its content and outer conceptual boundaries and applying them to specific incidents of self-defence are more complex than with necessity.[3] Flexibility is required. This is partly due to debates amongst scholars and states regarding the scope of self-defence. Most importantly, however, identifying from state practice the constituent elements of the proportionality calculus is challenging. States' views on proportionality are frequently hard to interpret and might be too closely tied up with political considerations to permit a clear distillation of firm legal principles. States or UN bodies 'tend to use the phrase "proportionality" indiscriminately, basing it on a gut feeling of when something was "over the top"';[4] or 'excessive'.[5] Furthermore, proportionality is a limiting factor in both the *jus ad bellum* and international humanitarian law ('IHL') and it is often unclear whether states are referring to either, or both, regimes when commenting on specific incidents. This is despite the fact that the meanings and purposes of proportionality are markedly different in each of these bodies of law.[6]

This latter uncertainty might be due to states relying on IHL, rather than the *jus ad bellum*, to regulate the use of defensive force, once necessity has been established.[7] The concern might also be that fully engaging with the *jus ad bellum* requirements puts defending states at a disadvantage vis-à-vis the attacker because of the potential limitation that the *jus ad bellum* imposes on a defending state's right

[1] Christian J Tams and James Devaney, 'Applying Necessity and Proportionality to Anti-Terrorist Self-Defence' (2012) 45(1) Israel L Rev 91, 106.

[2] Rosalyn Higgins, *Problems and Process: International Law and How We Use It* (OUP 1994) 230.

[3] This is particularly so with armed attacks by NSAs in the context of international terrorism. See Section 4.3.

[4] Noam Lubell, 'Comments on David Kretzmer's "The Inherent Right to Self-Defence and Proportionality in *Jus ad Bellum*"' (*EJIL: Talk!*, 17 April 2013) <http://www.ejiltalk.org/comments-on-david-kretzmers-the-inherent-right-to-self-defence-and-proportionality-in-jus-ad-bellum/> accessed 5 September 2020.

[5] States and scholars often refer to 'excessive' when considering proportionality. Examples are referred to throughout this chapter.

[6] See Section 3.4.1.

[7] See Section 3.5. Regarding the interaction between the two regimes, see Sections 2.6 and 3.4.

Necessity and Proportionality and the Right of Self-Defence in International Law. Chris O'Meara, Oxford University Press (2021). © Chris O'Meara. DOI: 10.1093/oso/9780198863403.003.0003

of defensive action.[8] The argument is that defending states are put under an unfair burden by the obligation to comply with the *jus ad bellum*, which the attacker (if it is a state) has already breached and may be disinclined to follow. During the negotiations regarding the Definition of Aggression, for example, a number of states expressed reservations that the inclusion of proportionality in the definition would put the defender at a disadvantage to the benefit of the attacker.[9] Regardless of whether this concern is empirically true, this theoretical imbalance of obligations is countered by a fuller understanding of proportionality as set out in this chapter. As will be seen, states do have leeway to defend themselves effectively, provided that they do not act excessively.

The uncertainties surrounding the proportionality requirement have not been helped by the jurisprudence of the International Court of Justice ('ICJ', or the 'Court'). As this chapter illustrates, the Court has provided confused and contradictory guidance regarding both the standard against which proportionality is to be measured and how the requirement is to be applied to specific incidents.[10] Despite these difficulties, an analysis of proportionality involving a critical review of state practice, case law and theory does bear fruit. The requirement's specific limitations remain to be developed through further state practice, but its core meaning is readily identifiable and meaningful conclusions regarding its content may be drawn.

As with necessity, the natural starting point for studying proportionality is the *Caroline* incident.[11] Supposing the necessity of the moment requires defensive action, Webster asserted that it would also be incumbent on a government purportedly acting in self-defence to show that it 'did nothing unreasonable or excessive; since the act, justified by the necessity of self-defence, must be limited by that necessity, and kept clearly within it'.[12] This is the genesis of the modern requirement that, following an armed attack, and where necessity (both general and specific) is established, the use of defensive force must also be proportionate. Necessity determines *whether* force may be used to respond to an actual or imminent armed attack[13] and *where* it must be directed, proportionality governs *how much* force is permissible.

[8] Judith Gardam, *Necessity, Proportionality and the Use of Force by States* (CUP 2004) 23–24; James A Green, 'Docking the *Caroline*: Understanding the Relevance of the Formula in Contemporary Customary International Law Concerning Self-Defense' (2006) 14(2) Cardozo J Int'l & Comp L 429, 457.

[9] UNGA Res 3314 (XXIX) (14 December 1974) (hereafter Definition of Aggression). See UNGA 'Special Committee on the Question of Defining Aggression', Third Session, Volume II, Summary Records of the 67th to 78th Meetings (19 October 1970) UN Doc A/AC.134/SR.67–78, 85–86 (USSR); 86–87 (Ghana); 87 (Syria).

[10] See in particular Sections 3.2.1.6 and 3.4.2.2.

[11] See Section 1.4.

[12] Letter from Mr Webster to Mr Fox (24 April 1841) *British and Foreign State Papers*, 1840–1841, Vol. XXIX, 1138.

[13] Regarding imminent armed attacks, see Section 2.5.1.2. This chapter proceeds on the basis that a right of pre-emptive self-defence might exist as a matter of *lex lata*. If not, such right has the potential to exist as *lex ferenda*.

Accordingly, it is proportionality that seeks to prevent a state from acting excessively, beyond a defensive purpose.[14] It restricts conflict from escalating in an ever-increasing cycle of violence and minimizes disruption to third parties and the international community.[15] How proportionality is applied to achieve these aims, and what may count as 'excessive', is explored in the following sections.

Proportionality's function is not universally viewed in the manner described in the preceding paragraph, however. Certain academics propose that proportionality forms part of the trigger of the right of self-defence, rather than conditioning the exercise of the right once it is triggered.[16] Such an approach harkens back to just war theory, in which proportionality factored in determining whether force was initially warranted.[17] This minority view is difficult to reconcile with both the ICJ's jurisprudence and with principle, however. In *Nicaragua*, the Court clearly associates proportionality with the exercise of the right once it has arisen, rather than whether or not the right is available in the first place.[18] The *sine qua non* for the right of self-defence is an armed attack.[19] To assert that proportionality also relates to whether the right is triggered, rather than conditioning the response, unnecessarily conflates proportionality with an armed attack.

Adopting the ICJ's approach, it remains the case that Webster's exposition of proportionality should be taken as a starting rather than an end point. On its own terms, the *Caroline* formula does not fully represent the complexities of how proportionality operates to moderate a defensive military response in the contemporary *jus ad bellum*. Most importantly, as set out in the next section, proportionality requires that defensive force is evaluated in relation to, or balanced against, a particular standard. What this standard should be is perhaps implicit in Webster's formulation, but there is scope for much greater explicit elaboration. Therefore, the first part of this chapter considers how proportionality applies to the right of self-defence, providing an answer to the operative question: 'proportionate to what?'. The examination will continue to how proportionality functions in practice and what factors indicate whether or not states acting in purported self-defence have complied with the requirement.

As will be seen, the devil is in the detail. Assessing proportionality is more complex and more context dependant than necessity. There are a greater number of

[14] Christopher Greenwood, 'Self-Defence and the Conduct of International Armed Conflict' in Yoram Dinstein (ed), *International Law at a Time of Perplexity: Essays in Honour of Shabtai Rosenne* (Martinus Nijhoff Publishers 1989) 273–274.

[15] Greenwood argues that proportionality is concerned with the preservation of international order and the minimization of the use of force. Ibid, 278.

[16] For example, Wedgwood suggests that proportionality is a strategic doctrine governing not only how a state employs force, but also whether it may do so. Ruth Wedgwood, 'Proportionality and Necessity in American National Security Decision Making' (1992) 86 Am Soc Int L Proc 58–61.

[17] See Gardam, *Necessity, Proportionality* (n 8) 35–36.

[18] *Military and Paramilitary Activities in and against Nicaragua* (*Nicaragua v US*) (Merits) [1986] ICJ Rep 14 (hereafter '*Nicaragua*') paras 194, 237.

[19] Ibid, para 237.

variables that must be applied and balanced in order to ascertain whether an act of self-defence is proportionate in the particular circumstances. Establishing a 'magical template' that is applicable to all defensive action is not possible.[20] Yet, just because something cannot be defined with absolute precision does not mean that 'anything goes'. States frequently employ proportionality as a marker of the legality of military action and, as the following study highlights, there is potential for achieving much greater determinacy regarding this core requirement of the *jus ad bellum*.

3.2 Proportionate to What?

Proportionality is often understood as balancing two principal variables, although the reality is more complex.[21] The first variable relates to a defending state's response to an armed attack. This might be described as the defensive 'action' or 'act',[22] the defensive 'use of force',[23] the defensive 'operation,[24] and so forth. The ICJ has referred in its jurisprudence to defensive 'measures', 'activities', 'actions' and 'operations'.[25] Such references *prima facie* pertain to the defending state's physical response: what the defending state is doing in pursuit of its defensive right. More accurately, however, it is better to view this variable as also including the *effect* of such defensive response.[26]

That the defensive action and its consequences together form the first variable is clear from state practice. As explored below, states tend to focus on (dis) proportionality in terms of the consequences of self-defence, most notably collateral civilian harm. The ICJ has also considered the consequential harm in its

[20] Tom Ruys, *'Armed Attack' and Article 51 of the UN Charter: Evolutions in Customary Law and Practice* (CUP 2010) 110; Gardam, *Necessity, Proportionality* (n 8) 21–22.

[21] Section 3.3 sets out how this balancing act, rather than being a purely binary exercise, accounts for a number of additional factors that go to whether a defensive act is excessive.

[22] For example, Noam Lubell, *Extraterritorial Use of Force Against Non-State Actors* (OUP 2010) 64.

[23] For example, Green, 'Docking the *Caroline*' (n 8) 457; Kimberley N Trapp, 'Back to Basics: Necessity, Proportionality and the Right of Self-Defence against non-State Terrorist Actors' (2007) 56(1) ICLQ 141, 146.

[24] For example, Raphaël Van Steenberghe, 'Proportionality under *Jus ad Bellum* and *Jus in Bello*: Clarifying their Relationship' (2012) 45(1) Israel L Rev 107, 115.

[25] See *Nicaragua* (n 18) paras 176, 237; *Case Concerning Oil Platforms (Iran v US)* (Judgment) [2003] ICJ Rep 161 (hereafter '*Oil Platforms*') paras 43, 51, 77; *Case Concerning Armed Activities on the Territory of the Congo (Democratic Republic of the Congo v Uganda)* (Judgment) [2007] ICJ Rep 168 (hereafter '*Armed Activities*') paras 112, 118, 120.

[26] Scholars sometime note that proportionality constrains the 'scale and effects of defensive action.' See Ruys, *'Armed Attack'* (n 20) 110; Christian Henderson, *The Use of Force and International Law* (CUP 2018) 234. These are in fact two distinct variables. The scale of the force might be related to its effects, but this will not always be so. For example, an intense bombardment of one isolated target might result in its destruction but have limited additional consequential effects. Likewise, a targeted and limited use of force has the potential to result in much greater harm depending on the nature of the target (for example, targeting an arms depot, resulting in a larger blast radius, or if a large number of civilians were in or nearby the target).

deliberations, rather than just the defensive acts themselves. In *Nuclear Weapons*, the Court noted the potential environmental damage caused by the use of nuclear weapons when considering necessity and proportionality.[27] In *Oil Platforms*, it concluded that the American response to the mining of a single military vessel, the *USS Samuel B. Roberts*, was disproportionate. This was framed in terms of the overall effect of the American response on Iran's military and civilian infrastructure and apparatus.[28] Therefore, whereas the first variable comprises the defensive acts and their outcomes, identifying the second variable is more complicated. The standard against which defensive force and its effects are to be measured (answering the question 'proportionate to what?') is the focus of the debate.

3.2.1 Quantitative or Teleological Proportionality?

There are two principal analytical approaches that are proposed by scholars to identify the second variable. These options are also discernible in the ICJ's reasoning and in state practice. This section begins by reviewing the two alternatives and the related scholarship and ICJ jurisprudence. A subsequent review of specific incidents of self-defence reveals a mixed approach in the practice of states.

3.2.1.1 Alternative Models and Academic Opinion

The first option is a quantitative understanding of proportionality that focuses on the relationship between the armed attack and the defensive response. A purely quantitative approach requires an equivalence or parity of scale and/or means between attack and defence: the response must be proportionate to the act that provoked it.[29] This 'tit for tat' or 'eye for an eye' conception of proportionality might better be described as 'armed attack proportionality', given that this is the variable against which the defensive force is being measured. However, it is generally referred to as 'quantitative proportionality', as it also seeks to balance the amount of harm suffered, or anticipated, by each side to the conflict. It dictates that the armed attack and the defence be commensurate in terms of relative injury, comprising human casualties and damaged incurred.[30]

[27] *Legality of the Threat or Use of Nuclear Weapons* (Advisory Opinion) [1996] ICJ Rep 226 (hereafter '*Nuclear Weapons*') paras 30–31. See further Section 3.3.7. The effects of nuclear weapons were the focus of great attention in the separate and dissenting opinions. See especially the dissent of Judge Weeramantry, paras 102–172.

[28] *Oil Platforms* (n 25) para 77. See Section 3.2.1.6.

[29] David Kretzmer, 'The Inherent Right to Self-Defence and Proportionality in *Jus Ad Bellum*' (2013) 24(1) EJIL 235, 238. See also Yoram Dinstein, *War, Aggression and Self-Defence* (6th edn, CUP 2017) 282, who asserts that in the case of 'on-the-spot reactions' and 'defensive armed reprisals,' proportionality points to a symmetry or approximation of scale and effects between the armed attack and defensive response. See Section 3.5, however, regarding his approach to 'wars of self-defence'.

[30] Tams argues that proportionality is 'a prohibition against measures that are excessive *in relation to the injury expected from the attack*'. Christian J Tams, 'The Necessity and Proportionality of

As such, the quantitative model balances offensive kinetic force (and its outcomes) against defensive kinetic force (and its outcomes).[31] Yet, a distinction should be made between the 'quantitative model' described here and 'material factors' that form part of establishing a quantitative balance. Material factors typically include harm to civilians and civilian objects, as well as other material damage arising from uses of force. The subsequent analysis reveals that material factors are often referenced by states when considering proportionality. However, it does not necessarily follow that the quantitative model as a whole is being relied upon as the determinant of legality in such cases. This distinction between 'material factors' and the 'quantitative model' is explored further in the following sections.

The second option is a teleological interpretation of proportionality. This model adopts a functional approach that is tied to the defensive needs of the defending state.[32] It may also be described as the 'means-end' test, measuring as it does the defensive force (the means) against the legitimate ends of using that force (being the purposes of self-defence).[33] Ago, in an often-quoted passage, explains teleological proportionality as follows:

> The requirement of the proportionality of the action taken in self-defence [. . .] concerns the relationship between that action and its purpose, namely - and this can never be repeated too often - that of halting and repelling the attack or even, in so far as preventive self-defence is recognized, of preventing it from occurring. It would be mistaken, however, to think that there must be proportionality between the conduct constituting the armed attack and the opposing conduct. The action needed to halt and repulse the attack may well have to assume dimensions disproportionate to those of the attack suffered. What matters in this respect is the result to be achieved by the 'defensive' action, and not the forms, substance and strength of the action itself.[34]

Scholars who advocate for the qualitative model of proportionality are very much in the minority.[35] The majority of academic opinion clearly favours the

Anti-Terrorist Self-Defence' in Larissa van den Herik and Nico Schrijver (eds), *Counter-Terrorism Strategies in a Fragmented International Legal Order: Meeting the Challenges* (CUP 2013) 373, 389.

[31] This assumes that the force involved is physical. Except as specifically referred to in this book, self-defence against cyber attacks is beyond the scope of the present study.

[32] Ruys, *'Armed Attack'* (n 20) 112.

[33] Kretzmer, 'Proportionality in *Jus Ad Bellum*' (n 29) 239.

[34] International Law Commission, 'Addendum—Eighth Report on State Responsibility by Mr. Roberto Ago, Special Rapporteur—The Internationally Wrongful Act of the State, Source of International Responsibility (Part 1)' (1980) UN Doc A/CN.4/318/Add.5-7 (hereafter 'Ago, "Addendum—Eighth Report on State Responsibility"') para 121. See also Elihu Lauterpacht, 'The Legal Irrelevance of the "State of War"' (1968) 62 Am Soc Int L Proc 58, 64.

[35] See, for example, Johanna Friman, *Revisiting the Concept of Defence in the Jus ad Bellum: The Dual Face of Defence* (Bloomsbury 2017) 86–93. This author remains unconvinced by Friman's reasoning, however. The state practice and legal theory set out in this chapter do not support her conclusion that the defensive response must essentially mirror the prior armed attack.

teleological model, requiring as it does a balance to be struck between the defensive responsive and a defensive purpose or necessity: halting, repelling or preventing an armed attack.[36] This model encapsulates Webster's assertion that defensive acts must not be 'unreasonable or excessive' and must be limited by the necessity that gave rise to them.[37] As such, defensive kinetic force and its outcomes are balanced against a defensive purpose, not only against offensive kinetic force and its outcomes, as with the quantitative model.

Some commentators, in referencing the teleological model, paraphrase it as measuring proportionality against the 'threat' posed to the defending state. For example, Greenwood asserted in the lead up to the second Iraq war in 2003 that:

[36] Claud HM Waldock, 'The Regulation of the Use of Force by States in International Law' (1951) 81 Collected Courses of the Hague Academy of International Law 451, 464; Ian Brownlie, *International Law and the Use of Force by States* (Clarendon Press 1963) 434; Higgins, *Problems and Process* (n 2) 231–232; Robert Jennings and Arthur Watts (eds), *Oppenheim's International Law: Volume I, Peace* (9th edn, Longman 1996) 422; Stanimir A Alexandrov, *Self-Defense Against the Use of Force in International Law* (Kluwer Law International 1996) 167; Dapo Akande, 'Nuclear Weapons, Unclear Law? Deciphering the *Nuclear Weapons* Advisory Opinion of the International Court' (1998) 68 BYIL 165, 191; William H Taft, 'Self-Defense and the *Oil Platforms* Decision' (2004) 29 Yale J Int'l L 295, 305; Gardam, *Necessity, Proportionality* (n 8) 142, 156–162; Antonio Cassese, 'Article 51' in Jean-Pierre Cot, Alain Pellet and Mathias Forteau, *La Charte des Nations Unies: Commentaire Article par Article* (3rd edn, Economica 2005) 1333; Elizabeth Wilmshurst, 'The Chatham House Principles of International Law on the Use of Force in Self-Defence' (2006) 55(4) ICLQ 963 (hereafter 'The Chatham House Principles') 969; Andreas Zimmermann, 'The Second Lebanon War: *Jus ad bellum, Jus in Bello* and the Issue of Proportionality' (2007) 11 Max Planck Yrbk UN L 99, 117, 123; Olivier Corten, *The Law Against War: The Prohibition on the Use of Force in Contemporary International Law* (Hart Publishing 2010) 470, 488–491; Ruys, *'Armed Attack'* (n 20) 94–95; Lubell, *Non-State Actors* (n 22) 65–66; Christopher Greenwood, 'Self-Defence' in *Max Planck Encyclopaedia of Public International Law* (OUP 2011) para 27; Van Steenberghe, 'Proportionality' (n 24) 113, 115; Keiichiro Okimoto, 'The Cumulative Requirements of *Jus ad Bellum* and *Jus in Bello* in the Context of Self-Defense' (2012) 11 Chinese JIL 45, 64; Michael Schmitt (ed), *Tallinn Manual on the International Law Applicable to Cyber Warfare* (CUP 2013) 62; Georg Nolte, 'Multipurpose Self-Defence, Proportionality Disoriented: A Response to David Kretzmer' (2013) 24(1) EJIL 283, 284; Tams, 'Necessity and Proportionality' (n 30) 388–389; Enzo Cannizzaro, 'Proportionality in the Law of Armed Conflict' in Andrew Clapham and Paola Gaeta (eds), *The Oxford Handbook of International Law in Armed Conflict* (OUP 2014) 332, 345–346; James A Green, 'The *Ratione Temporis* Elements of Self-Defence' (2015) 2(1) JUFIL 97, 101; Terry D Gill, 'When Does Self-Defence End?' in Marc Weller (ed), *The Oxford Handbook on the Use of Force in International Law* (OUP 2015) 737, 744; Christine Gray, *International Law and the Use of Force* (4th edn, OUP 2018) 159; International Law Association, Committee on the Use of Force, 'Final Report on Aggression and the Use of Force', Sydney Conference (2018) 12; Kimberley N Trapp, 'The Turkish Intervention Against the PKK in Northern Iraq–2007–08' in Tom Ruys and Olivier Corten (eds) with Alexandra Hofer, *The Use of Force in International Law: A Case-Based Approach* (OUP 2018) 689, 699; Craig Forcese, *Destroying the Caroline: The Frontier Raid that Reshaped the Right to War* (Irwin Law Inc 2018) 212, 235. Not all scholars cited here accept a right of anticipatory self-defence. Whereas 'halting' and 'repelling' are generally accepted as legitimate goals of self-defence, these commentators do not necessarily subscribe to the notion that a future armed attack may be 'prevented'. However, all the scholars referred to adopt a teleological understanding of proportionality: self-defence is limited by what is proportionate to the defensive objective and not by the requirement of strict equivalence of scale and/or means between the armed attack and resulting defensive acts. See also David Rodin, *War and Self-Defense* (OUP 2002) 114–115; Georg Nolte and Albrecht Randelzhofer, 'Ch.VII Action with Respect to Threats to the Peace, Breaches of the Peace, and Acts of Aggression, Article 51' in Bruno Simma and others (eds), *The Charter of the United Nations: A Commentary, Volume II* (3rd edn, OUP 2012) 1397, 1426.

[37] See Section 1.4.

> [i]f Iraq did pose such an immediate threat then, in my opinion, military action against Iraq *for the purpose of dealing with that threat* would be lawful. The degree of force used would have to be *proportionate to the threat and no more than necessary to deal with that threat* (including preventing a recurrence of the threat).[38]

The reference to 'threat' indicates one of the immediate advantages of the teleological model, which is its flexibility. This model avoids a purely retrospective view of proportionality that focuses solely on the completed armed attack. Rather than the only benchmark for proportionality being the harm already inflicted, a teleological appreciation of proportionality also accounts for the potential need to counter ongoing and imminent armed attacks.[39] By encapsulating the total threat to the defending state comprising past, present and future armed attacks,[40] this model accepts a possible quantitative imbalance between the defensive response and the armed attack that immediately prompted such response. Without this ability, states would be limited to only responding to past events, rather than having the flexibility to counter threats that are both current and which may be reasonably anticipated. A teleological approach takes 'due account of the future-looking character of self-defence measures and of the characterization, in Article 51, of self-defence as an "inherent right"'.[41]

These two conceptual models of proportionality might be presented by commentators as alternatives, but a review of state practice and *opinio juris* reveals a mixed picture. Depending on the context, states variously refer to the quantitative and/or teleological models of proportionality, as well material factors such as civilian harm that may speak to both.

3.2.1.2 State Practice—Consideration in Abstract Terms

When states reference proportionality in abstract terms, the variable against which they measure this requirement is sometimes unclear. In response to Israeli incursions into Lebanon in 1972,[42] for example, the representative of Argentina offered their view on the general meaning of proportionality:

[38] Christopher Greenwood, 'Memorandum: The Legality of Using Force Against Iraq' (24 October 2002) Select Committee on Foreign Affairs Minutes of Evidence <http://www.publications.parliament.uk/pa/cm200203/cmselect/cmfaff/196/2102406.htm> accessed 5 September 2020, para 26. Although Greenwood's position of the legality of this particular incident is questionable, his statement of the law pertaining to self-defence more generally is widely supported. In terms of 'preventing a recurrence of the threat', see Section 2.5.2.2. Brownlie also discusses proportionality in relation to the 'threat' faced. Brownlie, *Use of Force by States* (n 36) 261, 264. Such formulation assesses proportionality by reference to the goal that the defending state is entitled to seek to achieve. Greenwood, 'Self-Defence' (n 36) paras 26–27. Greenwood states these goals as including halting and repelling an armed attack and recovering occupied territory.

[39] This is the UK's position, for example. See Section 3.2.1.2.

[40] See Section 2.5.2.2 regarding the 'accumulation of events' theory.

[41] Tams, 'Necessity and Proportionality' (n 30) 388.

[42] See Section 3.2.1.3.

> the measures adopted in self-defence must be of a similar nature or reasonably in keeping with the means used in the illegal act against which action is being taken. Any use of force on a considerably larger scale or on a scale which goes beyond the events or the provocative circumstances obviously exceeds the general framework of self-defence and is considered illegal in accordance with the uses and practices of the law.[43]

This comment refers to the commensurability of the nature, means and scale of the attack and response, but offers little insight into how proportionality should be gauged in practice. The reference to the 'general framework of self-defence' might be interpreted as a reference to the overall governing principle that force must be defensive in nature. This might suggest that any finding of unlawfulness of a use of force is ultimately tied to the purpose of the right. Argentina's statement can be read as supporting either model of proportionality, therefore, or both.

During deliberations by the UN General Assembly ('UNGA') over the Definition of Aggression, the proportionality of self-defence was also referenced by a number of delegates. Discussing the right in abstract terms, some states noted that an exercise of self-defence should be proportionate to the armed attack.[44] Others clearly rejected the need for an precise balance between the two.[45] Although there was no detailed discussion, a number of states did express concern regarding incorporating proportionality into the Definition of Aggression because of perceived benefits this would offer to the attacker. In particular, on what appears to be a reference to the quantitative model, the view was that this would unduly restrict the victim state's choice of weapons and the scale of the defensive response.[46]

The Democratic Republic of the Congo ('DRC') representative initially expressed the view that 'the act of self-defence must be proportionate to the armed attack which gave rise to it',[47] again alluding to the quantitative model. He went on to say, however, that proportionality 'required the victim State to use only that amount of force necessary to halt the armed attack' and only when the defensive objective had been achieved would the right of self-defence end.[48] Other representatives adopted this ultimately teleological model, albeit that there was no extended consideration of its content.[49] These debates accordingly represent an inconsistency among states in characterising a proportionate defensive response in broad conceptual terms.

[43] UNSC Verbatim Record (27/28 February 1972) UN Doc S/PV.1644, para 26.

[44] UNGA 'Special Committee on the Question of Defining Aggression', Third Session, Volume I, Summary Records of the 52nd to 66th Meetings (19 October 1970) UN Doc A/AC.134/SR.52–66, 43 (Turkey); 61 (Yugoslavia); 88 (Madagascar); 91 (Cyprus).

[45] For example, UN Doc A/AC.134/SR.67–78 (n 9) 83 (Iraq); 88 (Guyana).

[46] Ibid, 85 (USSR); 86 (Ghana); 87 (Syria).

[47] Ibid, 81.

[48] Ibid, 81, 90.

[49] Ibid, 83 (Iraq); 84, 117 (UK); 89 (Italy). See also UN Doc A/AC.134/SR.52–66 (n 44) 53 (Ecuador).

The DRC's comments referred to in the preceding paragraph exemplify how a state might set out both alternative models of proportionality, yet ultimately tie proportionality to the defensive needs of the state. This is not uncommon. When states combine models, however, difficulties arise as to the proper meaning and application of proportionality. In 2004, for example, the UK Attorney General offered his thoughts on proportionality. On the topic of self-defence in response to imminent armed attacks, Lord Goldsmith stated that 'the force used must be proportionate to the threat faced *and* must be limited to what is necessary to deal with the threat'.[50] *Prima facie*, therefore, the UK's position on proportionality refers to both the quantitative and teleological models.

The first thing to note is that the reference to 'threat' could be interpreted narrowly, equating it to an individual armed attack that has already occurred. Alternatively, it could be interpreted broadly, such that 'threat' encompasses the wider circumstances, potentially including past, ongoing and imminent armed attacks.[51] The latter interpretation appeared to be the understanding of the UK Attorney General in 2017.[52] Whether we interpret 'threat' narrowly or broadly, however, there arises a possible dichotomy. This is where it is not possible for a defensive response to be proportionate to both the armed attacks(s) and the defensive necessity, as Lord Goldsmith's formulation appears to require. As noted above, achieving a defensive aim (*viz* removing the totality of the threat posed by accumulating past, ongoing and imminent armed attacks) might necessarily require an amount of defensive force that exceeds the armed attack that immediately prompted it.

Reading Lord Goldsmith's opinion as being cumulative of quantitative and teleological proportionality leads to confusion and should be avoided. His reference to the defensive necessity suggests that it is not his intention that the requirement of quantitative equivalence is determinative of the question of proportionality. To the contrary, his (and his successor's) reference to the need to 'deal with the threat' suggests that the purposive element is the overriding concern. This conclusion is also reflected in the UK Military Manual[53] and the UK practice referred to in the following sections.

[50] HL Deb 21 April 2004, vol 660, col 370 (emphasis added). Along similar lines, Cassese suggests that the defending state 'must use an amount of force strictly necessary to repel the attack and proportional to the force used by the aggressor'. Cassese, *International Law* (2nd edn, OUP) 355. Elsewhere, however, Cassese links the lawfulness of self-defence solely to achieving the defensive necessity. Cassese, 'Article 51' (n 36) 1333.

[51] Given that Lord Goldsmith clearly refers to 'armed attack' and 'attack' as distinct concepts throughout his speech, the broad interpretation of 'threat' is the most likely option.

[52] UK Attorney General's Speech at the International Institute for Strategic Studies, 'The Modern Law of Self-Defence' (11 January 2017) <https://www.gov.uk/government/uploads/system/uploads/attachment_data/file/583171/170111_Imminence_Speech_.pdf> accessed 5 September 2020, 7, 19–20. The UK Attorney General clearly sets out a view of self-defence where proportionality is measured against a 'threat' that includes imminent armed attacks.

[53] UK Ministry of Defence, *The Manual of the Law of Armed Conflict* (OUP 2005) (hereafter 'UK Military Manual') Sections 2.8, 13.2.

A more recent example of this dual reference in the context of general considerations of proportionality is found in the 2017 Australian Attorney-General's speech regarding imminent armed attacks. In it, he initially appears to adopt the quantitative model: 'Proportionality [...] acts as a restraint to ensure that any use of force in self-defence corresponds to the gravity of the imminent attack sought to be repelled.'[54] He goes on to explain, however, that proportionality is designed to ensure that 'an imminent armed attack cannot be used as a pretext to engage in a wider act of aggression', before proceeding to quote Webster that defending states must do 'nothing unreasonable or excessive, since the act justified by the necessity of self-defense, must be limited by that necessity, and kept clearly within it'.[55] The latter two references are not unequivocal, but appear to relate to a defensive purpose. This interpretation is supported by references in his speech to self-defence serving a protective function.[56]

These examples demonstrate that states may adopt either, or both, models of proportionality when considering its meaning in abstract terms. As noted in Section 2.5.1.2, states rarely make such general statements on international law. Yet, in order to avoid confusion, when states do engage with concepts that are central to the operation of the *jus ad bellum*, they should take great care in how they express their understanding of them.

3.2.1.3 State Practice—Specific Incidents and the Quantitative Model

State practice and *opinio juris* in the context of specific incidents of purported self-defence also reference both models of proportionality, as well as material factors. Starting with examples of allusions to the quantitative model, China labelled Israeli action during the 1956 Suez crisis as disproportionate to the 'wrongs' suffered by Israel, without elaborating further.[57] This was presumably a reference to attacks by the Egyptian fedayeen, however, to which Israel claimed to be acting in self-defence.[58] A number of states also concluded that the British raid on the Harib Fort in Yemen in 1964 was out of proportion to the acts that provoked it. The Ivory Coast pointed to the fact that British action had resulted in the loss of twenty-five lives and caused extensive material damage, which was not in any way commensurate with the death of two camels, which had ostensibly prompted the British raid.[59] These references could be characterized as reliance

[54] Australian Attorney-General, Senator the Hon. George Brandis QC, 'The Right of Self-Defence Against Imminent Armed Attack in International Law', Public Lecture at the T C Beirne School of Law, University of Queensland (11 April 2017) <https://www.ejiltalk.org/the-right-of-self-defence-against-imminent-armed-attack-in-international-law/> accessed 5 September 2020.

[55] Ibid.

[56] Ibid.

[57] UNSC Verbatim Record (30 October 1956) UN Doc S/PV.749, para 133.

[58] Ibid, para 33.

[59] UNSC Verbatim Record (6 April 1964) UN Doc S/PV.1108, paras 32, 35 (Morocco); paras 48–50 (Ivory Coast). This was denied by the British who insisted that they were responding in defence of the South Arabia Federation to a series of attacks from Yemeni territory and were also acting to prevent

on the quantitative model. However, the Harib Fort incident appears to be a case of marked asymmetry between attack and defence, based on both the scale and effects of the British action. Notably, other states based their criticism on a lack of defensive purpose.[60]

In 1968, the USA decried Israel's attack on Beirut airport in response to prior attacks against Israeli civilian aircraft as entirely disproportionate in magnitude to the act that preceded it.[61] The Americans understood disproportionality to be based on the degree of the destruction involved, and on the nature of the attack as compared to the purported act of self-defence. Whereas the former comprised acts of two individual terrorists, the latter was carried out by a sizeable military force operating under government orders. Regardless of this disparity, it is clear that the Americans viewed such action as being devoid of any justification whatsoever, disproportionate or not.[62] The British concern meanwhile was over the 'scale and intensity' of the Israeli action, without referencing the particular nature of it.[63]

Prima facie, the reference by both states to such material factors as comparative harm and the nature, scale and intensity of the force deployed by Israel may indicate reliance on the quantitative model of proportionality. They highlight the disparity between attack and defence. Likewise, American concern over Israeli action against non-state actors ('NSAs') in Lebanon in 1970 appeared to rest on the scale and effects of the Israeli operation, comprising the accompanying loss of life and destruction of property.[64] However, it is not clear that the quantitative model was determinative in either incident. The disparity in material factors could also speak to a lack of a defensive purpose. Moreover, states are not necessarily consistent over time in how they view proportionality. Even if the quantitative model informed the American response to these latter incidents, the USA has also explicitly adopted the teleological model of proportionality. This is evident in its claim of self-defence during the Vietnam War,[65] in its pleadings before the ICJ,[66] and to justify its recent military strikes against Daesh

further attacks from the same source. UNSC Verbatim Record (7 April 1964) UN Doc S/PV.1109, paras 2–45.

[60] See Section 3.2.1.4.

[61] UNSC Verbatim Record (29 December 1968) UN Doc S/PV.1460, para 73. The US employed the same language in the same year regarding Israeli anti-terrorist action in Jordan. UNSC Verbatim Record (21 March 1968) UN Doc S/PV.1402, para 5; UNSC Verbatim Record (24 March 1968) UN Doc S/PV.1407, para 7. In the same incident, Senegal expressed the view that self-defence had to be 'by means proportionate to those used by the aggressor [in its attack]'. UNSC Verbatim Record (7 August 1968) UN Doc S/PV.1436, para 132.

[62] UN Doc S/PV.1460 (n 61) para 73.

[63] UN Doc S/PV.1460 (n 61) para 81. The UK did not specifically refer to proportionality, although such comments clearly indicate concerns regarding this requirement.

[64] UNSC Verbatim Record (19 May 1970) UN Doc S/PV.1542, para 91.

[65] Office of the Legal Adviser, Department of State, 'Rights and Duties of States' (1972) 66 AJIL 836, 837.

[66] See Section 3.2.1.5.

in Syria.[67] The UK has similarly adopted the teleological model to justify its own actions.[68]

In 1972, Israel claimed a right of self-defence to justify its incursions into Lebanon in response to purported terrorist attacks by the Palestine Liberation Organization ('PLO').[69] The attacks had been on a relatively small scale, resulting in eight injuries and three deaths. In contrast, the Israeli response constituted a large-scale military operation comprising ground troops, tanks, aerial bombardments and artillery fire. It caused a number of deaths and substantial material harm.[70] In the ensuing UN Security Council ('UNSC') debates, states condemned Israel's action as disproportionate to the alleged terrorist acts that preceded them.[71] Sudan labelled them unequal and disproportionate.[72] The UK confined itself to expressing concern over the unjustifiable scale of Israel's military response.[73] The means and scale of the Israeli action, and its effects were the focus of discontent, suggesting a reliance on the quantitative model. Yet, this is again an example of manifest asymmetry between attack and defence. Furthermore, reference to these material factors were clearly combined with wider concerns over peace in the Middle East.

In respect of Israel's strike on the PLO headquarters in Tunis in 1985,[74] Thailand's conclusion that it was disproportionate rested on the disparity in the numbers of casualties on both sides.[75] Although this factor was raised, it is clear that Thailand would have condemned Israel's actions in any event, based on the unjustified violation of Tunisia's sovereignty and territorial integrity.[76] This was reflective of the general scepticism levied at Israel's response. The striking disparity between (high) Palestinian casualties and (low) Israeli casualties, coupled with widespread damage to civilian infrastructure and a dire humanitarian situation, is also a feature

[67] Letter dated 23 September 2014 from the Permanent Representative of the United States of America to the United Nations addressed to the Secretary-General (23 September 2014) UN Doc S/2014/695.

[68] See Sections 3.2.1.2, 3.2.1.4, 3.2.1.5.

[69] Letter dated 25 February 1972 from the Acting Permanent Representative of Israel to the United Nations addressed to the President of the Security Council (25 February 1972) UN Doc S/10550.

[70] Ibid; UN Doc S/PV.1644 (n 43) paras 8–14 (Lebanon); 19–22 (Argentina).

[71] See UNSC Verbatim Record (26 February 1972) UN Doc S/PV.1643, para 20 (Lebanon); para 166 (Belgium); UN Doc S/PV.1644 (n 43) para 142 (Italy). See also UNSC Verbatim Record (26 June 1972) UN Doc S/PV.1650, para 10 (France).

[72] UN Doc S/PV.1644 (n 43) para 210.

[73] UN Doc S/PV.1643 (n 71) para 134. The UK likewise referred to the 'scale' of Israeli action, highlighting concern over civilian casualties, when denouncing as unjustified Israeli against PLO targets in Lebanon in 1981. UNSC Verbatim Record (21 July 1981) UN Doc S/PV.2293, paras 47, 49.

[74] On this incident generally, see Erin Pobjie, Fanny Declercq and Raphaël Van Steenberghe, 'The Israeli Raid Against the PLO Headquarters in Tunis–1985' in Ruys and Corten, *The Use of Force in International Law* (n 36) 395.

[75] UNSC Verbatim Record (2 October 1985) UN Doc S/PV.2611, para 44. They noted that whereas fifteen Israelis were killed, over sixty lives were lost in Tunisia as a result of the Israeli response. The UK also concluded that the raid was disproportionate. UN Doc S/PV.2611, para 111. Again, however, this was within the context of a general rejection of the necessity of the Israeli action. Indonesia took a similar position. UNSC Verbatim Record (4 October 1985) UN Doc S/PV.2615, para 60. Israel, in defence of its actions, stated that it was necessary not only to count past victims in the proportionality calculus, but also potential future victims if 'this nerve-centre of terror is allowed to operate undisturbed'. UN Doc S/PV.2615, para 194.

[76] UN Doc S/PV.2611 (n 75) para 44.

of concern regarding Israel's interventions in Gaza in 2008–2009 and 2014. These material factors featured in a number of states' conclusions that such action was disproportionate.[77] The relative scale of the military action and resulting civilian harm were also apparent in the general condemnation of Israeli's incursions into Lebanon in 1982[78] and 2006.[79] Material factors, in particular relative civilian harm, are clearly present in each of these examples as indicators of disproportionality. However, this does not equate to states requiring a strict adherence to the quantitative model, meaning parity between attack and defence. In respect of the 2006 invasion, for example, states tended to view material harm to Lebanon as indicative of Israel acting beyond a defensive purpose, thereby pointing to an overriding reliance on the teleological model.[80]

Other incidents might serve as precedents for recourse to the quantitative model of proportionality, at least in part. In support of the American strike on the headquarters of the Iraqi Intelligence Service ('IIS') in Baghdad in 1993, France noted that it was 'proportionate to the action of the Iraqi secret service'.[81] The facts of the case do not support a conclusion of quantitative equivalence, however. In terms of methods, the foiled attempt on President Bush's life consisted of a car-bomb and other explosives, whereas the American response was the launch of twenty-three Tomahawk cruise missiles.[82] On relative scale and casualties, this is much more difficult. The American President was not killed, although the potential damage that could have been caused by the bomb was considerable.[83] The American response, however, resulted in the almost complete destruction of the IIS headquarters, at least three civilian deaths, civilian injury and the destruction of property.[84] Therefore, it is notable that France's approval of the American action was also closely tied to the need to combat terrorism and was set against a background of the desire by the international community to moderate Iraq's behaviour and to induce it to fulfil its international obligations.[85]

77 See UNSC Verbatim Record (31 December 2008) UN Doc S/PV.6060, 3 (UN Secretary General); 9 (South Africa); 9 (France); 10 (Indonesia); 13–14 (Vietnam); 15 (Burkina Faso); 16 (Costa Rica); 17 (Belgium); 18 (Egypt); UNSC Verbatim Record (6 January 2009) UN Doc S/PV.6061, 10 (Turkey); 14 (Austria); 15 (Vietnam). Regarding the 2014 Israeli action, deemed by most states to be disproportionate for the same reasons, see UNSC Verbatim Record (22 July 2014) UN Doc S/PV.7222. See further Gray, *Use of Force* (n 36) 230–231.

78 See UNSC Verbatim Record (5 June 1982) UN Doc S/PV.2374, paras 35–36 (Ireland).

79 See Sections 3.2.1.4 and 3.3.5.

80 See Section 3.3.5.

81 UNSC Verbatim Record (27 June 1993) UN Doc S/PV.3245, 13.

82 Ibid, 3–9; David Von Drehle and R Jeffrey Smith, 'U.S. Strikes Iraq for Plot to Kill Bush' *Washington Post* (27 June 1993) <http://www.washingtonpost.com/wp-srv/inatl/longterm/iraq/timeline/062793.htm> accessed 5 September 2020.

83 UN Doc S/PV.3245 (n 81) 5.

84 Von Drehle and Smith, 'U.S. Strikes Iraq for Plot to Kill Bush' (n 82). The numbers and details of civilian harm very. See, for example, Paulina Starski, 'The US Airstrike Against the Iraqi Intelligence Headquarters–1993' in Ruys and Corten, *The Use of Force in International Law* (n 36) 504, 522–523.

85 UN Doc S/PV.3245 (n 81) 13–14.

State practice reveals that material factors, most notably civilian harm, will influence conclusions regarding the (dis)proportionality of force used in self-defence. In reviewing relative harm, states do sometimes focus on quantitative balance or imbalance and might refer specifically to the nature, means and/or scale of the attack and response, in addition to their outcomes. Such references are not consistent, however, and may be oblique. These references also tend to factor most clearly in cases of manifest asymmetry. This latter fact naturally raises questions regarding whether the forcible action has a defensive purpose. In any event, and as a general rule, states have approached the issue of equivalence flexibly and have not required an exact balance between attack and defence.[86] States might have assessed proportionality by reference to a series of attacks and not just the armed attack that immediately preceded the defensive response,[87] and material factors might constitute one of several justifications for determining the lawfulness of a particular act. As discussed further below, states sometimes point to the equivalence, or lack thereof, between attack and defence, but it is rarely the sole or primary determinant of legality. Moreover, as will become clear in the next section, pursuing a defensive aim can take precedence over considerations of quantitative equivalence, particularly in the context of combatting NSAs.

3.2.1.4 State Practice—Specific Incidents and the Teleological Model

Reference to the teleological model of proportionality is also found in the practice and *opinio juris* of states. During the conflict between India and Pakistan over Kashmir in 1947–1948, Pakistan asserted that it did no more than the 'very least' to 'hold the line' and protect its security against India.[88] Whist not expressed in clear legal terms, its position appears to be that it was responding with a degree of force required to defend itself, and nothing beyond that.[89] In the same conflict, sporadic activities of Pathan tribesmen (allegedly directed by Pakistan) resulted in a full-scale response by India's regular army, denoting quantitate imbalance, but appearing to advance a defensive purpose.[90] The UNSC implicitly accepted India's action.[91]

The UK has also shown preference for the teleological model. It defended its raid on the Harib Fort in Yemen in 1964, *inter alia*, on the basis that it was proportionate to a defensive aim.[92] The UK's acts were widely condemned, however, and were

[86] Ruys, '*Armed Attack*' (n 20) 116.
[87] Ibid.
[88] UNSC Verbatim Record (8 February 1950) UN Doc S/PV.464, 29.
[89] Green, 'Docking the *Caroline*' (n 8) 458. Caution should be taken with examining this incident. Pakistan did not invoke self-defence to the UNSC until two years after the conflict began and was criticized by India for this omission. UNSC Verbatim Record (10 February 1950) UN Doc S/PV.466, 4. Self-defence is, nevertheless, the most obvious implication of Pakistan's position. See James A Green, 'The Article 51 Reporting Requirement for Self-Defense Actions' (2015) 55 Va JIL 563, 597–598.
[90] Green, 'Docking the *Caroline*' (n 8) 458.
[91] UNSC Res 47 (21 April 1948) UN Doc S/RES/47, requiring a Pakistani withdrawal from Kashmir, whilst allowing India to remain. Green, 'Docking the *Caroline*' (n 8) 458.
[92] UN Doc S/PV.1109 (n 59) 30–31.

deplored by the UNSC.[93] During the 1982 Falkland Islands conflict, the UK Prime Minister did not refer specifically to the requirements of necessity and proportionality, but was nevertheless clear in describing the UK's response pursuant to Article 51 UN Charter as being 'measured and controlled' and 'consistent with achieving our objective'.[94] The objectives, in line with demands from the UNSC, were ending the occupation and withdrawal of all Argentine troops from the Islands.[95] Despite a number of controversies pertaining to the British response (most notably the sinking of the *General Belgrano*[96]), it is significant when considering the UK's 'objective' that the British military action was generally regarded as proportionate to securing its defensive goal and comprised a lawful act of self-defence.[97] The UK maintained its position in relation to the first Gulf conflict of 1991. It defended the proportionality of coalition measures taken in the collective self-defence of Kuwait (under the auspices of UNSC authority), insisting that the force used corresponded to the aim of liberating Kuwait.[98] The UK's view was generally consistent with the forceful response taken by the coalition to achieve compliance with the UNSC resolutions that preceded it.[99] Proportionality was accordingly tied to the purpose of repelling the Iraqi attack and securing the withdrawal of Iraqi forces from Kuwait.

In contrast, but likewise adopting a teleological model of proportionality, Panama condemned Russia's intervention in Georgia in 2008. This reaction was based on the belief that the Russian operation exceeded the stated defensive aim (of protecting Russian citizens and peacekeeping forces) and was, therefore, disproportionate.[100] France meanwhile, appeared to focus simply on the civilian harm in

[93] UNSC Res 188 (9 April 1964) UN Doc S/RES/188.

[94] HC Deb 29 April 1982, vol 22, col 980.

[95] UNSC Res 502 (3 April 1982) UN Doc S/RES/502. See further Geoffrey Marston (ed), 'United Kingdom Materials on International Law 1982' (1983) 53(1) BYIL 337, 538–540. See also Section 2.8.2 of the UK Military Manual (n 53) noting the same under the heading of *jus ad bellum* proportionality.

[96] See Section 2.6.1.

[97] Michael J Levitin, 'The Law of Force and the Force of Law: Grenada, the Falklands, and Humanitarian Intervention' 27 (1986) Harv Int'l LJ 621, 638; Green, 'Docking the *Caroline*' (n 8) 459.

[98] UNSC Verbatim Record (14 February 1991) UN Doc S/PV.2977 (Part II) 73. The UK also stated that achieving this aim took account of the military capacity of Iraq. See further Section 3.3.1.

[99] Gardam, *Necessity, Proportionality* (n 8) 159. Whether this incident should be rightly characterized as an incident of self-defence and/or UNSC authorization to use force, however, is debatable. Its precedential value is consequently obscured. The USA claimed a right of individual and collective self-defence, which it reported to the UNSC. Letter dated 9 August 1990 from the Permanent Representative of the United States of America to the United Nations addressed to the President of the Security Council (10 August 1990) UN Doc S/21492. The UK followed suit. Letter dated 13 August 1990 from the Permanent Representative of the United Kingdom of Great Britain and Northern Ireland to the United Nations addressed to the President of the Security Council (13 August 1990) UN Doc S/21501. This right was affirmed by the UNSC. UNSC Res 661 (6 August 1990)) UN Doc S/RES/661. The UNSC later authorized 'all necessary means' to respond to the invasion. UNSC Res 678 (29 November 1990) UN Doc S/RES/678. See further Gardam, *Necessity, Proportionality* (n 8) 151; Ruys, *'Armed Attack'* (n 20) 101; Dinstein, *War, Aggression and Self-Defence* (n 29) 323–327; Erika de Wet, 'The Gulf War–1990-91' in Ruys and Corten, *The Use of Force in International Law* (n 36) 456.

[100] UNSC Verbatim Record (10 August 2008) UN Doc S/PV.5953, 15. Russia meanwhile offered a quantitative understanding of proportionality to justify its actions, coupled with a teleological elaboration of it: 'the use of force by the Russian side is strictly proportionate to the scale of the attack and

Georgia in reaching its conclusion that Russian actions were 'brutal and disproportionate'.[101] The Council of the European Union's Independent International Fact-Finding Mission on the Conflict in Georgia also adopted the teleological approach in reviewing the conflict, with civilian harm acting as an indicator of whether or not a defensive purpose was exceeded. It concluded that Russia's actions were neither necessary nor proportionate.[102]

State action against NSAs often reflects a teleological approach to proportionately. For example, Egypt linked proportionality to a defensive purpose to support its view that Israel's intervention in Lebanon in 1996 was an act of aggression.[103] Iran's claim to be operating against terrorist bases in Iraq in 1999 has already been noted. In its report to the UNSC, Iran explicitly defended the proportionality of its actions by reference to the defensive aim of responding to past armed attacks and preventing repetition.[104] It adopted the same approach in 2001.[105]

Israel's strikes against Hezbollah in Lebanon in 2006 also constitute an important case study of proportionality, both in terms of how states conceive of its general conceptual meaning and its granular content. This incident is discussed in detail in Section 3.3.5. For present purposes, it is notable that Russia's concern was framed in the following terms: 'the scale of [Israel's] use of force, the casualties and the destruction demonstrate that the actions stated for achieving this purpose go far beyond a counterterrorist operation'.[106] Proportionality was not specifically referenced, but this statement implicitly reflects Russia's teleological conception of this requirement, with material quantitative imbalance indicating a lack of defensive purpose. Qatar's attitude to this incident was the same. It remarked on the extent of civilian targets in reaching its conclusion that Israel's action had gone beyond a stated defensive objective.[107]

Although differing on the proportionality of its actions on the facts, Israel adopted this model to defend its actions: 'the proportionality of a response to an attack is to be measured not in regard to the specific attack suffered by a state but in

pursues no other goal but to protect the Russian [peacekeepers and citizens] and to prevent future armed attacks against them'. Letter dated 11 August 2008 from the Permanent Representative of the Russian Federation to the United Nations addressed to the President of the Security Council (11 August 2008) UN Doc S/2008/545.

[101] UNSC Verbatim Record (19 August 2008) UN Doc S/PV.5961, 6.

[102] The Council of the European Union's Independent International Fact-Finding Mission on the Conflict in Georgia, Report, Vol II (September 2009) <http://www.mpil.de/files/pdf4/IIFFMCG_Volume_II1.pdf> accessed 5 September 2020 (hereafter 'IIFFMCG Report') 248–249, 272–275.

[103] UNSC Verbatim Record (15 April 1996) UN Doc S/PV.3653, 14.

[104] Letter dated 12 July 1999 from the Permanent Representative of the Islamic Republic of Iran to the United Nations addressed to the Secretary-General (12 July 1999) UN Doc S/1999/781, 2.

[105] Letter dated 18 April 2001 from the Permanent Representative of the Islamic Republic of Iran to the United Nations addressed to the President of the Security Council (19 April 2001) UN Doc S/2001/381.

[106] UNSC Verbatim Record (21 July 2006) UN Doc S/PV.5493 (Resumption 1) 2.

[107] UNSC Verbatim Record (21 July 2006) UN Doc S/PV.5493, 14.

regard to what is necessary to remove the overall threat'.[108] This statement reflected Israel's prior justification when it acted to rescue its nationals in Uganda in 1976. The Israeli representative insisted that '[t]he means used were the minimum necessary to fulfil that purpose, as is laid down in international law'.[109] The scale of the 2006 Israel invasion and its effect on the civilian population meant that the quantitative imbalance between the attack and defence (*viz* the civilian harm on either side) was particularly stark. States emphasized these material factors, but the general consensus was that the Israeli action went well beyond the defensive purpose of countering Hezbollah. It was regarded as excessive and punitive.[110]

In contrast, in response to Turkey's 2008 Operation Sun, the European Union warned against a disproportionate military response. It called upon Turkey 'to limit its military activities to those which are absolutely necessary for achieving its main purpose—the protection of the Turkish population from terrorism'.[111] The statement is ambiguous. It talks of 'protection' rather than 'self-defence' and does not explicitly engage with legality. Yet, the clear implication is that the lawfulness (or, at least, the acceptability) of the Turkish operation was conditioned on Turkey not exceeding a defensive purpose. Moreover, although the Turkish intervention was quantitatively greatly in excess of the attacks by the Kurdistan Workers' Party ('PKK') that preceded it, the international community did not condemn it.[112] Instead, an overarching teleological approach appears to lead to a conclusion that Turkey's actions were an act of proportionate self-defence.[113]

The most recent state practice in response to international terrorism also reveals a clear overarching teleological approach to proportionality. In this context, purported defensive operations taken by states against terrorist NSAs will often be greatly in excess of the armed attack(s) that preceded them. State responses might contain far-reaching aims over and above repulsing ongoing armed attacks

[108] Israel Ministry of Foreign Affairs, 'Responding to Hezbollah Attacks From Lebanon: Issues of Proportionality' (25 July 2006) <http://www.mfa.gov.il/MFA/AboutIsrael/State/Law/Pages/Responding%20to%20Hizbullah%20attacks%20from%20Lebanon-%20Issues%20of%20proportionality%20July%202006.aspx> accessed 5 September 2020.

[109] UNSC Verbatim Record (9 July 1976) UN Doc S/PV.1939, 121. Israel did not explicitly reference proportionality, but this is implicit in the statement and from the context. This claim of self-defence is dubious (see Gray, *Use of Force* (n 36) 39), but the defending state expresses its actions to be bound by the requirement of a defensive purpose.

[110] See Section 3.3.5.

[111] 'EU Presidency Statement on the Military Action Undertaken by Turkey in Iraqi Territory' (25 February 2008) <www.eu2008.si/en/News_and_Documents/CFSP_Statements/February/0225MZZturkey.html> accessed 5 September 2020.

[112] The PKK's cross-border raids were on a small scale, albeit resulting in Turkish casualties. The eventual Turkish response, in contrast, consisted of the deployment of several thousand troops, aerial assaults and artillery support. For details, see Tom Ruys, '*Quo Vadit Jus ad Bellum*?: A Legal Analysis of Turkey's Military Operations Against the PKK in Northern Iraq' (2008) 9 Melbourne Journal of International Law334, 334–335, 362.

[113] Ibid, especially 362–363; Tams, 'Necessity and Proportionality' (n 30) 396. See also Trapp, 'The Turkish Intervention Against the PKK' (n 36) 700.

or preventing imminent ones. These aims have included removing a *de facto* government like the Taliban and the pursuit of the total destruction of NSA terrorist organizations like Al-Qaeda and Daesh. Such anti-terrorist operations might be accepted by a large number of states despite the fact that they comprise manifest quantitative imbalance between attack and defence. That such responses might be proportionate to a defensive purpose has also received implicit support from the UNSC (for example, in the form of UNSC Resolution 2249). These conclusions, and the applicable state practice are examined in detail in Chapter 4.

3.2.1.5 State Practice—Pleadings Before the ICJ

States have referred to both models of proportionality in their pleadings before the ICJ, whilst expressing a preference for the teleological model. In *Nuclear Weapons*, France explicitly relied on Ago's teleological characterization set out in Section 3.2.1.1, stating that necessity and proportionality required that measures of response to an attack be adjusted to the defensive aim.[114] In line with the practice referred to in the previous sections, the UK's position in this case was that a proportionate response related to the 'threat posed to the victim State', referring to the need for the victim to be able to 'defend himself and reverse the aggression'. It insisted that '[a] decision to use nuclear weapons would only be taken in extreme cases and on the basis of the ultimate duty of a State to defend its people and their homeland'.[115] Therefore, proportionality was to be judged against a defensive purpose.

New Zealand took the same approach as the UK, at least implicitly. It insisted that defensive acts be proportionate to the 'danger' that they are designed to meet.[116] San Marino, meanwhile, argued that self-defence must be proportionate to the 'provocation' or the 'offence',[117] which might be understood as the preceding armed attack. Mexico also asserted an apparently quantitative understanding to ensure that defensive acts are not 'excessive'.[118] However, it drew on the work of the International Law Commission ('ILC') on state responsibility to justify this

[114] *Nuclear Weapons* (n 27) Oral Proceedings, Verbatim Record, 1 November 1995, CR 95/23, 66.

[115] *Nuclear Weapons* (n 27) Oral Proceedings, Verbatim Record, 15 November 1995, CR 95/34, 34.

[116] *Nuclear Weapons* (n 27) Note Verbale dated 20 June 1995 from the Embassy of New Zealand, together with Written Statement of the Government of New Zealand, para 55. Such 'danger' appears to consist of both actual and imminent armed attacks and a right of self-defence to prevent the latter is explicitly asserted (at para 56). *Ipso facto*, a response to the cumulative 'danger' might include a quantitatively greater amount of force than the immediately preceding armed attack. This suggests a teleological approach.

[117] *Nuclear Weapons* (n 27) Oral Proceedings, Verbatim Record, 13 November 1995, CR 95/31, 20–21.

[118] 'The right of self-defense is [...] considered legal when proportional to the armed attack that gave rise to such defense.' *Nuclear Weapons* (n 27) Note Verbale dated 19 June 1995 from the Embassy of Mexico, together with Written Statement of the Government of Mexico, paras 57–58.

position, rather than the *jus ad bellum*, which obscures its analysis.[119] India referenced both models of proportionality in the alternative.[120]

In *Oil Platforms*, Iran also implicitly relied on Ago, appearing to accept a teleological model of proportionality that related to 'the needs of protection rather than the scale of the attack'.[121] This understanding was made more explicit when it drew a distinction between lawful self-defence and unlawful reprisals. The difference, it was stated, was a disproportionate use of force, being excessive in relation to a protective need.[122] Intriguingly, however, Iran later relied on the quantitative standard in its Reply:

> It is an uncontroversial requirement of self-defence that counter-force must not be excessive in relation to the first use of force. This means that the damage done by the counter-force must be commensurate with or generally comparable to that caused by the first use of force.[123]

It is not clear from the pleadings why Iran switched models. It might have been to highlight the 'gross lack of balance' between the damage caused by the alleged attacks on the USA and the harm that the USA inflicted in response.[124] The scale of the imbalance was certainly reflected in the Court's observations on proportionality.[125] Iran's approach perhaps refers to its belief that a *manifest* lack of symmetry between attack and defence is indicative of teleological disproportionality. The USA clearly understood Iran's position on proportionality to be teleological and explicitly agreed with this approach by, *inter alia*, also citing Ago's formulation.[126]

In *Wall*, whilst many states were as dismissive of Israel's claim of self-defence as the Court, some did engage with necessity and proportionality. Palestine, for example, in asserting that defensive force must be 'proportional to the actual or imminent harm',[127] appeared to adopt a mixed model, going beyond equivalence

[119] Ibid, para 58. The ICJ has also adopted this approach. See Section 3.2.1.6.

[120] '[A]ny use of force in self-defence has to be proportional to the means and ends involved or to the original wrongful use of force.' *Nuclear Weapons* (n 27) Letter dated 20 June 1995 from the Ambassador of India, together with Written Statement of the Government of India, 3.

[121] *Oil Platforms* (n 25) Memorial Submitted by the Islamic Republic of Iran, 8 June 1993, paras 4.21–4.23.

[122] Ibid, para 4.34.

[123] *Oil Platforms* (n 25) Reply and Defence to Counter-Claim Submitted by the Islamic Republic of Iran, 10 March 1999, para 7.62.

[124] Ibid, para 7.63.

[125] See Section 3.2.1.6.

[126] *Oil Platforms* (n 25) Counter-Memorial and Counter-Claim Submitted by the United States of America, 23 June 1997, para 4.32; *Oil Platforms* (n 25) Rejoinder Submitted by the United States of America, 23 March 2001, paras 5.48–5.51. The USA reported to the UNSC that its defensive response was 'necessary and proportionate *to the threat* posed by [. . .] hostile Iranian actions' (emphasis added). Letter dated 18 April 1988 from the Acting Permanent Representative of the United States of America to the United Nations addressed to the President of the Security Council (18 April 1988) UN Doc S/19791.

[127] *Legal Consequences of the Construction of a Wall in the Occupied Palestinian Territories* (Advisory Opinion) [2004] ICJ Rep 136 (hereafter '*Wall*') Written Statement Submitted by Palestine, 29 January 2004, paras 530, 533.

of attack and defence to encompassing the prospective need to avoid future harm. Indonesia, Malaysia, South Africa and Cuba, meanwhile, all clearly presented an understanding of proportionality linked to a defensive purpose.[128] Lastly on the ICJ's jurisprudence, the DRC in *Armed Activities* was another state to expressly rely on Ago's teleological model.[129] Uganda disagreed with the DRC's conclusions on the facts, but adopted the same interpretation of proportionality, insisting that its actions were 'directly related to [its] defensive objectives'.[130]

3.2.1.6 ICJ Jurisprudence

The quantitative model of proportionality *prima facie* dominates the ICJ's jurisprudence. However, it goes too far to represent this as the Court's definitive stance on this issue. A firm and coherent line of reasoning is not reflected in the relevant cases. The Court's approach was first laid down in *Nicaragua*, where it stated that 'self-defence would warrant only measures which are proportional *to the armed attack* and necessary to respond to it'.[131] The majorities also adopted this apparently quantitative rationale in *Oil Platforms* and *Armed Activities*, without going into further detail in either case.[132]

Although the quoted passage seems to represent the end of the matter, a further examination of *Nicaragua* demonstrates that the Court's understanding of proportionality is not so straightforwardly quantitative. As noted in Section 1.1, the issue of proportionality was moot in this case.[133] Regardless, the Court went on to opine that:

> Whatever uncertainty may exist as to the exact scale of *the aid* received by the Salvadorian armed opposition from Nicaragua, it is clear that [the United States' purported defensive conduct] could not have been proportionate *to that aid*.[134]

Conspicuous is the fact that, in this paragraph, the Court is not in fact striking a balance between an armed attack and a defensive use of force (including their

[128] *Wall*, ibid, Written Statement Submitted by the Government of the Republic of Indonesia, 30 January 2004, para 5; *Wall*, ibid, Written Statement of Malaysia, 30 January 2004, para 151; *Wall*, ibid, Written Statement Submitted by the Government of the Republic of South Africa, 30 January 2004, paras 36, 38, 59; *Wall*, ibid, Written Statement of the Republic of Cuba, 30 January 2004, 6 (although this latter example appears somewhat conflated with IHL principles).

[129] *Armed Activities* (n 25) Memorial of the Democratic Republic of the Congo, 6 July 2000, paras 5.26–5.31; *Armed Activities* (n 25) Reply of the Democratic Republic of the Congo, 29 May 2002, 230–231 (paras 3.159–3.160).

[130] *Armed Activities* (n 25) Rejoinder Submitted by the Republic of Uganda, 6 December 2002, paras 289–290.

[131] *Nicaragua* (n 18) para 176 (emphasis added).

[132] *Oil Platforms* (n 25) para 77; *Armed Activities* (n 25) para 147.

[133] The Court had decided that the provision of any aid by Nicaragua to the insurgents in El Salvador could not constitute an armed attack, thereby justifying the USA's invocation of collective self-defence. *Nicaragua* (n 18) para 230. Therefore, consideration of necessity and proportionality was not required for the Court to reach its decision.

[134] *Nicaragua* (n 18) para 237 (emphasis added). For the Court's summary of the American's putative defensive conduct, see paras 80, 81 and 86.

respective outcomes). Instead, the balance is stated as being made between wrongful conduct (being action not sufficient to reach the scale of gravity required by the Court for an armed attack) and defensive force. Consequently, there is a disconnect between what the Court says it is doing and what it is actually doing.

Balancing wrongful conduct against measures adopted by a state in response to such conduct, and requiring a degree of equivalence, points more clearly to the operation of countermeasures than to claims of self-defence. It is generally accepted that countermeasures must be proportionate to the act that provoked them,[135] an approach clearly followed by the ICJ in *Gabčíkovo-Nagymaros*.[136] Therefore, although the Court stipulates in *Nicaragua* that it is balancing attack and defence, this is not so. By balancing instead wrongful conduct against defensive force, it adopts an approach to proportionality that conflates self-defence with countermeasures.

To add to this confusion, it is possible to interpret the Court's focus as pertaining to the *provision* of the aid, rather than the aid in and of itself. On this basis, the majority may be understood as referring not to equivalence between the aid given and the American's military response, but rather whether the action taken by the USA was commensurate to the goal of stopping that aid.[137] If so, this is a teleological appreciation of proportionality, not a quantitative one. It suggests that the Court is measuring the application of purported defensive force against a particular purpose.

It is notable that Judge Higgins, in her separate opinion in *Nuclear Weapons*, offered the following interpretation of the majority's opinion in *Nicaragua*:

> the Court already made clear that the concept of proportionality in self-defence limits a response to what is needed to reply to an attack. This is consistent with the approach of Professor Ago […] that the concept of proportionality referred to was that which was proportionate to repelling the attack, and not a requirement of symmetry between the mode of the initial attack and the mode of response.[138]

In endorsing Ago's approach,[139] Judge Higgins rejects reliance on a purely quantitative model of proportionality. In so doing, she espouses a reading of the *Nicaragua* judgment that is unsupportive of the notion that proportionality requires equivalence between attack and defence. This reading of the majority opinion follows Judge Schwebel's dissent in *Nicaragua* where he also quoted Ago.[140] Accordingly,

[135] See International Law Commission ('ILC'), Draft Articles on Responsibility of States for Internationally Wrongful Acts, with Commentaries (2001) UN Doc A/56/10 ('ARSIWA') Art 51 and related commentary.

[136] *Gabčíkovo-Nagymaros Project (Hungary/Slovakia)* (Judgment) [1997] ICJ Rep 7, para 85.

[137] Gardam, *Necessity, Proportionality* (n 8) 158; James A Green, *The International Court of Justice and Self-Defence in International Law* (Hart Publishing 2009) 92.

[138] *Nuclear Weapons* (n 27) diss op Higgins, para 5.

[139] See Section 3.2.1.1.

[140] *Nicaragua* (n 18) diss op Schwebel, para 212.

the ICJ's position in *Nicaragua* is not as clear-cut as it might seem initially. In addition to the confusion regarding which variables the Court is balancing (in contrast to those it says it is balancing), there is scope to interpret its application of proportionality as not being based on a purely quantitative model. The Court's reasoning also potentially takes account of the need to pursue a defensive purpose.

Judge Higgins' aforementioned reading of *Nicaragua* is also implicit in the majority's opinion in *Nuclear Weapons*. Following an expansive review of international law, which included consideration of *jus ad bellum* necessity and proportionality, the Court could not reach a 'definitive conclusion as to the legality or illegality of the use of nuclear weapons by a State in an extreme circumstance of self-defence, in which its very survival would be at stake'.[141] Therefore, the Court's view that the 'proportionality principle may thus not in itself exclude the use of nuclear weapons in self-defence in all circumstances'[142] is expressed in relation to the defensive need of the state (*viz* countering an existential threat). That survival is the overarching purpose of self-defence was explicitly recognized by the Court as a 'fundamental right of every State',[143] thereby tying the right more generally to its purpose. It was this purpose that appeared to be ultimately decisive in respect of the question put to the Court. Judge Weeramantry adopted the same approach in his dissent. He likewise quoted Ago's teleological articulation of proportionality, by implication endorsing it.[144] In terms of the ICJ's more recent jurisprudence, Judge Kooijmans also chose to measure proportionality against a defensive purpose in his separate opinion in *Armed Activities*.[145]

Oil Platforms exemplifies the uncertainties regarding the Court's account of proportionality. Putting aside once again the general propriety of the Court's observations on this issue,[146] its application of the requirement leaves much to be desired. The majority distinguished between the American response to the missile attack on the *Sea Isle City*[147] and its response to the mining of the *USS Samuel B. Roberts*.[148]

[141] *Nuclear Weapons* (n 27) paras 41–44, 97, 105(E). The latter paragraph, being the operative part of the *dispositif*, was passed seven votes to seven, with the President's casting vote. This fact, and the number of separate and dissenting opinions, demonstrate the deep division within the Court on this highly controversial issue.

[142] Ibid, para 42.

[143] Ibid, para 96.

[144] Ibid, diss op Weeramantry, 518–519.

[145] '[Uganda's] actions moreover were grossly disproportionate to the professed aim of securing Uganda's border from armed attacks by anti-Ugandan rebel movements.' *Armed Activities* (n 25) sep op Kooijmans, para 34.

[146] As noted, in addition to finding an absence of an armed attack, the Court considered both responses by the USA to be unnecessary. *Oil Platforms* (n 25) paras 61, 64, 72, 76. Proportionality is accordingly irrelevant.

[147] The USA attacked the Reshadat offshore oil production installation. One platform was almost completely destroyed and another severely damaged. Ibid, para 47.

[148] The USA attacked the Nasr and Salman oil complexes. The former was nearly destroyed and the latter severely damaged. Ibid, paras 65–66. These attacks were part of the wider American response, codenamed Operation Praying Mantis, which was not at issue before the Court. This operation involved, *inter alia*, the destruction of two Iranian frigates and a number of other naval vessels and

In respect of the former, the Court concluded that, had it found the American attack to be necessary, such attack could potentially have been proportionate.[149] In contrast, the American military response to the latter incident could not have been proportionate.[150] The result of the Court's reasoning is that the damage or destruction of oil platforms in response to a missile attack on a single merchant vessel might have been proportionate, whereas the damage and destruction of oil platforms in response to the mining of a single military vessel was disproportionate. The Court offered no reasons for making this distinction.

Given that the USA's reactions in each case were essentially of the same character, and both were responses to an attack on a single vessel, it is difficult to see why the Court viewed only one reaction as potentially proportionate.[151] Material factors alone (*viz* focusing solely on relative harm) appear not to be the reason. The Court accepted that the missile attack on the *Sea Isle City* caused damage to the ship and injury to six crewmembers.[152] The mining of the *USS Samuel B. Roberts* resulted in the injury to ten American sailors (one seriously) and the ship was severely damaged.[153] *Prima facie*, therefore, the harm to the military vessel seems to be greater than that of the civilian vessel. Despite this disparity, the Court downplayed the damage to the *USS Samuel B. Roberts*. In commentating on the disproportionality of the USA's actions against the Iranian oil platforms, the Court places importance on the fact that the *USS Samuel B. Roberts* was 'a single United States warship, which was severely damaged but not sunk, and without loss of life'.[154] This comment appears to be based on the marked asymmetry between attack and defence and the fact that the American response had a punitive feel to it. If so, the Court's reasoning ultimately reflects an overarching teleological approach to proportionality.[155]

aircraft, in addition to the destruction of the two oil complexes that were the subject of the dispute. Ibid, paras 68, 77.

[149] Ibid, para 77.

[150] Ibid. Whereas the Court was clearly concerned with the overall reaction of the USA, this conclusion regarding disproportionality was expressed to be so regardless of whether the attacks on the Salman and Nasr platforms were considered in isolation, or as part of Operation Praying Mantis.

[151] Green, *The International Court of Justice* (n 137) 87.

[152] *Oil Platforms* (n 25) para 52. For further details of the alleged damage caused, see *Oil Platforms* (n 25) Counter-Memorial and Counter-Claim Submitted by the United States of America, 23 June 1997, para 1.65.

[153] UN Doc S/19791 (n 126). These facts appear to be accepted by the Court. *Oil Platforms* (n 25) para 67. The Court (at para 77) later characterized the damage as severe. For further details of the alleged damage caused, see *Oil Platforms* (n 25) Counter-Memorial and Counter-Claim Submitted by the United States of America, 23 June 1997, para 1.105.

[154] *Oil Platforms* (n 25) para 77.

[155] Simple asymmetry on its own would suggest a conclusion regarding proportionality based solely on the quantitative model. It is the factor of *marked* asymmetry in this incident that emphasizes the purpose element.

The difference in treatment by the Court of the two incidents might relate to the means of attack, whether by missile or mine.[156] This would make the governing factor the type of the weapon used in the armed attack that, as explored in Section 3.3.1, should not of itself be viewed as determinative of proportionality. If the Court's reasoning pertaining to the type of weapons used is that mines are inherently indiscriminate, meaning that *USS Samuel B. Roberts* could not have been the intended target,[157] then it is difficult to see how this factor pertains to proportionality. Logically, the question of intent relates to general and specific necessity: did the USA need to respond at all if it was not the intended victim and, if so, where should that response be directed? Alternatively, the Court might have made the distinction it did based on the nature of the object of the attack. In this case, an attack on a merchant vessel, being a civilian object, might be deemed by the Court to be qualitatively different to an attack on a military vessel.[158] Yet, it was the attack on the *USS Samuel B. Roberts,* and the not the *Sea Isle City*, that was treated by the Court as being the most grave, with the potential of constituting an armed attack.[159] Therefore, it is arguable whether the distinction regarding proportionality is justifiable. The Court may be criticized for not setting out the basis on which it makes such distinction.[160]

Reaching firm inferences from the jurisprudence on the Court's general approach to proportionality is problematic. The ICJ's reasoning lacks clarity and consistency as to whether it regards reviewing proportionality as a quantitative and/or teleological exercise. The relationship between the armed attack and the defensive response certainly forms part of the limited commentary in the cases that have come before the Court. However, it is uncertain to what extent asymmetry between material factors will be determinative in future cases and what other elements might be deemed relevant to an assessment of proportionality.

It is also worth noting that the Court has so far adopted an analysis that is purely retrospective, focusing on the harm already inflicted. In contrast, the state practice discussed throughout this book is generally not confined to a purely retrospective view. Instead, states tend to adopt a prospective approach that accounts for the overall threat it is facing. As such, the ICJ's approach reflects the specific facts of the cases put before it. The result is that there is no evident judicial framework or abstract realization of proportionality that might be readily applied to other

[156] Laursen, for example, appears to assume that the means of attack plays a role in distinguishing the two approaches. Andreas Laursen, 'The Judgment by the International Court of Justice in the *Oil Platforms* Case' (2004) 73 Nordic J Int'l L 135, 152–153.

[157] This is perhaps discernable in the Court's determination that the USA had not been the victim of an armed attack *by Iran*. *Oil Platforms* (n 25) para 61.

[158] See Green, *The International Court of Justice* (n 137) 87–88.

[159] The attack on the *Sea Isle City*, even taken together with other incidents cited by the USA, did not constitute an armed attack. *Oil Platforms* (n 25) para 64. In contrast, with regards to the *USS Samuel B. Roberts,* the Court (at para 72) accepted that mining a single military vessel might be sufficient to constitute an armed attack.

[160] Green, *The International Court of Justice* (n 137) 88.

cases with different facts. Perhaps all that we can say regarding the Court's general approach to proportionality thus far is that it is inclined to recognize the possibility that a defensive response is disproportionate if its intensity is in excess of the gravity of the armed attack.[161]

3.2.2 A Mixed Model of Proportionality

The foregoing analysis shows that understanding proportionality is not simply a matter of adopting one model to the complete exclusion of the other. The quantitative and teleological models both appear, in a somewhat inconsistent narrative, in state practice, ICJ jurisprudence and scholarship. This has led some commentators to conclude that there is a dual aspect to proportionality.[162] Although there is debate regarding which model dominates, some also conclude that state practice suggests that the *primary* determinant of legality is the defensive purpose to be achieved.[163] This latter conclusion certainly reflects the dominant feature of state practice, but the final picture is more nuanced. This section contends that proportionality operates in a way that goes beyond consideration of just the quantitative and teleological models. There is more than a dual aspect to its operation.

To begin, it is clear that states do not commonly rely on a purely quantitative model. States do not require precise equivalence between an armed attack and self-defence in terms of the nature, scale or means of the action taken, or their respective outcomes.[164] Material factors such as civilian harm are typically referenced in considerations of proportionality, but this does not equate to the adoption of the quantitative model to the exclusion of other considerations, such as achieving a defensive purpose. That states have this attitude is logical. An approach to proportionality that measures it exclusively on the basis of quantitative equivalence faces significant limitations.

The deficiencies are largely practical and relate to what degree of equivalence is required and how it is to be evaluated. One might argue that, in cases of minor,

[161] Claus Kress, 'The International Court of Justice and the "Principle of Non-Use of Force"' in Weller (ed), *The Oxford Handbook* (n 36) 561, 590.

[162] See, for example, Green, *The International Court of Justice* (n 137) 95; Enzo Cannizzaro, 'Contextualizing Proportionality: *Jus ad Bellum* and *Jus in Bello* in the Lebanese War' (2006) 88 International Review of the Red Cross 779, 784; Ruys, *'Armed Attack'* (n 20) 116; Gill, 'When Does Self-Defence End?' (n 36) 744. See also International Institute of Humanitarian Law, *San Remo Manual on International Law Applicable to Armed Conflicts at Sea* (1994) <https://ihl-databases.icrc.org/ihl/INTRO/560> accessed 5 September 2020, Arts 4–5.

[163] For example, Green, *The International Court of Justice* (n 137) 95; Raphaël Van Steenberghe, 'Self-Defence in Response to Attacks by Non-state Actors in the Light of Recent State Practice: A Step Forward?' (2010) 23(1) LJIL 183, 205–207. See also Cannizzaro, 'Contextualizing Proportionality' (n 162) 784; Gill, 'When Does Self-Defence End?' (n 36) 744. Cf Ruys *'Armed Attack'* (n 20) 117.

[164] See further Section 3.3.1. Even the state practice referred to in Section 3.2.1.3 does not point to such equivalence.

one-off skirmishes, the quantitative model is simple and intuitively logical. Higgins notes, for example, that in respect of such incidents 'it is easy to see that the response must be proportionate to the harm inflicted'.[165] On this basis, deploying a nuclear weapon in response to a raid across a border would be disproportionate.[166] That much seems obvious. Yet, absent extreme asymmetry, it is not clear how quantitative equivalence should be measured, particularly in terms of effects. Whether it comes down to tallying up harm on either side of a conflict in a mathematical fashion or involves another more complex quantification of relative injury is uncertain. How, for example, is one to place a value on dissimilar entities that have been harmed by the attacker and the defending state (whether they be human beings killed or injured, civilian buildings and infrastructure damaged and destroyed, and so forth), and at what point does approximate equivalence turn into disproportionality? It seems impossible to draw a line that is meaningful.

Employing only a quantitative model to establish if and when force becomes unacceptable points to arbitrariness. It also potentially deprives the state of the means to pursue to conclusion the purpose of its inherent right of self-defence.[167] In fact, limiting a defensive response to quantitative equivalence might give rise to further armed attacks. This is because the danger posed by the attacker is not necessarily countered in a way that ensures enduring peace. Ultimately, Higgins does accept that pursuing a legitimate defensive objective might mean that force is proportionate 'even though it is a more severe use of force than any single prior incident might have seemed to have warranted it'.[168] This reflects the fact that states tend to be more flexible in their appraisals, often including a retrospective and prospective appreciation that encompasses past, ongoing and (potentially) imminent armed attacks.[169] This approach is particularly notable in state practice relating to self-defence against NSAs, where defending states do not limit their defence quantitatively to completed armed attack(s) and the resulting harm. Their defensive responses invariably encompass a prospective element that are calibrated to counter the entirety of the perceived threat.[170]

When defending states face a continuing threat over a period of time from the same source, greater flexibility is required for assessing the proportionality of defensive responses, potentially allowing for the deployment of force on a larger scale to the immediately preceding armed attack. This is reflected in the state practice referred to in Section 3.2.1 and Chapter 4. In such circumstances, there is perhaps a greater need to tackle the source of the attacks. In extreme cases, the result might be the total military defeat of the attacker and, if it is a state, the removal of its

165 Higgins, *Problems and Process* (n 2) 231.
166 Ibid.
167 See further Cannizzaro, 'Proportionality in the Law of Armed Conflict' (n 36) 345–346.
168 Higgins, *Problems and Process* (n 2) 232.
169 Ruys, *'Armed Attack'* (n 20) 116.
170 See Chapter 4.

governing regime.[171] Assessing proportionality in such cases will naturally involve a greater number of factors, even if the armed attack and its effects are the starting point.[172]

Nevertheless, the state practice reviewed in Section 3.2.1 indicates that there must still be a rational connection between the outcomes of the attack and the defence.[173] Manifest asymmetry might indicate an excessive reaction. Civilian harm appears from state practice to be the most important indicator of excessiveness.[174] Yet, although marked quantitative asymmetry in civilian harm might, as an independent factor, constitute disproportionality for some states, there is no significant body of practice where quantitative imbalance alone has led to a determination of illegality.[175] As noted above in this section, such material factors *in and of themselves* cannot be tallied up in any meaningful manner so as to be determinative of proportionality. Rather, marked quantitative asymmetry will tend to act as an indicator of a lack of a defensive purpose. An obvious example is Israel's invasion of Lebanon in 2006.[176] Accordingly, material factors also speak to the teleological model of proportionality. Absent a satisfactory justification, when defensive action is greatly in excess of the armed attack and harm caused by it, such action risks being characterized as punitive and unlawful. Likewise, and conversely, states, courts and international organizations might point to quantitative equivalence in order to assist with establishing a defensive purpose.[177] Therefore, material factors are clearly important to appraising self-defence, but the ultimate governing factor is typically whether or not a defensive purpose is objectively identifiable.

It is this overriding teleological approach to proportionality that is the predominant feature of the scholarship, jurisprudence and (most importantly) state practice analysed in Section 3.2.1. Adherence to this model might even excuse manifest asymmetry between attack and defence. Examples include Operation Sun in 2008 and the ongoing Global Coalition action against Daesh in Syria.[178] The injury incurred, or expected, from an armed attack is certainly an important

[171] Ruys, *'Armed Attack'* (n 20) 116–117. Overthrowing a government would only be considered proportionate in those extreme and very rare cases where this was the only way to achieve the defensive aim. Corten, *The Law Against War* (n 36) 285.

[172] See Section 3.3.

[173] This is to be contrasted to the connection between the armed attack and the target of the defensive response, which is an issue for specific necessity. See Sections 2.6 and 3.4.2.

[174] See Sections 3.3.5 and 4.3.3.

[175] See Section 3.2.1.3.

[176] See Section 3.3.5.

[177] In *Oil Platforms* (n 25) for example, the USA favoured the teleological model, but the summation of its position was that 'it is clear that the U.S. actions were proportionate responses in self-defense to the Iranian armed attacks and continuing threat of hostile action'. *Oil Platforms* (n 25) Rejoinder Submitted by the United States of America, 23 March 2001, para 5.51.

[178] That other states largely appear to accept quantitative asymmetry in these incidents, see Sections 3.2.1.4 and 4.2.3.2.

part of the equation, but it is best thought of as offering a *prima facie* guideline to establishing a proportionate defensive response. Consequently, it might be true that a response that is disproportionate in scale to the initial attack is likely to be disproportionate to the goal of abating that attack,[179] but this will not always be so. Proportionality should not be thought of as limiting defensive action to that which is less than necessary to remove the threat.[180] We must be careful in assuming that the '*primary* determinant' of proportionality is the nature and gravity of the armed attack.[181] This approach risks placing undue emphasis on this particular aspect of the quantitative model at the expense of pursuing the defensive right to which proportionality speaks. Doing so can lead to hasty conclusions regarding the proportionate or disproportionate nature of a particular military response.

Assessing proportionality primarily by reference to the defensive need, whilst taking full account of relevant material factors (including relative harm), offers the best general theoretical model of proportionality. This approach accords more readily with the genesis and purpose of the right of self-defence and the need for states to respond flexibly to protect themselves in cases of emergency. States may respond legitimately on a retrospective and prospective basis and account for the wider threat comprising past, ongoing and imminent armed attacks. At the same time, this mixed model calls for a balance to be struck such that defensive military action does not result in harm that is completely out of proportion to the attack(s) that prompted it. Going one step further, however, it is clear that proportionality also accounts for wider interests that go beyond both the quantitative and teleological models of proportionality. These interests are considered in the next section.

3.3 Applying Proportionality and Identifying 'Excessiveness'

The balancing exercise described in Section 3.2 is not the end of how we should understand proportionality. States tend to justify the proportionality of their putatively defensive acts primarily by reference to a defensive purpose and other states focus on such purpose when reviewing the legality of such acts. Yet, it is also clear that the right of self-defence is not absolute, and the review of defensive actions

[179] Green, *The International Court of Justice* (n 137) 94–95.

[180] Greenwood, 'Self-Defence' (n 36) para 28, gives an example of territory captured by a surprise attack employing a limited use of force. Where the attacker goes on to reinforce its position, the defending state will be required to employ a far greater degree of force to reverse the situation. To prohibit it from doing so would be to reward the attacker and place the victim state in an unreasonable disadvantage. Greenwood asserts that there is no indication that international law requires such an unjust conclusion. Therefore, proportionality must allow the defending state to reverse the effects of the armed attack.

[181] As suggested by Ruys, *'Armed Attack'* (n 20) 117 (emphasis added). On the nature of an armed attack, however, see Section 3.3.1.

does not operate in a vacuum. Despite what some might think of as the 'superior right' of the defending state vis-à-vis the attacker,[182] other states do not regard the right of self-defence as a licence to harm others, especially civilians.[183] More generally, when other states, international courts and scholars review the proportionality of self-defence and whether or not it is 'excessive' (to quote Webster), they consider a range of issues.

This section reviews factors that are regarded as either permitted, or proscribed, by proportionality. The analysis includes factors that are *not* relevant to proportionality by way of additional clarification of how proportionality operates in practice and, in certain cases, to confront conclusions made by other scholars regarding what is relevant to the proportionality calculus. Where this is so, it is highlighted. The factors reviewed account, *inter alia*, for the needs and rights of the defending state, as well as those of the attacker.[184] They are evaluated to ensure that the purposes of self-defence are achieved (and nothing more) and that actions in self-defence do not cause excessive harm to those not participating in the conflict or impinge unduly on the interests of the wider international community. The relevance and relative importance of each factor will vary depending on the circumstances and they may overlap and interrelate in a manner that is not so neatly delineated as set out below. The subheadings are employed, however, for ease of analysis.[185]

The following review reveals that the pursuit of defensive purpose, although operating as the overarching consideration, is not unfettered. Even if a defending state is regarded as employing no more force than is necessary to achieve a defensive purpose, such force might nevertheless be deemed disproportionate if it causes undue harm to other interests, including third-party interests. A defending state cannot prioritize its right of self-defence over the concerns of the international community and pursue such right at any cost. These other interests act as a check on the pursuit of a defensive purpose. They constitute additional limitations on the exercise of the right of self-defence, acting to guard against excessive defensive responses. The result is an overriding teleological approach that primarily balances defences force and its outcomes against a defensive purpose *and* against these other interests.

[182] Cannizzaro, 'Contextualizing Proportionality' (n 162) 785.

[183] Christian J Tams and Wenke Brückner, 'The Israeli Intervention in Lebanon–2006' in Ruys and Corten, *The Use of Force in International Law* (n 36) 673, 686. See Section 3.3.5.

[184] That the attacker has rights under the *jus ad bellum* is, perhaps, controversial. Yet, in the case of an attacker that is a state, the following analysis shows that even when an attacking state breaches Art 2(4) of the UN Charter, it does not follow that it may be subjected to unchecked violence in response. In particular, excessive harm to its civilian population risks being regarded as an unlawful act of self-defence.

[185] The way in which these different interests relate to each other in the context of armed attacks by NSAs is very different. This relationship is discussed further in Section 4.3.

3.3.1 Scale, Nature, Methods and Means

Section 3.2.1 confirmed that, on the whole, states do not regard proportionality as confining the amount of defensive force to that employed in the armed attack that provoked it. There is no requirement of parity,[186] albeit that marked asymmetry might be indicative of disproportionality. State practice against armed attacks by NSAs referred to in Sections 3.2.1 and Chapter 4 most clearly reflects this general premise. Defending states do not match the scale of their defence to those of NSA attacks. This is a natural consequence of the teleological model acting as the primary determinant of proportionality. Proportionality operates to restrain excess and mitigate harm, but it would be illogical that the defending state's ability to protect itself is strictly limited by the capabilities of the attacker and the means and methods the latter adopts in its armed attack. The former should not be required to mirror the latter. This is particularly the case where a series of attacks are expected from the same source. In such cases, the defensive response might need to be of a greater magnitude than the armed attack that immediately prompted it in order to counter the threat taken as a whole.[187] Unreasonable confinement of the defending state, in favour of the attacker, serves only to encourage further violence and prolong conflict.[188]

In keeping with this logic, it is further asserted that there is no requirement that the defensive force be of the same nature as the armed attack.[189] The defending state is not obliged to use the same or similar weapons that were used in the attack.[190] Ground attacks employing one type of weapon, for example, may be met

[186] Daniel P O'Connell, *The Influence of Law on Sea Power* (Naval Institute Press 1975) 64; Ago, 'Addendum—Eighth Report on State Responsibility' (n 34) para 121; Judith Gardam, 'A Role for Proportionality in the War on Terror' (2005) 74 Nord J Int'l L 3, 13; The Chatham House Principles (n 36) 969; Michael Schmitt, '"Change Direction" 2006: Israeli Operations in Lebanon and the International Law of Self-Defense' (2008) 29(2) Mich J Int'l L 127, 153; Greenwood, 'Self-Defence' (n 36) para 28; Gray, *Use of Force* (n 36) 159–160.

[187] See Section 3.2.1.1.

[188] The military capacity of the attacker, including the nature and make-up of its armed forces, is not irrelevant to determining what a proportionate self-defence looks like, however. This fact was highlighted, for example, in the UK's justification for calibrating its role in liberating Kuwait from Iraqi occupation in 1991. The size, nature and make-up of Saddam Hussein's 'military machine' helped to determine what force was needed to liberate Kuwait. UN Doc S/PV.2977 (Part II) (n 98) 72. Therefore, the capabilities of the attacker might inform what is required to achieve a defensive purpose. This is an operational consideration for those planning military strategy, however. Legally such capabilities should not be thought of as an overarching limitation.

[189] Schmitt, *Tallinn Manual* (n 36) 62–63. One exception to this general principle might be the first use of nuclear weapons in response to a conventional armed attack. Given the likely effects of nuclear weapons on other states and the environment and the fact that a first use of nuclear weapons risks a response in kind (thereby escalating the conflict), such first use is only likely to be proportionate in the most extreme cases, where the very survival of the state is threatened (see *Nuclear Weapons* (n 27) paras 96–97). See further Greenwood, 'Self-Defence and the Conduct of International Armed Conflict' (n 14) 280–281.

[190] Ruys, *'Armed Attack'* (n 20) 123; Gray, *Use of Force* (n 36) 159–160. See also IIFFMCG Report (n 102), 272. Cf Greenwood, 'Self-Defence and the Conduct of International Armed Conflict' (n 14) 279–281; Gardam, *Necessity, Proportionality* (n 8) 171–172.

with an aerial response using another, and vice versa.[191] Judge Schwebel adopted this general position in his dissent in *Nicaragua*[192] and it has occasionally been expressly asserted by states. The Congo, for instance, maintains that 'all means of armed force a victim state had available were lawful, provided they were used only for defence'.[193] The UK has been emphatic on this point:

> [The UN Charter] says nothing whatever about any particular weapon or method which may be used for self-defence. Those who wrote the Charter expected victims of aggression to react as necessary to protect their territorial integrity and political independence, and they were very careful not to say how self-defence could be carried out.[194]

The USA, in citing this passage in its pleadings before the ICJ in *Nuclear Weapons*, appears to endorse this approach[195] and state practice responding to acts of terrorism clearly reflects it.[196] Asymmetric conflicts of this kind exhibit how the methods and means of attack employed by NSAs are not adopted by states in their defensive responses. No state fighting against Daesh would (or should) see itself bound to responding to acts of terror in kind. The methods of defence are incomparable to the modes of attack.

Proportionality, and the *jus ad bellum* more generally, do not prohibit or permit the use of any particular weapon, including nuclear weapons.[197] Therefore, a distinction should be drawn between whether a weapon might be said to be inherently disproportionate from a *jus ad bellum* perspective, and the manner in which it is used. On the first point, it is difficult to argue that any weapon might be deemed disproportionate per se under the *jus ad bellum*.[198] Such proposition is clearly supported by the ICJ's jurisprudence. In *Nuclear Weapons*, France maintained that neither necessity nor proportionality could preclude, *in abstracto*, the use of nuclear weapons in self-defence.[199] The ICJ accepted this view, adopting

[191] For example, the American strike on the IIS headquarters in 1993, where cruise missiles were used to respond to an attack employing a car bomb; Operation Enduring Freedom, whereby Al-Qaeda's attacks on 9/11 using hijacked aircraft were met with aerial attacks and the eventual ground invasion of Afghanistan.

[192] *Nicaragua* (n 18) diss op Schwebel, paras 212, 237.

[193] UN Doc A/AC.134/SR.67–78 (n 9) 90 (Congo).

[194] UNGA Verbatim Record (24 November 1961) UN Doc A/PV.1063, para 20.

[195] *Nuclear Weapons* (n 27) Letter dated 20 June 1995 from the Acting Legal Adviser to the Department of State, together with Written Statement of the Government of the United States of America, 19. The USA has also reserved the right to respond to cyber armed attacks with conventional means. William J. Lynn, III, Deputy Secretary of Defense, Speech Delivered at the National Defense University, Washington, D.C. (14 July 2011) <http://archive.defense.gov/speeches/speech.aspx?speechid=1593> accessed 5 September 2020.

[196] See Chapter 4.

[197] *Nuclear Weapons* (n 27) paras 39, 42, 105.

[198] Gardam, 'Proportionality in the War on Terror' (n 186) 19.

[199] *Nuclear Weapons* (n 27) Oral Proceedings, Verbatim Record, 1 November 1995, CR 95/23, 66.

the position that even nuclear weapons are not inherently disproportionate.[200] If the most devastating weapon of all does not automatically breach this requirement, then it is difficult to see why any other weapon because of its nature would do so. As such, it cannot be the nature of the weapon that is determinative of proportionality.

The regulation of weapons used in self-defence (or otherwise) is primarily and better dealt with by the tailored provisions of IHL and those conventions relating to the use of particular weapons.[201] A summary of the position may be stated as follows:

> It is necessary to reiterate here the undoubted right of the State that is attacked to use all the weaponry available to it for the purpose of repulsing the aggressor. Yet this principle holds only *so long as such weapons do not violate the fundamental rules of warfare embodied in those rules.* Within these constraints, and for the purpose of repulsing the enemy, the full military power of the State that is attacked can be unleashed upon the aggressor.[202]

Jus ad bellum proportionality instead considers the resulting harm caused by those weapons (and weighs it, primarily, against a defensive purpose). As will be made clear, its remit is the overall defensive response and its outcomes.[203] Force used in self-defence must be scaled to effect that purpose. The key point when looking at the methods of defence is whether a weapon's deployment is restricted to a defensive purpose. Where the use of a particular weapon or mode of response significantly escalates hostilities, this serves to counter such conclusion and points to a disproportionate use of force. The fact of escalation is key to such determination, but we should be clear that it is not the nature of the weapon or the mode of response, per se, that might result in escalation. It is how the weapon is used or the results of the mode adopted that might take a military response beyond a defensive purpose.[204]

Therefore, subject to adhering to the requirements of IHL and international law relating to the use of particular weapons, a state may use whatever force is required, including of scale and/or means to halt, repel or prevent an armed attack, *but no more.*[205] In fact, depending on the circumstances, using less force than the armed

[200] 'The proportionality principle may thus not in itself exclude the use of nuclear weapons in self-defence in all circumstances.' *Nuclear Weapons* (n 27) para 42.

[201] Certain weapons, such as chemical and biological weapons, are absolutely prohibited by the operation of IHL and specific weapon conventions. See International Committee of the Red Cross ('ICRC') 'Use of Weapons' <https://www.icrc.org/en/war-and-law/weapons> accessed 5 September 2020.

[202] *Nuclear Weapons* (n 27) diss op Weeramantry, 514.

[203] See in particular Section 3.4.2.

[204] See O'Connell, *The Influence of Law on Sea Power* (n 186) 64–5; Ruys, *'Armed Attack'* (n 20) 123; Gardam, *Necessity, Proportionality* (n 8) 171; Section 2.8.1 of the UK Military Manual (n 53). See further the analysis in Section 2.6.1 of this book regarding the sinking of the *General Belgrano*.

[205] Green, 'The *Ratione Temporis* Elements of Self-Defence' (n 36) 101.

attack might be sufficient to achieve such aim.[206] The latter point is crucial. If it is clear in the circumstances that 'less force' (in terms of the nature or scale of the response and/or the methods and means of warfare) could have been deployed to achieve the same result, this suggests that the force actually used was more than was necessary to achieve the defensive aim.[207] Depending on the particular context, the resulting conclusion might be that the measures taken were instead punitive.

3.3.2 Timing—A Distinct Element of Proportionality?

Once a military response has achieved the purpose of self-defence (*viz* halting, repelling or preventing an armed attack), the UNSC has taken effective action, or the situation has otherwise been resolved peaceably, the use of defensive force will no longer be necessary. This is due to an absence of general necessity. Although it is not this author's position, it is perhaps tempting to say that a use of force beyond this point in time is also disproportionate. That proportionality might also impose a time limit on self-defence is suggested in the ICJ's jurisprudence. In *Nicaragua*, the Court noted in its comments on proportionality that the American reaction 'continued long after the period in which any presumed armed attack by Nicaragua could reasonably be contemplated'.[208] The purported defensive response endured after the point in time that the defensive necessity had fallen away. The Court also appeared to view force beyond this point as disproportionate.

Yet, the Court's position on how the timing of a defensive response relates to proportionality is ambiguous. As set out in Section 2.5.2, it considered the timing of the American response principally on the basis of general necessity. Having found a lack of general necessity, it is unclear why it offered further observations on proportionality or considered temporal factors to be part of this requirement. Even assuming that there had been an armed attack, the fact that the American action continued 'long after' it is irrelevant if the response to it was unnecessary and, on that basis alone, unlawful. As such, the weight that should be placed on this observation on proportionality is questionable.

A number of commentators also adopt the view that temporal considerations might form part of both necessity and proportionally.[209] Yet, identifying a clear body of state practice to support such a conclusion is difficult. Examples include Argentina's condemnation of Israel's 'punitive expedition' in Lebanon in 1972. This

[206] Ago, 'Addendum—Eighth Report on State Responsibility' (n 34) para 121; Gardam, 'Proportionality in the War on Terror' (n 186) 12.

[207] In this regard, Kretzmer asks whether it was 'necessary in the sense that no less drastic means were available for achieving the same ends?'. Kretzmer, 'Proportionality in *Jus Ad Bellum*' (n 29) 277.

[208] *Nicaragua* (n 18) para 237.

[209] For example, Gardam, *Necessity, Proportionality* (n 8) 167; Ruys, '*Armed Attack*' (n 20) 119; Green, 'The *Ratione Temporis* Elements of Self-Defence' (n 36) 112–113; Gill, 'When Does Self-Defence End?' (n 36) 745–746.

statement was made, *inter alia*, on the basis that proportion had not been respected in terms of the scale of the action or its duration.[210] Argentina adopted a very strict understanding of proportionality in respect of Israel's action on this occasion. In addition to recognizing a temporal aspect to proportionality, Argentina also tied its operation largely to the quantitative model.[211] Its view on immediacy is similarly strict: 'no time must pass in deliberating or reflecting on the desirability of a reaction. This means that the reaction must immediately follow the illegal attack'.[212] These observations display an overly rigid understanding of both requirements and might be a result of the circumstances of the particular incident. As explored throughout this book, states and scholars do not generally share such a narrow view of either necessity or proportionality.

In *Armed Activities*, the DRC also argued that the excessive duration of the Ugandan intervention was indicative of its disproportionate nature.[213] However, the intervention consisted of Uganda's occupation of Congolese territory. As such, it is the specific factor of enduring occupation that might best explain this negative reaction. A further example, in response to Israel's action in Lebanon against Hezbollah in 1996, is Egypt's insistence that '[t]he scale, duration and objective of military activity must be proportionate to the reason for [self-defence]'.[214] No elaboration was offered, however.

We should not dismiss this state practice of course. Yet, these incidents highlight how difficult it is to discern from the particular context analytical clarity regarding the importance (or not) of temporal considerations. More often than not, states refer vaguely to the duration of a defensive response, without specifically identifying whether such factor pertains to necessity, proportionality, or any other legally pertinent requirement. For example, Ruys proposes the American intervention in the Dominican Republic in 1965 as a candidate in support of the contention that proportionality encompasses a temporal element. In such case, France insisted that any operation to evacuate citizens 'should be limited in objective, *duration* and scale'.[215] This is a classical formulation adopted by states when referring to defensive force, but France does not specifically mention either necessity or proportionality when noting these requirements. Likewise, states have tied the duration of armed conflict explicitly to a defensive necessity. This was the case with the USA during the Vietnam War.[216] Accordingly, commentators might

[210] UN Doc S/PV.1644 (n 43) para 29.

[211] '[T]he measures adopted in self-defence must be of a similar nature or reasonably in keeping with the means used in the illegal act against which action is being taken.' Ibid, para 26.

[212] Ibid, para 25.

[213] *Armed Activities* (n 25) Reply of the Democratic Republic of the Congo, 29 May 2002, 241–243 (paras 3.173–3.177).

[214] UN Doc S/PV.3653 (n 103) 14.

[215] Ruys, *'Armed Attack'* (n 20) 119–120, citing 'Political and Security Questions: Questions Relating to the Americas' (1965) UNYB 142 (emphasis added).

[216] Office of the Legal Adviser, 'Rights and Duties of States' (n 65) 837.

overstate the case and provide only scant state practice to support the notion that states view timing as a clear and distinct element of proportionality.[217] The ICJ and states undoubtedly view the duration of self-defence as relevant to its legality, but it is not so clear if and how it operates as an independent indicator of (dis) proportionality.

For this author, the blurring of the line between the requirements of necessity and proportionality should be resisted. They should not be used jointly or interchangeably as an all-inclusive statement of illegality. General necessity must be applied before proportionality. Proportionality is only meaningful where a use of force is and remains compliant with the requirements of general necessary. Where a use of force breaches the requirements of general necessity because it is employed beyond the point in time that the defensive necessity has ceased, such use of force is unlawful. It cannot also be disproportionate. Therefore, it is submitted that although the ICJ, certain commentators and states might refer (or be understood as referring) to proportionality in terms of the temporal duration of a particular act, in the pursuit of conceptual clarity, this is misleading.[218] It is not clear from state practice that proportionality, rather than general necessity, imposes a time limit on a defensive response.

3.3.3 Geography

Certain scholars also argue that proportionality imposes a geographical limitation on self-defence, meaning that defensive force 'must generally be confined to the area of the threat which it is designed to meet'.[219] However, whether and how geography factors into the review of the proportionality of self-defence is unclear, particularly in light of recent state practice against NSAs in the context of transnational terrorism. Moreover, this author contends that where a defensive response is directed is better understood as pertaining to specific necessity, not to considerations of proportionality.

[217] For example, Gardam, *Necessity, Proportionality* (n 8) 167, references the American intervention in Grenada in 1983 in support of the same contention, citing to Levitin, 'The Law of Force and the Force of Law' (n 97). Yet, Levitin's comments on the proportionality of the action appear to pertain to the overthrow of the Grenadian government, not the duration of the American response. See Levitin, 'The Law of Force and the Force of Law' (n 97) 650. Therefore, it is unclear on what basis Gardam interprets this state practice.

[218] The need to assess proportionality throughout the duration of a defensive act is separate to this issue and is discussed in Section 3.5.

[219] Greenwood, 'Self-Defence and the Conduct of International Armed Conflict' (n 14) 277. See also O'Connell, *The Influence of Law on Sea Power* (n 186) 65; Oscar Schachter, *International Law in Theory and Practice* (Martinus Nijhoff Publishers 1991) 153–154; Gardam, 'Proportionality in the War on Terror' (n 186) 14; Ruys, *'Armed Attack'* (n 20) 118–119.

3.3.3.1 ICJ Jurisprudence

In *Nicaragua*, the Court held that the USA's mining of Nicaraguan ports and attacks on oil installations, in response to Nicaragua's alleged support of Salvadorian rebels who were operating along El Salvador's border, was disproportionate.[220] Implicit in this determination is a geographical limitation, being that proportionality takes account of the distance between the target of defensive force and the source of the armed attack. Indeed, the Court questioned whether a strong patrol along the border of El Salvador and Honduras might have been the best way to respond to the attacks by the Salvadorian rebels.[221] However, it is unclear how the factor of distance featured in the majority's view on proportionality.

As noted, to the extent that the Court considered the necessity and proportionality of the USA's response in *Nicaragua*, it clearly focused on the former requirement. In fact, the mention of a patrol as an appropriate response to rebel activity in that border region can clearly be interpreted as a reference to the specific necessity of the American action. This is to say that the focus of the Court's concern was the lack of a nexus between the target of the American response and the source of the purported armed attack.[222] This is not simply a question of geographical proximity. As such, distilling a firm view from *Nicaragua* on the ICJ's view of any geographical element of proportionality is not straightforward.

At first glance, *Armed Activities* presents a clearer jurisprudential position on this issue. In this case, the Court observed that Uganda's taking of airports and towns many hundreds of kilometres from its border would not seem proportionate to the series of transborder attacks Uganda claimed had given rise to the right to use force in self-defence.[223] The geographical distance between attack and defence appears to form part of the Court's position on proportionality. Yet, putting aside the fact that the Court found that the right of self-defence had not arisen, vague comments contained in three lines of the Court's judgment do not provide a firm and reasoned position on this point.

It is not apparent that distance was the principal factor that led to the Court's conclusion. The nature of the target (*viz* towns and airports) seems equally important. As in *Nicaragua*, the lack of a nexus between attack and defence is readily apparent. Perhaps it was a combination of both factors that informed the Court's decision, but there is insufficient detail in the judgment to say either way. Furthermore, the Court rendered a view on proportionality before necessity, which is contrary to the logical application of these criteria and its other self-defence jurisprudence.[224] It is unclear why it did this. Given that the Court held that the taking of the airports and towns was unnecessary (understood as specific necessity), its views on

[220] *Nicaragua* (n 18) para 237.
[221] Ibid, para 156.
[222] See Section 2.6.
[223] *Armed Activities* (n 25) para 147.
[224] See Section 1.1.

proportionality are rendered nugatory.[225] If the targets of the defensive response were unnecessary, for whatever reason, any force used against them was unlawful. Therefore, although the Court appears to link geography and proportionality, its position on this relationship remains unsettled.

Nicaragua and *Armed Activities* provide insufficient indications regarding whether and how geography relates to proportionality. Moreover, both cases can also be explained on the basis of specific necessity: the object of purported defensive action was not connected to the alleged armed attacks. Perhaps the best that can be said from this jurisprudence is that geography has featured in the Court's reasoning regarding proportionality on the facts of the cases before it. The pertinent facts in each case were purported acts of self-defence against a state in response to, and far from, cross-border armed attacks by NSAs. Future jurisprudence is required to confirm the Court's position regarding how important the geographical element is more generally to the requirement of proportionality.

3.3.3.2 State Practice

State practice also indicates a possible requirement of a geographical nexus between attack and defence. When claiming a right of self-defence, states will sometimes emphasize that their actions were limited geographically. In seeking to vindicate Operation Sun in 2008, for example, Turkey asserted that its counter-terrorism efforts against the PKK were 'limited in scope, geography and duration', and accordingly confined their response to the border region where the attacks were occurring.[226] In reviewing military operations, other states might also allude to geography or distance to inform their responses. Following the 1964 Gulf of Tonkin incident, Czechoslovakia rejected the USA's declaration of self-defence, *inter alia*, on the basis that the American military response occurred hundreds of miles away from the alleged North Vietnamese attacks to which the USA claimed to be reacting.[227] Similarly, Senegal's general view on self-defence is that it is only exercisable at the 'actual site of aggression'.[228]

In none of these examples, however, is it clear that the states concerned viewed the factor of geography or distance as pertaining to proportionality. Such comments can equally be interpreted as relating to necessity (*viz* specific necessity).[229]

[225] Judge Kooijmans in his dissent also appears to characterize such actions as both unnecessary and disproportionate, but it is also unclear how geography factors in his conclusions. *Armed Activities* (n 25) sep op Kooijmans, para 34.

[226] Note Verbale dated 26 March 2008 from the Permanent Mission of Turkey to the United Nations Office at Geneva addressed to the Secretariat of the Human Rights Council (28 March 2008) UN Doc A/HRC/7/G/15. See further Ruys, *'Armed Attack'* (n 20) 119, 460–461.

[227] UNSC Verbatim Record (7 August 1964) UN Doc S/PV.1141, 5–6.

[228] UN Doc S/PV.1436 (n 61) para 132.

[229] O'Connell and Greenwood note, for example, that Portugal did not react to India's seizure of Goa in 1961 by seizing Indian shipping in European waters where Portugal enjoyed naval superiority. O'Connell, *The Influence of Law on Sea Power* (n 186) 65; Greenwood, 'Self-Defence and the Conduct of International Armed Conflict' (n 14) 277. However, this example of state practice might be better interpreted on the basis of specific necessity: reacting in self-defence against targets not connected to

This is to ask whether, in the particular circumstances, it was necessary for acts of self-defence to be directed beyond the area of the armed attack in order for a defensive purpose to be achieved. This distinction is evident in Jordan's pleadings before the ICJ in *Wall*. Jordan concluded that the wall was *unnecessary* for the purposes of self-defence on the basis that, geographically, it went far beyond Israel's territory, which it was designed to protect. Its conclusion that the wall was also disproportionate was formed on the basis not of its geographical location, but on the 'consequences and implications' of its construction. Such effects took the wall beyond a defensive purpose and assumed characteristics of punishment, humiliation and conquest.[230] Likewise, in *Armed Activities*, Uganda justified its actions, which extended well inside the DRC, on the basis of necessity (understood as specific necessity) rather than proportionality.[231]

Finally, on this point, it is worth noting a classic example that is often suggested as supporting the requirement of a geographical nexus within the proportionality assessment. The incident in question is the Falklands War. Specifically, that the UK did not engage Argentine warships in areas far removed from the Falkland Islands and, more significantly, the UK did not extend military operations against the Argentine mainland.[232] Higgins maintains that any British bombing of the Argentinian navy or air force while in Argentina or in port would have been regarded as disproportionate.[233] Ruys concludes that neither a large-scale British operation against the Argentine mainland, nor an Argentinian attack again the British mainland, would have been 'justified' (appearing to base such conclusions on an assessment of proportionality).[234] Such scholarly views on the conflict appear *prima facie* to be reflected in the UK Military Manual. In accepting that a use of force must be proportionate to the overall objective of self-defence, the Manual provides the following example: '[i]n the Falklands conflict [...] there were defined and limited goals: to re-take the occupied territories, not to pursue a war of conquest against Argentina'.[235]

the armed attack is unnecessary. In a similar vein, see Office of the Legal Adviser, 'Rights and Duties of States' (n 65) 837, pertaining to the USA's actions during the Vietnam War. See further Tom Ruys, 'The Indian Intervention in Goa–1961' in Ruys and Corten, *The Use of Force in International Law* (n 36) 85, 91–94, regarding whether the Goa incident should rightly be characterized as an incident of self-defence.

230 *Wall* (n 127) Written Statement of the Hashemite Kingdom of Jordan, 30 January 2004, para 5.275.

231 *Armed Activities* (n 25) Rejoinder Submitted by the Republic of Uganda, 6 December 2002, para 289.

232 Greenwood notes that it is unclear whether the latter policy was determined by a conclusion that such extension would be disproportionate, or merely reflected political and military considerations. Nevertheless, he concludes that the decision taken by the British not to extend the conflict beyond the Islands and surrounding waters undoubtedly assisted the UK in portraying its actions as being within the boundaries of self-defence. Greenwood, 'Self-Defence and the Conduct of International Armed Conflict' (n 14) 277.

233 Higgins, *Problems and Process* (n 2) 232.

234 Ruys, *'Armed Attack'* (n 20) 119.

235 UK Military Manual (n 53) Sections 2.8–2.8.2.

These comments on the Falklands War appear to be expressed in the context of proportionality. Yet, by assessing necessity first (which is the order of application advocated by this book) the same conclusions may be reached on the basis of specific necessity. It might equally be concluded that in order to liberate the remote Falkland Islands (which was the defensive objective), it was simply not necessary (*viz* specific necessity) for the British to target the Argentine mainland or Argentinian forces located there. Therefore, it is not clear from these examples why assertions are sometimes made that a geographical nexus naturally pertains to a proportionality assessment. State practice does not provide a clear account to support this contention.

3.3.3.3 Principle and General Application

The above analysis reveals an inconclusive picture regarding whether geographical considerations sit squarely within the purview of proportionality, as some scholars maintain. There is a lack of clarity and consistency on this point. Even if geography is regarded as an element of proportionality, the required proximity between the armed attack and the corresponding defensive force remains unclear. State practice and the ICJ jurisprudence suggests, however, that a geographical connection will be most relevant to border disputes and localized incidents of hostility. Any geographical nexus between attack and defence must accordingly be considered in light of the specific circumstances.

Schachter suggests that where a series of attacks in one area requires a defensive response on a larger scale to counter the source of an attack then it does not seem unreasonable to allow a state to retaliate beyond the immediate area of the attack.[236] Greenwood, along similar lines, notes that force falling short of 'total war' will generally incur a geographical restriction, although in the cases of 'total war' the proportionality requirement would no longer confine defensive measures to a restricted geographical locale.[237] Zimmermann likewise maintains that proportionality might allow for the targeting of command and control centres well away from a trans-border attack.[238] Again, absent a conclusive position based on state practice, such conclusions might also be better understood as issues of specific necessity, rather than proportionality. Repeated, or large-scale attacks, may simply require targeting on a larger scale to ensure an effective defensive response.

In any event, a requirement of confining a response to a particular locale must be viewed reasonably. It is contingent on context, and flexibility is required. It seems sensible to conclude that any geographical limitation would gradually lose its restraining influence in the case of repeated and/or large-scale attacks that threaten

236 Schachter, *International Law* (n 219) 153–154.

237 Greenwood, 'Self-Defence and the Conduct of International Armed Conflict' (n 14) 278. See also Ruys, *'Armed Attack'* (n 20) 119. See Section 3.3.6, however, regarding the effect on other states.

238 Zimmermann, 'The Second Lebanon War' (n 36) 123.

the existence of the state, or where there is reciprocal escalation of an armed conflict.[239] It is also reasonable to assume that, in an era of advanced weaponry, where intercontinental ballistic missiles can cross the globe, countering the source of an armed attack might require covering great distances. A nuclear missile launched from North Korea against the USA might justify a response in kind. In such circumstances, it would be nonsensical to suggest that geography, as an element of proportionality, acts as an independent limitation on action. Specific necessity, however, would confine the defensive response to the source of the armed attacks (being the launch sites and related infrastructure), rather than anywhere in North Korean territory.

In the context of self-defence against armed attacks by terrorist NSAs, state practice pertaining to combatting organizations such as Al-Qaeda and Daesh suggests that geography, as an element of proportionality (or otherwise) constitutes little or no meaningful restraint on state responses. Instead, specific necessity assumes the burden.[240] Therefore, confining a defensive response geographically may increasingly be difficult as customary international law adapts to a changing world. The importance of geography is being placed under ever-greater strain.[241]

3.3.4 Effects of the Use of Force on the Defending and Attacking States—General Considerations

Section 3.2.1.3 examined in detail the importance of the armed attack and how it factors in the proportionality equation. Strict quantitative equivalence between attack and defence (and their respective outcomes) is not required, but state practice shows that defending states and other states might nevertheless refer to the armed attack when considering the proportionality of a defensive response.

3.3.4.1 The Defending State

The scale and gravity of the actual or anticipated armed attack (including its actual or anticipated effects) on the defending state is a *prima facie* starting point when considering whether a defensive response is proportionate.[242] This will involve, as applicable, an evaluation of the overall damage, death and/or destruction to the defending state's military apparatus, combatants, civilians, territory, infrastructure and other property.[243] Also naturally feeding into its defensive reaction

[239] Ruys, *'Armed Attack'* (n 20) 119.

[240] See Section 4.3.2.

[241] For a review of a number of 'geography-defying' challenges for international law, see Daniel Bethlehem, 'The End of Geography: The Changing Nature of the International System and the Challenge to International Law' (2014) 25(1) EJIL 9.

[242] See Sections 3.2.1.3 and 3.2.2.

[243] For a general discussion of some of these factors, see Tams, 'Necessity and Proportionality' (n 30) 390–391.

is an evaluation by the defending state of whether an armed attack is a one-off, or is likely to be one of a series of attacks from the same source. The history and relations between the defending state and the attacker leading up to the attack, as well as the likelihood of success of the attacks themselves, are all necessarily relevant to this threat assessment. Serious threats need to be distinguished from those that have no chance of realization and will depend on the relative military strengths of the parties involved.[244] These latter considerations are teleological, going beyond a purely quantitative assessment of harm, to what is required to achieve a defensive purpose. These factors are not exhaustive but are indicative of how the peril faced by the defending state should be quantified in terms of the nature of the armed attack(s) it faces and their actual or likely effects. This informs how its defensive response should be conditioned.

3.3.4.2 The Attacking State

The actual or anticipated effects of self-defence on an attacker should also be evaluated in similar terms, taking into account many of the same factors.[245] This section considers the position of an attacker that is a state.[246] In general, Gardam describes the major considerations for proportionality being 'the level of destruction of enemy territory and the infrastructure of the State; overall collateral civilian damage and combatant casualties'.[247] As set out below, the position of the attacking state is clearly identifiable in state practice. This practice reflects the fact that the defending state's right to protect itself is not unlimited. An appraisal of the defending state's response to an armed attack takes into account the effects of its actions on the attacking state (particularly its citizens) and on the wider international community.

One candidate for establishing the outer limits of a general approach to judging the effects of self-defence on an attacking state is the suggestion that the wholesale destruction of an attacking state's military capability and the overthrow of a hostile regime are not warranted.[248] This conclusion will be true in the vast majority of cases, as it will go beyond a defensive purpose. It was noted in Section 3.2.2 that overthrowing a government would only be considered proportionate in those extreme and very rare cases where this was the only way to achieve the defensive aim. This controversial prospect was embodied, for example, in the diverging opinions over whether the removal of Cambodia's Khmer Rouge by Vietnam in 1978 could be considered a proportionate act of self-defence.[249] However, the conclusion must

[244] Ibid, 389.

[245] This section assumes that the identity of the attacker is known. It is often the case that both sides to a conflict claim a right of self-defence, as well as maintaining that the other side is the attacker. Ultimately, this is a question of fact.

[246] Section 4.3 considers the position of NSA attackers and that of the host state.

[247] Gardam, *Necessity, Proportionality* (n 8) 17.

[248] Gardam, 'Proportionality in the War on Terror' (n 186) 16.

[249] See Thomas M Franck, *Recourse to Force: State Action Against Threats and Armed Attacks* (CUP 2002) 150; Gregory H Fox, 'The Vietnamese Intervention in Cambodia–1978' in Ruys and Corten,

also be viewed in light of the *Nuclear Weapons* dictum regarding the potential right of states to resort to using nuclear weapons in self-defence when their survival is at stake. As such, *in extremis*, one might envisage the complete destruction of the attacker.[250] This outcome again reflects the overriding teleological element of proportionality. Outside of such marginal cases, defensive action might warrant the invasion of the attacking state's territory.[251] This further raises the issue of the proportionality of occupation by the defending state of territory that it has captured as a result of its defensive actions.

Occupation is subject to extensive IHL regulation, principally The Hague Regulations of 1907 and the Fourth Geneva Convention.[252] For the purposes of the *jus ad bellum*, occupation of territory by a defending state is rarely going to be necessary or proportionate. This is because the essence of self-defence is the protection of a state's own territory, and modern international law prohibits the use of force for the acquisition of territory.[253] Occupation of part of an attacking state's territory will only be lawful in exceptional circumstances, where the threat to the defending state is so great that it cannot be adequately resisted without occupation.[254] Prolonged occupation or annexation is never justified, however.[255] Occupation may only be potentially proportionate whilst the threat to the defending state subsists. Once an armed attack has been successfully halted, repelled or prevented, ongoing occupation will be unnecessary. Proportionality at that point is irrelevant.

3.3.5 Civilian Harm

The precise impact of overall combatant casualties on proportionality is unclear in state practice.[256] Conversely, it is uncontroversial that civilian casualties resulting from defensive action are fundamental to considerations of proportionality.[257]

The Use of Force in International Law (n 36) 242, 251. See further Section 4.2.3.1 regarding Operation Enduring Freedom and the removal of the Taliban.

250 This conclusion is easier to reach with respect to armed attacks by NSA terrorists. See Section 4.3.

251 Gardam, 'Proportionality in the War on Terror' (n 186) 15–16. Operation Desert Storm is an obvious example.

252 See Philip Spoerri, 'The Law of Occupation' in Clapham and Gaeta (eds), *The Oxford Handbook of International Law in Armed Conflict* (n 36) 182.

253 Greenwood, 'Self-Defence and the Conduct of International Armed Conflict' (n 14) 282. Greenwood gives the example of Israel's occupation of territories during the 1967 war as a possible example of where occupation was necessary.

254 Ibid. See also Cassese, 'Article 51' (n 36) 1333; Ruys, *'Armed Attack'* (n 20) 117.

255 Cassese, 'Article 51' (n 36) 1333; Gray, *Use of Force* (n 36) 164.

256 Gardam suggests that there is little evidence of restraint in this area. Gardam, 'Proportionality in the War on Terror' (n 186) 20. See also the IIFFMCG Report (n 102) 272, reaching the same conclusion. Regarding terrorist NSA casualties, see Section 4.3.

257 Gardam argues that civilian collateral damage is generally not specifically articulated as being relevant to proportionality. Gardam, 'Proportionality in the War on Terror' (n 186) 14. However, the

Watkin rightly explains that '[i]t is the strategic impact of large-scale civilian casualties and damage that appears to influence what might constitute a disproportionate exercise of the right to self-defense by a State'.[258] States purporting to act in self-defence, either against other states or NSAs, frequently stress that they have made every effort to minimize civilian casualties and civilian damage.[259] Most recently, the American-led Global Coalition against Daesh and other terrorist groups (hereafter 'Global Coalition') has defended a highly rigorous targeting selection process designed to avoid civilian casualties resulting from their operations in Syria and Iraq. They maintain that more resources go into target analysis and selection than into the airstrikes themselves.[260] The record of the Global Coalition on the issue of civilian casualties is controversial and contested, but the fact that states generally regard themselves subject to an obligation to minimize civilian harm when acting in self-defence is not.[261] In *Oil Platforms*, in justifying the proportionality of its actions, the USA even argued that it had rejected possible targets because 'their destruction threated an excessive level of casualties or of damage to civilian property'.[262]

state practice referred to in this section suggests otherwise. Furthermore, Gardam accepts elsewhere that compliance with proportionality entails an analysis of whether there has been an 'unacceptable level of civilian losses in order to achieve the legitimate aims'. Gardam, *Necessity, Proportionality* (n 8) 209. See also IIFFMCG Report (n 102) 272, counting collateral civilian damage as a highly relevant criterion.

[258] Kenneth Watkin, *Fighting at the Legal Boundaries: Controlling the Use of Force in Contemporary Conflict* (OUP 2016) 62.

[259] See, for example, UNSC Verbatim Record (2 April 1964) UN Doc S/PV.1106, para 54 (UK, in respect of its raid on Harib Fort); UNSC Verbatim Record (13 December 1971) UN Doc S/PV.1613, para 202 (India, in respect of the India-Pakistan conflict); UNSC Verbatim Record (15 April 1986) UN Doc S/PV.2674, 14–15 (USA, justifying its actions against Libya); UNSC Verbatim Record (13 February 1991) UN Doc S/PV.2977 (Part I) 43 (USA, in defence of its actions in the first Iraq War); UN Doc S/PV.2977 (Part II) (n 98) 74–75 (UK, in defence of its actions in the first Iraq War); Letter dated 26 June 1993 from the Permanent Representative of the United States of America to the United Nations addressed to the President of the Security Council (26 June 1993) UN Doc S/26003 (USA, in respect of its strike on the IIS headquarters); Letter dated 20 August 1998 from the Permanent Representative of the United States of America to the United Nations addressed to the President of the Security Council (20 August 1998) UN Doc S/1998/780 (USA, justifying its airstrikes against Al-Qaeda in Sudan and Afghanistan); Letter dated 7 October 2001 from the Permanent Representative of the United State of America to the United Nations addressed to the President of the Security Council (7 October 2001) UN Doc S/2001/946 (USA, justifying its actions against Al-Qaeda in Afghanistan); UN Doc A/HRC/7/G/15 (n 226) (Turkey, justifying Operation Sun); Letter dated 9 October 2019 from the Permanent Representative of Turkey to the United Nations addressed to the President of the Security Council (9 October 2019) UN Doc S/2019/804 (Turkey, justifying Operation Peace Spring).

[260] Global Coalition, 'Airstrikes, Civilian Casualties and Investigations' (13 November 2017) <http://theglobalcoalition.org/en/airstrikes-civilian-casualties-and-investigations/> accessed 5 September 2020. See further Chapter 4.

[261] Regarding the reported civilian harm and the proportionality of Global Coalition action in Syria, see Section 4.3.3.2.

[262] *Oil Platforms* (n 25) Counter-Memorial and Counter-Claim Submitted by the United States of America, 23 June 1997, paras 4.34.

Despite states undoubtedly recognizing the general obligation to minimize civilian harm, it is not apparent that states regard it as deriving uniquely from the *jus ad bellum*. IHL proportionality, focusing as it does on civilian collateral damage, may deflect attention from this factor under the *jus ad bellum*.[263] States might be referring to either regime, or both, when referencing this requirement. Alternatively, or in addition to constituting a legal obligation, minimizing civilian harm could be a consequence of policy. There might be a need to garner political support for the operation at hand, as well as support amongst the local civilian population.[264] Yet, such limitation is a logical consequence of *jus ad bellum* proportionality. Moreover, the fact that states will frequently cite the requirement to minimize civilian harm when justifying their purported acts of self-defence suggests that the requirement is (also) part of the *jus ad bellum* proportionality calculus. As such, although it is not an absolute limitation on state action in the *jus ad bellum*, it is one of the most important.[265]

This conclusion is clearly supported in the reactions of other states and international organizations to ostensibly defensive military operations. Where actions in self-defence lead to large numbers of civilian casualties, or where civilians are perceived by states to be the main victims of the military response, this factor might form the core of their negative reactions. Israel's invasion of Lebanon in 2006 constitutes one of the most frequently cited examples of disproportionate self-defence based in particular on civilian collateral damage.[266] It was reported that Israel's actions, justified as self-defence, resulted in 1,191 deaths and 4,409 injured.[267] Most of these casualties were civilians. In addition, more than 900,000 people were displaced and major damage was inflicted on civilian infrastructure, including large numbers of bridges and roads, and the Beirut International Airport. Private housing, water and electrical facilities, schools, medical facilities, factories, mosques and churches, television and radio transmission stations,

[263] Gardam, 'Proportionality in the War on Terror' (n 186) 14.

[264] It is argued that part of the rationale for the American desire for a 'zero-casualty standard' in Syria derives from the wars in Iraq and Afghanistan, where winning over the local population was considered critical to success. See Kristina Wong, 'US Aim for "Zero Civilian Casualties" Draws Criticism' *The Hill* (24 June 2015) <http://thehill.com/policy/defense/policy-strategy/245932-us-aims-for-zero-civilian-casualties-in-war-vs-isis> accessed 5 September 2020.

[265] Concern for civilians does not equate to requiring a complete absence of civilian harm. Such a position would not be a requirement of either the *jus ad bellum* or IHL. This point is discussed further below in this section.

[266] For detailed descriptions of the facts, international reaction and a range of legal opinion, see Cannizzaro, 'Contextualizing Proportionality' (n 162); Tom Ruys, 'Crossing the Thin Blue Line: An Inquiry into Israel's Recourse to Self-Defense against Hezbollah' (2007) 43 Stan J Int'l L 265; Zimmermann, 'The Second Lebanon War' (n 36); Gregor Wettberg, *The International Legality of Self-Defense Against Non-State Actors, State Practice from the U.N. Charter to the Present* (Peter Lang 2007) 114–123; Schmitt, '"Change Direction" 2006' (n 186); Van Steenberghe, 'Proportionality' (n 24); Gray, *Use of Force* (n 36) 213–216; 227–231; Tams and Brückner, 'The Israeli Intervention in Lebanon' (n 183) 673–688.

[267] Identical Letters dated 12 July 2006 from the Permanent Representative of Israel to the United Nations addressed to the Secretary-General and the President of the Security Council (12 July 2006) UN Doc A/60/937–S/2006/515. Reported figures vary. See further the references in n 266.

historical, archaeological and cultural sites were damaged or destroyed.[268] Israel also imposed air and naval blockades resulting in significant negative humanitarian, environmental and economic impacts.[269] On the Israeli side, forty-three civilians were killed and approximately 1,000 injured (seventy-five seriously), 6,000 homes were affected and 300,000 persons were displaced by Hezbollah's attacks on towns in northern Israel.[270]

Putting aside, for present purposes, controversies over the legality of Israel's claim of self-defence against Hezbollah,[271] most states in reacting to the Israeli invasion focused on the scope of such action. Proportionality was decisive to the assessment of its legality. It is clear that the principal concern for those states that criticized or condemned Israel's military response as disproportionate was the overall harm to Lebanese civilians and civilian infrastructure.[272] This was also true for those states and international organizations that did not go so far as to condemn Israel's action, but which nevertheless called for a proportionate response that avoided civilian damage.[273] The scale of the harm to Lebanon, most notably the collective impact on the civilian population and infrastructure, was deemed by most states to be out of proportion to both the immediate trigger that led to the Israeli invasion and to the broader threat posed by Hezbollah.[274] Lebanon

[268] Human Rights Council, 'Report of the UN Commission of Inquiry on Lebanon Pursuant to Human Rights Council Resolution S-2/1' (23 November 2006) UN Doc A/HRC/3/2 (hereafter 'HRC Lebanon Report') paras 11, 20, 76–79.

[269] Ibid, paras 268–275.

[270] Ibid, para 78.

[271] Although a majority of states, as well as the UN Secretary General and various international organizations, recognized that Israel was entitled to invoke self-defence against Hezbollah, controversies remain regarding that claim. For details and commentary, see the references in n 266.

[272] UNSC Verbatim Record (14 July 2006) UN Doc S/PV.5489, 7–8 (Russia); 9 (Argentina); 11 (China); 13 (Congo); 13 (Tanzania); 17 (Greece); 17 (France); UN Doc S/PV.5493 (n 107) 14 (Qatar); UN Doc S/PV.5493 (Resumption 1) (n 106) 4 (Peru); 11 (France); 18 (Switzerland); 19 (Brazil); 20 (Algeria); 24 (Jordan); 25 (Indonesia); 28 (Turkey); 30 (Djibouti); 33 (New Zealand); 34 (India); 35 (Chile); 36 (Venezuela); 41 (Guatemala); 45 (Mexico); Letter dated 19 September 2006 from the Permanent Representative of Cuba to the United Nations addressed to the Secretary-General (29 September 2006) UN Doc A/61/472–S/2006/780, para 145 (on behalf of the Non-Aligned Movement).

[273] UNSC Verbatim Record (13 July 2006) UN Doc S/PV.5488, 5 (UK); UN Doc S/PV.5489 (n 272) 12 (UK); 15 (Denmark); UN Doc S/PV.5493 (n 107) 19 (Slovakia); UN Doc S/PV.5493 (Resumption 1) (n 106) 7 (Denmark); 16 (Finland, on behalf of the EU. Bulgaria, Romania, Turkey, Croatia, the former Yugoslav Republic of Macedonia, Albania, Bosnia and Herzegovina, Serbia, Iceland, Ukraine and the Republic of Moldova also aligned themselves with the statement); 23 (Norway).

[274] The immediate trigger occurred on 12th July 2006. Hezbollah launched several rockets across the Blue Line into Israel. Hezbollah forces crossed into northern Israel, killed three Israeli Defense Forces soldiers, injured two and abducted two others. The conflict escalated thereafter, culminating in Israel's invasion. See UNSC, 'Report of the Secretary-General on the United Nations Interim Force in Lebanon' (21 July 2006) UN Doc S/2006/560 and the commentary referred to in n 266. Israel viewed the overall threat posed by Hezbollah and regional terrorism as much broader than this triggering event. See Steven Erlanger, 'With Israeli Use of Force, Debate Over Proportion' *The New York Times* (19 July 2006) <http://www.nytimes.com/2006/07/19/world/middleeast/19israel.html> accessed 5 September 2020. The aforementioned response by a majority of states suggests that, even accepting such characterization of a broader threat, Israel's response remained disproportionate. Gray agrees that the action was disproportionate, even if Hezbollah's past attacks could be taken cumulatively. Gray, *Use of Force* (n 36) 227. For the contrary view, asserting that the Israeli invasion was proportionate (especially when viewed in

had not actively supported Hezbollah's activities, yet the Israeli response led to destruction of large parts of Lebanese public and civilian infrastructure. In addition, the aerial and naval blockade targeted not only Hezbollah, but also the entire Lebanese population.[275] The deleterious effects of the blockade were noted by a number of states.[276] The European Union criticized Israel's disproportionate use of force, insisting that 'the imposition of an air and sea blockade on Lebanon cannot be justified'.[277] Therefore, Israel's actions were viewed by certain states as a collective punishment of Lebanon's civilians.[278] The UN Secretary General[279] and the UN Commission of Inquiry on Lebanon[280] also viewed Israel's acts in this way. The Non-Aligned Movement went so far as to condemn Israel's use of force against Lebanon as aggression.[281] Looking at the purported act of self-defence as a whole, the prevailing view on the overall disastrous effects on civilians of Israel's invasion is clear.[282]

This incident epitomizes how states and international organizations focus on civilian harm when assessing whether or not a purported act of self-defence is proportionate. It might be that for some states such harm, in and of itself, is sufficient to reach this conclusion. This would constitute a purely quantitative assessment, based on the asymmetry between attack and defence, including their respective effects. Alternatively, or additionally, such marked quantitative imbalance might be viewed as pointing to excessiveness vis-à-vis a defensive purpose. As noted in the preceding paragraph, a number of states adopted this view and regarded Israel's acts as punitive rather than defensive in nature. This approach reflects a teleological evaluation. Therefore, both material and qualitative elements of proportionality are readily apparent. It is submitted that, over and above the marked asymmetry in harm between attack and defence, the magnitude of civilian causalities and civilian

the context of the broader threat), see Schmitt, '"Change Direction" 2006' (n 186) in particular, 155–156, 163–164.

[275] Ruys, 'Crossing the Thin Blue Line' (n 266) 292.

[276] See UN Doc S/PV.5489 (n 272); UN Doc S/PV.5493 (Resumption 1) (n 106).

[277] Hassan M Fattah and Steven Erlanger, 'Israel Blockades Lebanon; Wide Strikes by Hezbollah' *The New York Times* (14 July 2006) <http://www.nytimes.com/2006/07/14/world/middleeast/14mideast.html> accessed 5 September 2020.

[278] UN Doc S/PV.5493 (Resumption 1) (n 106) 20 (Algeria); 24 (Norway); 25 (Indonesia); 26 (League of Arab States); 29 (Morocco); 30 (Iran); 32 (Djibouti); 42 (UAE); 44 (South Africa).

[279] UNSC Verbatim Record (20 July 2006) UN Doc S/PV.5492, 3, describing Israel's acts as excessive and disproportionate.

[280] HRC Lebanon Report (n 268) in particular, para 331.

[281] UN Doc A/61/472-S/2006/780 (n 272) paras 142–143.

[282] As noted, when reviewing the UNSC debates, it is not possible to separate clearly concerns over IHL proportionality from *jus ad bellum* proportionality. The legality of specific targets, for example, may be debated for the purposes of IHL and also from the perspective of specific necessity. If targeting fails the latter test, then proportionality is irrelevant. Regardless, it is the effect of the combination of all incidents of targeting that is the purview of *jus ad bellum* proportionality. For commentary regarding the targetability of bridges, roads, the Beirut International Airport and other elements of Lebanese infrastructure, see Zimmermann, 'The Second Lebanon War' (n 36) 133–135; Ruys, 'Crossing the Thin Blue Line' (n 266) 290–292. See also HRC Lebanon Report (n 268) in particular, paras 319–337.

damage is impossible to reconcile with achieving the defensive aim of combatting Hezbollah. In the words of the Russian delegate, 'the scale of the use of force, the casualties and the destruction demonstrate that the actions [...] go far beyond a counterterrorist operation'.[283]

Emphasis placed by other states and international organizations on excessive damage to civilians and civilian infrastructure is a consistent and longstanding theme in state practice. This is so in both interstate conflicts and in state action against NSAs operating in foreign territory. Other examples include the UK's raid on the Harib Fort in Yemen in 1964,[284] as well as Israel's response to terrorist attacks carried out by the PLO in 1978. In the latter case, Israeli action also included a large-scale military operation against Lebanon, resulting in the occupation of territory, the death and injury of civilians and the destruction of Lebanese infrastructure. The operation was broadly condemned and resulted in the UNSC calling for a cessation of military action and the withdrawal of Israeli forces from Lebanese territory.[285] Other Israeli interventions in Jordan and Lebanon over the years have invited similar criticism, focusing on the effects on civilians.[286] The same is apparent when Israel has claimed a right of self-defence against Hamas and other armed groups in the occupied Palestinian territories.[287] These represent examples amongst a number of other such incidents where states have expressed concerns over excessive civilian harm.[288] Turkey's Operation Sun in 2008 likewise

[283] UN Doc S/PV.5493 (Resumption 1) (n 106) 2.

[284] UN Doc S/PV.1106 (n 259) paras 66–67 (Iraq); UN Doc S/PV.1108 (n 59) para 27 (Morocco); paras 48–50 (Ivory Coast); UNSC Verbatim Record (8 April 1964) UN Doc S/PV.1110, paras 24–26 (Czechoslovakia).

[285] UNSC Res 425 (19 March 1978) UN Doc S/RES/425. See further UNSC Verbatim Record (19 January 1979) UN Doc S/PV.2113, para 116 (USSR); 'Political and Security Questions: Questions Relating to the Middle East' (1978) UNYB 288, 298–311.

[286] See UNSC Verbatim Record (16 November 1966) UN Doc S/PV.1320, paras 79–80 (UK); para 89 (USA); UNSC Verbatim Record (18 November 1966) UN Doc S/PV.1323, paras 9–11 (The Netherlands); UNSC Verbatim Record (24 November 1966) UN Doc S/PV.1327, paras 14–15 (Uganda); UN Doc S/PV.1643 (n 71) para 118 (France); para 39 (Italy); UN Doc S/PV.1644 (n 43) paras 162, 168 (Somalia); UNSC Verbatim Record (23 June 1972) UN Doc S/PV.1648, paras 120–121, 127 (Sudan); UN Doc S/PV.1650 (n 71) paras 9–11 (France); paras 99–100 (Italy); UNSC Verbatim Record (17 July 1981) UN Doc S/PV.2292, paras 28–30 (Lebanon); UNSC Verbatim Record (8 June 1982) UN Doc S/PV.2377, paras 34–35 (Ireland); para 41 (Japan); UN Doc S/PV.3653 (n 103) 9 (Germany) 10 (Russia) 23 (Afghanistan).

[287] As an occupying power, Israel's claims of self-defence against NSAs operating in occupied territory are highly questionable. See *Wall* (n 127) paras 70–79 for further analysis of this status. Nevertheless, in one incident in 2004, Russia recognized in principle Israel's claim of self-defence, yet condemned it as disproportionate on the basis of the 'massacre of innocent civilians'. This position was echoed by other states, such as Pakistan. UNSC Verbatim Record (4 October 2004) UN Doc S/PV.5049, 6 (Israel); 12–13 (Russia); 14 (Pakistan). See also UNSC Verbatim Record (31 December 2008) UN Doc S/PV.6060; UNSC Verbatim Record (6 January 2009) UN Doc S/PV.6061; UNSC Verbatim Record (22 July 2014) UN Doc S/PV.7222; UNSC Verbatim Record (26 April 2018) UN Doc S/PV.8244; UNSC Verbatim Record (15 May 2018) UN Doc S/PV.8256; UNSC Verbatim Record (30 May 2018) UN Doc S/PV.8272; UNSC Verbatim Record (26 March 2019) UN Doc S/PV.8489, 10–11 (South Africa); 17–18 (France).

[288] See, for example, 'Political and Security Questions: Matters Relating to Africa' (1979) UNYB 167, 219–220 (USA, in the context of the conflict between Zambia and Southern Rhodesia); 'Political and Security Questions: Africa' (1982) UNYB 255, 311–312, 315 (various states expressing concern

highlights the concern placed by the international community on the need to protect civilians. It stands, however, as an example of proportionate defensive action against NSAs in foreign territory. This is on the basis that, although the PKK incurred heavy losses, harm to Iraq's population and infrastructure was limited, despite the scale of the Turkish intervention.[289]

For states appraising the proportionality of claims of self-defence, collateral civilian harm accordingly acts as a consistent indicator of excessiveness. It will often be impossible to avoid such death and destruction, but this practice reveals how civilian harm is frequently the focus of the debate regarding the legality of asserted defensive action. State reactions confirm that a defensive purpose cannot be achieved at any cost. Other interests, in this case of civilians, must be accounted for. The difficulty is determining where states will draw the line. There is no absolute mathematical answer to this question. High levels of civilian casualties might point to a lack of defensive purpose, but such levels might equally be unavoidable if a defending state is to defend itself effectively. It must be recognized that the defending state's action will invariably be in defence of its own civilian population. Therefore, although civilians and civilian objects on the other side of a border may not be directly targeted under the *jus ad bellum* or IHL (and civilian harm must be kept to a minimum under both regimes), this does not entirely exclude civilian death or injury. Identifying excessiveness in such circumstances will be context dependant. This might be an unsatisfactory conclusion, but states assess proportionality flexibly and in light of the surrounding circumstances. The analysis regarding Global Coalition action against Daesh and other terrorist groups in Syria indicates that high levels of civilian harm might well be accepted where the threat to states is perceived to be particularly great.[290]

Although civilian harm is a clear indicator of excessiveness, the significance of possible long-term effects on the civilian population, including large refugee outflows that might result from conflict, is less clear from state practice.[291] Judge Higgins, in her Separate Opinion in *Wall,* considered the general effect of defensive force on the civilian population, over and above death and injury. In so doing, she doubted whether the building of a wall could constitute an act of self-defence.

over civilian harm arising out of South Africa's actions in a number of neighbouring countries); UNSC Verbatim Record (16 April 1986) UN Doc S/PV.2676, 12 (Ukraine, in respect of American airstrikes in Libya); UNSC Verbatim Record (21 December 1989) 14–15, 18, 28 (respectively, Finland, Algeria and Cuba regarding the USA's invasion of Panama); UN Doc S/PV.5961 (n 101) (France, in the context of the 2008 conflict in Georgia); IIFFMCG Report (n 102) 272–275; Identical Letters dated 4 November 2011 from the Permanent Representative of Turkey to the United Nations addressed to the Secretary-General and the President of the Security Council (9 November 2011) UN Doc S/2011/690 (Turkey, in respect of Israel's use of force against the *Mavi Marmara*).

289 Ruys, '*Quo Vadit Jus ad Bellum*?' (n 112) 362–363; Tams, 'Necessity and Proportionality' (n 30) 414.

290 See Sections 4.2.3.2 and 4.3.3.2.

291 Gardam, 'Proportionality in the War on Terror' (n 186) 20.

Even assuming it could, she went on to query whether the particular route selected could be necessary or proportionate given the '*attendant hardships* for Palestinians uninvolved in these attacks'.[292] This view was echoed by Judge Kooijmans[293] and suggests that the general impact on the lives of those affected by, but not taking part in, the conflict might also be taken into account in concluding whether or not defensive force is proportionate. Logically, this would appear to apply to the civilian populations of both the defending state and the attacker.

3.3.6 Effect on Third-Party Rights

3.3.6.1 General Considerations and State Responsibility

Despite not tending to feature in the literature on the subject, Gardam rightly reminds us that the impact of defensive force on the rights of other states is also relevant to a proportionality evaluation.[294] This factor speaks to the wider effects of an exercise of self-defence and how the interests of the international community operate to curtail the pursuit of that right. Undue interference with third-party interests might be deemed excessive. There are many ways in which other states might be affected by defensive force, including violations of sovereignty and territorial integrity. Temporary incursions by an aircraft or missile into another state's airspace, or the traversing of its territory by the defending state's military in order to reach their objective, are obvious examples. These breaches might be deliberate or accidental and will be of varying degrees of gravity. Most serious are those violations of territorial integrity that result in physical damage to another state's territory or harm to its civilian population. Additionally, blockades, exclusion zones or other military activity might interfere with economic, trade and other rights of states that have no involvement in the conflict. The potential effects of nuclear weapons have already been referred to and the widespread use of conventional weapons might be equally injurious. Regional instability caused by warfare also produces a range of deleterious consequences.

The issue of third-party rights is clearly relevant to the proportionality equation and takes us beyond considerations of a defensive purpose and the material factors referred to previously in this chapter. Recourse to the laws of state responsibility can assist with an understanding how third-party rights factor in the proportionality review. As noted in Section 2.2, the ILC recognizes that defensive force might affect other states, including neutral states, but it explicitly leaves open the question of whether Article 21 of the ARSIWA precludes the wrongfulness of self-defence vis-à-vis other states.[295] For the purposes of Article 25 of the ARSIWA, however, an

[292] *Wall* (n 127) sep op Higgins, para 35 (emphasis added).
[293] *Wall* (n 127) sep op Kooijmans, para 34.
[294] Gardam, *Necessity, Proportionality* (n 8) 17.
[295] ARSIWA (n 135) para 5 of the commentary to Art 21.

invocation of a state of necessity takes into account the interests of other states and the international community as a whole, in addition to the interests of the acting state.[296] That competing interests are accounted for in this way within the laws of state responsibility provides an instructive template for approaching the present enquiry.

The following analysis indicates that the rights and interests of other states, and of the international community as a whole, also form part of the determination of whether or not a defending state has acted excessively. Where the pursuit of the right of self-defence infringes upon other legally protected interests, it might be that such infringement is regarded as proportionate. Employing the justificatory language of circumstances precluding wrongfulness, the act of self-defence might be objectively justifiable as a 'lesser evil' when compared to the infringement of the other right. This is to say that the result achieved, being the defending state protecting itself and its citizens, provides a net benefit.[297] This will not always be the case, however, and self-defence will not always prevail. The following review also suggests that the right of self-defence is not to be regarded as a superior interest that invariably trumps all others. An exercise of self-defence might be considered to be excessive, depending on the circumstances. The situation is to be reviewed as a whole. The right of self-defence is weighed against other interests affected by the use of military force in light of the particular context.[298] These conclusions are explored further below.

3.3.6.2 Neutrality and Former Belligerent Rights

The relationship between defending states exercising their right of self-defence and how the rights of other states are affected under the UN Charter 'awaits full elaboration'.[299] Section 4.3.3 considers proportionality in the context of the effect of defensive action on host states. A related question is whether adhering to proportionality permits incursions into the territory of a neutral state.[300] Traditionally, the law of neutrality applies only in the context of international armed conflicts between two or more states, not to non-international armed conflicts between states and NSAs, transnational or otherwise.[301] It comprises rights and obligations for both belligerents and neutral non-belligerents. Essentially, this means that neutral

[296] ARSIWA (n 135) Art 25(1)(b) and para 17 of the related commentary. This balancing exercise is objective and based on a reasonable assessment.

[297] For an overview of the balancing and safeguarding of competing interests in the context of the ARSIWA (n 135) Art 25, together with commentary on the 'lesser evil' justification in this context, see Federica Paddeu, *Justification and Excuse in International Law* (CUP 2018) 400, 415–421.

[298] In the context of the ARSIWA (n 135) Art 25, see Paddeu, ibid, 415–421.

[299] Gardam, 'Proportionality in the War on Terror' (n 186) 21.

[300] For the purposes of this section, a distinction is made between states that are unwilling or unable to confront terrorist threats emanating from their territory and states that have no nexus whatsoever with the relevant conflict. This section relates to the latter type of state.

[301] Paul Seger, 'The Law of Neutrality' in Clapham and Gaeta (eds), *The Oxford Handbook of International Law in Armed Conflict* (n 36) 248, 253.

states must abstain from involvement in a conflict and treat the belligerents impartially. In return, the belligerents are required to respect a state's neutral status.[302] Most importantly, parties to an armed conflict must respect the sovereignty and territorial integrity of the neutral state and must not use force within neutral territory, including a neutral state's territorial waters and airspace.[303] The fundamental legal rationale is to guarantee that neutral states will sustain only minimal injury from warfare, so long as they in turn abide by the aforesaid obligations not to participate and not to discriminate.[304]

The law relating to neutrality holds an uncertain position in the post-UN Charter world.[305] In *Nuclear Weapons*, the ICJ affirmed the continued application of the law of neutrality, 'whatever its content', to all international armed conflicts, but expressed it to be subject to the provisions of the UN Charter.[306] This statement leaves its application vis-à-vis the *jus ad bellum* unsettled, including to what extent the rules of neutrality might affect the application of both necessity the proportionality.[307] As a general proposition, however, given the seriousness of intruding into the territory of a neutral state, it would only be where the need to take action there is 'very great indeed' that necessity and proportionality might be satisfied.[308] To be regarded as the 'lesser evil' and not excessive, the context would arguably need to be such that the violation of neutral territory was the *only* way for a state to defend itself.[309]

[302] Christine Chinkin, *Third Parties in International Law* (Oxford, Clarendon Press 1993) 300. For a general overview of the law of neutrality, see Seger, 'The Law of Neutrality' (n 301) 248–270; James Upcher, *Neutrality in Contemporary International Law* (OUP 2020).

[303] The general principle of neutrality is reflected in Art 1 of the Hague Convention V Respecting the Rights and Duties of Neutral Powers and Persons in Case of War on Land, 18 October 1907, 205 CTS 299. It states that '[t]he territory of neutral Powers is inviolable'. See further Seger, 'The Law of Neutrality' (n 301) 254–255. However, a belligerent can take defensive action on a neutral state's territory if such state allows its territory to be used by another belligerent state in violation of its duties of neutrality. Derek W Bowett, *Self-Defence in International Law* (Manchester University Press 1958) 167–174; Brownlie, *Use of Force by States* (n 36) 312–314.

[304] Dinstein, *War, Aggression and Self-Defence* (n 29) 27.

[305] See generally Chinkin, *Third Parties* (n 302) 299–314; Greenwood, 'Self-Defence and the Conduct of International Armed Conflict' (n 14) 283–286; Stephen C Neff, *War and the Law of Nations* (CUP 2005) 349–356.

[306] *Nuclear Weapons* (n 27) para 89.

[307] Within the context of collective security, the laws of neutrality are subject to the operation of Art 2(5) of the UN Charter. This requires all Member States of the UN to assist the UN in carrying out preventive or enforcement measures under the UN Charter, and to refrain from assisting any state against which such measures are taken. This operates as a 'rigorous caveat' to the law of neutrality. Dinstein, *War, Aggression and Self-Defence* (n 29) 186–187. Furthermore, if the UNSC were to make an authoritative determination regarding which party to a conflict prompted by self-defence was the aggressor, the logic of the Charter would suggest that all Member States of the UN must do whatever they can to assist the defending state and to foil the aggressor's designs. This also challenges the entitlement of states to neutrality. Dinstein, *War, Aggression and Self-Defence* (n 29) 187. Outside of these contexts, however, neutrality remains possible. See further Seger, 'The Law of Neutrality' (n 301) 261–263; Upcher, *Neutrality* (n 302) 18–21, 126–161.

[308] Greenwood, 'Self-Defence and the Conduct of International Armed Conflict' (n 14) 278.

[309] The ICJ has employed this logic, also in the context of considering necessity as a circumstance precluding wrongfulness. In *Wall* (n 127) para 140, the Court rejected the necessity of Israel's construction of the wall along the chosen route as it was not the *only* way to safeguard Israel's interests from peril.

The issue is not limited to territorial violations, however. Neutrality is perhaps most problematic in the context of interference with neutral shipping.[310] The laws of war and neutrality previously allowed belligerents considerable freedom to stop and search ships on the high seas, to seize and condemn in prize contraband, to operate long distance blockades and even to use force against neutral shipping.[311] It is debatable whether such rights remain available under the post-UN Charter *jus ad bellum* and might be compatible with necessity and proportionality. On the basis of the targeting analysis set out in Section 2.6, we may reasonably conclude that deliberate attacks on neutral shipping, whether military or civilian, are never justifiable. Targeting them will not satisfy the requirement of specific necessity. Proportionality is consequently irrelevant on this point.

More generally, necessity and proportionality should be viewed as narrowing the scope of former belligerent rights, even if they do not require that they be dispensed with entirely.[312] Blockades are an important example of this limitation. Being designed to prevent all vessels and/or aircraft from entering or exiting specified ports, airports or coastal areas belonging to, or under the control of, another state, blockades have the potential to impinge on the rights of neutral states.[313] Specifically, blockades might affect their freedom of navigation and aviation and, being enforced by military means, could constitute acts of aggression if not justified (for example, by self-defence).[314] O'Connell argues that the international community would nowadays not accept the long-distance blockades of the two World Wars. Such widespread interference with neutral shipping would be inconsistent with the theory of self-defence and would arguably constitute an unlawful use of force. He suggests, however, that close blockades (*viz* specific blockades of more limited scope) restricting ingress and egress of neutral shipping to and from a belligerent port, might be tolerated.[315] The UK appears to adopt this general approach.[316] The USA likewise recognized that its claim of self-defence during the Vietnam War in 1972 required more limited action than a blockade under

[310] For state practice examples and commentary, see Chinkin, *Third Parties* (n 302) 305–308.

[311] Greenwood, 'Self-Defence and the Conduct of International Armed Conflict' (n 14) 284; Penelope Nevill, 'Military Sanctions Enforcement in the Absence of Express Authorization?' in Weller (ed), *The Oxford Handbook* (n 36) 272, 274–279.

[312] Upcher, *Neutrality* (n 302) 211–212.

[313] For a general overview of the types of blockades, their history and their current legality, including under IHL, see Daniel P O'Connell, *The International Law of the Sea* (Oxford, Clarendon Press 1984) 1150–1158; Douglas Guilfoyle, 'The *Mavi Marmara* Incident and Blockade in Armed Conflict' (2011) 81(1) BYIL 171; Wolff Heintschel Von Heinegg, 'Blockades and Interdictions' in Weller (ed), *The Oxford Handbook* (n 36) 925, 927–934. For further discussion of neutral shipping, including under IHL, see Natalie Klein, *Maritime Security and the Law of the Sea* (OUP 2012) 287–300.

[314] Definition of Aggression (n 9) Art 3(c). They might also be authorized by the UNSC. Their legality additionally depends on compliance with IHL. See generally Von Heinegg, 'Blockades and Interdictions' (n 313) 927–934.

[315] O'Connell, *The International Law of the Sea* (n 313) 1155–1156. Upcher reaches a similar conclusion. Upcher, *Neutrality* (n 302) 207.

[316] See UK Military Manual (n 53) Section 13.3.

traditional IHL. In so doing, the USA explicitly adopted more restricted naval operations in order to protect the rights of neutrals. It saw this deference to neutrality as a key factor in justifying its defensive actions.[317]

Von Heinegg also recognizes the potential acceptance of blockades under the *jus ad bellum*, subject to compliance with necessity and proportionality. He argues, however, that there would need to be a clear nexus with the armed attack. This means that a blockade could not block all vessels or aircraft, but only those 'associated' with the self-defence situation.[318] This approach also represents a move from previously accepted traditional blockades to more limited interdiction operations. Such action would presumably include vessels transporting arms to, or otherwise supporting, the attacker. Although this latter conclusion is not clear from Von Heinegg's analysis, it is consistent with the UK Military Manual and the International Institute of Humanitarian Law's *San Remo Manual on International Law Applicable to Armed Conflicts at Sea*.[319] Iran has also followed the UK in asserting a right of stop and search in the exercise of the right of self-defence, if there are reasonable grounds to suspect a vessel of taking arms to the other side for use in a conflict.[320] Greenwood concludes this is probably permissible.[321]

Following its investigation into the blockade of the Gaza strip in 2010 and Israeli attacks on the flotilla of ships (including the *Mavi Marmara*) carrying humanitarian assistance to Gaza, the Human Rights Council's fact finding mission concluded that such action could not be justified on the basis of self-defence.[322] This determination was based on the fact that the flotilla was making no contribution to the war effort and posed no immediate security threat to Israel.[323] Therefore, the Israeli action went beyond a defensive purpose. By implication, an objectively identifiable defensive purpose might have rendered such action justifiable. If accepted, the foregoing analysis suggests that, even if 'a right of interference with third States' freedom of navigation should not lightly be presumed',[324] limited interference with neutral states might be notionally necessary. Proportionality will depend on the acceptance of the degree of interference in the particular circumstances. Widespread

[317] Office of the Legal Adviser, 'Rights and Duties of States' (n 65) 837–838. See further Neff, *War and the Law of Nations* (n 305) 353; Nevill, 'Military Sanctions' (n 311) 278.

[318] Von Heinegg, 'Blockades and Interdictions' (n 313) 931.

[319] UK Military Manual (n 53) Section 13.91; San Remo Manual (n 162) Arts 67, 118. Such action by a neutral state would, however, jeopardize its neutral status.

[320] HC Deb 5 February 1986, vol 91, col 278. This assertion by the UK was cited by Iran in support of its case before the ICJ in *Oil Platforms* (n 25). Memorial Submitted by the Islamic Republic of Iran, 8 June 1993, para 4.59.

[321] See Greenwood, 'Self-Defence and the Conduct of International Armed Conflict' (n 14) 284. See further Upcher, *Neutrality* (n 302) 178–187.

[322] Human Rights Council, 'Report of the International Fact-Finding Mission to Investigate Violations of International Law, Including International Humanitarian and Human Rights Law, Resulting from the Israeli Attacks on the Flotilla of Ships Carrying Humanitarian Assistance' (27 September 2010) UN Doc A/HRC/15/21, paras 56–61.

[323] Ibid.

[324] Ibid, para 55.

blockades of previous, pre-UN Charter years, are unlikely to satisfy either requirement, however.

A further controversial issue when considering the position of neutral states relates to maritime exclusion zones.[325] These zones might be established by a defending state to prevent the passage through a designated area of vessels and aircraft, including those of neutral countries, during conflict. In so doing, these zones *prima facie* impinge on an essential principle that neutral shipping is not to be denied the freedom of navigation on the high seas.[326] During the 1982 Falkland Islands conflict, for example, the UK invoked self-defence to justify its imposition of a 'total exclusion zone' around the Islands, which applied to both Argentine vessels and to any other ships or aircraft operating in support of the Argentine occupation. Any such ships or aircraft found within the zone, without authorization, were to be treated as hostile.[327]

Ostensibly, such action constituted an 'arbitrary interference' with the freedom of navigation and over-flight of aircraft and ships of non-parties to the conflict.[328] Yet, as Fenrick argues, the exclusion zone:

> was a reasonable temporary appropriation of a limited area of the high seas away from major shipping routes for self-defence purposes to prevent non-party clandestine participation in the conflict. The appropriation was accompanied by adequate notice, did not result in any casualties to the ships or aircraft of non-parties, and was terminated after a brief period […] once the British consolidated their position in the Falklands.[329]

Indeed, other than Argentina, only Russia officially protested against the British exclusion zone.[330] Therefore, assuming that there is an enduring defensive necessity that requires such a maritime operation, exclusion zones might be regarded as proportionate measures of self-defence, provided that they are limited, states are notified of their existence and the danger to neutral shipping is kept to a minimum.[331] The imposition of maritime exclusion zones as an act of self-defence

[325] See generally Sandesh Sivakumaran, 'Exclusion Zones in the Law of Armed Conflict at Sea: Evolution in Law and Practice' (2016) Int'l L Stud 153; Upcher, *Neutrality* (n 302) 207–211.

[326] See O'Connell, *The International Law of the Sea* (n 313) 1109–1112.

[327] Letter dated 28 April 1982 from the Permanent Representative of the United Kingdom of Great Britain and Northern Ireland to the United Nations addressed to the President of the Security Council (28 April 1982) UN Doc S/15006.

[328] William J Fenrick, 'The Exclusion Zone Device in the Law of Naval Warfare' (1986) 24 Canadian YBIL 91, 116.

[329] Ibid. Questioning the legality of the zone under the *jus ad bellum*, see Upcher, *Neutrality* (n 302) 209–210.

[330] M Binyon, 'Moscow Rebukes Britain' *The Times* (London, 15 May 1982) 1.

[331] O'Connell, *The International Law of the Sea* (n 313) 1110–1111; Greenwood, 'Self-Defence and the Conduct of International Armed Conflict' (n 14) 285. See further Christopher Michaelsen, 'Maritime Exclusion Zones in Times of Armed Conflict at Sea: Legal Controversies Still Unresolved'

nevertheless continues to occupy an ill-defined position under international law.[332]

The position of neutral states also poses a conundrum for proportionality in the context of the use of nuclear weapons. In *Nuclear Weapons*, the ICJ side-stepped this issue, failing to rule on the legality of the use of nuclear weapons on the basis of the laws of neutrality. It simply noted that the principle of neutrality 'has [. . .] been considered by some to rule out the use of a weapon the effects of which simply cannot be contained within the territories of the contending States'.[333] The issue of the effect of nuclear weapons on neutrality featured more extensively in the separate and dissenting opinions. Judge Shahabuddeen, for example, noted that neutrality was not understood to guarantee neutral states 'absolute immunity from the effects of armed conflict', but it was difficult to justify the use of nuclear weapons given their potentially devastating effects on neutral states.[334]

The consequences for the natural environment, as well as the territory, infrastructure and populations of neutral countries would naturally appear to factor into any assessment of proportionality. It logically follows that such considerations should also apply to all other weapons (biological, chemical and conventional) that might affect neutral states in this way. There is no obvious rationale why the nature of the weapon, rather than its effects, should limit how proportionality should be assessed. Nuclear weapons are simply the extreme example of what those effects might be.[335]

The position of other states, including the issue of neutrality and former belligerent rights, ultimately holds an uncertain place in the proportionality equation.[336] Further elaboration in the practice of states is required in order to draw firm conclusions. Their role in determining proportionality will be contingent on the context, however. Depending on the nature of the incident, other clearer indicators of excess, such as civilian harm, might factor more prominently in the appraisal of defensive action. The foregoing analysis suggests, however, that even if

(2003) 8(2) JC&SL 363, especially 379–380; Federica Paddeu, 'Self-Defence as a Circumstance Precluding Wrongfulness: Understanding Article 21 of the Articles on State Responsibility' (2015) 85 BYIL 90, 129.

332 See generally Michaelsen, 'Maritime Exclusion Zones' (n 331).

333 *Nuclear Weapons* (n 27) para 93.

334 Ibid, diss op Shahabuddeen, 44–46.

335 The likelihood and degree of deleterious transboundary effects are more apparent with nuclear, chemical and biological weapons. The effects of such weapons, by their nature, can be devastating and are harder to control. Yet, the invasion or bombardment of neutral territory with conventional weapons might be equally catastrophic.

336 Gardam maintains that former belligerent rights are not necessarily inconsistent with the right of self-defence and their legality depends on whether they are proportionate. Gardam, 'Proportionality in the War on Terror' (n 186) 23.

the pursuit of a defensive purpose has unavoidable repercussions for such states, it is not the case that defending states may freely prioritize their own defence above all other interests. Depending on the context, third party rights have the potential to limit defensive action. This conclusion is an example of proportionality accounting for how the exercise of self-defence impinges on the wider international community. Drawing on the operation of necessity as a circumstance precluding wrongfulness assists with how we might view the place of these rights within the proportionality equation. The justificatory notion of a 'lesser evil' reflects the balancing exercise that must be carried out between the right of self-defence and other rights that might be impaired by its exercise. This informs whether or not defensive action might be viewed as excessive.

3.3.7 Effect on the Environment

The impact on the environment of states using force is potentially significant.[337] During the 1991 Gulf War, for example, over 500 oil wells were deliberately set on fire and huge quantities of oil were pumped or spilled into the Gulf causing widespread environmental damage.[338] The type of weapons used might also raise environmental concerns. A notable case was the use of Agent Orange (a herbicide and defoliant) during the Vietnam War. More recently, a UN environmental report examined potential contamination caused by depleted uranium munitions during the Kosovo conflict.[339] As noted, in *Nuclear Weapons*, the Court concluded that existing international law does not specifically prohibit the threat or use of nuclear weapons.[340] It also considered that international environmental law should not be construed as depriving a state of its right of self-defence.[341] Nevertheless, it did note the 'powerful constraints' that IHL and international environmental law have placed on those states regarding environmental protection.[342] It insisted that such environmental law indicates 'important environmental factors that are properly to be taken into account in the context of the implementation of the principles and rules of the law applicable in armed conflict'.[343]

[337] See generally Philippe Sands and Jacqueline Peel with Adriana Fabra and Ruth MacKenzie, *Principles of International Environmental Law* (4th edn, CUP 2018) 828–840.

[338] Adam Roberts, 'Environmental Destruction in the 1991 Gulf War' (1992) 291 International Review of the Red Cross 538, 540–541.

[339] United Nations Environment Programme, 'Depleted Uranium in Kosovo: Post-Conflict Environmental Assessment' (2001) <http://postconflict.unep.ch/publications/uranium.pdf> accessed 5 September 2020.

[340] *Nuclear Weapons* (n 27) para 105(B).

[341] Ibid, para 30.

[342] Ibid, para 31. See n 345 and n 346 and accompanying text regarding IHL environmental protections.

[343] Ibid, para 33.

On this basis, the Court held that:

> States must take environmental considerations into account when assessing what is necessary and proportionate in the pursuit of legitimate military objectives. Respect for the environment is one of the elements that go to assessing whether an action is in conformity with the principles of necessity and proportionality.[344]

This paragraph is ambiguous. The reference to 'legitimate military objectives' in the first sentence suggests that environmental considerations relate to an IHL assessment of military necessity and proportionality, whereas the second sentence appears to refer to the *jus ad bellum*. The position remains unclear.

Furthermore, this assertion does not provide detail regarding how to assess the proportionality of a state using nuclear weapons in self-defence. Given the potentially catastrophic and enduring effects that such weapons could have on the natural environment, it is reasonable to conclude that their use can only be proportionate in the most extreme cases (*viz* where the survival of the state is at stake). Yet, if that is so, it might be questioned to what degree the leaders of a state subject to an existential threat would consider themselves under an obligation to respect the environment. How are they to weigh environmental protection against the necessity of protecting their country and their people from what presumably would need to be annihilation? In such circumstances, we might question whether it is truly meaningful to maintain that respect for the environment factors into the calculus.

For *jus ad bellum* proportionality, perhaps environmental considerations carry greater weight and operate as more meaningful limitations on defensive action in the context of the use of conventional weapons. This is to say in situations where the state is not facing an existential threat. In these cases, deploying certain types of conventional weapons might result in devastating environmental consequences, depending on how they are used and to what extent. Therefore, as a general rule, where a defending state has a choice of weapons to deploy to achieve an effective defence, proportionality logically dictates that those weapons that cause the least harm to the environment should be chosen. This conclusion accords with the analysis in the previous section that accounts for the interests of the wider international community that might be affected by a use of defensive force. An act of self-defence is likely to be more easily justified as a 'lesser evil' and not excessive if the impact on the environment (in which the international community in general has an interest) is minimized.

This approach is also in line with the IHL rules that limit the methods and means of warfare. These include the IHL principle of military necessity[345] and API

[344] Ibid, para 30.
[345] See Section 2.2.

that prohibits methods and means of warfare that are intended or may be expected to cause widespread, long-term and severe damage to the natural environment, as well as prohibiting attacks against the natural environment by way of reprisals.[346] In the future, in attempting to identify where the balance should be struck between states pursuing a right of self-defence and protecting the environment, the developing law relating to the latter will undoubtedly influence perceptions of what is proportionate.[347]

3.4 Overlaps and Distinctions

In order to formulate a clear conceptual understanding of *jus ad bellum* proportionality, it is imperative to identify the connections between IHL and the *jus ad bellum* and the distinctions that should be drawn between them. Scholars and states have yet to conquer this difficult challenge. Although scholars often prefer to refer to the more specific rules of IHL when commenting on proportionality, states generally do not distinguish between the two legal frameworks when employing that term.[348] Examining the differences and areas of possible confusion and conflation allows for an enhanced review of the jurisprudence, academic opinion and state practice.

3.4.1 *Jus ad Bellum* Proportionality v IHL Proportionality

IHL and the *jus ad bellum* both regulate a state's use of force. However, on the whole, these are distinct and separate branches of international law. The operation of IHL, for example, does not take account of the legality of a state's use of force under the *jus ad bellum* (*viz* whether self-defence is lawfully established).[349] This autonomy is 'holy gospel'[350] and is '[o]ne of the oldest and best established

346 Protocol Additional to the Geneva Conventions, 12 August 1949, and Relating to the Protection of Victims of International Armed Conflicts, 8 June 1977, 1125 UNTS 3 ('API') Arts 35(3) and 55. See further the ICRC's commentary of 1987 relating to Art 35(3) of API <https://ihl-databases.icrc.org/applic/ihl/ihl.nsf/Comment.xsp?action=openDocument&documentId=2F157A9C651F8B1DC12563CD0043256C> accessed 5 September 2020, paras 1440–1462. More generally on IHL protections of the environment, see Sands and others, *Principles of International Environmental Law* (n 337) 832–836.

347 Gardam, 'Proportionality in the War on Terror' (n 186) 24. For ongoing consideration by the ILC of protecting the environment during armed conflicts, see 'Summaries of the Work of the International Law Commission: Protection of the Environment in Relation to Armed Conflicts' <http://legal.un.org/ilc/summaries/8_7.shtml> accessed 5 September 2020.

348 Ruys, *'Armed Attack'* (n 20) 110–111.

349 The preamble to API (n 346) reaffirms 'that the provisions of the Geneva Conventions of 12 August 1949 and of this Protocol must be fully applied in all circumstances to all persons [. . .] without any adverse distinction based on the nature or origin of the armed conflict or on the causes espoused by or attributed to the Parties to the conflict'.

350 Schmitt, '"Change Direction" 2006' (n 186) 154.

axiomata of international law'.[351] That said, the operation of the one regime has the potential to influence the understanding of the other.[352] For present purposes, both systems of law share the concept of proportionality, but its role in each is different, as are the variables against which the relevant type of proportionality is measured.

As will be explored in more detail in Section 3.5, *jus ad bellum* proportionality measures the defending state's response *as a whole* primarily against its defensive purpose. This assessment also takes into account material factors such as resulting civilian harm and the impact of such response on wider third-party interests. In contrast, IHL proportionality requires an assessment of whether the expected civilian loss or injury, or damage to civilian objects, in each case resulting from a particular planned attack, would be excessive in relation to the concrete and direct military advantage anticipated.[353] This rule places an obligation on those planning attacks to assess the proportionality of their individual targeting decisions. Proportionality at this operational level employs different variables to *jus ad bellum* proportionality. Whereas *jus ad bellum* proportionality balances the defending state's total use of force against its overall defensive purpose and wider third-party interests, IHL proportionality balances anticipated collateral damage (being to civilians and civilian objects) against the expected outcome of specific attacks (that form part of the overall defensive operation).[354] The UK Military

[351] Terry D Gill, 'The *Nuclear Weapons* Advisory Opinion of the International Court of Justice and the Fundamental Distinction Between the *Jus ad Bellum* and the *Jus in Bello*' (1999) 12(3) LJIL 613, 614. For examples of commentary on this long debated and controversial topic, see Jasmine Moussa, 'Can *Jus ad Bellum* Override *Jus in Bello*? Reaffirming the Separation of the Two Bodies of Law' (2008) 90 International Review of the Red Cross 963; Van Steenberghe, 'Proportionality' (n 24); Okimoto, 'The Cumulative Requirements of *Jus ad Bellum* and *Jus in Bello*' (n 36). See also paras 215–216 of the ICRC's commentary of 2016 on the First Geneva Convention relating to Art 2 <https://ihl-databases.icrc.org/applic/ihl/ihl.nsf/Comment.xsp?action=openDocument&documentId=BE2D518CF5DE54EAC1257F7D0036B518> accessed 5 September 2020.

[352] See, for example, Section 2.6, including analysis of the meanings of 'military target', 'military objectives' and 'military advantage'.

[353] This core principle of IHL is encapsulated in Art 51(5)(b) of API (n 346). If collateral damage is expected to be excessive, then an attack is to be cancelled, suspended or re-planned. API, Arts 57(2)(a)(iii) and (2)(b).

[354] It is generally understood that collateral damage is assessed in relation to the anticipated military advantage from the attack as a whole and not only from isolated or particular parts of that attack. Ten contracting states (Australia, Belgium, Canada, France, Germany, Italy, the Netherlands, New Zealand, Spain and the UK) made formal declarations that the expression 'military advantage' employed in Arts 51, 52 and 57 of API (n 346) (as applicable) has this meaning. See the ICRC database relating to API: <https://ihl-databases.icrc.org/applic/ihl/ihl.nsf/States.xsp?xp_viewStates=XPages_NORMStatesParties&xp_treatySelected=470> accessed 5 September 2020. However, '"attack as a whole" is not used as meaning the whole military campaign that may be conducted in self-defence but rather as referring at best to a series of military actions which are part of the individual attack launched in the framework of such a campaign'. Van Steenberghe, 'Proportionality' (n 24) 116. See also Yoram Dinstein, *The Conduct of Hostilities under the Law of International Armed Conflict* (2nd edn, CUP 2010) 94–95.

Manual is but one resource that notes the importance of this distinction between the two regimes.[355]

Therefore, proportionality in the *jus ad bellum* operates at the macro level. It is concerned with the big picture and the totality of the wider defensive response. It is not concerned with single acts of force, unless such acts constitute evidence of a shift in the overall scale or scope of that response.[356] Proportionality in the *jus ad bellum* relates primarily to the generalities of self-defence, operating to protect against 'excessive overall reactions' by states.[357] The logic of this conclusion is based on the fact that uses of force that are uncontained and go beyond what is strictly necessary for states to protect themselves are likely to be disruptive to the international legal order. This goes back to the point made in Section 1.6.1 and this chapter more generally that proportionality accounts for, and seeks to balance, the interests of a number of different actors, including those of the wider international community. Accordingly, it has been suggested that the ultimate rationale of *jus ad bellum* proportionality (over and above proscribing excessive uses of force against the attacker) is the maintenance of international peace and security.[358] This conclusion is supported by the analysis set out in Section 3.3 regarding how essential interests of the international community are accounted for in determining whether defensive responses are excessive.

In contrast, IHL proportionality focuses on the micro level. Its purview is one-off incidents, being the specifics of individual targeting decisions. It requires a 'concrete and direct military advantage' from each and every military action to ensure that such use of force is not excessive in relation to civilian harm resulting from the particular attack (that forms part of the overall defensive operation). As such, whilst much of the decision making for the purposes of the *jus ad bellum* will be made strategically at the state level, the majority of the decision making that is relevant to the IHL calculus will happen much lower down the chain of command.[359]

Therefore, the rationale of IHL proportionality is not tied to the international order and the minimization of the use of force between states. Its purview is more localized and short term. Its primary concern is the effect of such force on individuals, not the effect on states in any abstract sense.[360] It offers humanitarian

[355] UK Military Manual (n 53) Section 2.8.

[356] The Chatham House Principles (n 36) 969; Ruys, *'Armed Attack'* (n 20) 110; Lubell, 'Comments on David Kretzmer' (n 4); Henderson, *The Use of Force and International Law* (n 26) 234. See further Section 3.3.1.

[357] Nolte and Randelzhofer, 'Ch.VII Action' (n 36) 1427.

[358] Greenwood, 'Self-Defence and the Conduct of International Armed Conflict' (n 14) 278; Gardam, *Necessity, Proportionality* (n 8) 16; Van Steenberghe, 'Proportionality' (n 24) 118–119.

[359] Gardam, *Necessity, Proportionality* (n 8) 21. See also Lubell, 'Comments on David Kretzmer' (n 4), noting the macro/micro distinction between IHL and the *jus ad bellum*.

[360] An exception that does account for protection of wider interests and international society more generally are the IHL rules pertaining to protection of cultural property. For an overview of these rules, see Roger O'Keefe, 'Protection of Cultural Property' in Clapham and Gaeta (eds), *The Oxford Handbook of International Law in Armed Conflict* (n 36) 492.

protection on an equal basis to all sides in a conflict, focusing on minimizing damage and suffering of non-combatants to the greatest degree possible during the exigencies of war.[361] It seeks at the micro level to balance the two cardinal principles of IHL: military necessity and humanity.[362] Consequently, the function, make up and rationale of proportionality in each regime are markedly different.[363]

It is understandable that the distinction between IHL and *jus ad bellum* proportionality is not always so readily apparent. After all, both legal regimes govern a state's use of force, acting to constrain it. Yet, although a breach of, or compliance with, one regime might lead to the same result in the other, this is not automatic. Starting with the effect of IHL violations on the *jus ad bellum*, it is perhaps reasonable to conclude that a violation of IHL proportionality indicates that *jus ad bellum* proportionality is also breached.[364] This might be the case, but a breach of IHL proportionality will not violate *jus ad bellum* proportionality as a matter of course. It would be illogical to conclude, for example, that a violation of IHL proportionality early on in a long defensive campaign renders the whole operation disproportionate under the *jus ad bellum*.[365]

This conclusion is based on the fact that the rules of IHL and the *jus ad bellum* operate at different levels. As IHL proportionality operates at the micro level of individual decision-making, a one-off or small number of IHL disproportionate targeting decision(s) might *or might not* render the whole defensive operation disproportionate at the macro level, where proportionality in the *jus ad bellum* operates. A 'global calculation' of excessiveness at the *jus ad bellum* level might accommodate individual instances of excess at the IHL level.[366] This will depend on the severity and number of IHL breaches when considered in the context of the overall defensive campaign. Where there are systematic rather than exceptional

[361] Greenwood, 'Self-Defence and the Conduct of International Armed Conflict' (n 14) 278; Van Steenberghe, 'Proportionality' (n 24) 118–119; Nolte and Randelzhofer, 'Ch.VII Action' (n 36) 1427; Okimoto, 'The Cumulative Requirements of *Jus ad Bellum* and *Jus in Bello*' (n 36) 49.

[362] See *Nuclear Weapons* (n 27) para 78.

[363] Van Steenberghe, 'Proportionality' (n 24) 115–118, refers to the distinction described in this paragraph as the 'general versus particular' dichotomy. For similar conclusions and further analysis, see further Akande, 'Nuclear Weapons' (n 36) 191–192; The Chatham House Principles (n 36) 969; Cannizzaro, 'Contextualizing Proportionality' (n 162) 786; Moussa, 'Can *Jus ad Bellum* Override *Jus in Bello*?' (n 351) 976–978; Okimoto, 'The Cumulative Requirements of *Jus ad Bellum* and *Jus in Bello*' (n 36).

[364] Van Steenberghe, 'Proportionality' (n 24) 117.

[365] Greenwood has suggested that an act that contravenes IHL cannot be a 'reasonable and proportionate measure of self-defence' under the *jus ad bellum*. Christopher Greenwood, 'The Relationship Between *Jus ad Bellum* and *Jus in Bello*' (1983) 9 Rev Int'l Stud 221, 231. However, he also accepts that neither body of law is logically dependent on the other. Given the logic of the latter conclusion, and the analysis set out in this section, it is this author's position that a contravention of IHL does not always breach the rules of the *jus ad bellum*.

[366] This conclusion assumes that targeting is *prima facie* lawful under both the *jus ad bellum* and IHL. As noted in Section 2.6.2, a lack of specific necessity is also likely to result in the absence of a 'military advantage' for the purpose of IHL. This denies targeting under both bodies of law. In such cases, an act of targeting can be neither IHL nor *jus ad bellum* proportionate. It will simply be unlawful under both legal regimes.

violations of IHL proportionality, these violations might also result in a breach of *jus ad bellum* proportionality. Consistent violations of IHL proportionality resulting in excessive civilian damage (weighed against a concrete and direct military advantage) will likely indicate that defence is not the aim of the military campaign.

Likewise, adherence to the IHL rules of proportionality on all individual targeting decisions during a defensive campaign might indicate *jus ad bellum* compliance, especially where collateral civilian harm is minimized in each case. Yet, such compliance might still breach *jus ad bellum* proportionality if, *on an overall assessment*, the combination of uses of force is excessive in relation to the defensive purpose.[367] Everything depends on how a specific act of targeting fits within the bigger defensive picture. This will be decided on a case-by-case basis. The Ethiopia-Eritrea Claims Commission followed this logic when, in adhering to the strict distinction between the *jus ad bellum* and IHL, it concluded that compliance with IHL does not preclude a breach of the *jus ad bellum*.[368] However, although a breach of IHL proportionality might not lead to a breach of *jus ad bellum* proportionality, it still constitutes a breach of IHL. It is an unlawful act that must not be carried out or, if in progress, must cease immediately. As such, depending on the circumstances, it may attract both state responsibility and individual criminal responsibility.[369]

Conversely, it has been suggested that compliance with *jus ad bellum* proportionality might prevent an attack on a target that would otherwise be lawful under IHL. Gardam proposes the example of an electricity grid that, she argues, might be targetable under IHL, but the destruction of which might be excessive in relation to achieving the aims of self-defence (thereby constituting a breach of *jus ad bellum* proportionality).[370] However, as explored in Section 2.6 and in this section, to be targetable under the *jus ad bellum*, specific necessity must first be satisfied. Specific necessity requires a connection between the armed attack and the defensive response (in this example, being the destruction of the electricity grid). To be targetable under IHL, there must also be a 'military advantage' to destroying the grid. If the grid is not connected with an armed attack, it is unlikely to offer a

[367] Greenwood, 'Self-Defence and the Conduct of International Armed Conflict' (n 14) 279, reaching a similar conclusion. See also Gardam, *Necessity, Proportionality* (n 8) 11; Okimoto, 'The Cumulative Requirements of *Jus ad Bellum* and *Jus in Bello*' (n 36) 58; Kretzmer, 'Proportionality in *Jus Ad Bellum*' (n 29) 278.

[368] 'If [...] a State initiating a conflict through a breach of the [*jus ad bellum*] is liable under international law for a wide range of ensuing consequences, the initiating State will bear extensive liability whether or not its actions respect [IHL]. Indeed, much of the damage for which Ethiopia claims [*jus ad bellum*] compensation involves conduct that the Commission previously found to be consistent with [IHL].' *Eritrea-Ethiopia Claims Commission—Final Award—Ethiopia's Damages Claims* (17 August 2009) Volume XXVI RIAA 631, para 316.

[369] See further below in this section and Section 3.5 regarding the ongoing and concurrent application of the *jus ad bellum* and IHL.

[370] Gardam, *Necessity, Proportionality* (n 8) 168–169.

'military advantage' during a defensive operation.[371] Consequently, the grid will not likely be targetable under IHL or the *jus ad bellum*. For the *jus ad bellum*, however, it is the operation of specific necessity and not proportionality that leads to this conclusion.

Therefore, the instinctive link between the two types of proportionality must be approached with caution. A contributor to any potential conflation or confusion is that IHL and *jus ad bellum* proportionality share common, ultimately humanitarian, characteristics. Both account for how force affects civilians and civilian objects and, thereby, seek to minimize civilian harm. As noted in Section 3.3.5, states often focus on this point when referring to proportionality and tend not to distinguish between IHL proportionality and *jus ad bellum* proportionality when so doing. This conflation, unhelpfully for those seeking conceptual clarity, leads to 'a sort of global assessment of proportionality'.[372]

Albeit that civilian harm is the principal variable against which the concrete and direct military advantage anticipated is measured for the purposes of IHL proportionality, it is only one of a number of factors and interests that go to whether a purported defensive purpose satisfies *jus ad bellum* proportionality. IHL proportionality is not concerned, for example, with broader considerations such as the effect on other states, including a host state where acts of self-defence are carried out against NSAs within its territory.[373] IHL incorporates environmental protections, but they are not a feature of IHL proportionality.[374] Moreover, as noted above, the *jus ad bellum* will review overall collateral civilian damage (and all the other aspects of proportionality discussed above) from the perspective of the defensive military operation as a whole, rather than in respect of each individual part of that operation, which is the purview of IHL.

The ICJ has contributed to the confusion regarding the distinction between the *jus ad bellum* and IHL by potentially suggesting that compliance with *jus ad bellum* proportionality is dependent upon conformity with IHL. In *Nuclear Weapons*, the Court stated that:

> a use of force that is proportionate under the law of self-defence, must, in order to be lawful, also meet the requirements of the law applicable in armed

[371] See Section 2.6.2. For differing views of how *jus ad bellum* proportionality and *jus in bello* proportionality interaction might relate to military advantage, see Eliav Lieblich, 'On the Continuous and Concurrent Application of *Ad Bellum* and *In Bello* Proportionality' in Claus Kress and Robert Lawless (eds), *Necessity and Proportionality in International Peace and Security Law* (OUP forthcoming 2020) 19–22 (page reference to manuscript available on SSRN: <https://papers.ssrn.com/sol3/papers.cfm?abstract_id=3284411> accessed 5 September 2020).

[372] Cannizzaro, 'Proportionality in the Law of Armed Conflict' (n 36) 348.

[373] This is not to say that these considerations are irrelevant for the purposes of IHL. The point is that they are not relevant to a calculation of IHL proportionality. See further Section 4.3.3.

[374] See Section 3.3.7. The environment more generally does not factor as a third-party interest in IHL proportionality as it might do in *jus ad bellum* proportionality, even though it is a protected interest under separate IHL prohibitions.

conflict which comprise in particular the principles and rules of humanitarian law.[375]

This passage might be interpreted to mean that in order for self-defence to be *jus ad bellum* proportionate, it must comply with IHL, including IHL proportionality.[376] This unnecessarily conflates the *jus ad bellum* and IHL, however.[377] The better view is that, *in order to be lawful*, any use of defensive force must be *jus ad bellum* proportionate and also comply with IHL. The UK adopted this conclusion in its statement to the Court.[378]

On this interpretation, to be a lawful use of force, the requirements of both the *jus ad bellum* and IHL (including proportionality in each) must be met, but independently.[379] There is support for this position in the *Nuclear Weapons* judgment itself. Compliance with the two regimes is set out separately and independently in the *dispositif*[380] and is also considered on this basis in the declaration of President Bedjaoui,[381] as well as several separate and dissenting opinions.[382] As such, the *jus ad bellum* and IHL should be regarded as imposing cumulative obligations whilst remaining as two essentially separate and independent bodies of international law.[383] Any suggestion that the *jus ad bellum* is subordinated to IHL, such that compliance with the former depends on adhering to the latter, fails to recognize the fundamental distinction between the two.[384]

375 *Nuclear Weapons* (n 27) para 42.

376 Kevin Jon Heller, 'The Use and Abuse of Analogy in IHL' in Jens David Ohlin (ed), *Theoretical Boundaries of Armed Conflict and Human Rights* (CUP 2016) 232, 252.

377 Moussa, 'Can *Jus ad Bellum* Override *Jus in Bello*?' (n 351) 974–977.

378 'Assuming that a State's use of nuclear weapons meets the requirements of self-defence, it must then be considered whether it conforms to the fundamental principles of the law of armed conflict regulating the conduct of hostilities.' *Nuclear Weapons* (n 27) Letter dated 16 June 1995 from the Legal Adviser to the Foreign and Commonwealth Office of the United Kingdom of Great Britain and Northern Ireland, together with Written Comments of the United Kingdom, 40 (para 3.44).

379 Moussa, 'Can *Jus ad Bellum* Override *Jus in Bello*?' (n 351) 975. See also Christopher Greenwood, 'International Law and the 'War Against Terrorism' (2002) 78 Int'l Aff (UK) 301, 313–314; Kretzmer, 'Proportionality in *Jus Ad Bellum*' (n 29) 240; Cannizzaro, 'Proportionality in the Law of Armed Conflict' (n 36) 347–348; Terry D Gill, 'Classifying the Conflict in Syria' (2016) 92 Int'l L Stud 353, 369.

380 *Nuclear Weapons* (n 27) paras 105(C), 105(D).

381 Ibid, declaration of President Bedjaoui, para 22.

382 Ibid, sep op Ranjeva, 301, 303; sep op Fleischhauer, paras 3, 5; diss op Shahabuddeen, 426–427; diss op Weeramantry, 519 (although, see also diss op Weeramantry, 514, which suggests a less clear separation); diss op Koroma, 562. See also sep op Guillaume, para 8, for some more nuanced views on this issue.

383 Gill, 'The *Nuclear Weapons* Advisory Opinion' (n 351) 618, 623; Van Steenberghe, 'Proportionality' (n 24) 115, 117; Okimoto, 'The Cumulative Requirements of *Jus ad Bellum* and *Jus in Bello*' (n 36) 50, 57, 70. As noted, this is subject to the interaction between the *jus ad bellum* and IHL on the issue of targeting. See Section 2.6.2.

384 For further discussion of this case and the relationship between IHL and the *jus ad bellum*, see Akande, 'Nuclear Weapons' (n 36); Gill, 'The Nuclear Weapons Advisory Opinion' (n 351); Moussa, 'Can *Jus ad Bellum* Override *Jus in Bello*?' (n 351); Van Steenberghe, 'Proportionality' (n 24) 121–123.

3.4.2 *Jus ad Bellum* Proportionality v *Jus ad Bellum* Necessity

Adopting the teleological or 'means-end' model as the primary determinant of proportionality emphasizes the rapport that necessity has with proportionality and explains the risk of conflation between the two. As Kretzmer rightly notes, '[m]eans can only be proportionate when they are necessary to achieve the legitimate ends'.[385] The result is a possible understanding of proportionality that 'the level of force used is not greater than that necessary to end the attack or remove the threat. As such it is another way of looking at the requirement of necessity'.[386] This conclusion brings us back to the conceptual circularity that exists between these two customary requirements.

3.4.2.1 Proportionality and General Necessity

This circularity and the potential for conflation between necessity and proportionality is limited, however. As initially set out in Section 2.3, understanding necessity and proportionality to be equivalent is only theoretically possible as between specific necessity and proportionality. There can be no conflation between proportionality and general necessity. The two are conceptually distinct. This can be explained as follows. If, following an armed attack, self-defence (in any form) is deemed unnecessary, such conclusion must result from a lack of general necessity. This might be because peaceful alternative means are available to resolve the situation, or the UNSC takes effective action to resolve it. In such circumstances, where there is no *prima facie* need for a state to act in self-defence, it is meaningless to say that a use of force is also disproportionate. Absent general necessity, any recourse to force is simply unlawful. An assessment of proportionality, as against a defensive aim, cannot be made as such aim is lacking. Consideration of specific necessity is also impossible in such circumstances.

If, in the alternative, some form of defensive response is necessary (for example, because peaceful options are not available and/or were unsuccessfully pursued, and/or the UNSC has not taken effective action), then it is meaningful to assess the proportionality of a defensive operation. This is because, once general necessity is satisfied, a defensive purpose is present. The two concepts function very differently, however. General necessity requires an assessment of whether any force is required to respond to an armed attack. Proportionality requires that the total force deployed (as a result of that general necessity) is not excessive. In summary, therefore, a use of force that satisfies general necessity may be proportionate or

385 Kretzmer, 'Proportionality in *Jus Ad Bellum*' (n 29) 239. See also Corten, *The Law Against War* (n 36) 488.

386 The Chatham House Principles (n 36) 969. See also Ruys, '*Armed Attack*' (n 20) 112; Kress, 'The International Court of Justice' (n 161) 587; Henderson, *The Use of Force and International Law* (n 26) 237.

disproportionate. However, a use of force that does not pass the general necessity test can be neither.

3.4.2.2 Proportionality and Specific Necessity

To address the potential conflation issue, we must examine the relationship between proportionality and specific necessity. To understand proportionality, and to identify distinctions between it and specific necessity, it is important to appreciate where any overlap might exist. The principal factor that might lead to a conclusion that defensive force is both 'necessary and proportionate', or 'unnecessary and disproportionate', is the nature of the targets of self-defence. As set out in Section 2.6, this book argues that specific necessity requires that such targets be military in nature (in line with IHL 'military objectives') and, in addition, be connected with the armed attack (thereby establishing a defensive purpose). The question is accordingly whether the nature of the target also factors in the proportionally equation.

The ICJ in *Oil Platforms*, in referring to both necessity and proportionality, stated that '[o]ne aspect of these criteria is the nature of the target of the force used avowedly in self-defence'.[387] Some commentators interpret this to mean that proportionality also requires the target to have a connection with the armed attack.[388] Others state that proportionality, like necessity, requires the target to be of a military nature.[389] The result of this approach is to conclude that both specific necessity and proportionality impose an identical limitation on the choice of targets. Such conclusion requires further examination.

As noted, following an armed attack and the satisfaction of general necessity, specific necessity must be established before a proportionality assessment is possible.[390] Where specific necessity is absent (for example, because the target is not military and/or not connected with the armed attack), *ipso facto* a use of force cannot possess a defensive purpose. It is meaningless in such cases to say that an unnecessary incident of targeting is also disproportionate. It will simply be an unlawful use of force. As an example, let us consider targets that are *prima facie* unnecessary for the purposes of the *jus ad bellum*. Obvious candidates are civilians and civilian objects that, by definition, are not (and cannot be) legitimate targets connected to the armed attack.[391] Targeting them directly is not capable of serving

[387] *Oil Platforms* (n 25) para 74.

[388] Okimoto, 'The Cumulative Requirements of *Jus ad Bellum* and *Jus in Bello*' (n 36) 64. Ruys asserts that as well as forming part of the necessity criterion, targeting 'equally fits into the proportionality framework.' Ruys, '*Armed Attack*' (n 20) 121.

[389] Sina Etezazian, 'The Nature of the Self-Defence Proportionality Requirement' (2016) 3(2) JUFIL 260, 284–288. Although, to the extent his analysis relates to proportionality, such conclusion appears to focus largely on the resulting civilian harm.

[390] See Sections 1.6.1 and 2.6.1.

[391] As set out in Section 2.6, this assumes that civilians are not directly participating in hostilities and that civilian objects are not being used for military purposes.

a defensive purpose and will always be unnecessary under the *jus ad bellum*, as well as constituting unlawful acts under IHL.[392] This conclusion, so far as it relates to the *jus ad bellum*, is not reached on the basis of a particular prohibition under that regime. The *jus ad bellum* contains no such specific rules. Rather, the conclusion is deduced from the general principles that logically flow from the foregoing analysis.[393] The ensuing question is whether such unnecessary targeting may also rightly be labelled as disproportionate.

Green and Waters suggest that it may be so labelled. In asserting that targeting is also inherent in the proportionality requirement, they argue that 'it is unlikely that a direct attack on a civilian target will be anything other than "excessive" when measured against the state's defensive need'.[394] Therefore, there is a potential argument to be made that targeting decisions may lead to a determination of defensive force being both unnecessary and disproportionate. Despite Green and Waters' conclusion being instinctively appealing, it is problematic. This is because, in the case of targeting civilians, there is no defensive need against which proportionality can be assessed. The difficulty lies in the order in which the necessity and proportionality evaluations are made. By considering necessity first, as this book argues we must do, the requirement of proportionality in such circumstances is rendered inapplicable. On this basis, where specific necessity is absent, as is the case with attacking a civilian target, a use of force cannot be proportionate, but neither can it be disproportionate.

Where specific necessity is present (because the target is military and connected to the armed attack) the applicability of proportionality is clear. The resulting harm caused by attacking a target that is specifically necessary can either be proportionate or disproportionate (when measured against the overarching defensive

[392] As a caveat, Green and Waters argue that the *jus ad bellum* rules on civilian targeting are not absolute in the same way as they are in IHL. James A Green and Christopher PM Waters, 'Military Targeting in the Context of Self-Defence Actions' 84 (2015) Nord J Int'l L 3, 23–24. The authors highlight that necessity and proportionality are relative criteria, to be assessed by reference to the defensive needs of the state. As such, in extreme situations of defensive need, such as where the very survival of the state is threatened (as recognized by the ICJ in *Nuclear Weapons* (n 27) paras 96–97), then their position is that attacking a civilian target would meet the necessity and proportionality requirements. They accept that such instances would be rare and that targeting in this way would still be unlawful under IHL. Nevertheless, their conclusion regarding the *jus ad bellum* seems hard to reconcile with the *Oil Platforms* (n 25) decision, however, and the general proposition that targets must be military. The use of nuclear weapons might well be necessary and proportionate in such *in extremis* circumstances, allowing for the targeting of a *military target* that leads to high levels of civilian collateral damage (which is a proportionality consideration). However, there is nothing in the ICJ jurisprudence, or the logic inherent in the necessity criterion, that would allow for the deliberate targeting of civilians or civilian objects in these circumstances.

[393] As Okimoto rightly notes, the *jus ad bellum* is silent as to which types of persons and objects may be attacked in self-defence, as well as regarding which weapons can or cannot be used. Okimoto, 'The Cumulative Requirements of *Jus ad Bellum* and *Jus in Bello*' (n 36) 69. It is rather IHL that provides these detailed rules. However, such rule is inherent in the requirement that self-defence is both necessary and proportionate.

[394] Green and Waters, 'Military Targeting' (n 392) 11–12. See also Okimoto, 'The Cumulative Requirements of *Jus ad Bellum* and *Jus in Bello*' (n 36) 65.

purpose and accounting for the various factors referred to in this chapter).[395] Therefore, it is unfortunate that the ICJ in *Oil Platforms* was not clearer on how the 'nature of the target' pertains to the requirements of necessity and proportionality separately. It did not offer any analysis regarding what relevance this has in practice for proportionality, or how the two requirements might be applied jointly to issues of targeting.[396]

If the concern that the Court and certain commentators are attempting to address is the *result* of an act of targeting, this is indeed a matter for proportionality. However, such concern does not relate to the nature of the target per se, but rather the consequence of targeting, including the ensuing collateral damage.[397] Gardam argues, for example, that proportionality regulates, *inter alia*, the 'means and methods of warfare' and the 'targets that are available to States in the exercise of [the right of self-defence]'.[398] Yet, she goes on to argue that, integral to decisions relating to these two factors, are the anticipated *scale of the damage and destruction that result from these decisions*.[399] These latter comments reflect the foregoing analysis that shows that proportionality's purview is the overall defensive picture, not the minutiae. As set out in Section 3.3.1, proportionality should not be understood as limiting the methods and means of warfare, nor should it limit the nature of the targets. Proportionality evaluates whether or not the total resulting harm caused by the methods and means of defence and targeting decisions are excessive in relation to the defensive purpose and other affected interests.

As such, both necessity and proportionality are measured against a defensive purpose, and might risk being conflated on this basis, but their respective purposes and operation are very different. Specific necessity relates to targeting. Proportionality evaluates the outcomes of all instances of (specifically necessary) acts of targeting and whether or not they are excessive. Determining the specific necessity of an act of targeting comes before, and is separate to, whether the consequences of that act are proportionate. This does not mean that proportionality is limited to a *post facto* assessment, but rather that both requirements are to be reviewed constantly, and in this order. Along similar lines, IHL sets out rules that relate to the definition of a 'military objective' for the purposes of targeting and separate rules that pertain to proportionality, the analysis of which is a consequence of targeting. For *jus ad bellum* proportionality, the relevance of the choice

395 Cf Gray, *Use of Force* (n 36) 159, who argues that if a use of force is 'not proportionate, it is difficult to see how it can be necessary'.

396 Even if the taxonomy adopted by this book is not accepted, including the distinction between 'specific' and 'general' necessity, it is evident that the nature of the target and its connection with an armed attack is an issue for necessity broadly defined. If there is no rational connection between the act(s) of self-defence and the armed attack, such force cannot be necessary. In the crudest sense, proportionality then considers everything else in assessing the overall defensive response, including the outcomes of that use of defensive force.

397 Cf Etezazian, 'The Nature of the Self-Defence Proportionality Requirement' (n 389) 25–28.

398 Gardam 'Proportionality in the War on Terror' (n 186) 18.

399 Ibid (emphasis added).

of weapons, and where they are targeted, is that the ensuing outcome must remain within the confines of a truly defensive response. If the resort to a particular weapon or targeting strategy represents a considerable escalation of hostilities, it is not the choice of weapon and/or target in and of itself that might fail the test of proportionality, but rather the fact of that escalation.[400]

3.5 Overall Assessment and Enduring Application

Dinstein argues that in certain circumstances assessing proportionality might be a one-off decision, rather than applying throughout hostilities. He proposes a right for states to wage an all-out 'war of self-defence' against armed attacks of a 'critical character' that justify such a response.[401] In wars of self-defence, the argument goes, proportionality is a threshold question. It applies solely to the initial decision to go to war: is a defensive war proportionate to the 'critical' armed attack? After that, the applicability of proportionality falls away. Once a war of self-defence has started, Dinstein maintains that the defending state may destroy the attacker's army or bring about the complete collapse of the enemy, regardless of the condition of proportionality.[402] This allows the defensive war to be carried out in a manner, and to an extent, that might greatly exceed both the attack that provoked it and the defensive need.

Lubell and Cohen have also questioned whether states accept that the *jus ad bellum* (as it currently stands) applies throughout the conflict. They suggest that 'once the conflict has begun, the parties will likely operate under the assumption they can use as much force as they want, and cause as much damage as they see fit, so long as they do not violate a specific rule of IHL'.[403] These authors do not provide any state practice to support this conclusion, however. Indeed, the state practice and associated analysis referenced throughout this chapter points to the contrary.[404] There is nothing to suggest that proportionality is restricted such that it does not regulate the entirety of a conflict. In his resolute defence of the continuous application of the *jus ad bellum*, Lieblich rightly notes that most commentators reject a static view of proportionality, instead favouring some form of continuous

[400] See Gardam 'Proportionality in the War on Terror' (n 186) 20. See further Sections 2.6 and 3.3.1.

[401] Dinstein, *War, Aggression and Self-Defence* (n 29) 282–283. He accepts that such right does not apply to armed attacks 'short of war', however.

[402] Ibid, 282–284.

[403] Noam Lubell and Amichai Cohen, 'Strategic Proportionality: Limitations on the Use of Force in Modern Armed Conflicts' (2020) 96 Int'l L Stud 159, 171–172. In advocating for a new concept of 'strategic proportionality', however, they submit (at 193) 'that the overall effects of the conflict measured in relation to the strategic objectives gained must be reevaluated continuously throughout the armed conflict'. They maintain this approach accords with common practice.

[404] See in particular the analysis regarding state concern with civilian harm in Section 3.3.5.

application of proportionality throughout the duration of hostilities prompted by self-defence.[405] This author agrees.

Any suggestion that proportionality is abrogated following a decision to go to war in self-defence is extremely concerning. It may be the case that an armed attack constituted by an all-out invasion requires the defending state to respond in kind, up to and including the total vanquishing of the attacking state. This might be required by the defensive purpose and the overarching teleological model of proportionality still properly describes and regulates such defensive necessity and its boundaries. We might also envisage scenarios where a defensive response of a significant magnitude is required to respond to armed attacks of a lesser magnitude. For example, a full-scale defensive war might be necessary to halt and prevent a series of minor attacks over a sustained period of time. Again, despite any quantitative imbalance vis-à-vis individual armed attacks, the overarching teleological model provides for a proper analytical assessment of the proportionality of this scenario. Yet, it is untenable to do away with the requirement of proportionality altogether once a defensive war has begun.

In the *jus ad bellum*, proportionality measures the defending state's response *as a whole*. It is concerned with the defending state's wider defensive operation.[406] In *Oil Platforms*, the Court confirmed that it 'cannot assess in isolation the proportionality of [a specific defensive act] to the attack to which it was said to be a response; it cannot close its eyes to the scale of the whole [defensive] operation.'[407] It is for this reason, as much as any other, that adherence to proportionality must be understood as an enduring requirement that applies throughout the entirety of a conflict arising out of an exercise of self-defence.[408] Evaluating the proportionality of a defensive response is only possible by reference to a period of time during which such response is occurring or, if the conflict is over, has occurred. It should not be viewed as relating solely to the initial decision to deploy defensive force, before handing over to IHL to govern the conduct of ongoing hostilities.[409]

Proportionality continues to apply even if the state is facing an existential threat. In *Nuclear Weapons*, the ICJ reaffirmed its application to acts of self-defence 'whatever the means of force employed',[410] specifically stating that proportionality may not exclude the use of nuclear weapons in self-defence in all circumstances.[411] It did not say that proportionality was inapplicable. Rather, the Court envisages an extreme situation of self-defence, where the very survival of

[405] Lieblich, '*Ad Bellum* and *In Bello* Proportionality' (n 371) 5–6 (page reference to SSRN manuscript).
[406] See further Section 3.4.1.
[407] *Oil Platforms* (n 25) para 77.
[408] Greenwood, 'The Relationship Between *Jus ad Bellum* and *Jus in Bello*' (n 365) 223; Gardam 'Proportionality in the War on Terror' (n 186) 5. See further Sections 3.4 and 3.5.
[409] See Section 3.4.1 regarding the joint application of IHL and the distinction between *jus ad bellum* proportionality and IHL proportionality.
[410] *Nuclear Weapons* (n 27) para 41.
[411] Ibid, para 42.

the state is at stake, where a defensive use of nuclear weapons might be considered proportionate.[412] Proportionality might be difficult, or even impossible, to measure or quantify in such circumstances.[413] Yet, the majority's conclusions in *Nuclear Weapons* point to an acceptance that a use of such a devastating weapon is permissible in order to fulfil the ultimate purpose of the right of self-defence, being the 'continued existence of its beneficiary'.[414] Even if one may disagree with the notion that the use of nuclear weapons can ever satisfy proportionality, the judgment reinforces the fact that, even in the most extreme of situations, it still has a role to play. The majority of the Court, and seemingly the states connected with the judgment, all accepted that the law continues to regulate conduct.[415]

As an enduring requirement, defensive action must be continuously monitored by the defending state to ensure that it is and remains proportionate and, *ipso facto*, lawful.[416] This *jus ad bellum* evaluation should run alongside monitoring of IHL compliance. It is notable that the rules relating to IHL proportionality themselves impose an ongoing obligation to appraise potential collateral damage and require the taking of precautions in attack.[417] It is logical that both regimes impose a similar obligation regarding the need to evaluate proportionality on a rolling basis, even if the meaning of such term in each regime is different.[418] Only when viewed in this way does *jus ad bellum* proportionality have the capacity to constrain defensive action. This enduring obligation means that proportionality in the *jus ad bellum* may operate to capture, at any point in time during an ongoing act of self-defence, 'a snapshot of the big picture'.[419] This snapshot necessarily involves retrospective, current and prospective elements. This is to ask what action has the defending state taken up until the point that the snapshot is taken (*viz* when the assessment of proportionality is being made), what is the state currently doing, and what will it need to do prospectively, in each case to meet its defensive objective?

The importance of the snapshot approach is likely to be realized as a practical decision-making tool. It can aid the defending state to take stock, assess the current situation, and then look forward and plan its ongoing defensive strategy. It enables, and requires, the defending state to determine what next steps may be taken to halt,

412 That both necessity and proportionality continue to apply to an exercise of self-defence using nuclear weapons, see *Nuclear Weapons* (n 27) diss op Shahabuddeen, 427.

413 *Nuclear Weapons* (n 27) diss op Weeramantry, 515.

414 Van Steenberghe, 'Proportionality' (n 24) 122. Akande likewise believes that '[i]t is difficult to hold that if the use of nuclear weapons is the *only* way of repelling an aggressor, that use is disproportionate to the objective of legitimate self-defence'. Akande, 'Nuclear Weapons' (n 36) 193.

415 *Nuclear Weapons* (n 27) para 22. That states explicitly viewed the *jus ad bellum*, as well as IHL, as regulating their conduct, see the pleadings referred to in Section 3.2.1.5.

416 Gardam, 'Proportionality in the War on Terror' (n 186) 5.

417 If collateral damage resulting from an attack is expected to be excessive, or if it becomes apparent that this would be the case, then the attack must be cancelled or suspended. API (n 346) Arts 57(2)(a)(iii) and (2)(b).

418 See Section 3.4.1.

419 Lubell, 'Comments on David Kretzmer' (n 4).

repel or prevent an armed attack, whilst still remaining within the boundaries of legality. This review cannot be undertaken as an exact science and, because of the changing nature of conflict (see below), it is not meaningful to look too far in the future. Accordingly, the idea of a snapshot should not be understood as a one-off event, but rather as a continuing process of assessment by the defending state that monitors the changing defensive need by reference to ongoing hostilities.

In the context of pre-emptive self-defence,[420] establishing what is proportionate to counter imminent armed attacks is challenging and involves a degree of conjecture. Gauging the magnitude and effects of an attack that has not yet occurred and determining what is required to achieve a defensive purpose in relation to such attack cannot be a precise undertaking. When the anticipated attack will start and finish might also be uncertain. States, and observers of state action, are thereby faced with a laborious undertaking in identifying the precise nature of the threat, how long it will endure, and what a reasonable defensive response looks like. As such, applying proportionality to defence against imminent armed attacks is 'somewhat of a haphazard process'.[421]

As with all acts of self-defence, a good faith effort must be made to calibrate carefully a response by reference to all reliable and credible intelligence available at the time the decision is taken. This requirement takes on greater significance with imminent armed attacks, due to the additional uncertainties. Ultimately, an assessment of the proportionality of pre-emptive self-defence will be made objectively on a *post facto* basis. It will be for third parties to judge, after the event, how they view the proportionality of the response. They will also need to decide on the basis of the available evidence whether an armed attack was in fact imminent and that the right of self-defence was available to the defending state at the relevant time. Given the inherent uncertainties pertaining to the availability and scope of a right of pre-emptive self-defence examined in Section 2.5.1.2, it might be that these threshold issues play the decisive role in determining the question of legality in such cases.

If the imminent armed attack is a threat of specific action,[422] or there is history between the defending state and the attacker, assessing proportionality might be easier. As noted in Section 2.5.1.2, claims of 'pure' anticipatory self-defence are rare. The prospect of imminent armed attacks tends to arise where there is an ongoing threat to a state that has already been the victim of a prior armed attack. As discussed in Section 2.5.2, Section 3.2.1, and Chapter 4, in such cases states might be entitled to respond on a cumulative basis to this persisting threat. Therefore, even if difficult, assessing the threat as a whole (*viz* looking at the entire period during which the threat subsists) must encompass consideration of imminent

420 See Section 2.5.1.2.
421 Gardam, *Necessity, Proportionality* (n 8) 179.
422 Ibid.

armed attacks. However, from a practical perspective, even if forming part of a series of armed attacks, states planning to counter an imminent armed attack are advised to exercise caution. This is because, as noted, formulating a proportionate response remains precarious. Where the details of the total threat are unclear, a defending state that is mindful of the legality of its actions might be wise to limit the initial stages of its defensive response to a high degree of quantitative equivalence vis-à-vis the anticipated imminent armed attack. Such strategy might serve to avoid a *post facto* determination that a defensive act was an overreaction and disproportionate.

Despite the difficulties presented by imminent armed attacks, assessing proportionality primarily against a defensive purpose and on an enduring basis provides a flexible and pragmatic model that takes into account the changing circumstances on the ground and the other interests referred to in this chapter that might indicate excessiveness. If we take the example of a defensive campaign against an ongoing threat, then there will be moments during this campaign when the level of violence rises and falls. Ruys, for instance, gives the example of the 2006 Israeli intervention in Lebanon where, over time, the circumstances gave rise to a 'mutually reinforcing cycle of violence' that, because of action on both sides, escalated well beyond an initial response to the abduction of two Israeli soldiers.[423] It is not the fact that Israel's campaign developed into an 'all-out war' with Hezbollah that automatically rendered the response disproportionate, however. Rather, it was the imposition of a naval blockade on Lebanon and the widespread targeting of civilian infrastructure and Lebanese military bases that clearly breached the proportionality requirement.[424]

This example serves to highlight why adherence to proportionality is necessarily an enduring requirement and may only be properly assessed as such. Evaluating compliance over the relevant period of time accounts for the vicissitudes of the factual context during that period. This is the case whether a proportionality calculus is made on a snapshot basis whilst a defensive act is ongoing, or when looking back at a defensive operation as a whole on a *post factum* basis. Viewing proportionality in this manner takes account of the fact that what is required to pursue a defensive objective will change over time as the nature and scale of the conflict ebbs and flows. Developments on the ground might mean that what is a proportionate response at one point in the conflict might later become disproportionate. As the threat to the defending state increases and decreases, so long as self-defence remains necessary, the corresponding defence must be calibrated accordingly. Proportionality only makes logical sense both theoretically, and as a matter of practical application, when conceptualized in this manner.

[423] Ruys, *'Armed Attack'* (n 20) 118.

[424] Ibid. See further Section 3.3.5.

3.6 Conclusions

Proportionality is often employed by states as a 'ritual incantation' to identify excess and illegality. State practice does not offer a consistent narrative regarding how proportionality is conceptualized and the ICJ jurisprudence likewise represents a mixed approach. Yet, the foregoing analysis clarifies proportionality's role in the exercise of self-defence. In response to an actual or imminent armed attack, general and specific necessity respectively determine *whether* force may be used, and *where* it must be directed. Proportionality proceeds to govern *how much* total force is permissible to achieve a defensive purpose. It guards against excessive reactions. It does this by appraising the act(s) of self-defence as a whole, not the specific targeting decisions, which are the domain of specific necessity and IHL. Therefore, proportionality is only relevant when there exists an actual or imminent armed attack and both general and specific necessity have first been satisfied. Like necessity, it is also an enduring requirement that subsists, and must be monitored, throughout the duration of a defensive operation.

State practice indicates that proportionality operates flexibly, is largely context-dependant, and accounts for a variety of interests that go beyond those of the defending state. Although proportionality balances defensive force and its outcomes primarily against a defensive purpose, its application is not the neat binary exercise that is sometimes suggested. It is not simply a question of referring to proportionality as either quantitative or teleological. Material factors arising out of defensive action play an important part in evaluating proportionality. In particular, widespread civilian harm will tend to be condemned by the international community as excessive. Manifest quantitative imbalance will indicate disproportionately, either in and of itself or, more likely, by signalling a lack of defensive purpose.

Moreover, states clearly do not view themselves as being able to do 'whatever it takes' to achieve a defensive purpose. Other interests operate to restrict how far defending states may go to defend themselves. They function as indicia of excessiveness (*viz* disproportionality). As a consequence, a proportionality analysis must account for how much these interests are affected by actions in self-defence. These interests include those of other states, as well as the environment and international peace and security more generally. The respective importance of defensive purpose, material factors and third-party interests varies and is contextual. State practice and jurisprudence suggests, however, that states and the ICJ will point to the most obvious indicator of illegality when considering whether or not an exercise of the right self-defence complies with the proportionality requirement. Civilian harm is likely to be the principal factor.

4

Necessity and Proportionality and Armed Attacks by Non-State Actors

4.1 Introduction

A right of self-defence against armed attacks by non-state actors ('NSAs') remains a disputed topic in the *jus ad bellum*. Most contentious is defensive force used against NSAs operating from the territory of a host state where the NSAs are acting independently and their acts are not attributable to that host state on the basis of Article 3(g) of the Definition of Aggression or the laws of state responsibility.[1] The defining issue is whether, for the right of self-defence to arise, an armed attack must necessarily be carried out (either directly or indirectly) by one state against another state. There is nothing in the ordinary meaning of Article 51 of the UN Charter that stipulates this precondition.[2] On the face of it, by not specifying the identity or nature of the attacker, the drafting of Article 51 would appear to accommodate (or at least not deny) armed attacks by NSAs, even when such attacks are not imputable to a state.[3]

However, the position is not so simple. Scholars have long debated the relationship between Articles 2(4) and 51 of the UN Charter. It has been suggested that as Article 2(4) prohibits states using military force against other states, Article 51 (which is the exception to the Article 2(4) prohibition) should likewise be read in a state-centric manner. Such a 'traditional' inter-state reading of Article 51 leads

[1] See UNGA Res 3314 (XXIX) (14 December 1974) (hereafter 'Definition of Aggression') and the International Law Commission's ('ILC') Draft Articles on Responsibility of States for Internationally Wrongful Acts, with Commentaries (2001) UN Doc A/56/10 ('ARSIWA'). For an overview of this topic, including the requisite legal threshold of attribution, see Tom Ruys, *'Armed Attack' and Article 51 of the UN Charter: Evolutions in Customary Law and Practice* (CUP 2010) 368–510. See further Christian J Tams, 'The Use of Force against Terrorists' (2009) 20(2) EJIL 359; Noam Lubell, *Extraterritorial Use of Force Against Non-State Actors* (OUP 2010); Daniel Bethlehem, 'Self-Defense Against an Imminent or Actual Armed Attack by Nonstate Actors' (2012) 106 AJIL 770; Kimberley N Trapp, 'Can Non-State Actors Mount an Armed Attack?' in Marc Weller (ed), The *Oxford Handbook on the Use of Force in International Law* (OUP 2015) 679; Christine Gray, *International Law and the Use of Force* (4th edn, OUP 2018) 139–150, 200–261; Christian Henderson, *The Use of Force and International Law* (CUP 2018) 308–346; Mary Ellen O'Connell, Christian J Tams and Dire Tladi, *Self-Defence Against Non-State Actors* (CUP 2019); Terry D Gill and Kinga Tibori-Szabó, 'Twelve Key Questions on Self-Defense against Non-State Actors' (2019) 95 Int'l L Stud 467.

[2] *Legal Consequences of the Construction of a Wall in the Occupied Palestinian Territories* (Advisory Opinion) [2004] ICJ Rep 136 (hereafter '*Wall*') sep op Higgins, para 33.

[3] International Law Association ('ILA') Committee on the Use of Force, 'Final Report on Aggression and the Use of Force', Sydney Conference (2018) 14.

Necessity and Proportionality and the Right of Self-Defence in International Law. Chris O'Meara, Oxford University Press (2021). © Chris O'Meara. DOI: 10.1093/oso/9780198863403.003.0004

some to conclude that an armed attack must be authored by a state for the right of self-defence to be triggered.[4] That self-defence is a limited inter-state right that cannot be exercised against NSAs is arguably a minority opinion.[5] Nevertheless, in *Wall*, the International Court of Justice ('ICJ', or the 'Court') famously adopted an inter-state reading of Article 51, opining that it 'recognizes the existence of an inherent right of self-defence in the case of *armed attack by one State against another State*'.[6] As the Court acknowledged, however, Article 51 had no relevance to that case, meaning that this assertion was unnecessary for the Court to reach its judgment. The *Wall* decision has been much criticized by scholars on this point and the Court appeared to back-track on its position in '*Armed Activities*', leaving open the issue of whether a state may lawfully respond defensively to NSA armed attacks that are not attributable to a state.[7]

Today, the issue remains open. State practice has not reached a consensus that provides a definitive answer. France, for example, confirmed in 2019 that it does not recognize a right of self-defence in response to acts perpetrated by NSAs that are not attributable, directly or indirectly, to a state.[8] Nevertheless, France accepts that it has deviated from this general rule in 'exceptional cases', invoking self-defence against NSAs having the characteristics of a 'quasi-State', as with its intervention in Syria against Daesh. France also acknowledges that state practice might shift towards a general acceptance of a right of self-defence against NSA armed attacks that are not attributable to a state.[9] Brazil and Mexico meanwhile have emphatically rejected any right of self-defence against armed attacks by NSAs absent state attribution.[10]

Such explicit rejections by states are uncommon, however. Although there remains a lack of unanimity, at worst we can say that military responses to armed attacks by NSAs without the required level of state attribution are 'not

[4] A state-centric reading of Art 51 is discussed in a number of the sources referred to in n 1. See, for example, Dire Tladi, 'The Use of Force in Self-Defence against Non-State Actors, Decline of Collective Security and the Rise of Unilateralism: Whither International Law?' in O'Connell, Tams and Tladi, *Self-Defence Against Non-State Actors* (n 1) 14; Christian J Tams, 'Self-Defence Against Non-State Actors: Making Sense of the 'Armed Attack' Requirement' in O'Connell, Tams and Tladi, *Self-Defence Against Non-State Actors* (n 1) 90, 115–116.

[5] Gill and Tibori-Szabó, 'Twelve Key Questions' (n 1) 487.

[6] See *Wall* (n 2) para 139 (emphasis added).

[7] *Case Concerning Armed Activities on the Territory of the Congo* (*Democratic Republic of the Congo v Uganda*) (Judgment) [2007] ICJ Rep 168 (hereafter '*Armed Activities*') para 147. See the references set out in n 1 for commentary on the *Wall* (n 2) and the other related ICJ jurisprudence.

[8] French Ministry of Defence, 'International Law Applied to Operations in Cyberspace' (2019) <http://www.defense.gouv.fr/content/download/567648/9770527/file/international%2Blaw%2Bapplied%2Bto%2Boperations%2Bin%2Bcyberspace.pdf> accessed 5 September 2020, 8–9.

[9] Ibid, 9.

[10] UNSC Verbatim Record (17 May 2018) UN Doc S/PV.8262, 44–45 (Brazil); Mexico, Statement to the United Nations General Assembly Sixth Committee, Agenda Item 85: Report of the Special Committee on the Charter of the United Nations and on the Strengthening of the Role of the Organization (12 October 2018) <http://statements.unmeetings.org/media2/19409927/mexico-s-.pdf> accessed 5 September 2020.

unambiguously unlawful'.[11] At best, we can point to an increasing (if not entirely coherent) body of state practice, as well as academic opinion, that indicates that states do possess a right of self-defence against armed attacks by NSAs, irrespective of a connection to a state.[12] On this latter view, self-defence is a right triggered by the act, rather than the actor.[13] State practice examples in support of this proposition stretch back to the *Caroline* incident of 1837,[14] but this trend is most clearly identifiable in state practice since 2001.

It is not the purpose of this book to examine this practice as it relates to the threshold question regarding the trigger of the right of self-defence. However, there are key case studies that both support the general premise that NSA armed attacks are capable of triggering a state's right of self-defence regardless of a state nexus, and which also have particular relevance to our review of necessity and proportionality. These incidents include Operation Enduring Freedom in 2001, Israel's invasion of Lebanon in 2006, Operation Sun in 2008, and the ongoing Global Coalition action against Daesh in Syria. Such practice is discussed throughout this chapter.[15] The latter incident is particularly instructive for present purposes given the number of states that have claimed a right of self-defence to justify their military operations against Daesh in Syria and the resulting reactions by other states and international organizations. It is, therefore, the focus of much of the ensuing analysis.

In summary at this point, we may reasonably conclude that claims of self-defence triggered by the actions of NSAs are increasingly made by states and accepted by the international community. The *lex lata* position remains unsettled, but there is growing acknowledgment that cross-border NSA armed attacks are capable of triggering a state's right of self-defence, absent any state involvement in such attacks. This stands as a general premise, however. Whether as *lex lata* or *lex ferenda*, the content and parameters of any right of self-defence against NSAs are still being worked out in state practice. Significant issues remain, most notably regarding how such right might lawfully be exercised and what are the consequences for the host state of force being used against NSAs within its territory.

[11] Ruys, *'Armed Attack'* (n 1) 487. Ruys reached this conclusion in 2010. Arguably, as explained in this section, the Global Coalition action against Daesh in Syria since 2014 has advanced the state practice analysis.

[12] Elizabeth Wilmshurst, 'The Chatham House Principles of International Law on the Use of Force in Self-Defence' (2006) 55(4) ICLQ 963 (hereafter 'The Chatham House Principles') 969–971; Institut de Droit International, Tenth Commission, 'Present Problems of the Use of Armed Force in International Law, Sub-Group on Self-Defence' (27 October 2007) <http://www.idi-iil.org/app/uploads/2017/06/Roucounas.pdf> accessed 5 September 2020, 214, Resolution 10; Nico Schrijver and Larissa van den Herik, 'Leiden Policy Recommendations on Counter-Terrorism and International Law' (2010) 57(3) NILR 531 (hereafter 'Leiden Policy Recommendations') 541–542; Noam Lubell, 'Fragmented Wars: Multi-Territorial Military Operations Against Armed Groups' (2017) 93 Int'l L Stud 215, 217–218; ILA, 'Final Report on Aggression and the Use of Force' (n 3) 14–15. See further the sources cited in n 1.

[13] ILA, 'Final Report on Aggression and the Use of Force' (n 3) 14.

[14] See Section 1.4.

[15] Further examples of state practice are referenced in the literature referred to in n 1.

If armed attacks carried out by NSAs absent a state nexus are or become capable of triggering a state's right of self-defence, the question for this book is how necessity and proportionality feature in the exercise of such right. The purpose of this chapter is to explore this question. It examines the role of these two requirements in the particular context of defensive action against NSAs, including how necessity and proportionality speak to some of the most controversial issues associated with this topic.

As a starting point, we should note that the analysis set out in Chapters 2 and 3 relating to interstate self-defence also applies in general terms to defensive action taken in response to armed attacks by NSAs operating from foreign territory. Yet, armed attacks by NSAs raise further particular issues for necessity and proportionality. In this context, their requirements are adapted and supplemented. As such, NSA armed attacks represent a particularly good medium through which the content and outer parameters of necessity and proportionality can be explored.[16] As will be made clear, necessity in particular plays a greater role outside of the interstate context where the requirement is likely to be satisfied more easily.[17] The content and operation of proportionality, however, are much more uncertain. Within the framework of self-defence against NSAs, proportionality is stretched to the very boundaries of meaningful application.

Much of the following analysis is set against the background of international terrorism. This is principally because the majority of state practice pertaining to NSA armed attacks has taken place in this context. There should be no confusion, however, between a right to respond defensively to armed attacks by NSAs who happen to be terrorists, and any responses to 'terrorism' (howsoever the latter concept might be defined).[18] There is no right of self-defence against 'terrorism', only against actual or (potentially) imminent armed attacks.[19] The fact that such attacks are being carried out for terrorist purposes does not affect the trigger of the right.[20] However, the threat posed by terrorism has consequential effects for how we should understand necessity and proportionality. Universally accepted as one of

[16] There are other areas of the *jus ad bellum* that also raise additional issues for these two concepts, including uses of force in cyber space and in outer space. Consideration of these topics is beyond the scope this book, however.

[17] Christian J Tams, 'The Necessity and Proportionality of Anti-Terrorist Self-Defence' in Larissa van den Herik and Nico Schrijver (eds), *Counter-Terrorism Strategies in a Fragmented International Legal Order: Meeting the Challenges* (CUP 2013) 373, 399–401.

[18] There is no commonly agreed legal definition of terrorism. See Ben Saul, 'Attempts to Define "Terrorism" in International Law' (2005) 52(1) NILR 57; Kimberley N Trapp, *State Responsibility for International Terrorism* (OUP 2011) 14–23; Marcello Di Filippo, 'The Definitions(s) of Terrorism in International Law' in Ben Saul (ed) *Research Handbook on International Law and Terrorism* (Edward Elgar 2014) 3; Kenneth Watkin, *Fighting at the Legal Boundaries: Controlling the Use of Force in Contemporary Conflict* (OUP 2016) 180–208.

[19] See Section 2.5.1.2. This Chapter proceeds on the basis that a right of pre-emptive self-defence might exist as a matter of *lex lata*. If not, such right has the potential to exist as *lex ferenda*.

[20] UN Charter, Art 51. See further Ruys, *'Armed Attack'* (n 1) 496–499.

the most serious threats to international peace and security,[21] the phenomenon has undoubtedly influenced how states and the UN Security Council ('UNSC') view the right of self-defence. As will be made clear, the factor of international terrorism feeds into what it means for states to comply with necessity and proportionality when responding to NSA armed attacks.

4.2 Necessity and Armed Attacks by NSAs

4.2.1 The Host State and Alternative Measures

When NSA armed attacks are not attributable to a host state, serious implications arise from a defending state using force against the responsible NSAs on the host state's territory. As in the interstate context, the starting point for considering the necessity of such action is to ascertain whether states have reasonable alternatives to using defensive force in the circumstances.[22] If force is required, the defending state should seek prior explicit consent from the host state to act militarily on its territory.[23] Absent consent, for action in self-defence to be necessary, the host state should generally be given the opportunity to comply with its international law obligations to prevent and suppress international terrorism. It might do so by acting on its own or working in cooperation with the defending state.[24] If the host state adopts measures against the NSAs within a reasonable time period and they are

21 UNGA Res 60/1 (16 September 2005) UN Doc A/Res/60/1, paras 81-91. See further Section 4.2.3.3.

22 Ideally, a defending state should request the host state to take adequate measures to forestall or halt (further) terrorist action and, in cooperation with the host state, take law enforcement measures to prevent terrorist acts from being perpetrated from host state territory. Terry D Gill, 'When Does Self-Defence End?' in Weller (ed), *The Oxford Handbook* (n 1) 737, 744; Tams, 'Necessity and Proportionality' (n 17) 403, 408–409. This presumptive approach is in keeping with the notion that terrorists are first and foremost criminals and, if possible, should be dealt with as such before states resort to force against them. Leiden Policy Recommendations (n 12) 539–540; Elizabeth Wilmshurst and Michael Wood, 'Self-Defense Against Nonstate Actors: Reflections on the "Bethlehem Principles"' (2013) 107 AJIL 390, 393. If law enforcement measures are capable of countering the terrorist acts, force will not be necessary. Leiden Policy Recommendations (n 12) 542.

23 What constitutes consent, including whether this might be implicit or intervention by invitation are much-debated topics. See, for example, Ademola Abass, 'Consent Precluding State Responsibility: A Critical Analysis' (2004) 53(1) ICLQ 211; Karine Bannelier-Christakis, 'Military Interventions against ISIL in Iraq, Syria and Libya, and the Legal Basis of Consent' (2016) 29(3) LJIL 743; Patrick M Butchard, 'Territorial Integrity, Political Independence, and Consent: The Limitations of Military Assistance on Request Under the Prohibition of Force' (2020) 7(1) JUFIL 35.

24 In *Armed Activities* (n 7) para 162, the ICJ confirmed as customary international law the requirement set out in UNGA Res 2625 (XXV) (24 October 1970) (hereafter 'Friendly Relations Declaration') that '[e]very State has the duty to refrain from organizing, instigating, assisting or participating in […] terrorist acts in another State or acquiescing in organized activities within its territory directed towards the commission of such acts, when the acts referred to in the present paragraph involve a threat or use of force'. This statement is an expression of the general premise that every state has an obligation not to allow knowingly its territory to be used for acts contrary to the rights of other states. *Corfu Channel* (*United Kingdom v Albania*) (Merits) [1949] ICJ Rep 4, para 51. This is not an absolute obligation, however. It is a duty to apply due diligence in preventing harm to other states stemming

effective to combat them, this *prima facie* renders unnecessary any action by the defending state.[25]

If seeking a solution via or in cooperation with the host state is an option, and has not been tried, it is unlikely that unilateral force against NSAs may be considered necessary.[26] Host state action, to use Webster's words, thereby offers a potential additional 'choice of means' to that seen in the interstate context. Alternative measures accordingly have the potential to play a much greater role in combatting NSAs than they do in the interstate context. The consequence is that general necessity, at least in theory, acts as a stronger limitation on states exercising their right of self-defence. The reality, however, might be somewhat different.

Whether peaceful options and/or host state action are in fact reasonable alternatives to defensive force will depend on the context, particularly the timing of the armed attack.[27] In terms of recourse to peaceful alternatives against the NSAs themselves, it might be that such action proves sufficient over time to counter an enduring threat. However, there is no suggestion in state practice that a defending state under direct attack from NSAs is required to forego its right of defensive response in favour of law enforcement. Therefore, a distinction must be made between long-term responses to degrade the capacity for future NSA armed attacks and the more immediate needs of a defending state to respond to current threats.[28]

from actions within the host state's own territory. It constitutes an obligation of means rather than results. Tom Ruys, 'Crossing the Thin Blue Line: An Inquiry into Israel's Recourse to Self-Defense against Hezbollah' (2007) 43 Stan J Int'l L 265, 285. The obligation to combat terrorism and prevent terrorist acts, and to cooperate with other states in so doing, is likewise reflected in various UNSC Resolutions (for example, UNSC Res 1373 (28 September 2001) UN Doc S/RES/1373, para 2) and nineteen multilateral terrorism suppression conventions (see UN Office of Counter Terrorism, 'International Legal Instruments' <https://www.un.org/counterterrorism/international-legal-instruments> accessed 5 September 2020). On the general approach to resolving the situation before force is used on a host state's territory, see further Ruys, *'Armed Attack'* (n 1) 505–506; Ashley Deeks, '"Unwilling or Unable": Toward a Normative Framework for Extra-Territorial Self-Defense' (2012) 52 Va JIL 483, 519–21; Henderson, *The Use of Force and International Law* (n 1) 324, 326.

25 For example, prior to Operation Sun in 2008, the Turkish President appeared to accept that if the Iraqi government acted against the PKK, it would not be necessary for Turkey to act in its place: 'We have made it very clear that if the terrorist shelters there are not destroyed, it is our legitimate right to destroy those shelters ourselves.' Michael Howard, 'Turkey Bombards Northern Iraq after Ambush' *The Guardian* (22 October 2007) <www.theguardian.com/world/2007/oct/22/turkey.iraq1> accessed 5 September 2020.

26 Lubell, *Non-State Actors* (n 1) 46.

27 See Section 2.5.1.

28 Pursuing peaceful alternatives vis-à-vis the NSAs themselves is not required by the UN Charter's emphasis on peaceful settlement of disputes, which only applies between states. See Section 2.4.1. Moreover, alternatives are unlikely, *on their own*, to prove effective in halting, repelling or preventing an armed attack. It is unrealistic, for example, to assume that diplomatic pressure or economic sanctions will be employable against terrorist organizations like Al-Qaeda or Daesh. Likewise, it is doubtful that law enforcement strategies and non-forcible options such as freezing bank accounts and funds will be sufficient alone to halt, repel or prevent armed attacks. This is especially so where the host state will not cooperate. Tams, 'Necessity and Proportionality' (n 17) 406–407. Domestic terrorism occurring exclusively within the confines of one national legal system is more likely to be countered by traditional law enforcement measures. With cross-border armed attacks by NSA terrorists such responses (coupled

There might also be an understandable reluctance on the part of the defending state to cooperate with a host state, or to rely on host state action, before resorting to force against the NSAs operating on host state territory. Deeks notes that although defending states tend to point to the fact that they first ask the host state to take steps to suppress NSA activities on their own territory before using force against the NSAs, this is not always the case. A request for the host state to take action might be considered to be futile or cause tangible harm to the defending state's national security.[29] For example, prior to the USA's intervention in Afghanistan in 2001 under the guise of Operation Enduring Freedom, the USA refused to negotiate, let alone cooperate, with the Taliban before launching its airstrikes.[30] The USA made a number of demands to the Taliban prior to using force, but there was no indication that the Americans felt legally obligated to resolve the issue peaceably, or that such demands were anything other than politically or strategically expedient.[31] The American approach is likely due to the Taliban's close relationship with Al-Qaeda and the view that Taliban support for the terrorist group made the 9/11 attacks possible.[32] George W Bush viewed the Taliban as an illegitimate and murderous regime and publicly condemned them on this basis.[33] Despite this refusal to cooperate with the Taliban, Operation Enduring Freedom was generally regarded as a lawful act of self-defence.[34]

Likewise, in the context of combatting Daesh and other terrorist groups in Syria since 2014, those states claiming a right of self-defence to justify their military operations within Syrian territory have refused to cooperate with President Assad.[35]

with other efforts like education and deradicalization programmes) are essential in dealing with the long-term threat, but they do not necessarily contribute to the immediate defensive needs of a state under attack, or threat of imminent attack. Where armed groups of NSAs have been sufficiently weakened by the application of military force, however, alternatives to force thereafter might be sufficient to tackle the long-term threat. See Section 4.2.4.1.

[29] Deeks, "Unwilling or Unable" (n 24) 521–525, noting that such procedural requirement is not absolute.

[30] George W Bush, 'Address Before a Joint Session of the Congress on the United States Response to the Terrorist Attacks of September 11' (20 September 2001) <https://www.govinfo.gov/content/pkg/WCPD-2001-09-24/pdf/WCPD-2001-09-24-Pg1347.pdf> accessed 5 September 2020, 1348.

[31] James A Green, *The International Court of Justice and Self-Defence in International Law* (Hart Publishing 2009) 81.

[32] Letter dated 7 October 2001 from the Permanent Representative of the United State of America to the United Nations addressed to the President of the Security Council (7 October 2001) UN Doc S/2001/946. See further Section 4.2.3.1.

[33] 'President Bush Addresses the Nation' *The Washington Post* (20 September 2001) <http://www.washingtonpost.com/wp-srv/nation/specials/attacked/transcripts/bushaddress_092001.html> accessed 5 September 2020.

[34] See Section 2.5.2.2.

[35] States invoking individual and/or collective self-defence to justify their actions against Daesh in Iraq and Syria include the following: Letter dated 23 September 2014 from the Permanent Representative of the United States of America to the United Nations addressed to the Secretary-General (23 September 2014) UN Doc S/2014/695; Identical Letters dated 25 November 2014 from the Permanent Representative of the United Kingdom of Great Britain and Northern Ireland to the United Nations addressed to the Secretary-General and the President of the Security Council (26 November 2014) UN Doc S/2014/851; Letter dated 31 March 2015 from the Chargé d'Affaires A.I. of the

Certain of these states have been very public about their reluctance to do so. The USA, for example, clearly rejected the offer of cooperation and coordination, explicitly stating that it was not looking for the approval of the Syrian regime.[36] This is despite potential initial indications on Syria's part of its ability to combat Daesh and its willingness to do so by coordinating military action.[37] This fact raises an interesting question of what it means to satisfy the necessity requirement in this context.[38] In particular, it is unclear from practice whether defending states consider themselves to be under a legal obligation to cooperate with a host state that

Permanent Mission of Canada to the United Nations addressed to the President of the Security Council (31 March 2015) UN Doc S/2015/221; Letter dated 24 July 2015 from the Chargé d'Affaires A.I. of the Permanent Mission of Turkey to the United Nations addressed to the President of the Security Council (24 July 2015) UN Doc S/2015/563; Letter dated 7 September 2015 from the Permanent Representative of the United Kingdom of Great Britain and Northern Ireland to the United Nations addressed to the President of the Security Council (8 September 2015) UN Doc S/2015/688; Letter dated 9 September 2015 from the Permanent Representative of Australia to the United Nations addressed to the President of the Security Council (9 September 2015) UN Doc S/2015/693; Identical Letters dated 8 September 2015 from the Permanent Representative of France to the United Nations addressed to the Secretary-General and the President of the Security Council (9 September 2015) UN Doc S/2015/745; Letter dated 3 December 2015 from the Permanent Representative of the United Kingdom of Great Britain and Northern Ireland to the United Nations addressed to the President of the Security Council (3 December 2015) UN Doc S/2015/928; Letter dated 10 December 2015 from the Chargé d'Affaires A.I. of the Permanent Mission of Germany to the United Nations addressed to the President of the Security Council (10 December 2015) UN Doc S/2015/946; Letter dated 11 January 2016 from the Permanent Representative of Denmark to the United Nations addressed to the President of the Security Council (13 January 2016) UN Doc S/2016/34; Letter dated 10 February 2016 from the Chargé d'Affaires A.I. of the Permanent Mission of The Netherlands to the United Nations addressed to the President of the Security Council (10 February 2016) UN Doc S/2016/132; Letter dated 3 June 2016 from the Permanent Representative of Norway to the United Nations addressed to the President of the Security Council (3 June 2016) UN Doc S/2016/513; Letter dated 7 June 2016 from the Permanent Representative of Belgium to the United Nations addressed to the President of the Security Council (9 June 2016) UN Doc S/2016/523; Letter dated 24 August 2016 from the Permanent Representative of Turkey to the United Nations addressed to the President of the Security Council (25 August 2016) UN Doc S/2016/739.

[36] Justin Sink, 'White House Won't Commit to Asking Congress for Syria Strike' *The Hill* (25 August 2014) <http://thehill.com/policy/defense/215905-white-house-wont-commit-to-asking-congress-for-syria-strike> accessed 5 September 2020.

[37] For commentary on this point, see Ryan Goodman, 'International Law on Airstrikes against ISIS in Syria' (*Just Security*, 28 August 2014) <https://www.justsecurity.org/14414/international-law-airstrikes-isis-syria/> accessed 5 September 2020; Goodman (December 2014); Ryan Goodman, 'Taking the Weight off of International Law: Has Syria Consented to US Airstrikes?' (*Just Security*, 23 December 2014) <https://www.justsecurity.org/18665/weight-international-law-syria-consented-airstrikes/> accessed 5 September 2020; Gray, *Use of Force* (n 1) 241. It later became clear that Syria was strongly opposed to Global Coalition action on its territory. Before the UNSC, Syria insisted that it was combatting terrorism and that any counter-terrorism efforts had to be coordinated with the Syrian government. UNSC Verbatim Record (19 September 2014) UN Doc S/PV.7271, 43; UNSC Verbatim Record (19 November 2014) UN Doc S/PV.7316, 33. Syria has since condemned Global Coalition airstrikes and complained to the UNSC of aggression against it. See, for example, Identical Letters dated 17 September 2015 from the Permanent Representative of the Syrian Arab Republic to the United Nations addressed to the Secretary-General and the President of the Security Council (21 September 2015) UN Doc S/2015/719; Identical Letters dated 9 November 2015 from the Permanent Representative of the Syrian Arab Republic to the United Nations addressed to the Secretary-General and the President of the Security Council (16 November 2015) UN Doc S/2015/851.

[38] See further Section 4.2.2 regarding necessity and the 'unwilling or unable' doctrine.

is purportedly willing. The refusal to cooperate with President Assad might have been because his regime had lost control over significant parts of Syrian territory (affecting its ability to counter the threat) and/or doubts as to whether Assad was acting in good faith regarding any cooperation.[39] Akin to the USA's view of the Taliban, states might also have had concerns regarding cooperating with, and potentially strengthening, an illegitimate regime that stands accused of crimes against humanity and war crimes.[40] The EU's position, for example, was that the policies and actions of the Assad regime meant that it could not be a partner in the fight against Daesh.[41]

This latter possibility reflects a regime interaction issue and the need to interpret international law systemically. *Jus ad bellum* necessity should not be interpreted so as to require a defending state to cooperate with, and thereby support, host states that breach international humanitarian law ('IHL') and whose officials potentially face international criminal law liability. Indeed, such collaboration by a defending state might engage its own international responsibility for a breach of the obligation to respect, and to ensure respect for, the Geneva Conventions and IHL more generally.[42] The International Committee of the Red Cross ('ICRC') maintains that, as a matter of customary international law, this obligation is not limited to the Geneva Conventions, but applies to the entire body of international humanitarian law binding upon a particular state.[43] Where IHL violations are 'likely or foreseeable', defending states might be responsible for providing support that could be construed as encouraging breaches of IHL.[44] If the breaches of IHL also constitute a serious breach of peremptory norms of international law, the laws of state responsibility would likewise prohibit aid or assistance to the responsible state (*viz* Syria)

[39] The USA accused the Syrian regime of focusing on combatting opposition groups rather than fighting terrorists. UNSC Verbatim Record (17 April 2018) UN Doc S/PV.8236, 7.

[40] See the various reports of the Human Rights Council's Independent International Commission of Inquiry on the Syrian Arab Republic (hereafter 'HRC Syrian Commission of Inquiry'), which was mandated in 2011 to investigate alleged violations of international human rights law in Syria and to establish the facts and circumstances that may amount to such violations and of the crimes perpetrated: <http://www.ohchr.org/EN/HRBodies/HRC/IICISyria/Pages/IndependentInternationalCommission.aspx> accessed 5 September 2020.

[41] UNSC Verbatim Record (22 October 2015) UN Doc S/PV.7540 (Resumption 1) 14.

[42] Common Art 1 to the Geneva Conventions. See further the 2016 commentary of the International Committee of the Red Cross ('ICRC') on the First Geneva Convention relating to Art 1 <https://ihl-databases.icrc.org/applic/ihl/ihl.nsf/Comment.xsp?action=openDocument&documentId=72239588AFA66200C1257F7D00367DBD> accessed 5 September 2020.

[43] ICRC Art 1 commentary, ibid, para 126. The ICRC's interpretation of this obligation is not without its critics, however. It has been described as 'expansive' and 'aspirational'. See Monica Hakimi, 'US Responsibility Arising From Russian Violations of the Law of Armed Conflict' (*Just Security*, 21 September 2016) <https://www.justsecurity.org/33075/u-s-responsibility-arising-russian-violations-law-armed-conflict/> accessed 5 September 2020; Ryan Goodman, 'Two U.S. Positions on the Duty to Ensure Respect for the Geneva Conventions' (*Just Security*, 26 September 2016) <https://www.justsecurity.org/33166/u-s-positions-duty-ensure-respect-geneva-conventions/> accessed 5 September 2020.

[44] *Military and Paramilitary Activities in and against Nicaragua* (*Nicaragua v US*) (Merits) [1986] ICJ Rep 14 (hereafter '*Nicaragua*') paras 220, 256.

that maintains the situation created by that serious breach. In fact, these rules go further and impose a positive obligation on states to cooperate in order to bring to an end such breaches.[45]

Operation Enduring Freedom and Global Coalition action in Syria appear to reflect this rationale.[46] However, in the latter case, the lack of sufficient detail surrounding the relevant states' positions on this topic means that it is difficult to conclude whether cooperation with Assad was a reasonable alternative to using force. After all, Assad did go on to cooperate with other nations, such as Russia and Iran, purportedly in its fight against Daesh.[47] Ultimately, the USA took the view that the Syrian regime could not, and would not, confront Daesh effectively.[48] Such inability was arguably confirmed by UNSC Resolution 2249.[49] Despite the legal controversies involved with intervention in Syrian territory against Daesh, a large number of states have claimed a right of self-defence against Daesh, clearly believing that they are not, as a matter of law, required to cooperate and coordinate with the host state before they do so.[50]

This most contemporary state practice highlights that the particular factual context is crucial when considering necessity and the resort to peaceable alternatives in the context of combatting terrorist NSAs. Emphasis is *prima facie* placed on host state action to tackle the threat emanating from its territory, but this is not always practicable. The necessity of the defending state taking action might instead be established, or at least arguable. The main additional considerations for necessity pertaining to cross-border terrorist attacks by NSAs are the nature of the group of NSAs being combatted, and of the regime on whose territory they operate. In particular, the focus is on the relationships between the defending state and the host state, and between the host state and the NSAs. The risk to the defending state of cooperating with a host state, in terms of whether the former's international responsibility might be engaged because of unlawful acts of the latter, is also a feature of more recent state practice. These issues are central to how states view their obligation to pursue (or not) peaceful alternatives and cooperate (or not) with host states. They bring an extra dimension to the contemplation of alternative measures.

[45] See ARSIWA (n 1) Arts 40, 41 and related commentary.

[46] On whether cooperating with the Assad regime would amount to illegal assistance, see Claus Kress, 'The Fine Line Between Collective Self-Defense and Intervention by Invitation: Reflections on the Use of Force against "IS" in Syria' (*Just Security*, 17 February 2015) <https://www.justsecurity.org/20118/claus-kreb-force-isil-syria/> accessed 5 September 2020.

[47] Whether the purpose of such collaboration was primarily to combat Daesh or Assad's domestic opponents is highly debatable, however. For an overview of Russian and Iranian involvement and objectives, see Terry D Gill, 'Classifying the Conflict in Syria' (2016) 92 Int'l L Stud 353, 356–357.

[48] UN Doc S/2014/695 (n 35); UNSC Verbatim Record (20 November 2015) S/PV.7565, 4. See further Section 4.2.2.

[49] See Section 4.2.3.3.

[50] See further Section 4.2.3.2.

4.2.2 'Unwilling or Unable'

The corollary to the general premise that primacy of action against NSAs lies with the host state is the suggestion that:

> where a state is unable or unwilling to assert control over a terrorist organisation located in its territory, the State which is a victim of the terrorist attacks would, as a last resort, be permitted to act in self-defence against the terrorist organisation in the State in which it is located.[51]

This so-called 'unwilling or unable doctrine' is not a new phenomenon. Indeed, that the American government was either unwilling or unable to prevent aggression against Canada was a feature of the British justifications for destroying the *Caroline* back in 1837.[52] However, as with the threshold question of whether states possess a right of self-defence against NSAs, that unwillingness or inability on the part of the host might be used to justify an exercise of self-defence against NSAs operating on its territory remains a highly controversial and contested issue in the modern *jus ad bellum*, both conceptually and as a matter of practical application.[53]

At best, state practice provides a mixed picture regarding the doctrine's place in the *lex lata*. Only a limited number of states explicitly or implicitly endorse the doctrine.[54] Amongst scholars, there is a clear divide. Some defend the doctrine.[55] They note, *inter alia*, that where there is a '*manifest and persistent unwillingness or inability to prevent non-State attacks*', self-defence will be justifiable: a host state cannot perpetually hide behind its sovereign inviolability.[56] Other commentators are sceptical, however, regarding the sufficiency of current state practice. They also note the difficulties with determining a host state's 'inability' or 'unwillingness' to

[51] The Chatham House Principles (n 12) 970.

[52] See Craig Forcese, *Destroying the Caroline: The Frontier Raid that Reshaped the Right to War* (Irwin Law Inc 2018) 35, 74, 149–150.

[53] For an overview, see Henderson, *The Use of Force and International Law* (n 1) 322–333; Gill and Tibori-Szabó, 'Twelve Key Questions' (n 1) 494–503.

[54] See Elena Chachko and Ashley Deeks, 'Which States Support the "Unwilling and Unable" Test?' (*Lawfare*, 10 October 2016) <https://www.lawfareblog.com/which-states-support-unwilling-and-unable-test#UnitedKingdom> accessed 5 September 2020; Jutta Brunnée and Stephen J Toope, 'Self-Defence against Non-State Actors: Are Powerful States Willing but Unable to Change International Law' (2018) 67 ICLQ 263.

[55] See, for example, The Chatham House Principles (n 12) 969–970; Leiden Policy Recommendations (n 12) 540; Bethlehem, 'Self-Defense Against an Imminent or Actual Armed Attack by Nonstate Actors' (n 1) 776; Deeks, 'Unwilling or Unable' (n 24); Kimberley N Trapp, 'Actor-Pluralism, the 'Turn to Responsibility' and the *Jus ad Bellum*: "Unwilling or Unable" in Context' (2015) 2(2) JUFIL 199; Kress, 'The Fine Line' (n 46).

[56] Ruys, *'Armed Attack'* (n 1) 505–506. '[A] state's territorial integrity should not act, *for its own sake*, to shield NSAs so as to provide them with the (legal and physical) space within which to violate individual rights to life and physical integrity, even if those threatened are across a border.' Trapp, 'Actor-Pluralism' (n 55) 211. See also Ruti G Teitel, *Humanity's Law* (OUP 2011) 219, noting the increasing acceptance of the compromise or suspension of the Westphalian norms of sovereignty and territorial integrity where human rights are at stake.

respond to terrorist threats emanating from its territory and the dangers associated with defending states unilaterally invoking these terms to breach the sovereignty and territorial integrity of host states.[57] Scholarship in this latter vein also reflects on how the doctrine favours militarily powerful states to the detriment of weaker states, particularly in the Global South.[58] These debates remain unresolved. In the contemporary context of combatting terrorism, Sands rightly notes that the challenge for international law is to ensure that the rules balance the legitimate interests of those states that feel vulnerable to international terrorism and those states that feel vulnerable to the response to that threat, especially unilateral responses.[59] Further state practice is required to clarify the place, or otherwise, of the unwilling or unable doctrine in contemporary international law and whether the operation of such doctrine might be capable of responding to these concerns.

For present purposes, a determination of unwillingness and/or inability on the part of the host state satisfies (if the doctrine is accepted as *lex lata*) or would satisfy (if *lex ferenda*) the necessity requirement of self-defence against NSAs carrying out cross-border armed attacks. That there has been, or will be, an armed attack that requires a defensive response (assuming any gravity threshold is met) is a general necessity issue (*viz* whether there is a need for some form of defensive response). Host state unwillingness and/or inability deny the defending state an alternative means of redress, meaning that force is the only way to remove the threat. Specific necessity accounts for military action taken against NSA targets on host state territory. These conclusions are discussed further below.

If accepted, self-defence against NSAs on the territory of another state absent its consent should nevertheless be viewed as an exception, exercisable only in cases of the most compelling emergency.[60] This general premise recognizes the difference between the bilateral situation of interstate self-defence, where defending state(s) respond directly against armed attacks by the attacking state(s), and the situation in self-defence against NSAs, where the host state is essentially a third party. In the latter situation, the unwilling or unable doctrine has the potential to act as an

[57] Kevin Jon Heller, 'Ashley Deeks' Problematic Defense of the "Unwilling or Unable" Test' (*Opinio Juris*, 15 December 2011) <http://opiniojuris.org/2011/12/15/ashley-deeks-failure-to-defend-the-unwilling-or-unable-test/> accessed 5 September 2020; Olivier Corten, 'The "Unwilling or Unable" Test: Has it Been, and Could it be, Accepted?' (2016) 29(3) LJIL 777; Gray, *Use of Force* (n 1) 243–248 Craig Martin, 'Challenging and Refining the "Unwilling or Unable" Doctrine' (2019) 52(2) Vand J Transnat'l L 387. See also the academic response initiated by Olivier Corten in 2016 entitled 'A Plea Against the Abusive Invocation of Self-Defence as a Response to Terrorism', which rejects the 'unable' element of the doctrine. <http://cdi.ulb.ac.be/wp-content/uploads/2016/06/A-plea-against-the-abusive-invocation-of-self-defence.pdf> accessed 5 September 2020.

[58] See, for example, Dawood I Ahmed, 'Defending Weak States against the Unwilling or Unable Doctrine of Self-Defense' (2013) 9 JILIR 1; Ntina Tzouvala, 'TWAIL and the "Unwilling or Unable" Doctrine: Continuities and Ruptures' (2015) 109 AJIL Unbound 266.

[59] Philippe Sands, *Lawless World: America and the Making and Breaking of Global Rules from FDR's Atlantic Charter to George W. Bush's Illegal War* (Viking Penguin 2005) 203, in the context of responding to terrorism more generally.

[60] Leiden Policy Recommendations (n 12) 543.

additional constraint on the exercise of self-defence. In accounting for the position of the host state, it has the capacity to constitute a further barrier to be overcome, taking necessity beyond its operation in the interstate context.[61]

If necessity is established as a result of unwillingness or inability, it is argued that a resulting lawful exercise of self-defence against the NSAs within host state territory excuses a limited breach of the host state's sovereignty and territorial integrity.[62] A further controversial question is whether host state unwillingness and/or inability, and the relationship between the host state and the NSAs, also account for a defending state's right of action *against* the host state itself, including its military personnel and apparatus and civilian infrastructure. The targeting rules considered in Section 2.6 suggest that specific necessity requires the defensive force to be aimed at, and only at, the NSAs responsible for the armed attack. This includes their personnel, equipment, bases and other resources located in host state territory. Where the host state has not sent, directed or controlled the NSAs (and NSA acts are not otherwise imputable to the host state), the host state should not be considered the source of the attack.[63] Accordingly, directly targeting the host state's infrastructure and apparatus is *prima facie* unnecessary. Recent state practice suggests, however, that important caveats apply to this general rule.

In practice, it might not to be easy to distinguish between targeting the NSAs and not targeting the host state. Unless the NSAs are operating in a remote location, it is unlikely that the host state (including its infrastructure, apparatus and civilian population) will remain totally unaffected by a defending state's military action. Effects might be by way of collateral damage, where the host state is not directly targeted, but suffers harm. This scenario will be discussed further in Section 4.3.3 in the context of proportionality. Going one step further, in order to ensure that actions in self-defence are effective, the defending state might consider it necessary to target elements of the host state in addition to the NSAs. Gardam argues that it might be difficult to establish to what degree a host state is complicit in allowing its resources, territory and infrastructure to be used by NSAs. Consequently, defending states will inevitably regard themselves as requiring a degree of latitude in the selection of targets in such cases.[64] Gardam maintains that targeting the infrastructure of the host state 'will not be justifiable unless it can be demonstrated that they contribute in some way to the terrorist activities'.[65]

[61] ILA, 'Final Report on Aggression and the Use of Force' (n 3) 16. The ability of necessity to act as an effective additional constraint on state action in this context depends on establishing a clearer unwilling or unable test. See Deeks, "Unwilling or Unable" (n 24).

[62] See Kimberley N Trapp, 'Back to Basics: Necessity, Proportionality and the Right of Self-Defence against non-State Terrorist Actors' (2007) 56(1) ICLQ 141, 147; Lindsay Moir, 'Action Against Host States of Terrorist Groups' in Weller (ed), *The Oxford Handbook* (n 1) 720, 735; Henderson, *The Use of Force and International Law* (n 1) 323. See further Section 4.3.3.

[63] Ruys, *'Armed Attack'* (n 1) 496.

[64] Judith Gardam, 'A Role for Proportionality in the War on Terror' (2005) 74 Nord J Int'l L 3, 21.

[65] Ibid. This is set out in the context of her views on proportionality. It is submitted, however, that such analysis is better understood as relating to specific necessity.

Other scholars support the notion that where the host state is unwilling or unable to meet its international law obligations to prevent and suppress international terrorism, then this might have implications for whether the defending state may also direct force against host state targets, in addition to NSA targets.[66] The authors of the Leiden Policy Recommendations maintain that:

> measures of self-defence against suspected terrorists must be directed primarily against the terrorist groups responsible for the armed attack in question or their facilities. Only in exceptional circumstances will self-defence justify the use of force against the armed forces or facilities of the [host state], for example, in circumstances where the [host state] is supporting suspected terrorists, as in Afghanistan in 2001.[67]

The state practice reviewed in the next section appears broadly supportive of this statement.

4.2.3 Targeting the Host State—State Practice

The controversial unwilling or unable doctrine is not universally or even consistently referred to by states when justifying their acts against NSAs in foreign territory.[68] Yet, the view that unwillingness or inability, as a factual matter, might lead to targeting elements of the host state in addition to the NSAs does find support in post-9/11 state practice in response to armed attacks by Al-Qaeda (and associated groups) and Daesh. Such practice points to a potential relaxation of the specific necessity requirements within the context of trans-border terrorism.

4.2.3.1 Operation Enduring Freedom

The first example, referred to in the Leiden Policy Recommendations quote at the end of Section 4.2.2, is Operation Enduring Freedom. The American-led action in Afghanistan beginning in 2001 as a response to 9/11 is difficult to reconcile with the specific necessity analysis set out in Section 2.6. In this incident, in addition to targeting the source of the armed attacks (*viz* Al-Qaeda), the coalition also targeted the military installations, personnel and apparatus of the Taliban regime, which was the *de facto* government of Afghanistan at the time.[69] The action led to the

[66] For example, Lubell, *Non-State Actors* (n 1) 47. It is unclear from the analysis, however, whether this conclusion holds true despite due diligence on the part of the host state, rather than achieving effective results.

[67] Leiden Policy Recommendations (n 12) 542. Support for NSAs clearly amounts to an unwillingness to combat them. Although expressed as a requirement of proportionality, it is submitted that these views on targeting are also better understood under the rubric of specific necessity.

[68] See Section 4.2.2.

[69] See UN Doc S/2001/946 (n 32); Sean D Murphy (ed), 'Contemporary Practice of the United States Relating to International Law' (2002) 96 AJIL 237, 246–247, 250.

overthrow of the Taliban and its replacement with a transitional government supported by UN peacekeepers.[70] This was despite the fact that, whilst the Taliban was considered to have wilfully and unlawfully harboured Al-Qaeda, it had not sent, directed or controlled them, thereby giving rise to attribution.[71] Therefore, the Taliban was not regarded as being directly responsible for the 9/11 armed attacks, only for acquiescing in terrorism[72] and making the attacks possible.[73] Yet, despite divided scholarly opinion, states and international organizations (including the UNSC) generally accepted the coalition action in Afghanistan as lawful. This acceptance appeared to include the targeting of the Taliban.[74]

There is no definitive interpretation of this incident of state practice, in terms of establishing an agreed justification for targeting the Taliban in addition to Al-Qaeda.[75] One option is to say that action against the Taliban was simply necessary to achieve the defensive purpose of defeating Al-Qaeda, given the support that the Taliban provided the terrorist group.[76] Indeed, the USA and the UK appeared to

[70] See 'Political and Security Questions: Asia and the Pacific' (2001) UNYB 254, 255–272; Murphy, 'Contemporary Practice of the United States' (n 69) 250–251; Gray, *Use of Force* (n 1) 231–233.

[71] The Taliban refused the UNSC's demand (acting under Chapter VII of the UN Charter) to hand over Osama bin Laden. See UNSC Res 1267 (15 October 1999) UN Doc S/RES/1267, para 2. The failure was expressly noted by the UNSC. See UNSC Res 1390 (28 January 2002) UN Doc S/RES/1390. See further Murphy, 'Contemporary Practice of the United States' (n 69) 243–244, 248; Ruys, *'Armed Attack'* (n 1) 440.

[72] Although not amounting to an armed attack, acquiescence in terrorist acts involving a threat or use of force itself constitutes an unlawful threat or use of force in breach of Art 2(4) of the UN Charter. See Friendly Relations Declaration (n 24); UNSC Res 748 (31 March 1992) UN Doc S/RES/748. Following 9/11, this general approach was encapsulated in UNSC Res 1373 (n 24) para 2.

[73] See UN Doc S/2001/946 (n 32); Letter dated 7 October 2001 from the Chargé D'Affaires A.I. of the Permanent Mission of the United Kingdom of Great Britain and Northern Ireland to the United Nations addressed to the President of the Security Council (7 October 2001) UN Doc S/2001/947. Regarding attribution, see references in n 74 and n 76.

[74] See Section 2.5.2.2. See further Trapp, 'Back to Basics' (n 62) 149–156; Ruys, *'Armed Attack'* (n 1) 495, 503–510, including in relation to the question of attribution and the controversies surrounding targeting the Taliban in addition to Al-Qaeda.

[75] On the question of indeterminacy, see Marko Milanovic, 'Self-Defense and Non-State Actors: Indeterminacy and the *Jus ad Bellum*' (*EJIL:Talk!*, 21 February 2010) <https://www.ejiltalk.org/self-defense-and-non-state-actors-indeterminacy-and-the-jus-ad-bellum/> accessed 5 September 2020.

[76] Other justifications focus on establishing a link between the armed attacks and the state of Afghanistan. One argument along these lines is that the Taliban was complicit in Al-Qaeda's actions, with complicity satisfying a lower standard of attribution, thus giving rise to a right of self-defence directly against the Taliban. See Tams, 'The Use of Force against Terrorists' (n 1) 385 (albeit not in the context of this particular incident). This approach is conceptually flawed, however. It unnecessarily conflates the primary rules of the *jus ad bellum* with the secondary rules of state responsibility. Kimberley N Trapp, 'The Use of Force against Terrorists: A Reply to Christian J Tams' (2009) 20(4) EJIL 1049; Nicholas Tsagourias, 'Self-Defence Against Non-State Actors: The Interaction Between Self-Defence as a Primary Rule and Self-Defence as a Secondary Rule' (2016) 29(3) LJIL 801, 806–807. Another possible justification is that the Taliban's 'substantial involvement' in Al-Qaeda's activities (per Art 3(g) of the Definition of Aggression (n 1)) makes it the author of the 9/11 armed attacks and, therefore, subject to a defensive response. See Tsagourias, 'Self-Defence Against Non-State Actors', 816–819, arguing that substantial state involvement (whether acts or omissions) with NSAs that commit armed attacks might satisfy this requirement where the state knows that the NSA is willing to commit attacks and such aid or assistance facilitates this. Making a similar argument, see also Tom Ruys and Sten Verhoeven, 'Attacks by Private Actors and the Right of Self-Defence' (2005) 10(3) JC&SL 289, 314–317. Alternatively, sheltering and refusing to surrender Al-Qaeda might be viewed as endorsement of the 9/11 attacks, thereby

take the view that they could not destroy Al-Qaeda without removing the Taliban.[77] The Americans justified taking defensive action against the Taliban on the basis that they had made the 9/11 attacks possible by allowing parts of Afghanistan to be used by Al-Qaeda as a base of operations.[78] This allowed Al-Qaeda to use Afghan territory to plot and prepare for the attacks and the Taliban were unwilling to prevent this.[79] The UK likewise noted the Taliban's support.[80] The UK House of Commons Foreign Affairs Committee concluded that 'the defeat of the Taliban did achieve its major objective, which was to destroy Al-Qaeda's support base in Afghanistan and significantly to weaken the organization'.[81]

We might hesitate, however, in accepting this incident as a precedent based on necessity for future action against a host state, absent attribution to it of an armed attack. The particular circumstances of Operation Enduring Freedom mean that it has been viewed as an exception to anti-terrorist self-defence state practice, which has been understood as justifying force against NSA terrorists, not against states.[82] Relevant factors include the magnitude of the Al-Qaeda terrorist attacks, the unique symbiosis between Al-Qaeda and the Taliban and the express recognition of the right of self-defence by the UNSC.[83] This conclusion is explored further in the following section.

4.2.3.2 Global Coalition Action in Syria

More recent state practice, in the form of the global response to Daesh, suggests that Operation Enduring Freedom is indeed *sui generis*, at least in relation to directly targeting manifestations of the host state. Such practice also highlights the potential for specific necessity to act as a restraint on a defending state's actions when responding to NSA armed attacks on the territory of a host state. The American-led Global Coalition operating against Daesh and other terrorist groups in Iraq and Syria was established in September 2014.[84] At the time of writing, it consists of a

constituting the Taliban as accessories-after-the-fact and justifying direct defensive action against them. Yoram Dinstein, *War, Aggression and Self-Defence* (6th edn, CUP 2017) 243, arguing the incident is consequently interstate. This latter conclusion does not appear to be the position of the USA or the UK, however.

[77] Christopher Greenwood, 'International Law and the "War Against Terrorism"' (2002) 78 Int'l Aff (UK) 301, 309.

[78] UN Doc S/2001/946 (n 32). As to whether this amounts to a lower 'harbouring' standard of attribution, and analysis of the attribution issue more generally, see Henderson, *The Use of Force and International Law* (n 1) 314–316, 319–322.

[79] John B Bellinger, 'Legal Issues in the War on Terrorism', speech delivered at The London School of Economics and Political Science (31 October 2006) <https://2009-2017.state.gov/s/l/2006/98861.htm > accessed 5 September 2020.

[80] UN Doc S/2001/947 (n 73).

[81] House of Commons Foreign Affairs Committee, *Foreign Policy Aspects of the War Against Terrorism* (HC 2001-02, 384) para 87.

[82] Tams, 'Necessity and Proportionality' (n 17) 411.

[83] Ruys, *'Armed Attack'* (n 1) 435, 495.

[84] The number of terrorist groups operating in Iraq and Syria is diverse and complex. The main groups, however, are Daesh, Al-Qaeda and Al-Qaeda-associated forces. See Gill, 'Classifying the

coalition of eighty-two states and international organizations, including the Arab League, NATO and the European Union. Its stated mission is to degrade and ultimately defeat Daesh in Syria and Iraq.[85] The Global Coalition action in Syria represents a factually and legally complex picture for the application of the *jus ad bellum*, as well as IHL and international human rights law. Such action takes place in the same territory as a bloody civil war and is further complicated by other non-Global Coalition actors fighting Daesh and other terrorist groups in the same areas. These include Russia, Iranian-back militia groups and the Syrian regime itself.[86]

The Global Coalition's intervention within Syria consists of air strikes, as well as operations on the ground by special forces and other military personnel.[87] Given the lack of information regarding ground operations over the years, including related troop numbers, the better documented air strikes provide a surer footing for analysing Global Coalition military action in Syria.[88] As of September 2020, reports suggest that the Global Coalition has carried out approximately 19,800 airstrikes in Syria since 2014.[89] Regardless of the precise number, even a cursory glance at the

Conflict in Syria' (n 47) 357–359; Gray, *Use of Force* (n 1) 237–248. See also Olivier Corten, 'The Military Operations Against the "Islamic State" (ISIL or Da'esh)–2014' in Tom Ruys and Olivier Corten (eds) with Alexandra Hofer, *The Use of Force in International Law: A Case-Based Approach* (OUP 2018) 873.

[85] See generally the Global Coalition website: <http://theglobalcoalition.org/en/home/> accessed 5 September 2020. There is controversy regarding the precise ultimate aim of some coalition partners. For example, the USA has appeared set on regime change in Syria. See Krishnadev Calamur, 'The Trump Administration Appears to Embrace Regime Change in Syria' *The Atlantic* (6 April 2017) <https://www.theatlantic.com/international/archive/2017/04/us-syria-policy/522117/> accessed 5 September 2020. Given that the Assad government is also combatting Daesh in Syria, regime change goes beyond a defensive purpose. It is unlikely to be either necessary or proportionate to achieving the defensive goal of defeating Daesh. See further Section 1.6.2.

[86] For a factual overview of the conflict, including its history and commentary on the principal protagonists, see Gill, 'Classifying the Conflict in Syria' (n 47) 354–362, 373–377; Michael P Scharf, Milena Sterio and Paul R Williams, *The Syrian Conflict's Impact on International Law* (CUP 2020) 4–16, 30–33.

[87] See, for example, Josie Ensor, 'US Special Forces Carry Out Secret Ground Raid Against ISIL in Syria, 'Killing at Least 25 Jihadists' *The Telegraph* (9 January 2017) <http://www.telegraph.co.uk/news/2017/01/09/us-special-forces-carry-ground-raid-against-isil/> accessed 5 September 2020; 'US Sends Hundreds of Marines to Syria to Support Fight Against ISIS' *The Guardian* (9 March 2017) <https://www.theguardian.com/us-news/2017/mar/09/us-sends-hundreds-of-marines-to-syria-to-support-fight-against-isis> accessed 5 September 2020.

[88] Regarding the ambiguity regarding troop numbers, see Global Coalition, 'Full Transcript of Media Q&A with Major General Jones' (28 June 2017) <http://theglobalcoalition.org/en/full-transcript-of-media-q-a-with-major-general-jones/> accessed 5 September 2020; Dan Lamothe, 'There are Four Times as Many U.S. Troops in Syria as Previously Acknowledged by the Pentagon' *The Washington Post* (6 December 2017) <https://www.washingtonpost.com/news/checkpoint/wp/2017/12/06/there-are-four-times-as-many-u-s-troops-in-syria-as-previously-acknowledged-by-the-pentagon/?utm_term=.830a0949682d> accessed 5 September 2020. On Turkey's ground operations in Syria, see n 104 and n 140.

[89] Global Coalition official figures, which were last updated on 9 August 2017, reported just over 11,200 air strikes in Syria. U.S. Department of Defense, Operation Inherent Resolve, Airstrike Updates <https://www.defense.gov/OIR/> accessed 5 September 2020. The BBC put the official figure at 19,288 in March 2019. 'IS Fight: US-Led Coalition Says it Killed 1,300 Civilians in Syria and Iraq' *BBC* (31 May 2019) <https://www.bbc.co.uk/news/world-middle-east-48473979> accessed 5 September 2020. Estimates by Airwars as of September 2020 suggest that this figure is approximately 19,800. Airwars, 'US-Led Coalition in Iraq & Syria' <https://airwars.org/conflict/coalition-in-iraq-and-syria/> accessed 5 September 2020.

strike release reports since 2014 quickly reveals the scale of the targeting of public and private objects and infrastructure within Syrian territory.[90] These include bridges, tunnels, factories, 'Daesh-held buildings', 'Daesh headquarters', 'Daesh vehicles', 'fighting positions', 'storage facilities' and 'supply routes'. Economic targets are also evident, such as oil collection facilities that have provided the necessary funds for Daesh to govern the areas that have been captured and to carry out military operations.[91]

Putting aside for the moment the issue of the proportionality of these air strikes and the ensuing collateral civilian damage,[92] the current issue is whether, as a general matter, targeting Syrian infrastructure and apparatus in this way might satisfy the test of specific necessity.[93] First, let us consider the Global Coalition's use of force against the military apparatus and personnel of Syrian and pro-Syrian forces. There are a handful of examples. They include air and artillery strikes against such forces operating inside so-called 'de-confliction zones', as well as the shooting down of unmanned aerial vehicles and a SU-22 fighter-bomber.[94] In these cases, it is noteworthy that the reason given by the Global Coalition for targeting Syrian

[90] Operation Inherent Resolve, 'Strike Releases' <https://www.inherentresolve.mil/Releases/Strike-Releases/> accessed 5 September 2020. Global Coalition partners also publish details of their individual activities. For example, UK Ministry of Defence, 'British Forces Air Strikes in Iraq and Syria: Monthly List' <https://www.gov.uk/government/publications/british-forces-air-strikes-in-iraq-monthly-list> accessed 5 September 2020.

[91] For example, 'Operation Tidal Wave II deprived ISIS of 80% of its oil collection facilities as well as $25 million a month in oil revenue which negatively impacted ISIS military operations and halted enemy expansion.' Combined Joint Task Force, Operation Inherent Resolve, 'History' <http://www.inherentresolve.mil/Portals/14/Documents/Mission/HISTORY_17OCT2014-JUL2017.pdf?ver=2017-07-22-095806-793> accessed 5 September 2020. Regarding whether such economic targets constitute 'military objectives' for the purposes of IHL, see n 175.

[92] See Section 4.3.3.

[93] The aim is not to analyse individual instances of targeting, but rather the general policy adopted by the Global Coalition.

[94] For details of these incidents, see Tom Ruys, Luca Ferro and Carl Vander Maelen (eds), 'Digest of State Practice: 1 January—30 June 2017' (2017) 4(2) JUFIL 371, 391–394; Tom Ruys, Carl Vander Maelen and Sebastiaan Van Severen (eds), 'Digest of State Practice: 1 January—30 June 2018' (2018) 5(2) JUFIL 324, 343–344. For a review of whether such targeting renders the Syrian conflict international or non-international in nature, see the ICRC's commentary of 2016 on the First Geneva Convention relating to Art 2 <https://ihl-databases.icrc.org/applic/ihl/ihl.nsf/Comment.xsp?action=openDocument&documentId=BE2D518CF5DE54EAC1257F7D0036B518> accessed 5 September 2020, paras 257–264; Dapo Akande, 'Classification of Armed Conflicts: Relevant Legal Concepts' in Elizabeth Wilmshurst (ed), *International Law and the Classification of Conflicts* (OUP 2012) 32, 70–79; Terry D Gill, 'Letter to the Editor from Professor Terry Gill on Classification of International Armed Conflict' (*Just Security*, 14 October 2016) <https://www.justsecurity.org/33569/letter-editor-prof-terry-gill-classification-international-armed-conflict/> accessed 5 September 2020; Kenneth Watkin, 'The ICRC Updated Commentaries: Reconciling Form and Substance, Part II' (*Just Security*, 30 August 2016) <https://www.justsecurity.org/32608/icrc-updated-commentaries-reconciling-form-substance-part-ii/> accessed 5 September 2020; Adil Haque, 'Between the Law of Force and the Law of Armed Conflict' (*Just Security*, 13 October 2016) <https://www.justsecurity.org/33515/law-force-law-armed-conflict/> accessed 5 September 2020. See further n 114 and accompanying text. Note that the American, French and British airstrikes against Syrian government targets in 2017 and 2018 in response to alleged Syrian deployments of chemical weapons is a separate, and also controversial, issue. See Ruys, Ferro and Maelen, 'Digest of State Practice 2017', 396–402.; Ruys, Maelen and Van Severen, 'Digest of State Practice 2018', 352–368.

and pro-Syrian forces directly has been the defence of Global Coalition and/or partnered forces.[95] The Global Coalition has consistently insisted that its mission is to defeat Daesh in Iraq and Syria and that it does not seek to fight the Syrian regime or forces partnered with them.[96]

In fact, the Global Coalition has gone so far as to publicly admit error in unintentionally targeting Syrian government forces.[97] This admission does not explain away all Global Coalition action in and against Syria, however. The nature, purpose and justification of the so-called 'de-confliction zones' are unclear and reports of the USA occupying a Syrian airfield and Syrian oil fields raise troubling legal issues, not least for necessity and proportionality.[98] Yet, the general trend implies that the Global Coalition does not deem it necessary as a matter of policy to engage the military of the Syrian regime and its partners in order to carry out its defensive operation against Daesh.[99] Instead, they will only engage them directly if the Coalition's defensive operation is threatened with force.

This approach by the Global Coalition is consistent with previous practice. States have frequently asserted a right of self-defence against NSAs in foreign territory and justified their actions by stating that their targeting is limited to the NSAs and they are not using force against the host state itself.[100] This was the case, for

[95] Ruys, Ferro and Maelen, 'Digest of State Practice 2017' (n 94) 391–394; Ruys, Maelen and Van Severen, 'Digest of State Practice 2018' (n 94) 343. An analysis of the legality of this justification is beyond the scope of this book. See Adil Haque, 'On the Precipice: The U.S. and Russia in Syria' (*Just Security*, 19 June 2017) <https://www.justsecurity.org/42297/precipice-u-s-russia-syria/> accessed 5 September 2020.

[96] See Ruys, Ferro and Maelen, 'Digest of State Practice 2017' (n 94) 391–394; Maelen and Van Severen, 'Digest of State Practice 2018' (n 94) 343. See also the documents cited in n 35.

[97] Spencer Ackerman, 'US Military Admits it Mistakenly Targeted and Killed Loyalist Syrian Forces' *The Guardian* (29 November 2016) <https://www.theguardian.com/world/2016/nov/29/us-military-airstrikes-mistake-syria-assad-deir-ez-zor> accessed 5 September 2020. This action was criticized by Russia and Syria and condemned by Venezuela before the UNSC. UNSC Verbatim Record (25 September 2016) UN Doc S/PV.7777, 10 (Russia); 14 (Venezuela); 22 (Syria). See also: 'Syrian War: US Military Strikes Pro-Assad Convoy Amid Clashes with Coalition Forces, Officials Say' *ABC News* (18 May 2017) <http://www.abc.net.au/news/2017-05-19/us-strikes-syria-convoy-threatening-us-backed-forces/8540070> accessed 5 September 2020.

[98] In the absence of additional details, further conclusions are difficult to draw regarding he occupation of the airfield. See, however, Jonathan Horowitz, 'Is the US Allowed to Control a Syrian Airfield?' (*Just Security*, 27 January 2016) <https://www.justsecurity.org/28988/allowed-control-syrian-airfield/> accessed 5 September 2020; Tess Bridgeman, 'About that "Deconfliction Zone" in Syria: Is the United States on Firm Domestic and International Legal Footing?' (*Just Security*, 15 June 2017) <https://www.justsecurity.org/42183/deconfliction-zone-syria-united-states-firm-domestic-international-legal-footing/> accessed 5 September 2020. Regarding the occupation of Syrian territory, including oilfields, see Section 4.3.3.1.

[99] Regarding scholarly support for this general position, Dinstein agrees that host state armed forces must not be engaged and host state 'installations' must be exempt from attack. Dinstein, *War, Aggression and Self-Defence* (n 76) 300. He does not provide reasons for such conclusion, however. This author suggests that the best interpretation of state practice is that it is due to specific necessity. Such explanation is supported, for example, by Tsagourias, 'Self-Defence Against Non-State Actors' (n 76) 823. Tams and Devaney, however, characterize this as an issue of proportionality. Christian J Tams and James Devaney, 'Applying Necessity and Proportionality to Anti-Terrorist Self-Defence' (2012) 45(1) Israel L Rev 91, 105.

[100] Indeed, Trapp notes that up until 2007 all invocations of self-defence against terrorists since 2001 had operated on this basis. Trapp, 'Back to Basics' (n 62) 155.

example, with American action against Al-Qaeda in Sudan and Afghanistan in 1998.[101] Israel has also consistently made this claim in its fight against the Palestine Liberation Organization ('PLO') and Hezbollah.[102] During the 2006 invasion of Lebanon, Israel insisted that it was not attacking the government of Lebanon, but rather the military assets of Hezbollah located in that country. It went on to assert that it had avoided striking Lebanese military assets, unless they were used to assist Hezbollah.[103] Turkey's Operation Olive Branch in 2018 and Operation Peace Spring in 2019 stand as more recent examples. Turkey justified both operations as self-defence against terrorist groups operating in Syria. In so doing, Turkey expressly stated that its military actions were limited to terrorist targets, whilst also emphasizing its commitment to the territorial integrity and political unity of Syria.[104] Iranian anti-terrorist operations in northern Iraq and Syria over the years have relied on similar justifications.[105]

All of these interventions against NSAs in foreign territory are controversial and different positions may be taken regarding their legality. Yet, self-limiting statements of this kind are illustrative of what defending states consider to be the defensive necessity (even if not explicitly characterized in these terms). If the armed attacks and enduring threat originate from the NSAs, then defensive targeting should be limited accordingly. Therefore, state practice supports the general proposition that the governmental and military apparatus and infrastructure of the host state (and its allies) are not to be targeted directly whilst acting in self-defence against NSAs on the territory of the host state. Absent attribution of the armed

[101] Letter dated 20 August 1998 from the Permanent Representative of the United States of America to the United Nations addressed to the President of the Security Council (20 August 1998) UN Doc S/1998/780.

[102] In relation to action against the PLO, see UNSC Verbatim Record (17 March 1978) UN Doc S/PV.2071, paras 52–58 (Israel); UNSC Verbatim Record (2 October 1985) UN Doc S/PV.2611, paras 65–67 (Israel).

[103] Israel Ministry of Foreign Affairs, 'Behind the Headlines: Israel's Counter Terrorist Campaign' (15 August 2006) <http://www.mfa.gov.il/MFA/ForeignPolicy/Issues/Pages/Israels%20counter%20terrorist%20campaign%20-%20FAQ%2018-Jul-2006.aspx> accessed 5 September 2020.

[104] See, for example, Identical Letters dated 20 January 2018 from the Chargé d'Affaires A.I. of the Permanent Mission of Turkey to the United Nations addressed to the Secretary-General and the President of the Security Council (22 January 2018) UN Doc S/2018/53 (Operation Olive Branch); Letter dated 9 October 2019 from the Permanent Representative of Turkey to the United Nations addressed to the President of the Security Council (9 October 2019) UN Doc S/2019/804 (Operation Peace Spring). For an overview of these two incidents, including state reactions to them, see Ruys, Maelen and Van Severen, 'Digest of State Practice 2018' (n 94) 344–352; Patrick M Butchard (ed), 'Digest of State Practice: 1 July—31 December 2019' (2020) 7(1) JUFIL 156, 192–201.

[105] See, for example, Letter dated 11 September 2018 from the Permanent Representative of the Islamic Republic of Iran to the United Nations addressed to the President of the Security Council (11 September 2018) UN Doc S/2018/830; Letter dated 3 October 2018 from the Permanent Representative of the Islamic Republic of Iran to the United Nations addressed to the Secretary-General and the President of the Security Council (3 October 2018) UN Doc S/2018/891; Letter dated 18 April 2001 from the Permanent Representative of the Islamic Republic of Iran to the United Nations addressed to the President of the Security Council (19 April 2001) UN Doc S/2001/381.

attack, it is difficult to argue that targeting such sovereign trappings of 'the state' will ever be necessary to support a self-defence claim.

Narrow exceptions to this general rule are potentially twofold. First, are the aforementioned claims of local force protection during defensive operations.[106] Further clarity is required, however, regarding the facts of these controversial incidents, as well as their acceptability in international law. A possible second exception, exemplified by the targeting of the Taliban during Operation Enduring Freedom, might be where there is complicity between the host state and the NSAs, or the former is somehow supporting or protecting the latter. This remains a unique and unclear potential precedent, however, and its purview is debatable. Absent a very close connection indeed, there can be no defensive purpose served by directly targeting the host state in this manner.[107]

However, the Syria incident does show that states participating in the Global Coalition action against Daesh accept that certain elements within the host state are potentially targetable. Such targets are reflected in the strike release reports referred to above. They exemplify the difficulties with trying to separate permissible 'NSA targets' from impermissible 'host state targets'. *Prima facie*, many of these targets are capable of satisfying the test of specific necessity, regardless of whether we consider such targets to be inherently civilian, or public/state owned. This is on the basis that they are either under the control of Daesh and are being used by them to conduct their armed activities (for example, 'ISIL-held buildings', 'ISIL headquarters', 'fighting positions', and so forth), or directly contribute to these activities and the ongoing threat that such activities pose to Global Coalition partners (for example, bridges, tunnels, factories, oil collection facilities, and so forth). Destroying, capturing or neutralizing such targets either directly affects Daesh's capacity to conduct military operations or cuts off the financing that allows them to continue.[108] Therefore, these targeting decisions are potentially necessary for the effective exercise of the right of self-defence against the NSAs, which is the primary purpose of such action. Any effect on the assets or persons of the host state is incidental to this necessity.[109]

In attempting to draw a line between permissible 'NSA targets' and impermissible 'host state targets' there is a strong argument to be made that when public property is under the control of NSAs (and not under the effective control of the host state), it can no longer be identified with that of 'the state'. This accords with Global Coalition action that is, as a matter of policy, limited to targeting Daesh, and only Daesh, in order to counter the threat that they pose. This is the position

[106] See n 95.

[107] *A fortiori* if the failure to combat the NSAs is due to inability, rather than unwillingness, on the part of the host state. Directly targeting the host state's military would serve only to further impair that ability. This could not logically be regarded as necessary.

[108] See further Section 2.6; n 175 and accompanying text.

[109] See Tsagourias, 'Self-Defence Against Non-State Actors' (n 76) 823, also adopting this position. The permissible extent of such incidental effects is an issue for proportionality. See Section 4.3.3.

explicitly adopted by the Global Coalition[110] and separately by a number of Coalition partners.[111] It also reflects the position of the Global Coalition that their military operations are carried out in areas controlled by Daesh (and, *ipso facto*, not in control of the Syrian government), in partnership with Syrian allies on the ground and aimed at liberating the local Syrian population.[112]

For the purposes of specific necessity, where the Global Coalition targets public or private buildings that have been captured or occupied by Daesh or, in the case of objects like bridges and roads, are being used by Daesh, this is not to be equated with targeting the state of Syria itself.[113] The Global Coalition should only be regarded as using force against the Syrian state when it engages its armed forces directly, attacks national assets that are under Syrian state control, or occupies its territory. The fact that the Global Coalition is avoiding doing all of these things as a matter of policy, albeit without a perfect success rate, provides support for the general premise. Drawing an analogy with the classification of conflicts under IHL also supports this conclusion. Gill argues that where intervening states direct their force solely against the NSAs, albeit without consent on host state territory, the IHL classification is one of a non-international armed conflict between the intervening state(s) and the NSAs, not an international armed conflict between the intervening state(s) and the host state.[114] Applying the same rationale to *jus ad bellum* necessity is logical and accounts for the Global Coalition state practice in Syria.

This argument is strongest with respect to those areas where the Syrian government has lost effective control of its territory. In these circumstances, the necessity

[110] Global Coalition, 'Q&A Session: Transcript of Major General Jones' Opening Remarks, June 26, 2017' (27 June 2017) <http://theglobalcoalition.org/en/qa-session-transcript-of-major-general-jones-opening-remarks-june-26-2017/> accessed 5 September 2020.

[111] See the reports of self-defence to the UNSC referred to in n 35; Brian Egan, Legal Adviser, U.S. Department of State, 'International Law, Legal Diplomacy, and the Counter-ISIL Campaign: Some Observations', Speech to the 110th Annual Meeting of the American Society of International Law (1 April 2016) (2016) 92 Int'l L Stud 235 (hereafter 'USA State Department Legal Adviser Speech 2016') 240–241.

[112] Combined Joint Task Force—Operation Inherent Resolve, Fact Sheet, 'Our Mission' <http://www.inherentresolve.mil/Portals/14/Documents/Mission/20170717-%20Updated%20Mission%20Statement%20Fact%20Sheet.pdf?ver=2017-07-17-093803-770> accessed 5 September 2020.

[113] Syria has complained, however, that by striking Syrian service, economic, industrial and productive infrastructure, the Global Coalition has demonstrated hostile intentions towards it. See, for example, Identical Letters dated 11 January 2016 from the Permanent Representative of the Syrian Arab Republic to the United Nations addressed to the Secretary-General and the President of the Security Council (12 January 2016) UN Doc S/2016/31.

[114] Gill, 'Classifying the Conflict in Syria' (n 47) 367–373. In contrast, Akande maintains that a use of force on the territory of another state, without its consent, is a use of force against that state. Akande, 'Classification of Armed Conflicts' (n 94) 70–79. This is the case, he argues, even if such force is directed only against the NSAs and not against the governmental structures of that state. The result is an international armed conflict between the two states. The ICRC's commentary of 2016 on the First Geneva Convention relating to Art 2 (n 94) paras 224, 260–263, also adopts this approach. Akande accepts, however, that his is the minority view, with most commentators focusing on the nature of the parties to a conflict (where the conflict is between a state and NSAs, for example, this renders it a non-international armed conflict). Conflict classification is an objective test, yet Akande's conclusion also runs contrary to the state practice referred to in this chapter that suggests that defending states do not consider themselves as being in an armed conflict with the host state, regardless of the latter's lack of consent for anti-terrorist operations to be carried out on its territory.

of taking action is greatest, given the inability of the Syrian regime to counter Daesh activities in such areas.[115] Indeed, certain Global Coalition states have explicitly referred to ungoverned space and/or a lack of effective territorial control to rationalize their interventions in Syria against Daesh.[116] That host states lack effective control over territory is an increasing feature of state justifications for transborder military actions against NSAs.[117] Other examples include Iran's reference to Iraq's lack of effective control over its northern territory to justify military action there in response to transborder terrorist attacks.[118] Turkey has relied on the same argument to vindicate its military operations in northern Iraq against the Kurdistan Workers' Party ('PKK')[119] and Israel made a similar claim regarding its strikes against Hezbollah in Lebanon in 2006.[120] In response to the latter incident, the importance of Lebanon extending control over its territory was generally emphasized by states and the UNSC.[121] The lack of effective control over territory is also a feature of the implicit endorsement of Global Coalition action in Syria offered by UNSC Resolution 2249,[122] as well as the ostensibly supportive observations made by the UN Secretary General.[123]

Therefore, state practice arising out of the Syrian incident suggests that self-defence against armed attacks by NSAs might necessarily involve damage to, and destruction of, a host state's apparatus and infrastructure. This points to an increasing acceptance by the states involved of harm to a host state. Yet, in contrast to Operation Enduring Freedom, Global Coalition action against Daesh does

[115] Yet, even if necessary, targeting NSAs in territory in which the host state lacks effective control might still be regarded as breaching that state's sovereignty. Tsagourias, 'Self-Defence Against Non-State Actors' (n 76) 811. See further Section 4.3.3.

[116] For example, Memorandum to the Foreign Affairs Select Committee, 'Prime Minister's Response to the Foreign Affairs Select Committee's Second Report of Session 2015-16: The Extension of Offensive British Military Operations to Syria' (November 2015) <https://old.parliament.uk/documents/commons-committees/foreign-affairs/PM-Response-to-FAC-Report-Extension-of-Offensive-British-Military-Operations-to-Syria.pdf> accessed 5 September 2020, 2, 9. See also the reports of self-defence sent to the UNSC referred to in n 35.

[117] Tams, 'Self-Defence Against Non-State Actors' (n 4) 148.

[118] Letter dated 29 July 1996 from the Permanent Representative of the Islamic Republic of Iran to the United Nations addressed to the Secretary-General (29 July 1996) UN Doc S/1996/602.

[119] See Identical Letters dated 27 June 1996 from the Chargé d'Affaires A.I. of the Permanent Mission of Turkey to the United Nations addressed to the Secretary-General and to the President of the Security Council (2 July 1996) UN Doc S/1996/479, 2; Identical Letters dated 3 January 1997 from the Permanent Representative of Turkey to the United Nations addressed to the Secretary-General and to the President of the Security Council (3 January 1997) UN Doc S/1997/7, 2. Turkey did not make an express claim of self-defence in these instances, but the language employed is approximate. Gray, *Use of Force* (n 1) 147–148.

[120] Identical Letters dated 12 July 2006 from the Permanent Representative of Israel to the United Nations addressed to the Secretary-General and the President of the Security Council (12 July 2006) UN Doc A/60/937–S/2006/515.

[121] UNSC Res 1701 (11 August 2006) UN Doc S/RES/1701, para 3; Ruys, *'Armed Attack'* (n 1) 451–453.

[122] The Resolution exhorted Member States to take action on the territory of Syria under the control of Daesh. UNSC Res 2249 (20 November 2015) UN Doc S/RES/2249. See further Section 4.2.3.3.

[123] See n 149 and accompanying text.

not, as a matter of policy, involve the deliberate targeting of the host state. There are limits on how far states will go in the pursuit of a defensive purpose. Although there may be any number of explanations for such limits, one of the most obvious is specific necessity. Put simply, it is not necessary to target directly manifestations of the Syrian state in order to defend against the Daesh threat.

The distinction between Operation Enduring Freedom and Global Coalition action in Syria partly comes down to the relationship in each case between the host state and the NSAs. In the former case, the active harbouring of the Taliban regime and the refusal to hand over Osama bin Laden meant that to combat Al-Qaeda effectively, it was also deemed necessary to target the Taliban. In contrast, there is no suggestion that President Assad has a positive relationship with Daesh or other terrorist organizations. To the contrary, the Syrian government has insisted that it is 'waging a relentless war on the terrorists'.[124] Therefore, the issue in the latter case is not one of unwillingness, but rather inability (or perceived inability) to deal with the threat effectively.[125] Global Coalition action is accordingly supplementing stated host state policy, rather than conflicting with it (and doing so largely in territory beyond the control of the Assad regime). Therefore, targeting Syrian armed forces is not necessary to achieve a defensive purpose. This explains why the Syrian military has not been deliberately targeted as a matter of policy, but rather sporadically by accident or as a result of claims of local force protection. Degrading the Syrian military would only increase the inability of the regime to deal with the Daesh threat.

Regarding the extent of state practice in support of these general propositions, of the approximately seventy eight states taking part in the Global Coalition, eleven have publicly claimed to be acting in self-defence against Daesh in Syria and have reported this to the UNSC.[126] The fact that not all Global Coalition partners operating in Syria have explicitly made this claim, or made a report, is indicative of the inconsistent state practice in this area. This makes assessing such practice difficult, especially as the absence of a report to the UNSC may speak to whether or not a state genuinely believes itself to be acting in self-defence.[127] However, the actions of Global Coalition partners, both those that have explicitly claimed a right

[124] Identical Letters dated 18 January 2016 from the Chargé d'Affaires A.I. of the Permanent Mission of the Syrian Arab Republic to the United Nations addressed to the Secretary-General and the President of the Security Council (22 January 2016) UN Doc S/2016/46, 2.

[125] See further Sections 4.2.1 and 4.2.2. The unwilling and unable doctrine in the context of the fight against Daesh is particularly controversial. This is partly because President Assad has asserted that he is actively fighting Daesh (and has requested the assistance of other states to do so), potentially suggesting that he is complying with the obligation of due diligence to combat terrorist threats originating from Syrian territory. Moreover, only a handful of states have explicitly, or implicitly, invoked the unable or unwilling doctrine in justifying their acts of self-defence against Daesh in Syria. See Corten, 'The "Unwilling or Unable" Test' (n 57), in particular 778, 780–785, 791–793.

[126] See n 35.

[127] *Nicaragua* (n 44) para 200.

of self-defence and those that have not, as well as the reactions of other states, speak directly to the issue of targeting in the course of defensive operations.

A number of Global Coalition states have taken part in airstrikes in Syria, whilst others have provided weapons, equipment, training and other material support as part of the military action taken against Daesh.[128] In terms of active participation in airstrikes, from North America the USA was assisted by Canada.[129] European partners have included the UK,[130] France,[131] Germany,[132] Denmark,[133] The Netherlands,[134] Norway[135] and Belgium.[136] From north Africa, Morocco sent warplanes,[137] and several Arab countries have carried out, or supported, air strikes. The latter include Saudi Arabia, the UAE, Jordan, Bahrain and Qatar.[138] Australia has also taken part,[139] with Turkey undertaking both air and ground operations against Daesh and Kurdish groups that it regards as terrorist organizations.[140] Italy and Estonia have materially contributed to these military activities.[141] Furthermore, a

[128] See generally the Global Coalition website <https://theglobalcoalition.org/en/> accessed 5 September 2020.

[129] UN Doc S/2015/221 (n 35). Canada later withdrew its fighter jets following the election of Prime Minister Trudeau in October 2015 but continues to participate in Operation Inherent Resolve. Justin Trudeau, Prime Minister of Canada, 'Canada's New Approach to Addressing the Ongoing Crises in Iraq and Syria and Impacts on the Region: Promoting Security and Stability', Prime Minister of Canada (8 February 2016) <http://pm.gc.ca/eng/news/2016/02/08/canadas-new-approach-addressing-ongoing-crises-iraq-and-syria-and-impacts-region> accessed 5 Septembers 2020.

[130] UN Doc S/2015/688 (n 35); UN Doc S/2015/928 (n 35).

[131] UN Doc S/2015/745 (n 35).

[132] UN Doc S/2015/946 (n 35).

[133] UN Doc S/2016/34 (n 35).

[134] UN Doc S/2016/132 (n 35).

[135] UN Doc S/2016/513 (n 35).

[136] UN Doc S/2016/523 (n 35).

[137] 'Moroccan F16s Undertake 20 Missions against 'Islamic State': British Magazine' *Morocco World News* (3 February 2015) <http://www.moroccoworldnews.com/2015/02/150884/moroccan-f16s-undertake-20-missions-islamic-state-british-magazine-2/> accessed 5 September 2020.

[138] U.S. Department of Defense, 'US Military, Partner Nations Conduct Airstrikes in Syria' (23 September 2014) <www.defense.gov/news/newsarticle.aspx?id=123234> accessed 5 September 2020. None of these Arab states have communicated reports of self-defence to the UNSC or otherwise made explicit the legal basis for their actions in Syria. Prior to the start of the Global Coalition action, however, the Arab League stressed 'the right of each member state, in accordance with its wish, to provide all means of self-defense, including military support to back the steadfastness of the Syrian people and the free army'. Arab League, 24th Summit, 21–27 March 2013, '24th Arab Summit Issues Doha Declaration' <http://arableaguesummit2013.qatarconferences.org/news/news-details-17.html> accessed 5 September 2020.

[139] UN Doc S/2015/693 (n 35).

[140] See UN Doc S/2015/563 (n 35); Gul Tuysuz and Zeynep Bilginsoy, 'Ministry: Turkey Joins Coalition Airstrikes against ISIS in Syria' *CNN* (29 August 2015) <http://edition.cnn.com/2015/08/29/europe/turkey-airstrikes/> accessed 5 September 2020; UN Doc S/2016/739 (n 35); Humeyra Pamuk and Jeff Mason, 'Turkish Tanks Roll into Syria, Pushing Islamic State out of Key Border Town' *Reuters* (24 August 2016) <http://uk.reuters.com/article/uk-mideast-crisis-turkey-operation-idUKKCN10Z07L> accessed 5 September 2020. Regarding the large-scale anti-Kurdish offences entitled Operation Olive Branch and Operation Peace Spring, see n 104 and accompanying text.

[141] UNSC Verbatim Record (30 September 2015) UN Doc S/PV.7527, 38 (Italy); UNSC Verbatim Record (14 April 2016) UN Doc S/PV.7670 (Resumption 1) 34 (Estonia). In 2019, Italy hailed the success of Global Coalition action against Daesh in Iraq and Syria. UNSC Verbatim Record (9 July 2019) UN Doc S/PV.8569, 29.

number of states have explicitly supported the Global Coalition's intervention in Syria in deliberations before the UNSC,[142] as has the European Union.[143] Other states have given implicit backing.[144]

The UNSC also gave implicit approval of defensive action against Daesh by way of UNSC Resolution 2249.[145] What is more, the UNSC has since reiterated its call to the international community to combat Daesh and other terrorist groups.[146] Far from condemning Global Coalition action, the UNSC has instead noted the progress made in taking back Daesh controlled territory in Syria. In so doing, the UNSC has expressed grave concern that areas remained under Daesh control and noted the negative impact of Daesh's continued presence, ideology and actions in the region. The UNSC linked the devastating humanitarian impact on the civilian populations to the acts of Daesh and other terrorist organizations, not to the actions of the Global Coalition.[147] It is also notable that the UNGA has avoided criticizing the Global Coalition. As 'world-wide juries', the reaction of these two UN bodies is significant.[148]

The UN Secretary General has followed this trend. He noted the lack of Syrian consent when the airstrikes began in September 2014 (without further comment on this point) and the need for those involved in the campaign to abide by IHL. He went on to remark, however, that the Syrian government was informed beforehand, that the strikes took place in areas not under the effective control of the government and that 'these extremist groups pose an immediate threat to international peace and security'.[149] At the very least, such statement shows an acceptance of the necessity of the Global Coalition intervention and, at best, might be interpreted as supportive of it. Since then, the focus of UN bodies in relation to Syria has generally related to such matters as the (non-)compliance with IHL and international

[142] UNSC Verbatim Record (21 October 2014) UN Doc S/PV.7281, 25 (Rwanda); UN Doc S/PV.7316 (n 37) 35 (Iraq); 65 (Albania); UN Doc S/PV.7527 (n 141) 55 (Bulgaria); 73 (Ukraine).

[143] See UN Docs S/PV.7281 (n 142) 42; S/PV.7540 (Resumption 1) (n 41) 14.

[144] For example, Lithuania has stated that '[i]t is incumbent upon individual Member States to take the steps needed to protect the Syrian people—steps that they are legally entitled to take—and to establish a no-fly zone over part of Syria'. Letter dated 17 March 2015 from the Permanent Representative of Lithuania to the United Nations addressed to the President of the Security Council (18 March 2015) UN Doc S/2015/190, 2–3. Japan has called upon Russia to limit its air strikes against Daesh targets in Syria. In so doing, it appears to accept, as a general principle, the legality of targeting Daesh in that country. It goes on to note, however, that targeting non-Daesh targets 'would be a cause for concern'. UN Doc S/PV.7540 (Resumption 1) (n 41) 19. Angola welcomed 'the broad-based international coalition to fight the so-called Islamic State/Daesh and other terrorist groups.' UNSC Verbatim Record (18 December 2015) UN Doc S/PV.7588, 14. See also UNSC Verbatim Record (8 February 2018) UN Doc S/PV.8178, 11 (Sweden); 12 (Kazakhstan).

[145] This Resolution is discussed in detail in Section 4.2.3.3.

[146] See, for example, UNSC Res 2254 (18 December 2015) UN Doc S/RES/2254, para 8; UNSC Res 2332 (21 December 2016) UN Doc S/RES/2332, 2.

[147] UNSC Res 2332 (n 146) 2.

[148] Tsagourias, 'Self-Defence Against Non-State Actors' (n 76) 824.

[149] Ban Ki-Moon, 'Remarks at the Climate Summit Press Conference (including comments on Syria)' (23 September 2014) <https://www.un.org/sg/en/content/sg/speeches/2014-09-23/remarks-climate-summit-press-conference-including-comments-syria> accessed 5 September 2020.

human rights law in the ongoing conflict, the use of chemical weapons, responding to the dire humanitarian situation on the ground, and facilitating the peaceful settlement of the conflict.[150] Other than the positions of individual states noted in the following paragraphs, the legality or legitimacy of the Global Coalition operating within Syrian territory has been noticeably absent in the deliberations of UN bodies.

Support for the Global Coalition intervention in Syria has clearly not been universal. During the many UNSC meetings held since 2014 that have considered the situation in Syria, a limited number of states have expressed general concern for action taken absent UNSC authorization, as well as the effect on the sovereignty, independence and territorial integrity of Syria.[151] These pronouncements may point to unease regarding Global Coalition military action in Syria, but they also recognize the threat posed by Daesh and do not go so far as to question the legality of such action. Similarly, Sweden has urged the Global Coalition to take 'greater care' in order to protect civilians in Syria but stopped short of directly criticizing the military operation. Kazakhstan took a similar line.[152] Both states have since expressed greater implicit support.[153]

Beyond the UNSC, the Non-Aligned Movement ('NAM') has adopted a more equivocal approach. In 2016, they condemned the actions of Daesh and other Al-Qaeda affiliated groups in Syria and elsewhere, recognizing the threat posed by terrorism to the region and the world.[154] Significantly, the NAM did not offer any comments on the Global Coalition intervention in Syria. Without referencing any specific bodies, states or acts, they simply affirmed, under the general heading of terrorism, that they 'totally reject[ed] targeting other States under the pretext of combating terrorism'.[155] In 2019, the NAM repeated its condemnation

[150] See, for example, Human Rights Council, 'Report of the Independent International Commission of Inquiry on the Syrian Arab Republic' (8 August 2017) UN Doc A/HRC/36/55; UN News Centre, 'Syria: UN Relief Officials Condemn Targeting of Civilians, Infrastructure as Airstrikes Hit Raqqa' (22 August 2017) <http://www.un.org/apps/news/story.asp?NewsID=57396#.WlNLuFSFhqd> accessed 5 September 2020; UNSC Res 2332 (n 146) 2; UNSC Verbatim Record (7 September 2018) UN Doc S/PV.8345; Human Rights Council, 'Report of the Independent International Commission of Inquiry on the Syrian Arab Republic' (2 July 2020) UN Doc A/HRC/44/61; UNSC Res 2504 (10 January 2020) UN Doc S/RES/2504.

[151] See UN Doc S/PV.7271 (n 37) 15 (Argentina); 17–18 (Chile); 20 (China); UNSC Verbatim Record (27 March 2015) UN Doc S/PV.7419, 53 (Pakistan); S/PV.7527 (n 141) 48–49 (Brazil); Hazem Sabbagh, 'South African Ambassador: Syria is an Independent Sovereign State, Can Handle its Own Affairs' *Syrian Arab News Agency* (22 June 2015) <http://sana.sy/en/?p=45877> accessed 5 September 2020. See further Corten, 'The "Unwilling or Unable" Test' (n 57) 789, citing a number of state reactions that point to a general concern regarding the infringement of state sovereignty.

[152] UNSC Verbatim Record (27 April 2017) UN Doc S/PV.7931, 5–6 (Sweden); UNSC Verbatim Record (27 June 2017) UN Doc S/PV.7983, 6 (Kazakhstan).

[153] UN Doc S/PV.8178 (n 144) 11 (Sweden); 12 (Kazakhstan).

[154] 17th Summit of Heads of State and Government of the Non-Aligned Movement, 'Final Document' (17–18 September 2016) <http://cns.miis.edu/nam/documents/Official_Document/XVII-NAM-Summit-Final-Outcome-Document-ENG.pdf> accessed 5 September 2020, paras 258, 258.29.

[155] Ibid, para 258.34.

of violence and terrorism perpetrated by Daesh and Al-Qaida affiliated groups,[156] as well as its general rejection of the threat or use of force in violation of the UN Charter and international law against NAM countries 'under the pretext of combating terrorism or to pursue its political aims'.[157] Once more, however, no mention was made of the Global Coalition's military operations in Syria. Indeed, whilst the NAM condemned 'all violations and acts of terrorism committed by [foreign terrorist fighters] in Iraq, Syria, Libya and elsewhere, *The Heads of State and Government welcomed all victories achieved in the fight to eradicate the threat posed by this phenomenon*'.[158]

We should be hesitant in attributing legal significance to silence regarding particular incidents, and these NAM statements may be interpreted in a number of ways.[159] However, the NAM's hesitance to condemn Global Coalition action contrasts with previous incidents where they have unequivocally stated their objections to expansive military interventions.[160] Furthermore, as the ILC reminds us, '[f]ailure to react over time to a practice may serve as evidence of acceptance as law (*opinio juris*), provided that States were in a position to react and the circumstances called for some reaction'.[161] Given the pertinence of this ILC statement to the Syrian incident and the NAM's restrictive reading of Article 51 of the UN Charter,[162] one might have expected more deliberate language referencing the Global Coalition, had the NAM in fact disapproved of their intervention in Syria.

A smaller group of states have been more emphatic in their negative reactions. Despite not initially submitting a complaint to the UNSC, Syria became increasingly critical, going on to denounce the Global Coalition's intervention as aggression and illegal intervention.[163] Its closest ally in the conflict, Russia, has

[156] 18th Summit of Heads of State and Government of the Non-Aligned Movement, 'Final Document' (25–26 October 2019) <https://namazerbaijan.org/pdf/BFOD.pdf> accessed 5 September 2020, paras 360.39–360.40.

[157] Ibid, para 360.46.

[158] Ibid, para 356 (emphasis added).

[159] Regarding the significance of silence, see Chapter 2, n 213.

[160] Following the 1999 NATO bombings of Kosovo, the Group of 77 and China were swift to reject the so-called 'right' of humanitarian intervention. Group of 77 South Summit, 'Declaration of the South Summit' held in Havana, Cuba (10–14 April 2000) <https://www.g77.org/summit/Declaration_G77Summit.htm> accessed 5 September 2020, para 54.

[161] See Conclusion 10, para 3, and related commentary of the ILC's draft conclusions regarding the identification of customary international law. UNGA, 'Report of the International Law Commission, Sixty-Eighth Session' (2 May–10 June and 4 July–12 August 2016) UN Doc A/71/10, Chapter V.

[162] The NAM's position is that 'Article 51 of the Charter is restrictive and should not be rewritten or reinterpreted'. UNSC Verbatim Record (15 February 2016) UN Doc S/PV.7621, 34.

[163] There are numerous examples of letters sent to, and statements made before, the UNSC to this effect. See, for example, Identical Letters dated 17 September 2015 from the Permanent Representative of the Syrian Arab Republic to the United Nations addressed to the Secretary-General and the President of the Security Council (21 September 2015) UN Doc S/2015/719; Identical Letters dated 9 November 2015 from the Permanent Representative of the Syrian Arab Republic to the United Nations addressed to the Secretary-General and the President of the Security Council (16 November 2015) UN Doc S/2015/851 (2015); Identical Letters dated 26 August 2016 from the Permanent Representative of the Syrian Arab Republic addressed to the Secretary-General and the President of the Security Council (30

also condemned the Global Coalition for unlawful acts of aggression.[164] Iran has characterized their actions as illegal.[165] Other states have followed suit, including Ecuador,[166] Cuba,[167] Venezuela,[168] Egypt,[169] China[170] and Bolivia.[171] Therefore, there are a number of states that have expressly rejected the right of other states to intervene in Syria, absent consent, in order to combat Daesh. Yet, it is notable that Russia and China have only taken their opposition so far. In their capacity as permanent members of the UNSC, and as agents of the international community,[172] they have not vetoed UNSC resolutions (like UNSC Resolution 2249) that are implicitly supportive of anti-terrorist military action within Syrian territory.

Moreover, where states have denounced Global Coalition action, such negative reactions have tended to be phrased in general terms. This makes it hard to engage with the legal question of whether and how they relate to claims of self-defence and, more specifically, the necessity of targeting elements of Syria's civilian infrastructure and apparatus controlled or used by Daesh. Yet, given the nature and scale of Global Coalition action and the fact that it began in 2014, there has been a relative lack of specific and direct condemnation by other states. This is despite the fact that the Syrian incident has been a constant feature of the UNSC agenda ever since. In that time, only a small number of states have explicitly characterized Global Coalition action as unlawful.

In summary, albeit not unequivocal, a careful review of the numerous UNSC deliberations and other sources concerning the situation in Syria since 2014 shows substantial support for the Global Coalition military action against Daesh within Syrian territory. Crucially, this consists of state backing, as well as implicit support

August 2016) UN Doc S/2016/745; UNSC Verbatim Record (13 February 2017) UN Doc S/PV.7882, 46–47; UNSC Verbatim Record (12 April 2017) UN Doc S/PV.7921, 18–20.

164 UN Doc S/PV.8262 (n 10) 26–27.

165 Heather Saul, 'Syria Air Strikes: Iran "Says US Attacks on Isis are Illegal"' *Independent* (23 September 2014) <http://www.independent.co.uk/news/world/middle-east/syria-air-strikes-iran-says-us-attacks-on-isis-are-illegal-9751245.html> accessed 5 September 2020.

166 'Ecuador Rejects US offensive in Syrian Territory', Ecuadorian Ministry of Foreign Affairs and Human Mobility (23 September 2014) <https://www.cancilleria.gob.ec/blog/2014/09/23/ecuador-rechaza-ofensiva-estadounidense-en-territorio-sirio/> accessed 5 September 2020.

167 'We reject unilateral actions and those taken outside the United Nations, such as those of the United States, which is launching air strikes across boundaries of sovereign States in clear violation of international law.' UN Doc S/PV.7281 (n 142) 62.

168 'We denounce the current attempt to apply the same formula in Syria as was done in Iraq and Libya.' UN Doc S/PV.7419 (n 151) 24.

169 Omar Fahmy and Yara Bayoumy, 'Egypt Defends Syria's Territorial Unity after Turkey Moves against IS' *Reuters* (29 July 2015) <http://uk.reuters.com/article/uk-mideast-crisis-syria-egypt-idUKKCN0Q31AY20150729> accessed 5 September 2020.

170 '[The USA's] gross violations of Syria's sovereignty have resulted in the further spread of the terrorist threat.' UNSC Verbatim Record (10 January 2017) UN Doc S/PV.7857, 22.

171 '[W]e see that completely illegal, unilateral military actions are still occurring, [. . .] undermining the sovereignty and integrity of the Syrian Arab Republic and Government efforts to combat Da'esh.' UNSC Verbatim Record (22 May 2017) UN Doc S/PV.7944, 7.

172 UN Charter, Art 24.

from principal UN organs (or, at least, a lack of condemnation from them). To the extent that this reaction is viewed as a positive endorsement, its precise parameters are nevertheless debatable. The position of the unwilling or unable doctrine, for example, is particularly contentious and the legal basis for military action in Syria varies from defending state to defending state. Yet, this incident points to an acceptance of a general right to use defensive force against Daesh in Syria. This is despite a lack of attribution of armed attacks to that state, or substantial involvement by the Assad regime in Daesh's activities (per Article 3(g) of the Definition of Aggression). The Syrian example furthers the general trend of state practice since 9/11 regarding the threshold issue of a right of self-defence against NSAs and is indicative of the international community's stance towards international terrorism as reflected in, and supported by, UNSC Resolution 2249 and subsequent resolutions.[173]

Furthermore, the post-9/11 state practice suggests that where the host state is unwilling or unable to tackle the NSA threat itself (including where it is acquiescing in such threat), defending states might deem it necessary to target non-military elements of a host state being used or occupied by the NSAs that were directly responsible for the armed attack. In these cases, the defending state has no choice of means but to use force both on, and potentially against, the territory of the host state in order to achieve an effective defensive outcome. Such necessity is reflected in UNSC Resolution 2249, where the UNSC unanimously recognized the need to 'eradicate' Daesh safe havens in Syria.[174] This conclusion sits as a general premise, however. At present, firm parameters are difficult to deduce from the aforementioned state practice regarding which particular aspects of the host state's civilian apparatus and infrastructure are viewed by states as lawful targets for the purposes of the *jus ad bellum*. A review of the strike release reports suggests that the members of the Global Coalition carrying out military strikes generally consider that targets must be directly connected to, or supportive of, the military activities of Daesh.[175] Yet, whether as a factual matter they are also connected with

[173] Wood, for example, argues that Resolution 2249 reflects the UNSC's unanimous approval of a right of self-defence against armed attacks by NSAs unattributable to a state. Michael Wood, 'The Use of Force in 2015 With Particular Reference to Syria' (2016) Hebrew University of Jerusalem Legal Studies Research Paper Series No. 16-05, 8. See further Section 4.2.3.3.

[174] Wood notes that the UNSC's reference to taking all necessary measures on Syrian territory under the control of Daesh to eradicate Daesh safe havens 'may be an important statement of what is necessary and proportionate in the circumstances.' Ibid, 8. See further Section 4.3.1.

[175] As noted, to be lawful, targets must also constitute military objectives for the purposes of IHL. See Section 2.6. A controversial category of targets includes objects, such as oil facilities, tankers and so forth, that contribute to financing Daesh's military activities. If the oil production facilities generate revenue that sustain Daesh's operations, this might make an 'effective contribution to military action' for the purposes of targeting them under Art 52(2) of Protocol Additional to the Geneva Conventions, 12 August 1949, and Relating to the Protection of Victims of International Armed Conflicts, 8 June 1977, 1125 UNTS 3. The position will depend on the precise connection between the oil production facilities and the military action. On this basis, such facilities are to be contrasted with 'war sustaining' objects that, although a controversial issue, are not generally viewed as targetable under IHL. See International Law Association Study Group on the Conduct of Hostilities in the 21st Century, 'The Conduct of

actual or imminent armed attacks and serve an identifiable defensive purpose is unclear.[176] Further clarification from states on this point would be welcome.

4.2.3.3 UNSC Involvement—A Limiting Factor

That defending states might lawfully be able to use force in, and potentially against, host sates when combatting terrorist NSAs naturally raises very serious concerns. Once general necessity is established, for states to be able to operate in this manner points to an expansive right of self-defence. Yet, there does appear to be a significant limiting factor on the ability of defending states to target elements of the host state in this way. This factor is the central role played by the UNSC in these specific incidents and in the global response to terrorism more generally. The Global Coalition action in Syria is an obvious example. During 2014 and 2015, and in line with its previous practice, the UNSC consistently condemned the acts of Daesh and other terrorist groups, whilst calling upon all Member States to act collectively to combat the threat to international peace and security caused by terrorist acts.[177] The UNSC proceeded to adopt unanimously Resolution 2249, which reaffirmed that 'terrorism in all forms and manifestations constitutes one of the most serious threats to international peace and security'. It called upon all Member States to 're-double and coordinate their efforts to prevent and suppress terrorist acts [. . .] and to eradicate the safe haven [that terrorists] have established over significant parts of Iraq and Syria'.[178]

Resolution 2249 does not authorize the use of force against Daesh and other named terrorist groups.[179] Instead, the UNSC *called upon* the international community 'to take all necessary measures, in compliance with international law' to respond to the stated terrorist threat.[180] Yet, such exhortation implicitly applies

Hostilities and International Humanitarian Law: Challenges of 21st Century Warfare' (2017) 93 Int'l L Stud 322, 340–342. The USA takes a different approach to 'war sustaining' objects. For commentary in the context of the fight against Daesh, see Kenneth Watkin, 'Sustaining the War Effort: Targeting Islamic State Oil Facilities' (*Just Security*, 3 October 2014) <https://www.justsecurity.org/15890/sustaining-war-effort-targeting-islamic-state-oil-facilities/> accessed 5 September 2020; Beth Van Schaack, 'Targeting Tankers Under the Law of War (Part 1)' (*Just Security*, 2 December 2015) <https://www.justsecurity.org/28064/targeting-tankers-law-war-part-1/> accessed 5 September 2020. As to whether Daesh's money is a legitimate target, see Daphné Richemond-Barak, 'Is Money a Legitimate Target?' (*Just Security*, 10 February 2016) <https://www.justsecurity.org/29255/money-legitimate-target/> accessed 5 September 2020.

[176] See Section 2.6.

[177] See, for example, UNSC Res 2178 (24 September 2014) UN Doc S/RES/2178; UNSC Res 2195 (19 December 2014) UN Doc S/RES/2195; UNSC Res 2199 (12 February 2015) UN Doc S/RES/2199; UNSC Res 2214 (27 March 2015) UN Doc S/RES/2214.

[178] UNSC Res 2249 (n 122). See further UN Doc S/PV.7565 (n 48).

[179] The Resolution was not passed under Chapter VII of the UN Charter, nor does it authorize or decide that force should be used. See further Dapo Akande and Marko Milanovic, 'The Constructive Ambiguity of the Security Council's ISIS Resolution' (*EJIL:Talk!*, 21 November 2015) <https://www.ejiltalk.org/the-constructive-ambiguity-of-the-security-councils-isis-resolution/> accessed 5 September 2020; Wood, 'The Use of Force' (n 173) 7.

[180] UNSC Res 2249 (n 122).

to each state employing its right of self-defence in response to armed attacks. The UNSC's adopted language confers a degree of legitimacy on states making this claim. Wood, for example, characterizes Resolution 2249 as an endorsement of claims of self-defence against Daesh in Syria and Tams argues that it lent 'international authority' to forcible responses contemplated by states.[181] Similarly, Akande and Milanovic maintain that Resolution 2249's constructive ambiguity might provide political cover for military intervention, without endorsing any particular legal basis for such action.[182] Significantly, following the passing of UNSC Resolution 2249 in 2015, six states invoked it in support of their claims of self-defence against Daesh in Syria, explicitly referencing the Resolution in their Article 51 reports of self-defence to the UNSC.[183] More specifically, this practice can be interpreted as these states accepting a collective determination of the necessity of action against Daesh in Syria. As a factual matter, the UNSC is confirming Syria's unwillingness or inability to counter Daesh on its territory.[184]

The UNSC's role in this incident is not unique. In response to 9/11, it explicitly recognized and reaffirmed the right of self-defence, thereby providing implicit support for the ensuing Operation Enduring Freedom.[185] Prior to this, the UNSC had insisted that the Taliban cease supporting terrorism and take effective action to combat it, including by cooperating with the international community.[186] The UNSC had also demanded that the Taliban hand over the mastermind of the attacks,[187] determined that the Taliban was itself a threat to international peace and security,[188] and condemned the Taliban for allowing its territory to be used as a base for the export of terrorism and for providing a safe haven for terrorists.[189] As such, there was more than mere unwillingness or inability on the part of host state (*viz* Afghanistan) that gave rise to a necessity of self-defence.

[181] Wood, 'The Use of Force' (n 173) 8, noting that no one at the UNSC meeting that adopted the Resolution suggested otherwise; Tams, 'Self-Defence Against Non-State Actors' (n 4) 151.

[182] Akande and Milanovic, 'Constructive Ambiguity' (n 179).

[183] UN Doc S/2015/928 (n 35) (UK); UN Doc S/2015/946 (n 35) (Germany); UN Doc S/2016/34 (n 35) (Denmark); UN Doc S/2016/132 (n 35) (The Netherlands); UN Doc S/2016/513 (n 35) (Norway); UN Doc S/2016/523 (n 35) (Belgium). Although not unanimous, or necessarily explicit, the views of a number of individual UNSC members of UNSC Resolution 2249 can also be interpreted as it being supportive of military action against Daesh in Syria. See UN Doc S/PV.7565 (n 48) 2 (France); 4 (USA); 5 (Nigeria); 6–7 (Jordan); 7 (Angola) 8–9 (UK).

[184] Along similar lines, Hakimi and Cogan argue that the six states are using UNSC Res 2249 to establish, as a legal fact, that the preconditions for defensive force have been met. Monica Hakimi and Jacob Katz Cogan, 'A Role for the Security Council on Defensive Force?' (*EJIL:Talk!*, 21 October 2016) <https://www.ejiltalk.org/a-role-for-the-security-council-on-defensive-force/> accessed 5 September 2020. See also Henderson, *The Use of Force and International Law* (n 1) 327. For the effect of this Resolution on proportionality, see Section 4.3.1.

[185] UNSC Res 1368 (12 September 2001) UN Doc S/RES/1368; UNSC Res 1373 (n 24).

[186] UNSC Res 1267 (n 71) para 1.

[187] Ibid, para 2.

[188] This was because the Taliban had failed to respond to demands to 'stop providing sanctuary and training for international terrorists and their organizations, and [to] cooperate with efforts to bring indicted terrorists to justice.' Ibid; UNSC Res 1214 (8 December 1998) UN Doc S/RES/1214, para 13.

[189] UNSC Res 1378 (14 November 2001) UN Doc S/RES/1378.

State practice associated with Operation Enduring Freedom and the ongoing Global Coalition action against Daesh in Syria points to an increased acceptance by a large number of states of the necessity of taking defensive action against NSAs that results in material harm to the host state. Such action might even include the direct targeting of elements of a host state. State support for this proposition is conditioned, however. The UNSC's response to the nature of the terrorist threat and to the particular host state is significant in each of these incidents. They are not simply cases of unilateral determinations of inability or unwillingness and ensuing actions by a state, or groups of states.

First, these incidents of practice arise in the context of international terrorism that the UNSC has reacted to in a very specific manner. Second, they are limited to cases where the host state has failed to take effective remedial action against NSAs at the express behest of the international community, acting through the UNSC.[190] As Zimmerman notes, where the UNSC requests the host state to take action against armed groups operating within its territory, and it fails to do so, this constitutes a specific form of qualified inaction on the latter's part.[191] A similar pattern also occurred prior to Israel's invasion of Lebanon in 2006. On a number of occasions, the UNSC called upon Lebanon to exercise effective control over its territory and to prevent attacks over the Blue Line into Israel. This action might account for the initial widespread support for Israel's intervention, which was later broadly condemned as disproportionate due to the scale of the operation.[192]

Third, as noted, in such cases the UNSC has implicitly established as a factual matter the necessity of defending states taking action within the host state's territory. It has expressed a collective view, as agent of the international community, on the unwillingness or inability of the host state to tackle the terrorist threat. Such a collective determination of necessity acts as an additional limiting factor on the ability of defending states to take action in and against a host state. Therefore, any ensuing harm to the host state is the price of repeated failure to live up to the collective demands placed upon such states by international law and the international community.[193]

[190] This is most clearly seen in the case of the Taliban and Al-Qaeda. With Syria, there is an argument that President Assad has been actively fighting Daesh and other terrorist groups and has enlisted the help of its allies, Russia and Iran, to do so. However, Global Coalition action in Syria suggests that much of the international community view these efforts as being ineffective. UNSC Res 2249 (n 122) confirms this view.

[191] Andreas Zimmermann, 'The Second Lebanon War: *Jus ad bellum, Jus in Bello* and the Issue of Proportionality' (2007) 11 Max Planck Yrbk UN L 99, 120–121. Zimmerman does not specify that the failure by the host state is to take *effective* action against the NSAs at the UNSC's behest, yet this is the natural implication.

[192] See, for example, UNSC Res 1583 (28 January 2005) UN Doc S/RES/1583, para 4; UNSC Res 1614 (29 July 2005) UN Doc S/RES/1614, para 6; UNSC Res 1655 (31 January 2006) UN Doc S/RES/1655, para 8. See further Section 3.3.5.

[193] As to the proportionality of that harm, see Section 4.3.3.

4.2.4 NSA Armed Attacks—Timing and Imminence

4.2.4.1 Temporal Duration of the Right of Self-Defence

Identifying the period of time over which the right of self-defence against terrorist NSAs subsists is more complex than in the interstate context. Factually determining when the goals of self-defence are achieved is much less clear. From a temporal perspective, what does the end point look like? In contrast to traditional interstate conflict, terrorists tend not to disarm or sign formal instruments of surrender in order to enter into a political process ensuring peace. Moreover, groups such as Al-Qaeda and Daesh are unlikely to renounce their ideology and give up their terrorist activities.[194] As a general premise, however, even if the eradication of international terrorism is the stated goal of the international community, self-defence cannot stand as the legal justification for it. Under the *jus ad bellum*, the right of self-defence does not provide a basis for a permanent war footing or a long-term solution to the security threat posed by terrorist NSAs.[195]

Section 3.3.2 posits that general necessity, rather than proportionality, most naturally imposes an independent time limit on the exercise of self-defence. In the context of international terrorism, general necessity's potential as a meaningful *jus ad bellum* restraint on state action is readily apparent. At some point, states will have degraded and dismantled the operational capacity and supporting networks of terrorist organizations like Daesh to such an extent that they will have been effectively destroyed and will no longer be able to attempt or launch strategic attacks.[196] It is unlikely that it will be possible to identify the precise moment in time when this happens, and the concept of 'defeat' is open to varying interpretations.[197] For example, despite the liberation of all Daesh-held territory in Iraq and Syria, Global Coalition states in 2019 and 2020 confirmed the enduring threat posed by Daesh and the Coalition's commitment to ensuring its lasting defeat and preventing its resurgence.[198] What this means in practice is not specified.

[194] These issues were noted in The White House, 'Report on the Legal and Policy Frameworks Guiding the United States' Use of Military Force and Related National Security Operations' (December 2016) <https://www.justsecurity.org/wp-content/uploads/2016/12/framework.Report_Final.pdf> accessed 5 September 2020, 11; Jeh Charles Johnson, General Counsel of the U.S. Department of Defense, 'The Conflict Against Al-Qaeda and its Affiliates: How Will it End?', Speech at the Oxford Union (30 November 2012) <https://www.lawfareblog.com/jeh-johnson-speech-oxford-union> accessed 5 September 2020.

[195] Achieving a long-term solution to international terrorism, including a politically stable environment in the countries concerned, should not be viewed as part of the emergency right that is self-defence. Rather, a solution should be sought through collective action via the UNSC and other international bodies, working in conjunction with host states.

[196] White House, 'Report on the Legal and Policy Frameworks' (n 194) 11–12.

[197] Ibid. Blank provides a general overview of the issues surrounding an enduring right of self-defence against terrorist NSAs and what it means to defeat them. Laurie Blank, 'The Extent of Self-Defence against Terrorist Groups: For How Long and How Far?' (2017) 47 Israel YB Hum Rts 265, especially 282–316.

[198] U.S. Department of State, 'Statement by Ministers of the Global Coalition to Defeat ISIS/Daesh' (6 February 2019) <https://www.state.gov/statement-by-ministers-of-the-global-coalition-to-defeat-isis-daesh/> accessed 5 September 2020; U.S. Department of State, 'Joint Statement on the Ninth

Nevertheless, as the USA has recognized, there is likely be a tipping point when the military operation against a particular group of NSAs has had such an effect that a counterterrorist law enforcement operation will be capable of replacing it.[199] This conclusion was reached in the context of whether the USA was in a non-international armed conflict with Al-Qaeda for the purposes of IHL.[200] Yet, the same logic is compelling when considering *jus ad bellum* general necessity and the duration of the right of self-defence. When hostilities are reduced to such a level that armed conflict can be replaced by law enforcement, force is not the only reasonable option and will be unnecessary (other than to counter further imminent armed attacks). This might be so in one particular territory or region, or globally. As such, focusing on general necessity has the potential to assuage concerns regarding the (im)possible application of proportionality in these circumstances.[201] As general necessity is the first requirement to be satisfied, it bears the burden of ensuring that a defensive response is temporally limited. Unfortunately, the capacity of general necessity to operate in this way is being put under pressure by how states and the UNSC approach the question of imminence.

4.2.4.2 Imminence

Armed attacks by terrorist NSAs tend to be one-off or temporally limited surprise attacks, rather than forming a military campaign with a clear beginning and end. This means that defending state responses are likely to take place after such attacks have ended, or before they have begun.[202] Where armed attacks form part of an enduring threat, the right to respond defensively depends on whether further armed attacks are imminent.[203] Imminent armed attacks by terrorists are often much more difficult to identify than traditional interstate threats,[204] although the accumulation of events doctrine might assist states to knit together past, ongoing and imminent armed attacks in order to maintain a right of self-defence against terrorists conducting a campaign over time.[205] This ability is controversial, however. Its

Anniversary of the Syrian Uprising' (15 March 2020) <https://www.state.gov/joint-statement-on-the-ninth-anniversary-of-the-syrian-uprising/> accessed 5 September 2020.

199 Johnson, 'The Conflict Against Al-Qaeda' (n 194).

200 On the classification of non-international armed conflicts and applicable IHL, see Dieter Fleck, The Law of Non-International Armed Conflict' in Dieter Fleck (ed), *The Handbook of International Humanitarian Law* (3rd edn, OUP 2013) 581. Regarding the issues with identifying the end of such conflicts, see Dustin A Lewis, Gabriella Blum and Naz K Modirzadeh, 'Indefinite War: Unsettled International Law on the End of Armed Conflict', The Harvard Law School Program on International Law and Armed Conflict (2017) <https://dash.harvard.edu/handle/1/30455582> accessed 5 September 2020, especially 51–66, 96–105.

201 See Section 4.3.

202 Tams, 'Necessity and Proportionality' (n 17) 394.

203 See Section 2.5.1.2.

204 Noam Lubell, 'The Problem of Imminence in an Uncertain World' in Weller (ed), *The Oxford Handbook* (n 1) 697, 707.

205 See Section 2.5.2.2.

adoption risks widening the ambit of self-defence to unacceptable dimensions and states abusing this right.

As noted in Section 2.5.1.2, a right of self-defence against imminent armed attacks is not understood to include responses to non-specific, potential, or perceived threats. Yet, in the context of countering NSA terrorist threats, state practice suggests a broad interpretation of imminence. It is noteworthy that UNSC Resolution 2249 stipulates that Daesh 'has the capability and intention to carry out further attacks'.[206] This reference *prima facie* pertains to an ongoing threat, comprising possible future attacks. Weller refers to this Resolution as recognizing a 'permanent imminence' of armed attacks. He concludes that, in considering Daesh's track record and confirming that it represents a permanent and active threat of further attack, the UNSC appears to relieve individual states from having to fulfil the criteria for self-defence. 'It is no longer necessary to demonstrate that they are acting in response to an actual or imminent armed attack and in a situation of instant and overwhelming necessity leaving no choice of means and no moment of deliberation.'[207] The UK parliament has also expressed concerns regarding the notion of permanent imminence in respect of the UK's response to individuals that have been identified as posing a terrorist threat.[208]

States intervening in Syria against Daesh and others have generally been hesitant to rely on imminence alone to justify self-defence.[209] They have instead opted, in whole or in part, for the more easily established justification of the collective self-defence of Iraq.[210] Nevertheless, in support of their right of action, such states have also tended to refer to the ongoing 'threat' posed by Daesh. Such threat is identified as being either to that state specifically, and/or to other states, and/or to international peace and security more generally.[211] As noted, a number of states have explicitly referenced UNSC Resolution 2249 to support such claim.[212] Therefore, there may be situations where specific future armed attacks against a particular

[206] UNSC Res 2249 (n 122).

[207] Marc Weller, 'Permanent Imminence of Armed Attacks: Resolution 2249 (2015) and the Right to Self Defence Against Designated Terrorist Groups' (*EJIL:Talk!*, 25 November 2015) <https://www.ejiltalk.org/permanent-imminence-of-armed-attacks-resolution-2249-2015-and-the-right-to-self-defence-against-designated-terrorist-groups/> accessed 5 September 2020.

[208] Joint Committee on Human Rights, *The Government's Policy on the Use of Drones for Targeted Killing* (2015-16, HL 141, HC 574) para 3.39.

[209] See Section 2.5.1.2, however, regarding claims made by the USA and the UK. See also Identical Letters dated 22 February 2015 from the Permanent Representative of Turkey to the United Nations addressed to the Secretary-General and the President of the Security Council (23 February 2015) UN Doc S/2015/127.

[210] See the reports to the UNSC of self-defence referenced in n 35.

[211] UN Doc S/2014/695 (n 35) (USA); UN Doc S/2015/221 (n 35) (Canada); UN Doc S/2015/563 (n 35) (Turkey); UN Doc S/2015/745 (n 35) (France); UN Doc S/2015/928 (n 35) (UK); UN Doc S/2015/946 (n 35) (Germany); UN Doc S/2016/34 (n 35) (Denmark); UN Doc S/2016/132 (n 35) (The Netherlands); UN Doc S/2016/513 (n 35) (Norway); UN Doc S/2016/523 (n 35) (Belgium).

[212] See Section 4.2.3.3.

state are not identified, yet NSA terrorists are deemed by states and the UNSC as posing an ongoing threat justifying an enduring exercise of self-defence.

Where this is so, imminence and necessity more broadly are stretched to the extremes of their conceptual boundaries.[213] The concern is that they are being disregarded as requirements for lawful self-defence against the threat posed by terrorist NSAs. Alternatively, and more optimistically, we might say that this state practice points to the continuing general necessity of some form of defensive response against an enduring terrorist threat. Given the particular nature of that threat, and the absence of effective UNSC action and peaceful alternatives, this conclusion recognizes that states simply have no choice of means to counter it. Such a view is still disconcerting, however. It constitutes an extremely broad conception of self-defence, stretching it far beyond a temporary right to respond to a situation of emergency. It also risks ignoring the analysis set out in Section 4.2.4.1 that when hostilities are reduced to such a level that they can be replaced by law enforcement, force is not the only reasonable option, and will be unnecessary. If states have indeed accepted this expansive view of self-defence, or might adopt it in the future, the burden falls to specific necessity to govern whether a particular defensive response is lawful in the circumstances. This is to ask whether the exercise of self-defence is necessary against a particular terrorist group operating in a particular state at any given time. This is a very heavy burden for specific necessity to bear. These conclusions are discussed further in the next section.

4.3 Proportionality and Armed Attacks by NSAs

When defending states evidently abuse their right of self-defence, other states might adopt a near-unanimous view of the disproportionality of that action. Israel's invasion of Lebanon in 2006 is an obvious case in point.[214] However, despite this example, armed attacks by NSAs generally pose significant challenges to the interstate conception of proportionality set out in Chapter 3. Proportionality operates in state-on-state self-defence to avoid large-scale wars, yet recent state practice in the context of international terrorism suggests a much more liberal approach to this requirement. As will be seen below, states often act beyond their immediate defensive needs when combatting NSA terrorists. Their responses might encompass preventing potential future armed attacks by eliminating the NSA terrorists entirely. Customary international law is evolving on this point, and it remains to be seen where it will settle.

[213] Controversially, Bethlehem argues that states must be able to act in self-defence where there is evidence of further imminent terrorist attacks, even if there is no specific evidence of where such attack will take place or of the precise nature of the attack. Bethlehem, 'Self-Defense Against an Imminent or Actual Armed Attack by Nonstate Actors' (n 1) 772.

[214] See Section 3.3.5.

The following study reveals that proportionality is not irrelevant to regulating state responses to international terrorism. Yet, the analysis does divulge the deficiencies in the ability of proportionality to control state action against terrorist NSAs and reveals it to be weak.[215] Therefore, a solution is offered that focuses on necessity. As a general premise, the main challenges to the interstate understanding of proportionality relate to measuring the danger posed to the defending state by actual and future NSA armed attacks and whether, in this context, the legitimate purposes of self-defence are consequently broader. In addition, as with necessity, much of the debate focuses on the host state, in particular how it is affected by a defending state's defensive acts on its territory.

4.3.1 A More Permissive Response vis-à-vis Terrorist NSAs

Post-9/11 state practice suggests that states consider that they have greater flexibility in acting in self-defence against terrorist NSAs than they do against other states. Recent incidents reveal how states might take extensive action to defend themselves against what they perceive to be a terrorist 'threat'.[216] In such cases, the putative defensive response might be greatly in excess of the corresponding armed attack(s), encompassing far-reaching aims. Indeed, irrespective of the objective dangers of terrorism, states might consider it legitimate to eliminate the terrorist threat entirely.[217] With a few notable exceptions referenced in this chapter, practice also shows how other states and international organizations will tend to give defending states much greater leeway in their responses to armed attacks from terrorist NSAs when compared to interstate self-defence. This attitude is particularly evident in cases where there has been a history of attacks from NSAs and the fear of repeated attacks is well founded.[218]

Expansive responses to counter further threats from the same source were discussed in Section 2.5.2.2. Examples included Turkey's Operation Sun in 2008 and the American-led response to 9/11. The latter incident is particularly noteworthy.

[215] See Tams and Devaney, 'Necessity and Proportionality' (n 99) 102, reaching the same conclusion.

[216] This section maintains that the 'threat' of international terrorism appears to account for a more permissive attitude to proportionality than is seen in the interstate context. The term 'threat' has been referred to in various contexts throughout this book and is discussed further below in this section. As has been made clear, however, to allow for a lawful defensive response such threat must comprise past, ongoing and/or imminent armed attacks. See further Section 2.5.2.2 regarding the accumulation of events doctrine. As noted in Section 4.2.4, however, the often-sporadic nature of NSA armed attacks makes evaluating the totality of a terrorist NSA threat, and whether it is current or has ended, very difficult.

[217] Tams, 'Necessity and Proportionality' (n 17) 411–412, arguing that the strong international response to terrorism has led to a normative reorientation that means that terrorist threats are invariably considered grave, even where the likelihood of attack or risk to the defending state is realistically not great. The state practice set out in this chapter, and the book more generally, supports this conclusion.

[218] Tams, 'Necessity and Proportionality' (n 17) 413.

Although not authorizing force, the UNSC explicitly recognized and reaffirmed the inherent right of individual and collective self-defence in response to Al-Qaeda's acts of terror. It also concluded that any act of international terrorism is a threat to international peace and security and should be combatted by 'all means'.[219] This was the prelude to the invasion of Afghanistan under the auspices of Operation Enduring Freedom and the removal of the Taliban regime. Crucially, such response was widely supported by the international community.[220]

The Global Coalition action against Daesh in Syria (examined in detail in Sections 4.2.3.2 and 4.3.3.2) constitutes the most recent and illuminating example of a defensive response that is, *prima facie*, vastly in excess of the threat faced by those states purportedly acting in self-defence. Therefore, it is deserving of particular scrutiny. It was noted in Section 4.2.3.2 that state practice since 2014 appears to show substantial support for the Global Coalition military action against Daesh within Syrian territory. The UNSC's adoption of Resolution 2249 is illustrative of the more permissive attitude towards the anti-terrorist operations. In this Resolution, the UNSC determined unanimously that terrorist groups such as Daesh, together with all acts of terrorism, constitute a global and unprecedented threat to international peace and security.[221] As noted, the UNSC also asserted that the named terrorist groups have the capability and intention to carry out further attacks, which might be read as confirming the 'permanent imminence' of future armed attacks.[222] Remarkably, the UNSC also called for the eradication of safe havens that such groups had established over significant parts of Iraq and Syria.[223]

The language adopted by the UNSC leaves states considerable discretion to act in accordance with its exhortation. The UNSC's approach also informs an understanding of the nature of the threat and the required response. UNSC Resolution 2249 endorses the view that self-defence might include as a legitimate aim the total elimination of the NSA terrorists or, at a minimum, eradicating all safe havens from which they benefit. The Resolution may thus be read as the unanimous view of the UNSC, acting on behalf of the international community, regarding what is a proportionate response in the circumstances.[224] This perspective is significant, particularly for those six states that have explicitly referenced UNSC Resolution 2249 to support their claim of acting in self-defence against Daesh in Syria.[225] The eventual destruction of Daesh is also the common mantra of the eighty-two members of the Global Coalition.[226] This collective view prevails even if it cannot

[219] UNSC Res 1368 (n 185); UNSC Res 1373 (n 24).
[220] See Section 4.2.3.1.
[221] UNSC Res 2249 (n 122).
[222] See Section 4.2.4.2.
[223] UNSC Res 2249 (n 122).
[224] Wood, 'The Use of Force' (n 173) 7.
[225] See n 183.
[226] 'Together, the Coalition is committed to degrading and ultimately defeating Daesh.' Global Coalition website <http://theglobalcoalition.org/en/home/> accessed 5 September 2020.

sensibly be asserted that the NSAs pose an existential threat to the states that respond defensively against them. As such, this practice reflects the notion that proportionate defensive responses against terrorist NSAs (or at least NSAs like Daesh and Al-Qaeda) may be greater than a comparable threat in the interstate context where, absent an existential threat, an equivalent goal would usually be regarded as disproportionate.[227]

It is not this author's position, but it is tempting conclude that, in the context of transnational terrorism, the aims of self-defence are more broadly defined.[228] If this view is adopted, such that destroying NSAs is an accepted purpose of self-defence, this pushes the right far beyond the boundaries of an emergency act of protection. A stated purpose of 'destruction' unacceptably blurs the line between lawful self-defence and unlawful armed reprisals. Moreover, it deprives proportionality of meaning. A defensive act cannot be proportionate to 'destruction'. Therefore, the eradication of NSAs should not be viewed as a defensive aim any more than regime change, or occupation.[229] Destruction is a means, rather than an end. This is to say that it might well be necessary to destroy the group of NSAs, but the necessity arises from a defensive purpose: halting, repelling or preventing armed attacks. Destruction is potentially proportionate to achieving that purpose, but this will rarely be the case. Necessity and proportionality can only possess meaning and have the capacity to restrain state action if the defensive purpose is understood in this way. Otherwise, military operations against NSAs are rendered unrestricted.

UNSC Resolution 2249 reflects that fact that defensive action against terrorist NSAs might be deemed to be more permissive, yet it must nevertheless be restrained. The call to Member States in the Resolution is not to take unlimited action against Daesh and other named groups. The UNSC asks states to take all necessary measures *in compliance with international law*. Although not specified, by implication this must include the provisions of the UN Charter (most pertinently Article 51), as well as customary international law (including the requirements of necessity and proportionality). Moreover, the objects of the defensive response are specified groups,[230] and the area of operation is geographically confined to the territories of Iraq and Syria.[231] These limitations accord with the general principles of necessity and proportionality as they apply to the right of self-defence.[232]

227 See Sections 3.3.4.2 and 3.5.

228 See, for example, Tams, 'Necessity and Proportionality' (n 17) 412–413.

229 See Section 1.6.2.

230 Being Daesh, Al Qaida and its associates, and other UNSC designated groups.

231 Para 5 of UNSC Res 2249 (n 122) purports to further limit the geographical scope of action to Iraqi and Syrian territory *under the control* of Daesh.

232 As noted in Section 4.2.3.3, the Resolution implicitly speaks to this right. Absent UNSC authorization to use force (which the Resolution does not provide) and absent Syrian government consent (which has not been forthcoming) the right of self-defence is the only available legal justification to use force against Daesh on Syrian territory.

Therefore, the UNSC's statements should not be read as an open-ended endorsement of combatting terrorist NSAs or terrorism in an abstract sense. Phrases such as the 'war on terror', the 'fight against terrorism', and the like, are often expressed by states and commentators, but this goes well beyond what is permitted by the terms of the UN Charter and applicable custom. States have no right of self-defence against an 'ism', only against an actual or (potentially) imminent armed attack. Fighting terrorism as a concept negates the limitations imposed by necessity and proportionality. It is impossible for these requirements to have any meaningful application in respect of combatting a nebulous abstraction like 'terrorism in all forms and manifestations'. Dispensing with necessity and proportionality would be contrary to the exhortation in UNSC Resolution 2249 to comply with the law.

As set out in Section 1.6.2, our understanding of the goals of self-defence should remain limited to the defensive: halting, repelling and/or preventing an armed attack. However, what in the interstate context might be viewed as legitimate to achieve these aims might take on different dimensions in the context of terrorist NSA armed attacks. States and the UNSC undoubtedly recognize greater elasticity in this context, at least in respect of tackling armed groups such as the PKK, Al-Qaeda, Daesh, and the like. The UNSC's general approach to terrorism is particularly interesting for a proportionality analysis. As noted, the issue of international peace and security forms part of the overall balancing of interests that proportionality seeks to achieve. That the UNSC has determined that terrorist NSAs pose a threat to such peace and security perhaps accounts for the more permissive attitude that the UNSC and states generally adopt vis-à-vis those states that combat them.

The nature of the actors, and the perceived harm that they threaten, appear to be determinative of this permissive attitude. States are not considering the threat of harm to only one state, or even a group of states. It is viewed as a global threat faced by all states and it is thought to be enduring. Moreover, the threat goes beyond an interstate paradigm to one where non-states are seeking to destabilize, and even destroy, states and the global order more generally.[233] Such states are victims of actual or imminent armed attacks, and/or are acting in defence of other direct victims, but their defensive action is also potentially in the collective interests of the international community.[234] They act with the international community's implicit

[233] Regarding Daesh, including its partly apocalyptic ideology, see Daniel Byman, 'Understanding the Islamic State—A Review Essay' (2016) 40(4) International Security 127, 136–9. For an overview of the goals of Al Qaeda, see Daniel Byman, *Al Qaeda, the Islamic State, and the Global Jihadist Movement: What Everyone Needs to Know* (OUP 2015) 47–51.

[234] In contrast, in the context of state responsibility, the ability of 'non-injured states' to respond on an *actio popularis* basis in the collective interest is circumscribed. There is no clearly recognized right to take collective countermeasures against a wrongdoing state. ARSIWA (n 1) paras 2–6 of the commentary to Art 54. In any event, countermeasures may not involve the threat or use of force. ARSIWA (n 1) Art 50(1)(a). With self-defence against armed attacks by NSA terrorists, however, the target of collective military action is not a state (even if the NSA target operates on the territory of a state) and the implicit support of the UNSC (acting as agent of the international community) means that the UNSC is part of the collective response, not excluded from it.

endorsement to counter a threat to that community and to restore international peace and security.[235]

We should hesitate, however, in accepting that a group of defending states, such as the Global Coalition, may legitimately act in place of the collective security function of the UNSC.[236] The UNSC's approach to terrorist NSAs, and the steps taken by defending states in support of it, have significant implications for how we might conceive of the proportionality of defensive action against these actors when compared to self-defence against states. Yet, practice suggests that there are restrictions even in this context. The notion of a defending state having greater latitude to respond to a terror threat to it, and the entire world, has been advanced before. Israel adopted this approach, and its role in the 'war on terror', to justify its invasion of Lebanon in 2006.[237] The majority of the international community refused to allow Israel to stretch the boundaries of proportionality too far, however. They employed proportionality as a rhetorical tool to condemn Israel's actions.[238] Although there appears to be a more permissive attitude to proportionality in the context of responses to terrorist NSA armed attacks, there are limits to how far defending states can take the notion that they are acting in the collective interest to counter them.

4.3.2 Geography

The post-9/11 responses to terrorist attacks by a number of defending states have taken acts of self-defence far beyond their own borders. The objects of defensive force have often been thousands of kilometres away from the defending state and the armed attacks to which they purport to respond. This reflects the fact that terrorist attacks will typically occur on the defending state's territory, but the terrorists themselves may be operating from safe havens in third countries on the other side of the globe. American action against Al-Qaeda and affiliated groups in Afghanistan and other parts of the world following the 9/11 terrorist attacks on American territory clearly illustrates this fact. More recently, the Global Coalition military action against Daesh in Iraq and Syria is occurring far away from many of the countries that have invoked individual and/or collective self-defence to justify

[235] The number of states and international organizations involved in the Global Coalition, coupled with the implicit support of the UNSC, points to this action being in pursuit of this shared goal. By analogy, see further Henderson, *The Use of Force and International Law* (n 1) 234–235, noting that proportionality is more permissive in the context of force *authorized* by the UNSC. Defending state action that goes beyond the bounds of necessity and proportionality of course risks disrupting international peace and security.

[236] Albeit that such state action is perhaps a product of the absence of explicit UNSC authorization to use military force against terrorist NSAs, as well as the UNSC's preference to date for adopting non-military sanctions against terrorist NSAs and employing peaceful measures to counter terrorism on a general thematic basis. See Tams, 'Necessity and Proportionality' (n 17) 401.

[237] UN Doc A/60/937–S/2006/515 (n 120).

[238] See Section 3.3.5.

their actions there (most notably the USA, Canada, Australia and the various European Coalition partners).[239]

Proportionality, conceptualized in interstate terms, struggles to accommodate this response and remain consequential to self-defence against terrorist NSAs.[240] In particular, the response to international terrorism casts doubt on whether proportionality imposes a requirement of a geographical nexus between the armed attack and defensive response, or whether customary international law applicable to self-defence against terrorist NSAs is evolving to accommodate more flexible notions pertaining to the distance between them. Alternatively, are the rules applicable in the interstate context being breached? That the UNSC appears to be encouraging (and certainly not condemning) anti-terrorist action well beyond the borders of the defending states, and that other states have generally supported military operations against terrorist NSAs in Afghanistan, Syria and elsewhere suggests that geography plays much less of a role in this context, or perhaps no role at all.

This conclusion is reflective of the global reach of international terrorism and is a consequence of the nature of the terrorist organizations themselves. Such groups often function across, and irrespective of, borders. They may be based in, and operate from, a number of different states and work with affiliates and like-minded groups around the globe.[241] When facing a threat of this nature, one of the fundamental questions for proportionally appears to be whether the defending state may mount a military response in various theatres of operation or countries that, together, constitute the same conflict.[242] Fulfilling a defensive need might mean that limiting a defensive response to a particular locale makes no sense when faced with a threat of this type. Such limitation might render the defensive response inadequate. Multiple military actions in a number of states might be the only effective way to counter the threat.

If a geographical restriction does exist in respect of armed attacks by NSAs that are disparate and splintered in this way, the challenge for clarifying any role for proportionality is to identify from state practice criteria to establish the locale to which the defensive response is to be confined. The question is whether this is possible given the foregoing commentary regarding the global responses to terrorism and, more fundamentally, whether it desirable. Arguably, the more meaningful and readily applicable limitation on state action in cases where a defending state is seeking to combat NSAs in a number of different territories is not proportionality

[239] See Section 4.2.3.2. Assertions of collective self-defence of Iraq may be regarded as geographically proximate to the armed attacks. However, a number of these states are also claiming individual self-defence in relation to terrorist attacks on their own soil.

[240] See Section 3.3.3.

[241] Al Qaeda is the classic example. See Byman, *Al Qaeda, the Islamic State, and the Global Jihadist Movement* (n 233) 95–98; 141–161.

[242] Lubell, *Non-State Actors* (n 1) 66.

at all, but necessity.[243] Before the proportionality of a response against a group of NSAs as a whole may be evaluated, the general necessity of any forceful response must be first established, followed by the specific necessity of targeting that group within a particular state. The right of self-defence that has previously arisen, or been claimed, in order to fight a group in one territory may not *automatically* be exported to another part of the world. Despite the so-called 'global war on terror', the USA at least appears to adopt this general premise.[244]

Absent host state consent, the right of self-defence must exist independently every time a defending state wishes to use force within the territory of another state. As explored in Sections 4.2.2 and 4.3.3, the host state's right to sovereignty and territorial integrity remains intact unless established otherwise.[245] If general necessity is absent because the 'new' host state is willing and able to combat the NSAs, the right to exercise self-defence is also absent in respect of the particular group of NSAs operating from within that territory. Proportionality is then a moot point. This fact places added emphasis on the disputed unable or unwilling doctrine, which operates as the main hurdle to the right of self-defence in this context.[246]

4.3.3 Effect on the Host State and its Citizens

If the necessity of a defending state acting against NSAs on the territory of the host state can be established,[247] the ensuing question is how, and to what extent, the position of the host state factors in assessing the proportionality of self-defence. The violation of a host state's sovereignty in the pursuit of a defensive purpose is a highly contentious issue. Yet, as with neutral states, recent state practice suggests that host states might be viewed as having to endure, to a degree, defending state action against NSAs on their territory.[248] Where the line is to be drawn, however,

[243] Note that targeting members of the same group on a territory without the consent of a host state is an issue for the *jus ad bellum*. It is separate from the question of whether members of the same group are targetable under IHL.

[244] '[I]nternational law not only requires a State to analyze whether it has a legal basis for the use of force against a particular non-State actor—which I'll call the "against whom" question—but also requires a State to analyze whether it has a legal basis to use force against that non-State actor in a particular location—which I'll call the "where" question.' USA State Department Legal Adviser Speech 2016 (n 111) 240.

[245] On expanding self-defence into new states, see Lubell, 'The Problem of Imminence' (n 204) 222–227.

[246] See Section 4.2.2.

[247] Whether intrusion into the territory of the host state can ever satisfy the requirement of proportionality is dependent on whether necessity can first be satisfied. The necessity analysis largely depends on the acceptance of the unwilling or unable doctrine to excuse the limited breach of the host state's territory. See Section 4.2.2.

[248] See Section 3.3.6.2. Where a host state violates its international law obligations to prevent and suppress terrorism, this might be equated with the position of a neutral state that violates the laws of neutrality. In such cases, a belligerent can take defensive action on a neutral state's territory if it allows such territory to be used by another belligerent state in violation of its duties of neutrality. Derek W Bowett, *Self-Defence in International Law* (Manchester University Press 1958) 167–174; Ian Brownlie,

remains unclear. Whereas general necessity preserves such acts of self-defence as exceptional measures of last resort, proportionality acts to minimize their effect on the host state.

State practice on this issue is limited, but the investigation below combines what practice is available with an analytical framework that seeks to describe how the effect on the host state (including its civilian population and infrastructure) might point to excessiveness. The analysis set out in Section 3.3.6.1 regarding the justificatory language of circumstances precluding wrongfulness is also helpful in this context. Depending on the circumstances, an act of self-defence *might* be objectively justifiable as a 'lesser evil' when compared to the infringement of a host state's rights and the effect on its citizens.

4.3.3.1 General Considerations

A number of general propositions that derive from the incidents of state practice referred to throughout this book inform the following analysis. The first is that, absent attribution of NSA armed attacks to a host state, defending states do not claim a right to act *against* the host state when taking action against NSAs operating in that state's territory, although they implicitly assert a right to violate the host sate's sovereignty and territorial integrity.[249] Instead, defending states tend to justify their acts by emphasizing that they limit their targeting to NSAs, and do not target host state military personnel and apparatus. With Operation Enduring Freedom standing as an exception, their actions largely conform to this rule.[250] Second, it is only where there has been widespread damage to the host state and harm to its civilians that other states and international organizations label ostensible defensive conduct as disproportionate.[251] Finally, the perceived threat from terrorist NSAs invariably informs the manner in which states will respond defensively and how the proportionality of such response is consequently assessed.[252]

From a proportionality perspective, where defending states limit their defensive actions by only targeting NSAs and their base of operations within the territory of the host state, the use of defensive force nevertheless violates, at a minimum, the host state's sovereignty and territorial integrity.[253] Although not to be readily

International Law and the Use of Force by States (Clarendon Press 1963) 312–314. See also International Institute of Humanitarian Law, *San Remo Manual on International Law Applicable to Armed Conflicts at Sea* (1994) <https://ihl-databases.icrc.org/ihl/INTRO/560> accessed 5 September 2020, Art 22. The propriety of the transposition of this rule into the *jus ad bellum* is debatable (see Tsagourias, 'Self-Defence Against Non-State Actors' (n 76) 812), but Global Coalition state practice in Syria might provide support for such position. See further Deeks, "Unwilling or Unable" (n 24) 497–501, considering neutrality in respect of the unwilling or unable doctrine.

249 Tams, 'Necessity and Proportionality' (n 17) 410.

250 See Section 4.2.3.1.

251 See Section 3.3.5. See further Tams, 'Necessity and Proportionality' (n 17) 410.

252 See Section 4.3.1.

253 Trapp, 'Back to Basics' (n 62) 145. Tsagourias suggests that lawful defensive force does not breach Art 2(4) or constitute unlawful intervention because it is not targeted at the host state, but rather at the

dismissed, if (and only if) necessity can be established in such circumstances to excuse the harm caused to the host state by way of a limited and temporary breach of its sovereignty and territorial integrity, then the minimal material effect on the host state is potentially proportionate.[254] *A fortiori* if the protection of the defending state's own citizens is regarded as an obligation.[255] Without this resulting outcome, the right of self-defence is nullified and international law would require a defending state to sacrifice the life of its citizens to the principles of sovereignty and territorial integrity.[256]

On this analysis, proportionality acts in tandem with necessity to restrain the use of force against the NSAs, and to limit the impact on the host state. Adherence to these requirements maintains a balance between two equally foundational principles of international law: sovereignty (and the attendant right of territorial integrity) and the right of self-defence. Schmitt argues that:

> International law does not require an either-or resolution of these counterpoised norms. Rather, when principles clash, law seeks that accommodation which best achieves their respective underlying purposes. Although the territorial state need not suffer unconstrained violations of its borders, neither does the victim state have to sit idly by while insurgents and terrorists attack it with impunity from abroad.[257]

Necessity and proportionality thereby 'operate as a mediator between the competing security interests of States victim to armed attacks by non-State terrorist actors operating from foreign territory, and States in whose territory terrorists operate'.[258] State practice, particularly with respect to the operation and content of the unwilling or unable doctrine, is yet to provide firm guidelines regarding how this

NSAs, and is not interned to coerce the host state. Tsagourias, 'Self-Defence Against Non-State Actors' (n 76) 822–823. See Section 4.2.3.2 regarding the implications for IHL conflict classification.

[254] Where necessity is not established, proportionality is irrelevant. The use of force, even if targeted solely at the NSAs, will breach Art 2(4). It will be an unlawful use of force against the host state, even though the apparatus or infrastructure of the state is not damaged and none of its armed forces are engaged.

[255] In *Wall* (n 2) para 141, the ICJ stated as a general premise that Israel had 'the right, and indeed *the duty*, to respond in order to protect the life of its citizens' (emphasis added). Trapp argues that states not only have an obligation to respect rights, but to ensure respect for those rights. As regards the right to life and physical integrity, this obligation means, *inter alia*, that individuals are entitled to expect that the state that exercises jurisdiction over them will do everything within its capacity to protect them from an existential threat, whatever its source. Trapp, 'Actor-Pluralism' (n 55) 209.

[256] Schmitt argues that 'the unwillingness or inability of one State to meet its legal obligations cannot deprive other States of the most important right found in international law, the right to defend oneself against an armed attack'. Michael N Schmitt, 'Preemptive Strategies in International Law' (2003) 24 Mich J Int'l L 513, 542.

[257] Michael Schmitt, 'Drone Attacks under the *Jus ad Bellum* and *Jus in Bello*: Clearing the "Fog of Law"' (2010) 13 YIHL 311, 316.

[258] Trapp, 'Back to Basics' (n 62) 146–147.

mediation is operationalized on a general basis. Practice suggests, however, that states nonetheless recognize that there is a balance to be struck such that defensive force is exercisable, but not excessive. This analysis reflects the 'lesser evil' justification referred to above. Therefore, as with Operation Sun in 2008, where harm to the host state and its citizens is minimal, the conclusion is that defensive action might be regarded as proportionate.[259]

This conclusion is most easily reached where the defensive force does not result in any physical harm to the host state's military forces or apparatus, its civilian population, or public infrastructure. An example might be a targeted missile strike by a drone on a desert camp, where only the NSAs and their property are damaged or destroyed. As the state practice referred to in particular in Sections 3.2.1 and 4.2 demonstrates, however, it will not always be the case that the host state and its citizens are insulated from defensive reactions within host state territory. Incidental collateral damage may result from self-defence against the NSAs, or even direct damage if elements of the host state itself are targeted.

The meeting of the two foundational principles of sovereignty and self-defence referred to above also holds true for these cases where the host state and its citizens are materially harmed. However, such material effects mean that the balance might be perceived to shift such that other states and international organizations conclude that the defending state's actions are excessive (*viz* disproportionate). Israel's intervention in Lebanon in 2006 is the conspicuous example.[260] In such cases, the pursuit of self-defence is not perceived to be the lesser evil. Therefore, the defensive response must be carefully crafted to achieving the destruction of the NSAs, with the minimum impact on the host state, its population and infrastructure.[261] Moreover, the use of defensive force must not amount to punishment for the host state's unwillingness or inability to combat the NSAs. This would go beyond a defensive purpose.[262]

Further state practice is required in order to clarify how far the foregoing analysis might settle in the *lex lata*, with the issue of necessity (and unwilling or unable in particular) being the key point of controversy. Regarding any assessment of proportionality, the major concern is the death and injury to the host state's civilians resulting from the defensive riposte. Section 3.3.5's review of state practice affirms that civilian collateral damage is the predominant feature of the practice of those states seeking to justify purported uses of defensive force, as well as of the reactions of other states and international organizations that scrutinize them.

[259] See Section 3.2.1.4.

[260] See Section 3.3.5.

[261] Gardam, 'Proportionality in the War on Terror' (n 64) 17; Ruys, *'Armed Attack'* (n 1) 509.

[262] Likewise, force intended to coerce the host state to abide by its international law obligations to prevent and suppress international terrorism would go beyond the remit of self-defence. Unilateral inducement to abide by international law is the province of countermeasures, which may not involve the threat or use of force. ARSIWA (n 1) Art 50(1)(a).

Concern over civilian harm sits in stark contrast to the death of the NSA terrorists themselves, however. Terrorist casualties are largely accepted by states, provided that civilian casualties and civilian collateral damage are avoided.[263] Even the total destruction of terrorist groups appears to be acceptable to the international community.[264] Accordingly, from the *jus ad bellum* perspective, terrorist NSA casualties might not be counted as part of the proportionality calculus at all. Alternatively, even very high terrorist casualty figures are generally accepted and not regarded as excessive.[265] In either case, the potential for proportionality to act as a restraining influence is severely reduced. This sits in contrast to the position in interstate self-defence, where proportionality accounts for the needs and rights of the attacker, as well as those of the defending state.[266]

Turning to other effects on the host state that are relevant to considerations of proportionality over and above civilian harm, the 2006 Lebanon incident also demonstrates unease amongst scholars regarding the geographical scope of the Israeli response. For some, the initial Israeli action taken in southern Lebanon appeared to abide by the principle of proportionality, given that Hezbollah's attacks had originated from that area. Later measures taken far beyond this zone, however, were viewed as problematic from this perspective.[267] Such concerns are in keeping with the argument that actions in self-defence, particularly along a border, should generally be confined geographically vis-à-vis the armed attacks that provoked them.[268] However, as noted, this is perhaps better understood as an issue of specific necessity. It is difficult to reconcile with a defensive objective the destruction of civilian and military infrastructure well away from, and unconnected with, the armed attack.[269]

Finally, minimizing the impact on the host state also requires that any incursion into its territory is temporally limited. As soon as the defensive objective is attained (*viz* once the threat is effectively countered), the cross-border operation must be terminated and all forces withdrawn.[270] As with the effects on an attacking state,

[263] Tams, 'Necessity and Proportionality' (n 17) 412. Tams cites the example of Turkey's Operation Sun in 2008. Resulting PKK casualties were twenty times the number of Turkish nationals killed in attacks preceding the invasion, yet the invasion generally was not considered excessive and was, in fact, lauded by states. Tams, 'Necessity and Proportionality' (n 17) 395–396.

[264] See Section 4.3.1.

[265] How 'terrorists' are identified and deemed to be targetable for the purposes of the *jus ad bellum* and IHL determines how this calculus is made. As noted, civilians not directly participating in hostilities may not be directly targeted under either regime. See further Section 2.6.

[266] See Section 3.3.

[267] Enzo Cannizzaro, 'Contextualizing Proportionality: *Jus ad Bellum* and *Jus in Bello* in the Lebanese War' (2006) 88 International Review of the Red Cross 779, 784; Zimmermann, 'The Second Lebanon War' (n 191) 124; Ruys, 'Crossing the Thin Blue Line' (n 24) 290–292.

[268] See Section 3.3.3.

[269] Ibid. This is a general premise. Depending on the circumstances, command and control centres and other military targets well away from the armed attack might well be legitimate targets that satisfy the requirements of specific necessity. This is most likely in large-scale and enduring conflicts. Regardless, the issue of targeting is still better analysed under the rules of specific necessity and IHL, rather than proportionality.

[270] Michael Schmitt, 'Preemptive Strategies in International Law' (2003) 24(2) Mich J Int'l L 513, 543.

temporary occupation of parts of the host state might be considered necessary depending on the circumstances, but it must remain proportionate to the defensive objective. Despite the more permissive attitude towards combatting terrorist NSAs, widespread occupation of territory beyond the area of NSA operations is likely to be considered disproportionate.[271] Moreover, enduring occupation after the defensive object is achieved will be unnecessary, with proportionality being irrelevant in such cases.[272] Therefore, it is disconcerting that the USA has confirmed its intention to maintain a military presence in Syria to prevent the re-emergence of Daesh, as well as keeping captured Syrian oil fields, ostensibly to protect them from Daesh.[273] The American measures have led to Syria complaining to the UNSC of America's occupation and plundering of Syrian natural resources in violation of international law.[274] Undoubtedly, open-ended occupation by the USA long after the threat to it has been significantly diminished goes well beyond an immediate defensive purpose.[275] It is similarly problematic that, following its Operation Peace Spring in 2019, Turkey established a so-called 'safe zone' within Syrian territory, patrolled by Turkish and Russian troops.[276] The protection of long-term security interests is not the purview of self-defence. Rather, once the defensive objective is attained, the onus reverts to host state action, international cooperation and measures not involving the use of force.[277]

4.3.3.2 Global Coalition Action in Syria

Assuming for the purposes of our analysis that the Global Coalition military campaign against Daesh in Syria is capable of satisfying the criterion of general necessary, this incident of state practice nevertheless poses a significant challenge when considering the effects of defensive action against NSAs on the host state. This is particularly so when we consider collateral civilian damage. Despite the

[271] As a general premise, Schmitt argues that it would be 'unlawful to deploy forces into locations void of terrorists or insurgents.' Schmitt, 'Drone Attacks' (n 257) 317.

[272] See Section 3.3.4.2.

[273] Secretary of State Rex W Tillerson, 'Remarks on the Way Forward for the United States Regarding Syria', U.S. Department of State, 17 January 2018, <https://www.state.gov/secretary/remarks/2018/01/277493.htm#https://www.state.gov/secretary/remarks/2018/01/277493.htm> accessed 5 September 2020; The White House, 'Remarks by President Trump on the Situation in Northern Syria' (23 October 2019) <www.whitehouse.gov/briefings-statements/remarks-president-trump-situation-northern-syria/> accessed 5 September 2020; The White House, 'Remarks by President Trump at the International Association of Chiefs of Police Annual Conference and Exposition | Chicago, IL' (28 October 2019) <https://www.whitehouse.gov/briefings-statements/remarks-president-trump-international-association-chiefs-police-annual-conference-exposition-chicago-il/> accessed 5 September 2020.

[274] Identical Letters dated 4 August 2020 from the Permanent Representative of the Syrian Arab Republic to the United Nations addressed to the Secretary-General and the President of the Security Council (6 August 2020) UN Doc S/2020/775.

[275] Daesh is not totally defeated in Syria and elsewhere and it is still considered a global threat. Yet, at the time of writing, it has lost the territory it once held in Iraq and Syria, including its capital Raqqa. 'UK Action to Combat Daesh', UK Government <https://www.gov.uk/government/topical-events/daesh/about> accessed 5 September 2020.

[276] See Butchard, 'Digest of State Practice 2019' (n 104) 190–191, 199.

[277] See Sections 1.6.2 and 4.2.4.1.

Global Coalition's insistence that it takes great efforts to minimize civilian harm, their strike reports reveal the extent of the targeting within and against the Syrian state.[278] Undoubtedly, the campaign has caused considerable damage to the civilian population and infrastructure, including high numbers of reported casualties. A symbolic milestone constituted Global Coalition airstrikes that contributed to the almost complete destruction of Daesh's self-proclaimed capital, Raqqa.[279] Syria accused the Global Coalition of deliberately destroying 90 per cent of the city, causing widespread civilian harm and perpetrating massacres against Syrian citizens.[280] Russia stated that the Global Coalition 'flattened' Raqqa, whilst remarking upon the resulting civilian casualties and lack of international concern regarding Global Coalition action.[281] In 2019, Amnesty International reported over 1,600 civilian lives lost as a result of Global Coalition airstrikes, decrying how the so-called 'most precise air campaign in history' in fact left Raqqa the most destroyed city in modern times.[282] Amnesty went so far as to suggest that Global Coalition airstrikes are indicative of possible war crimes.[283] The Global Coalition denies this allegation,[284] however, and the USA has defended the legality of Global Coalition action before the UNSC.[285]

How then should we approach assessing the proportionality of the Global Coalition intervention in Syria? Given the ongoing campaign, and the continued fight against Daesh globally, it is too early to say whether or not states and international organizations will ultimately conclude that the defensive action was proportionate. Even if one were to attempt to take a 'snapshot' of the proportionality of the ongoing response, it is doubtful given the particular circumstances of this

[278] See Section 4.2.3.2.

[279] Quentin Sommerville and Riam Dalati, 'The City Fit for No-One: Inside the Ruined 'Capital' of the Islamic State Group' *BBC News* (27 September 2017) <https://www.bbc.co.uk/news/resources/idt-sh/the_city_fit_for_no_one_raqqa_syria_islamic_state_group> accessed 5 September 2020. Regarding reported civilian casualties resulting from Global Coalition airstrikes, see the Airwars website: <https://airwars.org> accessed 5 September 2020. See also the Syrian Observatory for Human Rights website: <http://www.syriahr.com/en/> accessed 5 September 2020.

[280] UNSC Verbatim Record (14 February 2018) UN Doc S/PV.8181, 11; UNSC Verbatim Record (22 February 2018) UN Doc S/PV.8186, 19; UNSC Verbatim Record (16 March 2018) UN Doc S/PV.8206, 9; Letter dated 7 January 2019 from the Permanent Representative of the Syrian Arab Republic to the United Nations addressed to the Secretary-General and the President of the Security Council (8 January 2019) UN Doc S/2019/15.

[281] UN Doc S/PV.8186 (n 280) 4; UNSC Verbatim Record (27 March 2018) UN Doc S/PV.8217, 15.

[282] Amnesty International, 'Syria: Unprecedented Investigation Reveals US-led Coalition Killed More Than 1,600 Civilians in Raqqa "Death Trap"' (25th April 2019) <https://www.amnesty.org/en/latest/news/2019/04/syria-unprecedented-investigation-reveals-us-led-coalition-killed-more-than-1600-civilians-in-raqqa-death-trap/> accessed 5 September 2020.

[283] Amnesty International, '"War of Annihilation": Devastating Toll on Civilians, Raqqa-Syria' (5 June 2018) <https://www.amnesty.org/download/Documents/MDE2483672018ENGLISH.PDF> accessed 5 September 2020.

[284] Global Coalition, 'Coalition Response to Amnesty Report on Civilian Casualties in Raqqa' (5 June 2018) <http://theglobalcoalition.org/en/coalition-response-to-amnesty-report-on-civilian-casualties-in-raqqa/> accessed 5 September 2020.

[285] UN Doc S/PV.8236 (n 39) 7.

incident that a clear answer is discernible. Nevertheless, the following analysis suggests a number of observations and possible conclusions.

The first possibility is to label this incident as a violation of *jus ad bellum* proportionality. This verdict is partly based on what appears to be gross quantitative imbalance between the amount of harm suffered, or anticipated, as a result of Daesh armed attacks and the harm caused by the military response of the Global Coalition.[286] Although the extent of civilian casualties is debated, it is clear that cities like Raqqa have been decimated and large numbers of its citizens killed and forced to flee. There have even been reports of whole buildings being targeted and destroyed in the pursuit of killing individual Daesh fighters.[287] Such targeting decisions might be IHL compliant and, therefore, explain the actions of Global Coalition partners. Yet, regardless of whether this is in fact the case, the outcomes of such targeting decisions raise real concerns for *jus ad bellum* proportionality when they are reviewed cumulatively.

Moreover, if Amnesty International's reports are proved correct, the potential violations of IHL set out therein might indicate a breach of *jus ad bellum* proportionality. This is particularly likely if any violations are systematic and widespread.[288] Undoubtedly, the overall effect of Global Coalition action on Syria and its people has been severe. This is despite the lack of Syria's acquiescence in, or support for, Daesh's activities. Rather, its inability (or perceived inability) to deal with the threat has led to such devastating harm. As such, it is arguable that like Israel's invasion of Lebanon in 2006, the Global Coalition intervention in Syria goes beyond what is necessary to achieve a defensive purpose.

If perhaps instinctive, this conclusion might nevertheless be too hasty. Global Coalition action against Daesh in Syria sits in marked contrast to Israel's intervention in Lebanon in 2006. First, is the complexity of the Syrian civil war and the sheer number of interlocutors fighting within Syrian territory, all with competing agendas and all causing death and damage to civilians and civilian infrastructure.[289] The Assad regime, its allies and Daesh have all been accused of targeting the civilian population directly, as well as causing widespread collateral damage. Therefore, this factual matrix poses an evidential conundrum regarding 'who did what'. Even if it were possible to separate the effects of the ongoing civil war from the harm resulting from the purported counterterrorism actions of a number of states acting on claims of self-defence, a proportionality assessment of the Global Coalition action remains challenging. This is due to the other stark difference between the Syrian conflict and the 2006 Lebanese invasion. The latter incident was in response to the threat faced by one state (Israel) and was confined to the territory of

[286] The threat posed by Daesh to states is undoubtedly great, but it cannot be compared to the nature and scale of the defensive response, as clearly articulated in the strike reports of the Global Coalition.

[287] As reported in Sommerville and Dalati, 'The City Fit for No-One' (n 279).

[288] See Section 3.4.1.

[289] See Section 4.2.3.2.

another state (Lebanon).[290] In contrast, the Global Coalition consists of a number of states that are purporting to act in self-defence against a threat not only to such states, but which is characterized by the UNSC as an ongoing global threat to international peace and security.[291]

As noted in Section 4.3.1, since 9/11 great latitude has been given by other states and international organizations to states acting in self-defence against terrorist NSAs. Such actions might be regarded as also being in the collective interests of the international community. Despite concern over civilian harm, and regardless of the legality of particular instances of targeting under both IHL and specific necessity, a significant number of states appear to accept that the fight against Daesh necessitates a response of this scale and effects. Such states might be taken as acknowledging that the price to be paid for combatting the NSA terrorist threat to them, and the international community as a whole, includes cities like Raqqa being destroyed and its citizens killed and forced to flee. After all, retaking Raqqa was regarded as a breakthrough in the fight against Daesh. The Global Coalition hailed the 'liberation' of the former capital of Daesh's so-called 'caliphate'.[292] Russia, whilst blaming the Global Coalition for Raqqa's 'methodical destruction', credited the Global Coalition with 'smoking out' Daesh from the city.[293] Its destruction also presumably constitutes the eradication of a key safe haven, as per the exhortation of UNSC Resolution 2249.[294]

Ultimately, the tragic humanitarian fallout from the Syrian incident has not prevented the Global Coalition from pursuing its goal of defeating Daesh, and there has been a paucity of other states labelling the purported defensive action as excessive. Ostensibly, there appears to be widespread recognition that if the ultimate defensive goal is the annihilation of Daesh, then there is no other way to achieve this aim. Although not unequivocal, this suggests the possibility that they consider the harm caused to Syria and its civilian population to be notionally proportionate to that necessity.

This permissive attitude renders the proportionality assessment rather surreal. It also raises the unpleasant prospect of an increased willingness on the part of certain states and international organizations to place issues of security above the human rights and humanitarian protections of those civilians affected by defensive action. It suggests an unfortunate rebalancing of the 'lesser evil' equation, tipping it in favour of self-defence to the detriment of the rights of the host state and the

[290] This is despite Israel's insistence that the threat it faced was also faced by the world. UN Doc A/60/937–S/2006/515 (n 120). See Section 4.3.1.

[291] The status of the threat was reaffirmed by the UNSC in September 2019, despite the territorial defeat of Daesh in Iraq and Syria. See UNSC Res 2490 (20 September 2019) UN Doc S/RES/2490.

[292] Global Coalition, 'Syrian Democratic Forces Liberate Raqqa' (20 October 2017) <http://theglobalcoalition.org/en/syrian-democratic-forces-liberate-raqqa/> accessed 5 September 2020.

[293] UN Doc S/PV.8186 (n 280) 4.

[294] Although, it is doubtful whether the UNSC envisaged such an outcome in its call for states to act against Daesh.

rights and lives of its civilian population. The result is the prioritization of the interests of the citizens of the defending state(s) over those of the host state. If this is the case, then self-defence in the NSA terrorist context is conceived of very differently than in the traditional interstate setting. This conclusion is extremely troubling for the humanitarian situation of those innocent civilians caught up in anti-terrorism conflicts.

Therefore, determining the (dis)proportionality of Global Coalition action is no easy task. It is further complicated by how the Global Coalition approaches the issue of civilian harm in this context, and what that means for assessing proportionality. As noted, the Global Coalition insists that it is not targeting the Syrian state or its people, but only Daesh. The strike reports, taken on face value, confirm that targets are confined to civilian buildings, infrastructure and apparatus that are used or controlled by Daesh and consequently outside of the Syrian state's effective control.[295] These targets are also justified as military objectives under IHL,[296] which raises the question of whether IHL is the principal, or only, concern of the military when carrying out these strikes.[297] The issue for *jus ad bellum* proportionality, however, is whether damage and destruction to such targets should count as harm to Daesh, or harm to the host state (Syria), or both. State practice does not provide a clear answer.

The distinction is crucial, however. As noted, state practice indicates that states tend not to concern themselves with harm to terrorist NSAs, nor to buildings, infrastructure and apparatus that belong to them or are under their control. Accordingly, purported defensive actions are more likely to be characterized as proportionate by states if the harm is viewed as pertaining to the NSAs, rather than to the host state. As noted in Section 4.2.3.2, when public property is under the control of NSAs, and not under the effective control of the host state, it should not be identified with that of the host state. This perhaps accounts for the action taken in Syria, as well as the attitude of other states in their responses to it. If states principally view damage and destruction in those areas that Daesh controls as harm to Daesh itself, and (at most) only secondarily as harm to Syria, then Global Coalition action as a whole is more likely to be regarded as proportionate. The harm to 'Syria' under such appreciation is much less than might otherwise seem.

As noted above, the facts regarding the amount of collateral civilian injury and death are highly contested. Regardless of whether the Global Coalition and

[295] See Section 4.2.3.2. Gill, 'Classifying the Conflict in Syria' (n 47) 375, agrees that Global Coalition actions are directed almost exclusively against Daesh, which controlled a significant portion of Syrian territory, population and infrastructure, rather than Syrian government-held territory, population or infrastructure.

[296] Global Coalition, 'Airstrikes, Civilian Casualties and Investigations' (13 November 2017) <http://theglobalcoalition.org/en/airstrikes-civilian-casualties-and-investigations/> accessed 5 September 2020.

[297] However, see Section 2.6 regarding the need for targeting also to serve a defensive purpose to be compliant with *jus ad bellum* specific necessity.

other states view the harm caused by Global Coalition action as relating principally to Daesh, and not Syria, greater clarity is required regarding the extent of such civilian death and injury and which party to the conflict caused it. Part of the *jus ad bellum* proportionality analysis will then hang on the IHL status issue of whether an individual was in fact a civilian, or directly participating in hostilities ('DPIH').[298] The *jus ad bellum* contains no such specific rules to distinguish between them. However, in addition to IHL rules governing DPIH status, the *jus ad bellum* does require that targeting also serves a defensive purpose.[299] Yet, without further details of the civilian harm, it is difficult to conclude whether such harm will feature as it has in previous incidents as an indicator of excessiveness that other states would not normally accept.

Forming a final view on the proportionality of the ongoing assault on Daesh in Syria and beyond in order to destroy a threat that the UNSC has deemed to be global and enduring, is akin to being confronted with the Gordian knot. As a starting point, determining the factual elements of the Syrian incident as they relate to actions of the Global Coalition will require further investigation.[300] Even then, it is highly questionable whether any state, court or international body has the capacity to reach a definitive conclusion regarding the proportionality of the response of a large proportion of the international community to such threat. The permissive attitude of states and international organizations in the context of international terrorism suggests, however, that they are likely to take a more relaxed attitude to proportionality in the case of Syria than they would within the context of an interstate exercise of self-defence. This is despite the disparity between the (relatively minimal) threat that is faced by many of the defending states and their citizens from the NSAs, and the (extensive) harm to the host state and its citizens that results from action to counter that threat.

This conclusion is extremely troubling for the general balance that proportionality seeks to achieve. It also points to the ability of militarily powerful states to intervene in their less powerful neighbours in the name of self-defence. Therefore, the Syrian incident showcases the need for greater clarity in the law to enable better regulation of such conduct. Pending that development, the incident demonstrates the emphasis that must be placed on specific necessity and IHL as potential constraints on state behaviour. These are likely to be more meaningful markers of legality of state action in such complex scenarios. This, perhaps unsatisfactory, conclusion is discussed further in Chapter 5, together with proposals for legal development.

298 See Section 2.6.1.

299 Ibid.

300 The HRC Syrian Commission of Inquiry (n 40) has already produced a number of vital reports. Their work is ongoing and welcome, not only for the purposes of their mandate, but also as a potential aid to examine the state practice pertaining to the Syrian incident.

4.4 Conclusions

The existence, content and parameters of any right of self-defence against NSAs is still being worked out in state practice. Nevertheless, when compared to interstate self-defence, necessity is revealed to have the potential to play a much greater role in the ability of states to act in self-defence against NSAs in foreign territory. *Prima facie*, the focus is on the primacy of host state action against the NSAs operating on its territory. However, the host state's relationship with both the NSAs and the defending state is central to the question of whether host state action represents a reasonable alternative to defensive force in the particular circumstances. The latter association determines whether consent to, or cooperation with, the host state to counter the terrorist threat constitutes a viable option. Whether the host state is seen as a legitimate partner, or cooperation with it will engage the international responsibility of the defending state, might also determine the necessity of defensive action.

The highly contentious unwilling or unable doctrine is central to the ability of defending states to act against NSAs in foreign territory. Debates over its existence in the *lex lata*, as well as regarding its possible content and practical operation are ongoing, however. If accepted by states, it constitutes an additional barrier to a defending state resorting to military action. Regardless of whether this principle explains state practice against NSAs in foreign territory, such practice suggests that defending states are not to target directly the governmental and military apparatus and infrastructure of the host state (and its allies) whilst acting in self-defence against NSAs on the territory of the host state. This practice highlights the importance of specific necessity in such cases. Drawing on the principles of IHL, it defines what is a permissible NSA target and an impermissible host state target.

How far any defensive action on the host state's territory may ultimately go is an issue for proportionality. The potential for this requirement to operate as a restraint on state action is much more uncertain in the case of states combatting international terrorism, however. In this context, the meaning of proportionality is stretched, and its review is more permissive. States often act globally, on an enduring basis, and beyond their immediate defensive needs. Their responses may receive the blessing of the international community, in whose interests they might also be perceived to be acting. This is a troubling development in international law and makes identifying the lesser evil much more difficult. The law is in flux, but it appears that the right of self-defence in the context of international terrorism may unfortunately be prioritized above third-party interests and the human rights and humanitarian protections of civilians.

5
Conclusions

Claims of self-defence are habitual when states resort to force beyond their own borders. Although the *jus ad bellum* does not contain absolute and rigid rules regarding what amounts to lawful self-defence, states invariably accept that their extraterritorial military operations are governed by international law and the requirements of necessity and proportionality. Even states that argue for an expansive right of self-defence recognize this fact. As a breach of either requirement renders ostensibly defensive action unlawful, increased determinacy regarding the scope and substance of necessity and proportionality is crucial to how force might be constrained by operation of international law. Necessity and proportionality are revealed to be flexible, however, with their application and appraisal contingent on the particular facts of each case. Therefore, establishing general rules for their application is challenging. Despite these challenges and the fact that the law is in flux, this book provides greater precision regarding the conceptual meaning of necessity and proportionality, as well as their normative scope and content. Their operation is highly contextual, but the analytical framework set out herein allows for a more coherent exposition of both requirements.

The *Caroline* incident of 1837 endures as the *locus classicus* of international law governing the exercise of the right of self-defence. Webster's formula, albeit not synonymous with the contemporary *lex lata*, encapsulates its core elements. Once the availability of the right of self-defence is triggered by an actual or (potentially) imminent armed attack, necessity and proportionality condition the exercise of the right. More specifically, necessity determines *whether* defensive force may be used to respond to an armed attack and *where* it must be directed. Proportionality governs *how much* total force is permissible. Crucially, this book contends that the two requirements are conceptually distinct and must be applied in the foregoing order and on an ongoing basis throughout the duration of an armed conflict prompted by self-defence. Their operation ensures that the purposes of self-defence are met, and nothing more.[1] At the same time, necessity and proportionality guard against defensive force being unduly disruptive to third-party interests and international peace and security more broadly.

[1] The purposes of self-defence have been established as halting, repelling and (if a right of pre-emptive self-defence is accepted) preventing an armed attack. See Section 1.6.2.

Necessity and Proportionality and the Right of Self-Defence in International Law. Chris O'Meara, Oxford University Press (2021). © Chris O'Meara. DOI: 10.1093/oso/9780198863403.003.0005

The new taxonomy proposed by this book of 'general necessity' and 'specific necessity' captures the two distinct elements of the necessity requirement that are reflected in state practice, the jurisprudence of the International Court of Justice ('ICJ') and scholarship. Drawing these brighter lines and applying the order of application referred to in the previous paragraph challenges states, international organizations, courts and scholars to consider what it is specifically about a purported act of self-defence that is necessary or unnecessary, proportionate or disproportionate. This approach avoids the tendency to determine and describe the legality of resorting to force in a 'catch-all' manner that fails to distinguish between these requirements, and requires a more detailed articulation of the law and its application to the facts. This serves to clarify the *jus ad bellum*'s operation and review.

The notion of general necessity reflects Webster's 'no choice of means' formulation and whether the pursuit of peaceable options is reasonable in the circumstances. State practice reveals a nuanced application of this premise, however. States do consider defensive force to be a measure of last resort, but they have yet to provide a consistent approach to what this means in practice, beyond this generally accepted presumption. The importance of alternatives to force in determining the legality of purported defensive force is highly contextual. Recourse or otherwise to peaceable options may stand as evidence of general necessity, but it may not factor at all in either the justification for, or review of, military action.

Ultimately, general necessity will be satisfied where, in the particular circumstances, there is a reasonable need for a defending state to respond to an armed attack using force. This will typically be established per se in the case of an ongoing armed attack, where recourse to peaceable resolution will not usually constitute a reasonable alternative to force. Therefore, the ability of general necessity to act as a meaningful restraint on the exercise of self-defence is limited. This is especially so in the context of armed attacks against terrorist non-state actors ('NSAs') where, in the face of a perceived enduring threat, general necessity is revealed to be a weak limitation on state action.

In contrast, specific necessity operates as a clear restriction on the exercise of the right of self-defence. It confines defensive action to military targets connected with the armed attack, thereby ensuring that their capture, neutralization or destruction is limited to a defensive purpose. A lack of this nexus suggests that a use of force has a purely punitive purpose, rendering it unlawful. Specific necessity's importance as a separate and distinct element of necessity has been underappreciated to date. Accordingly, there is potential for future development regarding how states conceive of the targeting requirements of the *jus ad bellum* and how these rules run alongside international humanitarian law ('IHL') to impose parallel and cumulative obligations.

Proportionality is shown, as a general precept, to prohibit excessive uses of defensive force. By operating to restrain the outcomes of a defending state's overall defensive response, it has the potential to contribute to the preservation of international peace and security. It seeks to minimize the disruption of defensive action to the international order and to the rights of those that operate within it. Proportionality is the more complex of the two requirements, however, with its content and outer boundaries lacking detail when compared to necessity. It is also more difficult to apply in practice. Yet, states tend to use this term as their preferred measure of the legality of self-defence. As a rhetorical tool,[2] it will likely be employed to determine whether or not a state's use of putatively defensive force is deemed excessive by other states. This is so, even if it is not always clear whether the reference to (dis)proportionality is to the *jus ad bellum*, or IHL, or both.

Despite this lack of clarity and the fact that state practice does not offer a consistent narrative, a number of conclusions are apparent regarding how states view *jus ad bellum* proportionality. This book shows that states do not commonly require precise equivalence between an armed attack and self-defence in terms of the nature, scale or means of the action taken, or its outcomes. When justifying and appraising defensive action, states primarily balance the defensive response and its outcomes (as a whole) against the legitimate purposes of self-defence. Consequently, states may respond defensively on a retrospective and prospective basis, whilst considering the wider threat comprising past, ongoing and (potentially) imminent armed attacks. Yet, its application is not the neat binary exercise proposed by some academic commentators, but rather involves weighing a diversity of interests. Therefore, it is not simply a question of referring to proportionality as either quantitative or teleological.

A mixed model of proportionality calls for a balance to be struck so that defensive military action does not result in harm that is completely out of proportion to the armed attack(s) that prompted it. There must be a rational connection between the two. In addition, when other states, courts and scholars review proportionality, third-party interests are also accounted for. These interests constitute potential additional limitations on the exercise of the right of self-defence, although the importance of neutrality and former belligerent rights, as well as the effect of defensive action on the environment, require further elaboration in state practice. What is apparent is that defending states cannot prioritize their right to self-defence over the rights and interests of other states, and of the international community more broadly, and pursue it at any cost. Civilian collateral harm will typically stand as the principal factor that leads to a conclusion that an act of self-defence is excessive (*viz* disproportionate).

This book has also elaborated on the often-overlooked relationship between IHL and the *jus ad bellum*. These are essentially separate regimes of international law, but they have the potential to affect the understanding and operation of each other. The issue of IHL and the *jus ad bellum* operating together to regulate targeting is

[2] Judith Gardam, 'A Role for Proportionality in the War on Terror' (2005) 74 Nord J Int'l L 3, 25.

referred to above. In addition, this author has explained that *jus ad bellum* proportionality operates at the macro level of generality, with IHL proportionality being concerned with the micro level of individual targeting decisions. The exception is where widespread or systematic breaches of IHL constitute evidence of a shift in the overall scale or scope of a defensive response. Crucially, the analysis confirms that the *jus ad bellum* and IHL are two separate and independent bodies of international law but impose cumulative obligations that regulate the entire defensive operation and must be consistently applied and monitored over that period. A clearer appreciation of this relationship between IHL and the *jus ad bellum* provides scope for further theoretical development of how these legal regimes interrelate more generally, as well as contributing to real-world decision-making regarding resorting to, conducting and reviewing acts of self-defence.

Finally, this book has examined necessity and proportionality as they apply to self-defence in response to armed attacks by NSAs operating in foreign territory, principally in the context of international terrorism. Against this background, their requirements are adapted and supplemented. This author notes the potential of general necessity to play a greater role outside of the interstate context, where the requirement is likely to be satisfied more easily. This is because the option of seeking a solution via or in cooperation with the host state theoretically constitutes an additional limiting factor. However, this potential is not as strong as is sometimes suggested in the literature. Whether host state action stands as a reasonable alternative to the defending state using force is highly contextual. It is contingent on the timing of the armed attack and the relationships between the defending state and the host state, and between the host state and the NSAs. The risk to the defending state of its international responsibility being engaged by cooperating with a host state is also revealed to be a feature of more recent state practice.

Moreover, the response by states and the UN Security Council ('UNSC') to international terrorism has severely tested the application of both necessity and proportionality as conceived of in the interstate context. State practice points to the continuing general necessity of some form of defensive response against what is perceived to be an enduring terrorist threat. This account takes the right of self-defence beyond being a temporary right to respond to emergency situations. In terms of proportionality, states often act beyond their immediate defensive needs in their responses to international terrorism. They may take preventive action against potential future armed attacks by seeking to eliminate the NSA terrorists entirely. It is clear that there is a much more permissive attitude on the part of states and the UNSC when reviewing such action. The law is in flux, but it appears that the right of self-defence in this context might be prioritized above the rights and interests of the host state and its civilians. A clear balance between these rights and interests, and a meaningful role for proportionality, are yet to be worked out in practice. The Syrian conflict stands as a worrying example of potential imbalance and the resulting detriment to humanitarian protections.

Pending clarification of the *lex lata* through further state practice, this author argues that the burden falls to specific necessity to constrain military action and to regulate the legality of a particular defensive response. Relatively speaking, specific necessity is the *jus ad bellum* tool with the most determinacy. Where general necessity and/or proportionality are in doubt, specific necessity has the greatest potential to govern whether self-defence is permissible against a particular terrorist group operating in a particular state. It is for this reason that the highly controversial unwilling or unable debate is so crucial.[3] Although the law is unsettled, post-9/11 state practice suggests that where a host state is unwilling or unable to tackle the NSA threat itself, defending states may deem it necessary to target persons and objects on its territory. This ability raises concerns for the effect of defensive action on the host state, and for international peace and security more generally. However, drawing on principles of IHL, specific necessity establishes what is a permissible NSA target and an impermissible host state target. This author's analysis suggests that defending states do not regard themselves as having a general licence to target governmental and military apparatus and infrastructure of the host state (and its allies) when acting in self-defence against NSAs on its territory. Targeting is confined to non-military elements of a host state that are outside its effective control (*viz* targets being used or occupied by the NSAs that were responsible for the armed attack). This limits the potential impact on the host state itself.

Normatively, the arguments and conclusions set out in this book provide a basis for how future scholarship and jurisprudence might better conceive of and develop the right of self-defence. This book provides a scholastic and judicial tool for tackling some of the long-standing debates in the *jus ad bellum* relating to, *inter alia*, a right of self-defence against NSAs, responding defensively to imminent armed attacks, and whether there is a gravity threshold that triggers the right. The additional detail and nuance offer scope to move away from the focus to date on the armed attack and the examination of these controversies through that particular lens. The attention of scholars and international courts and tribunals should instead turn to the elements of self-defence that constitute the most prominent features of state practice and *opinio juris*: necessity and proportionality.

These requirements best represent how states view their right of self-defence, explain their actions publicly and review the acts of other states. A more coherent and determinate realization of necessity and proportionality speaks directly to this fact and the operation of self-defence. This realization provides a better theoretical statement of the law and constitutes a more effective and practicable determinant of

[3] The unwilling or unable doctrine relates to both general and specific necessity, although it is submitted that specific necessity is clearer in the practice of states. Therefore, it has the greatest potential at this point in time to regulate conduct.

the legality of state responses to armed attacks. Therefore, the analytical framework set out in this book offers the opportunity for a doctrinal switch that recognizes necessity and proportionality, and not the armed attack, as the core regulating requirements of the exercise of self-defence.[4] It challenges academics and judges to engage more fully with the detail of state practice and to avoid certain conflations and inaccuracies of the past.

It has been suggested that '[t]he maintenance of world peace and security depends importantly on there being a common global understanding, and acceptance, of when the application of force is both legal and legitimate'.[5] International law provides the independent standard for judging the legitimacy of international actions.[6] Most importantly, therefore, the analytical framework set out in this book provides tools for states to justify and legitimize more clearly their actions. It also establishes a structure and procedure for other states, international organizations and courts to review more effectively putative acts of self-defence and to assess compliance with the law. Instead of pointing to the most obvious indicator of illegality (as has been the tendency of states and the ICJ to date), this analytical framework requires consideration of the armed attack, followed by general necessity, specific necessity and proportionality, in that order.

Adopting this systematic approach assists with improved and more transparent decision-making. Coupled with the greater normative determinacy provided by this book, the proposed method has the potential to contribute to the clarity, coherency and predictability that underpin the operation of the *jus ad bellum* and the maintenance and legitimacy of the international rule of law.[7] The *jus ad bellum* remains, by its nature, an essentially indeterminate legal regime, but this development might help to curtail the number of occasions when states resort to using force and lead to fewer instances of excess when they do so.

Although this book offers a clearer and more coherent statement of the *lex lata*, there is of course scope to strengthen the potential of necessity and proportionality to restrain how states employ defensive force. Recent efforts by states to engage with *jus ad bellum* issues are accordingly very welcome and indicate the potential

[4] See further James A Green, *The International Court of Justice and Self-Defence in International Law* (Hart Publishing 2009) 109, 209, making a similar argument.

[5] 'A More Secure World: Our Shared Responsibility', Report of the High-Level Panel on Threats, Challenges and Change, UN Doc A/59/565 (2004) para 184.

[6] Philippe Sands, *Lawless World: America and the Making and Breaking of Global Rules from FDR's Atlantic Charter to George W. Bush's Illegal War* (Viking Penguin 2005) 238.

[7] A degree of indeterminacy will be present in any legal system and, for international law, it is arguable that indeterminacy is central to its acceptability, allowing for the legal rules to fulfil the purposes for which they are adopted. Martti Koskenniemi, *From Apology to Utopia: The Structure of International Legal Argument* (CUP 2006) 591. However, increased determinacy means; reporting greater potential for law to exert a more powerful pull towards compliance. See Thomas M Franck, 'Legitimacy in the International System' (1988) 82(4) AJIL 705; Ashley Deeks, '"Unwilling or Unable": Toward a Normative Framework for Extra-Territorial Self-Defense' (2012) 52 Va JIL 483, especially 508–514.

for future legal development in this direction.[8] Better articulation by states of their understanding of legal rules benefit the operation of the *jus ad bellum* and promote its advancement. In particular, defending states should articulate their reasons for using force, what information and facts these decisions were based on and what they consider to be the legitimate goals of self-defence in the circumstances. Defending states should explain in detail why their actions are necessary and proportionate and provide data and information to support their claims.

Such information should ideally be included in every report of self-defence to the UNSC, as required by Article 51 of the UN Charter.[9] The UNSC and other states should actively scrutinize claims of self-defence and, where absent, insist on explanations and available supporting evidence. They need to engage with the detail. Debates before the UNSC are the natural place for this dialogue to happen and should occur as a matter of course following a state resorting to force. Calls by states for improvements regarding how the UNSC handles Article 51 communications should be acted upon.[10] In particular, there is scope to reform how the UNSC records Article 51 communications, makes other states aware of their existence and formally responds to such communications in UNSC sessions. These measures would address concerns regarding the lack of information, publicity and transparency in the Article 51 reporting process.[11]

[8] For example, Brian Egan, Legal Adviser, U.S. Department of State, 'International Law, Legal Diplomacy, and the Counter-ISIL Campaign: Some Observations', Speech to the 110th Annual Meeting of the American Society of International Law (1 April 2016) (2016) 92 Int'l L Stud 235 (hereafter 'USA State Department Legal Adviser Speech 2016'); UK Attorney General's Speech at the International Institute for Strategic Studies, 'The Modern Law of Self-Defence' (11 January 2017) <https://www.gov.uk/government/uploads/system/uploads/attachment_data/file/583171/170111_Imminence_Speech_.pdf> accessed 5 September 2020; Australian Attorney-General, Senator the Hon. George Brandis QC, 'The Right of Self-Defence Against Imminent Armed Attack in International Law', Public Lecture at the T C Beirne School of Law, University of Queensland (11 April 2017) <https://www.ejiltalk.org/the-right-of-self-defence-against-imminent-armed-attack-in-international-law/> accessed 5 September 2020.

[9] Brazil has called for this level of information to be provided in all Art 51 communications, as well as more generally advocating for improvement to the UNSC's working methods regarding such communications. See UNSC Verbatim Record (6 February 2018) UN Doc S/PV.8175, 24–25; Brazil, Statement to the United Nations General Assembly Sixth Committee, Agenda Item 85: Report of the Special Committee on the Charter of the United Nations and on the Strengthening of the Role of the Organization (15 October 2018) <http://statements.unmeetings.org/media2/20303642/brazil-85.pdf> accessed 5 September 2020.

[10] See ibid. Mexico has also suggested that the UNGA's Special Committee on the Charter of the United Nations and on the Strengthening of the Role of the Organization might consider improvements to the Art 51 reporting process. UNGA, 'Report of the Special Committee on the Charter of the United Nations and on the Strengthening of the Role of the Organization' UN GAOR 73rd Session Supp No 33, UN Doc A/73/33 (2018) para 83.

[11] These concerns have been expressed by Mexico to the UNSC. See UN Doc S/PV.8175 (n 9) 58. See further Pablo Arrocha Olabuenaga, 'An Insider's View of the Life-Cycle of Self-Defense Reports by U.N. Member States' (*Just Security*, 2 April 2019) <https://www.justsecurity.org/63415/an-insiders-view-of-the-life-cycle-of-self-defense-reports-by-u-n-member-states/> accessed 5 September 2020; Dustin A Lewis, Naz K Modirzadeh and Gabriella Blum, 'Quantum Of Silence: Inaction and *Jus Ad Bellum*', The Harvard Law School Program on International Law and Armed Conflict (2019) <https://pilac.law.harvard.edu/quantum-of-silence> accessed 5 September 2020, 49–70.

Statements in other public fora that relate to the legality of self-defence are also to be encouraged. Such public explanations, or 'legal diplomacy', enable better international cooperation and joint action between states, as well as a common understanding of international law and a way to manage differences in interpreting obligations that are binding upon states.[12] There is no substitute for better engagement by states with these issues, although this author accepts that such action, and a transparent dialogue, might not be forthcoming or produce an obvious consensus amongst states regarding the applicable rules. As such, legal development would be aided by work that could build on the framework set out in this book. An equivalent of the Definition of Aggression might be too much to hope for by way of an attempt to codify the principles of necessity and proportionality, but there is certainly scope for bodies such as the International Law Commission to develop further their meaning and operation. Projects akin to the Chatham House Principles, the Tallinn Manual[13] and the Leiden Policy Recommendations could offer states the raw materials to advance the law further.[14] Therefore, this book represents an important step in understanding necessity and proportionality, but it is not the end of the story. The need for ever greater clarity is clear. As the *jus ad bellum* evolves to meet new challenges, states, scholars and the ICJ must focus on these requirements to enable international law to regulate more effectively how states exercise their right of self-defence.

[12] USA State Department Legal Adviser Speech 2016 (n 8) 237, 244–245. See further Christian J Tams, 'The Necessity and Proportionality of Anti-Terrorist Self-Defence' in Larissa van den Herik and Nico Schrijver (eds), *Counter-Terrorism Strategies in a Fragmented International Legal Order: Meeting the Challenges* (CUP 2013) 419–421; Nico Schrijver and Larissa van den Herik, 'Leiden Policy Recommendations on Counter-Terrorism and International Law' (2010) 57(3) NILR 531, 540–544, considering certain of these issues and the prospect of normative development.

[13] Michael Schmitt (ed), *Tallinn Manual on the International Law Applicable to Cyber Warfare* (CUP 2013).

[14] For a relatively recent example of a state actively engaging with, and recognizing the importance of, such projects (in this case the Tallinn Manual 2.0), see 'Keynote Address by the Minister of Defence, Ms. Ank Bijleveld, Marking the First Anniversary of the Tallinn Manual 2.0 on the 20th of June 2018' (21 June 2018) <https://english.defensie.nl/downloads/speeches/2018/06/21/keynote-address-by-the-minister-of-defence-ms.-ank-bijleveld-marking-the-first-anniversary-of-the-tallinn-manual-2.0-on-the-20th-of-june-2018> accessed 5 September 2020. A further example is reliance by states on the Bethlehem Principles. See Section 2.5.1.2.

Bibliography

Abass, A, 'Consent Precluding State Responsibility: A Critical Analysis' (2004) 53(1) ICLQ 211

Ahmed, DI, 'Defending Weak States against the Unwilling or Unable Doctrine of Self-Defense' (2013) 9 JILIR 1

Akande, D, 'Nuclear Weapons, Unclear Law? Deciphering the *Nuclear Weapons* Advisory Opinion of the International Court' (1998) 68 BYIL 165

Akande, D and Liefländer, T, 'Clarifying Necessity, Imminence, and Proportionality in the Law of Self-Defence' (2013) 107 AJIL 563

Akande, D and Milanovic, M, 'The Constructive Ambiguity of the Security Council's ISIS Resolution' (*EJIL:Talk!*, 21 November 2015) <https://www.ejiltalk.org/the-constructive-ambiguity-of-the-security-councils-isis-resolution/>

Alder, MC, *The Inherent Right of Self-Defence in International Law* (Springer 2013)

Alexandrov, SA, *Self-Defense Against the Use of Force in International Law* (Kluwer Law International 1996)

All Party Parliamentary Group on Drones Inquiry Report, 'The UK's Use of Armed Drones: Working with Partners' (July 2018) <http://appgdrones.org.uk/wp-content/uploads/2014/08/INH_PG_Drones_AllInOne_v25.pdf>

Anssari, M and Nussberger, B, 'Compilation of States' Reactions to U.S. and Iranian Uses of Force in Iraq in January 2020' (*Just Security*, 22 January 2020) <https://www.justsecurity.org/68173/compilation-of-states-reactions-to-u-s-and-iranian-uses-of-force-in-iraq-in-january-2020/>

Aust, A, *Handbook of International Law* (CUP 2005)

Australian Attorney-General, Senator the Hon. George Brandis QC, 'The Right of Self-Defence Against Imminent Armed Attack in International Law', Public Lecture at the T C Beirne School of Law, University of Queensland (11 April 2017) <https://www.ejiltalk.org/the-right-of-self-defence-against-imminent-armed-attack-in-international-law/>

Bannelier-Christakis, K, 'Military Interventions against ISIL in Iraq, Syria and Libya, and the Legal Basis of Consent' (2016) 29(3) LJIL 743

Bellinger, JB, 'Legal Issues in the War on Terrorism', speech delivered at the London School of Economics and Political Science (31 October 2006) <https://2009-2017.state.gov/s/l/2006/98861.htm>

Bethlehem, D, 'Not By Any Other Name: A Response to Jack Goldsmith on Obama's Imminence' (*Lawfare*, 7 April 2016) <https://www.lawfareblog.com/not-any-other-name-response-jack-goldsmith-obamas-imminence>

Bethlehem, D, 'The End of Geography: The Changing Nature of the International System and the Challenge to International Law' (2014) 25(1) EJIL 9

Bethlehem, D, 'Principles of Self-Defense—A Brief Response' (2013) 107 AJIL 579

Bethlehem, D, 'Self-Defense Against an Imminent or Actual Armed Attack by Nonstate Actors' (2012) 106 AJIL 770

Blank, L, 'The Extent of Self-Defence against Terrorist Groups: For How Long and How Far?' (2017) 47 Israel YB Hum Rts 265

Bowett, DW, 'Reprisals Involving Recourse to Armed Force' (1972) 66 AJIL 1

Bowett, DW, *Self-Defence in International Law* (Manchester University Press 1958)

Bowett, DW, 'Collective Self-Defence under the Charter of the United Nations' (1955–6) 32 BYIL 130

Boyle, J, 'Making Sense of Self-Defence in the War on Terror' (2014) 1 JUFIL 55

Breau, SC and Jachec-Neale, A (eds), *Testing the Boundaries of International Humanitarian Law* (British Institute of International and Comparative Law 2006)

Bridgeman, T, 'About that "Deconfliction Zone" in Syria: Is the United States on Firm Domestic and International Legal Footing?' (*Just Security*, 15 June 2017) <https://www.justsecurity.org/42183/deconfliction-zone-syria-united-states-firm-domestic-international-legal-footing/>

Brierly, JL, 'International Law and Resort to Armed Force' (1932) 4 The Cambridge Law Journal 308

Briggs, HW, *The Law of Nations* (2nd edn, Appleton-Century-Crofts 1952)

Brownlie, I, *International Law and the Use of Force by States* (Clarendon Press 1963)

Brunnée, J and Toope, SJ, 'Self-Defence against Non-State Actors: Are Powerful States Willing but Unable to Change International Law' (2018) 67 ICLQ 263

Butchard, PM, 'Territorial Integrity, Political Independence, and Consent: The Limitations of Military Assistance on Request Under the Prohibition of Force' (2020) 7(1) JUFIL 35

Butchard, PM (ed), 'Digest of State Practice: 1 July—31 December 2019' (2020) 7(1) JUFIL 156

Butler, WE (ed), *The Non-Use of Force in International Law* (Nijhoff Publishers 1989)

Byers, M, 'The Intervention in Afghanistan–2001' in Ruys, T, Corten, C, and Hofer, A (eds) *The Use of Force in International Law: A Case-Based Approach* (OUP 2018) 625

Byman, D, 'Understanding the Islamic State—A Review Essay' (2016) 40(4) International Security 127

Byman, D, *Al Qaeda, the Islamic State, and the Global Jihadist Movement: What Everyone Needs to Know* (OUP 2015)

Cannizzaro, E, 'Proportionality in the Law of Armed Conflict' in Clapham, A and Gaeta, P (eds) *The Oxford Handbook of International Law in Armed Conflict* (OUP 2014) 332

Cannizzaro, E, 'Contextualizing Proportionality: *Jus ad Bellum* and *Jus in Bello* in the Lebanese War' (2006) 88 International Review of the Red Cross 779

Cannizzaro, E and Palchetti, P (eds), *Customary International Law on the Use of Force: A Methodological Approach* (Martinus Nijhoff 2005)

Cannizzaro, E and Rasi, A, 'The US Strikes in Sudan and Afghanistan–1998' in Ruys, T, Corten, C and Hofer, A (eds) *The Use of Force in International Law: A Case-Based Approach* (OUP 2018) 541

Cassese, A, *International Law* (2nd edn, OUP 2005)

Cassese, A, 'Article 51', in Cot, J-P, Pellet, A and Forteau, M (eds) *La Charte des Nations Unies: Commentaire Article par Article* (3rd edn, Economica 2005)

Cassese, A (ed), *The Current Legal Regulation of the Use of Force* (Martinus Nijhoff Publishers 1986)

Castren, E, *The Present Law of War and Neutrality* (Academia Scientiarum Fennica 1954)

Chachko, E and Deeks, A, 'Which States Support the "Unwilling and Unable" Test?' (*Lawfare*, 10 October 2016) <https://www.lawfareblog.com/which-states-support-unwilling-and-unable-test#UnitedKingdom>

Chinkin, C, *Third Parties in International Law* (Clarendon Press 1993)

Clapham, A and Gaeta, P (eds), *The Oxford Handbook of International Law in Armed Conflict* (OUP 2014)

Constantinou, A, *The Right of Self-Defence Under Customary International Law and Article 51 of the United Nations Charter* (Ant. N. Sakkoulas 2000)

Corten, O, 'The "Unwilling or Unable" Test: Has it Been, and Could it be, Accepted?' (2016) 29(3) LJIL 777

Corten, O, 'Necessity' in Weller, M (ed), *The Oxford Handbook on the Use of Force in International Law* (OUP 2015) 861

Corten, O, *The Law Against War: The Prohibition on the Use of Force in Contemporary International Law* (Hart Publishing 2010)

Crawford, J, *State Responsibility: The General Part* (CUP 2013)

Crawford, J, Pellet, A and Redgwell, C, 'Anglo-American and Continental Traditions in Advocacy before International Courts and Tribunals' (2013) 2(4) CJICL 715

D'Amato, A, 'Israel's Air Strike against the Osiraq Reactor: A Retrospective' (1996) 10 Temp Int'l & Comp LJ 259

Darcy, S, 'Retaliation and Reprisal' in Weller, M (ed), *The Oxford Handbook on the Use of Force in International Law* (OUP 2015) 879

De Vattel, E, *The Law of Nations, Or, Principles of the Law of Nature, Applied to the Conduct and Affairs of Nations and Sovereigns* (1797, reprinted Indianapolis: Liberty Fund 2011)

De Wet, E, 'The Gulf War–1990-91' in Ruys, T, Corten, C and Hofer, A (eds) *The Use of Force in International Law: A Case-Based Approach* (OUP 2018) 456

Deeks, A, '"Imminence" in the Legal Adviser's Speech' (*Lawfare*, 6 April 2016) <https://www.lawfareblog.com/imminence-legal-advisers-speech>

Deeks, A, 'Multi-Part Tests in the *Jus ad Bellum*' (2015–2016) 53 Hous LR 1035

Deeks, A, '"Unwilling or Unable": Toward a Normative Framework for Extra-Territorial Self-Defense' (2012) 52 Va JIL 483

Di Filippo, M, 'The Definitions(s) of Terrorism in International Law' in Ben Saul (ed), *Research Handbook on International Law and Terrorism* (Edward Elgar 2014) 3

Dinstein, Y, *War, Aggression and Self-Defence* (6th edn, CUP 2017)

Dinstein, Y, *War, Aggression and Self-Defence* (5th edn, CUP 2011)

Dinstein, Y, *The Conduct of Hostilities under the Law of International Armed Conflict* (2nd edn, CUP 2010)

Dinstein, Y, *War, Aggression and Self-Defence* (4th edn, CUP 2005)

Dinstein, Y, *War, Aggression and Self-Defence* (3rd edn, CUP 2001)

Dinstein, Y (ed), *International Law at a Time of Perplexity: Essays in Honour of Shabtai Rosenne* (Martinus Nijhoff Publishers 1989)

Egan, B, Legal Adviser, U.S. Department of State, 'International Law, Legal Diplomacy, and the Counter-ISIL Campaign: Some Observations', Speech to the 110th Annual Meeting of the American Society of International Law (1 April 2016) (2016) 92 Int'l L Stud 235

Etezazian, S, 'The Nature of the Self-Defence Proportionality Requirement' (2016) 3(2) JUFIL 260

Evans, MD (ed), *International Law* (5th edn, OUP 2018)

Falk, RA, *The Vietnam War and International Law, Volume 3* (Princeton University Press 2015)

Fenrick, WJ, 'The Exclusion Zone Device in the Law of Naval Warfare' (1986) 24 Canadian YBIL 91

Fleck, D (ed), *The Handbook of International Humanitarian Law* (3rd edn, OUP 2013)

Fleck, D, The Law of Non-International Armed Conflict' in Fleck, D (ed), *The Handbook of International Humanitarian Law* (3rd edn, OUP 2013) 581

Forcese, C, *Destroying the Caroline: The Frontier Raid that Reshaped the Right to War* (Irwin Law Inc 2018)

Fox, GH, 'The Vietnamese Intervention in Cambodia–1978' in Ruys, T, Corten, C and Hofer, A (eds) *The Use of Force in International Law: A Case-Based Approach* (OUP 2018) 242

Franck, TM, 'On Proportionality of Countermeasures in International Law' (2008) 102 AJIL 715

Franck, TM, *Recourse to Force: State Action Against Threats and Armed Attacks* (CUP 2002)

Franck, TM, 'Terrorism and the Right of Self-Defense' (2001) 95 AJIL 839

Franck, TM, 'Legitimacy in the International System' (1988) 82(4) AJIL 705

Franck, TM, 'Who Killed Article 2(4) or: Changing Norms Governing the Use of Force by States' (1970) 64 AJIL 809

Friman, J, *Revisiting the Concept of Defence in the Jus ad Bellum: The Dual Face of Defence* (Bloomsbury 2017)

Gardam, J, 'A Role for Proportionality in the War on Terror' (2005) 74 Nord J Int'l L 3

Gardam, J, *Necessity, Proportionality and the Use of Force by States* (CUP 2004)

Gazzini, T, *The Changing Rules on the Use of Force in International Law* (Manchester University Press 2005)

Gill, TD, 'Letter to the Editor from Professor Terry Gill on Classification of International Armed Conflict' (*Just Security*, 14 October 2016) <https://www.justsecurity.org/33569/letter-editor-prof-terry-gill-classification-international-armed-conflict/>

Gill, TD, 'Classifying the Conflict in Syria' (2016) 92 Int'l L Stud 353

Gill, TD, 'When Does Self-Defence End?' in Weller, M (ed), *The Oxford Handbook on the Use of Force in International Law* (OUP 2015) 737

Gill, TD, 'The Temporal Dimension of Self-Defence: Anticipation, Pre-emption, Prevention and Immediacy' (2006) 11(3) JC&SL 361

Gill, TD, 'The *Nuclear Weapons* Advisory Opinion of the International Court of Justice and the Fundamental Distinction Between the *Jus ad Bellum* and the *Jus in Bello*' (1999) 12(3) LJIL 613

Gill, TD and Tibori-Szabó, K, 'Twelve Key Questions on Self-Defense against Non-State Actors' (2019) 95 Int'l L Stud 467

Glennon, MJ, 'The Fog of War: Self-Defense, Inherence, and Incoherence in Article 51 of the United Nations Charter' (2002) 25(2) Harvard Journal of Law & Public Policy 539

Goodman, R, 'Two U.S. Positions on the Duty to Ensure Respect for the Geneva Conventions' (*Just Security*, 26 September 2016) <https://www.justsecurity.org/33166/u-s-positions-duty-ensure-respect-geneva-conventions/>

Goodman, R, 'Assad: Willing to Risk Direct Confrontation with U.S. Over Moderate Rebels—and Stronger Opposition to US Airstrikes' (*Just Security*, 27 January 2015) <https://www.justsecurity.org/19419/syria-assad-risk-direct-confrontation-moderate-rebels-opposition-airstrikes/>

Goodman, R, 'Taking the Weight off of International Law: Has Syria Consented to US Airstrikes?' (*Just Security*, 23 December 2014) <https://www.justsecurity.org/18665/weight-international-law-syria-consented-airstrikes/>

Goodman, R, 'International Law on Airstrikes against ISIS in Syria' (*Just Security*, 28 August 2014) <https://www.justsecurity.org/14414/international-law-airstrikes-isis-syria/>

Gray, C, *International Law and the Use of Force* (4th edn, OUP 2018)

Gray, C, 'The Conflict in Georgia–2008' in Ruys, T, Corten, C, and Hofer, A (eds) *The Use of Force in International Law: A Case-Based Approach* (OUP 2018) 712

Gray, C, 'The Limits of Force' (2016) 376 Collected Courses of the Hague Academy of International Law 101

Gray, C, 'Targeted Killing Outside Armed Conflict: A New Departure for the UK?' (2016) 3(2) JUFIL 198

Gray, C, 'The International Court of Justice and the Use of Force' in Tams, CJ and Sloan, J (eds) *The Development of International Law by the International Court of Justice* (Oxford Scholarship Online 2014) 237

Gray, C, 'President Obama's 2010 US National Security Strategy and International Law on the Use of Force' (2011) Chinese JIL 35

Gray, C, *International Law and the Use of Force* (3rd edn, OUP 2008)

Green, JA, 'Initial Thoughts on the UK Attorney General's Self-Defence Speech' (*EJIL:Talk!*, 13 January 2017) <https://www.ejiltalk.org/initial-thoughts-on-the-uk-attorney-generals-self-defence-speech/>

Green, JA, 'The *Ratione Temporis* Elements of Self-Defence' (2015) 2(1) JUFIL 97

Green, JA, 'The Article 51 Reporting Requirement for Self-Defense Actions' (2015) 55 Va JIL 563

Green, JA, 'Questioning the Peremptory Status of the Prohibition of the Use of Force' (2011) 32 Michigan Journal of International Law 215

Green, JA, *The International Court of Justice and Self-Defence in International Law* (Hart Publishing 2009)

Green, JA, 'Self-Defence: A State of Mind for States?' (2008) 55 NILR 181

Green, JA, 'Docking the *Caroline*: Understanding the Relevance of the Formula in Contemporary Customary International Law Concerning Self-Defense' (2006) 14(2) Cardozo J Int'l & Comp L 429

Green, JA, 'The *Oil Platforms* Case: An Error in Judgment?' (2004) JC&SL 357

Green, JA and Waters, CPM, 'Military Targeting in the Context of Self-Defence Actions' 84 (2015) Nord J Int'l L 3

Greenwood, C, 'Self-Defence' in *Max Planck Encyclopaedia of Public International Law* (OUP 2011)

Greenwood, C, 'International Law and the 'War Against Terrorism' (2002) 78 Int'l Aff (UK) 301

Greenwood, C, 'Memorandum: The Legality of Using Force Against Iraq' (24 October 2002) Select Committee on Foreign Affairs Minutes of Evidence <http://www.publications.parliament.uk/pa/cm200203/cmselect/cmfaff/196/2102406.htm>

Greenwood, C, 'New World Order or Old—The Invasion of Kuwait and the Rule of Law' (1992) 55 MLR 153

Greenwood, C, 'Self-Defence and the Conduct of International Armed Conflict' in Dinstein, Y (ed), *International Law at a Time of Perplexity: Essays in Honour of Shabtai Rosenne* (Martinus Nijhoff Publishers 1989) 273

Greenwood, C, 'International Law and the United States' Air Operation Against Libya' (1987) 89 W Va L Rev 933

Greenwood, C, 'The Relationship Between *Jus ad Bellum* and *Jus in Bello*' (1983) 9 Rev Int'l Stud 221

Greig, DW, 'Self-Defence and the Security Council: What Does Article 51 Require?' (1991) 40 ICLQ 366

Guilfoyle, D, 'The Gulf of Tonkin Incident–1964' in Ruys, T, Corten, C and Hofer, A (eds) *The Use of Force in International Law: A Case-Based Approach* (OUP 2018) 108

Guilfoyle, D, 'The *Mavi Marmara* Incident and Blockade in Armed Conflict' (2011) 81(1) BYIL 171

Hakimi, M, 'The UK's Most Recent Volley on Defensive Force' (*EJIL:Talk!*, 12 January 2017) <https://www.ejiltalk.org/the-uks-most-recent-volley-on-defensive-force/>

Hakimi, M, 'US Responsibility Arising From Russian Violations of the Law of Armed Conflict' (*Just Security*, 21 September 2016) <https://www.justsecurity.org/33075/u-s-responsibility-arising-russian-violations-law-armed-conflict/>

Hakimi, M and Cogan, JK, 'A Role for the Security Council on Defensive Force?' (*EJIL:Talk!*, 21 October 2016) <https://www.ejiltalk.org/a-role-for-the-security-council-on-defensive-force/>

Halberstam, M, 'The Right to Self-Defence Once the Security Council Takes Action' (1996) 17(2) Mich J Int'l L 229

Haque, A, 'On the Precipice: The U.S. and Russia in Syria' (*Just Security*, 19 June 2017) <https://www.justsecurity.org/42297/precipice-u-s-russia-syria/>

Haque, A, 'Imminence and Self-Defense Against Non-State Actors: Australia Weighs In' (*Just Security*, 30 May 2017) <https://www.justsecurity.org/41500/imminence-self-defense-non-state-actors-australia-weighs/>

Haque, A, 'The United Kingdom's "Modern Law of Self-Defence"—Part I' (*Just Security*, 12 January 2017) <https://www.justsecurity.org/36235/united-kingdoms-modern-law-self-defence-part/>

Haque, A, 'Between the Law of Force and the Law of Armed Conflict' (*Just Security*, 13 October 2016) <https://www.justsecurity.org/33515/law-force-law-armed-conflict/>

Hargrove, JL, 'The *Nicaragua* Judgment and the Future of the Law of Force and Self-Defence' (1987) 81 AJIL 135

Heller, KJ, 'The Use and Abuse of Analogy in IHL' in Ohlin, JD (ed), *Theoretical Boundaries of Armed Conflict and Human Rights* (CUP 2016) 232

Heller, KJ, 'Ashley Deeks' Problematic Defense of the "Unwilling or Unable" Test' (*Opinio Juris*, 15 December 2011) <http://opiniojuris.org/2011/12/15/ashley-deeks-failure-to-defend-the-unwilling-or-unable-test/>

Henderson, C, *The Use of Force and International Law* (CUP 2018)

Henderson, C, 'The 2010 United States National Security Strategy and the Obama Doctrine of "Necessary Force"' (2010) JC&SL 403

Henderson, C and Green, JA, 'The *Jus ad Bellum* and Entities Short of Statehood in the Report on the Conflict in Georgia' (2010) 59 ICLQ 129

Henkin, L, 'The Invasion of Panama Under International Law: A Gross Violation' (1991) 29 Colum J Transnat'l L 293

Henry, E, 'The Falklands/Malvinas War–1982' in Ruys, T, Corten, C and Hofer, A (eds) *The Use of Force in International Law: A Case-Based Approach* (OUP 2018) 361

Henry, E, 'Alleged Acquiescence of the International Community to Revisionist Claims of International Customary Law (With Special Reference to the *Jus Contra Bellum* Regime)' (2017) 18 Melbourne Journal of International Law 260

Hernández, GI, *The International Court of Justice and the Judicial Function* (OUP 2014)

Higgins, R, *Problems and Process: International Law and How We Use It* (OUP 1994)

Higgins, R, *The Development of International Law Through the Political Organs of the United Nations* (OUP for the Royal Institute of International Affairs 1963)

Horowitz, J, 'Is the US Allowed to Control a Syrian Airfield?' (*Just Security*, 27 January 2016) <https://www.justsecurity.org/28988/allowed-control-syrian-airfield/>

Human Rights Council, 'Report of the Special Rapporteur on Extrajudicial, Summary or Arbitrary Executions, Philip Alston' (2010) UN Doc A/HRC/14/24/Add.6

International Institute of Humanitarian Law, *San Remo Manual on International Law Applicable to Armed Conflicts at Sea* (1994) <https://ihl-databases.icrc.org/ihl/INTRO/560>

International Law Association, 'Statement of Principles Applicable to the Formation of General Customary International Law', Report of the Committee on Formation of Customary (General) International Law (2000)

International Law Association, Committee on the Use of Force, 'Final Report on Aggression and the Use of Force', Sydney Conference (2018) <https://www.ila-hq.org/images/ILA/DraftReports/DraftReport_UseOfForce.pdf>

International Law Association, Study Group on the Conduct of Hostilities in the 21st Century, 'The Conduct of Hostilities and International Humanitarian Law: Challenges of 21st Century Warfare' (2017) 93 Int'l L Stud 322

International Law Commission, Draft Articles on Responsibility of States for Internationally Wrongful Acts, with Commentaries (2001) UN Doc A/56/10

International Law Commission, 'Second Report on State Responsibility, by Mr. James Crawford, Special Rapporteur' (1999) UN Doc A/CN.4/498 and Add.1-4

International Law Commission, 'Addendum—Eighth Report on State Responsibility by Mr. Roberto Ago, Special Rapporteur—The Internationally Wrongful Act of the State, Source of International Responsibility (Part 1)' (1980) UN Doc A/CN.4/318/Add.5-7

Jennings, R, 'The *Caroline* and *McLeod* Cases' (1938) 32(1) AJIL 82

Jennings, R and Watts, A (eds), *Oppenheim's International Law: Volume I, Peace* (9th edn, Longman 1996)

Kammerhofer, J, 'Uncertainty in the Formal Sources of International Law: Customary International Law and Some of Its Problems' (2004) 15(3) EJIL 523

Kamto, M, 'The US Strikes Against Libya–1986' in Ruys, T, Corten, C and Hofer, A (eds) *The Use of Force in International Law: A Case-Based Approach* (OUP 2018) 408

Kearley, T, 'Raising the *Caroline*' (1999) 17 Wisconsin Int'l LJ 325

Klein, N, *Maritime Security and the Law of the Sea* (OUP 2012)

Koskenniemi, M, *From Apology to Utopia: The Structure of International Legal Argument* (CUP 2006)

Kress, C, 'The International Court of Justice and the "Principle of Non-Use of Force"' in Weller, M (ed), *The Oxford Handbook on the Use of Force in International Law* (OUP 2015) 561

Kress, C, 'The Fine Line Between Collective Self-Defense and Intervention by Invitation: Reflections on the Use of Force against 'IS' in Syria' (*Just Security*, 17 February 2015) <https://www.justsecurity.org/20118/claus-kreb-force-isil-syria/>

Kress, C and Nussberger, BK, 'The Entebbe Raid–1976' in Ruys, T, Corten, C and Hofer, A (eds) *The Use of Force in International Law: A Case-Based Approach* (OUP 2018) 220

Kretzmer, D, 'The Inherent Right to Self-Defence and Proportionality in *Jus Ad Bellum*' (2013) 24(1) EJIL 235

Kritsiotis, D, 'The Legality of the 1993 US Missile Strike on Iraq and the Right of Self-Defence in International Law' (1996) 45(1) ICLQ 162

Kwakwa, E, 'South Africa's May 1986 Military Incursions into Neighboring African States' (1987) 12 Yale J Int'l L 421

Laursen, A, 'The Use of Force and (the State of) Necessity' (2004) 37 Vand J Transnat'l L 485

Laursen, A, 'The Judgment by the International Court of Justice in the Oil Platforms Case' (2004) 73 Nordic J Int'l L 135

Lauterpacht, E, 'The Legal Irrelevance of the "State of War"' (1968) 62 Am Soc Int L Proc 58

Lederman, M, 'The Egan speech and the Bush Doctrine: Imminence, Necessity, and "First Use" in the *Jus ad Bellum*' (*Just Security*, 11 April 2016) <https://www.justsecurity.org/30522/egan-speech-bush-doctrine-imminence-necessity-first-use-jus-ad-bellum/>

Lederman, M, 'ASIL Speech by State Legal Adviser Egan on International Law and the Use of Force Against ISIL' (*Just Security*, 4 April 2016) <https://www.justsecurity.org/30377/asil-speech-state-legal-adviser-international-law-basis-for-limits-on-force-isil>

Levitin, MJ, 'The Law of Force and the Force of Law: Grenada, the Falklands, and Humanitarian Intervention' 27 (1986) Harv Int'l LJ 621

Lewis, DA, Blum, G and Modirzadeh, NK, 'Quantum of Silence: Inaction and *Jus ad Bellum*', The Harvard Law School Program on International Law and Armed Conflict (2019) <https://pilac.law.harvard.edu/quantum-of-silence>

Lewis, DA, Blum, G and Modirzadeh, NK, 'Indefinite War: Unsettled International Law on the End of Armed Conflict' The Harvard Law School Program on International Law and Armed Conflict (2017) <https://dash.harvard.edu/handle/1/30455582>

Lieblich, E, 'On the Continuous and Concurrent Application of *Ad Bellum* and *In Bello* Proportionality' in Kress, C and Lawless, R (eds) *Necessity and Proportionality in International Peace and Security Law* (OUP forthcoming 2020) (manuscript available on SSRN: <https://papers.ssrn.com/sol3/papers.cfm?abstract_id=3284411>)

Lobel, J, 'The Use of Force to Respond to Terrorist Attacks: The Bombing of Sudan and Afghanistan' (1999) 24 Yale J Int'l L 537

Lowe, V, '"Clear and Present Danger": Responses to Terrorism' (2005) 54 ICLQ 185

Lubell, N, 'Fragmented Wars: Multi-Territorial Military Operations Against Armed Groups' (2017) 93 Int'l L Stud 215

Lubell, N, 'The Problem of Imminence in an Uncertain World' in Weller, M (ed), The *Oxford Handbook on the Use of Force in International Law* (OUP 2015) 697

Lubell, N, 'Comments on David Kretzmer's "The Inherent Right to Self-Defence and Proportionality in *Jus ad Bellum*"' (*EJIL:Talk!*, 17 April 2013) <http://www.ejiltalk.org/comments-on-david-kretzmers-the-inherent-right-to-self-defence-and-proportionality-in-jus-ad-bellum/>

Lubell, N, *Extraterritorial Use of Force Against Non-State Actors* (OUP 2010)

Lubell, N and Cohen, A, 'Strategic Proportionality: Limitations on the Use of Force in Modern Armed Conflicts' (2020) 96 Int'l L Stud 159

Lynn, III, WJ, Deputy Secretary of Defense, Speech Delivered at the National Defense University, Washington, D.C. (14 July 2011) <http://archive.defense.gov/speeches/speech.aspx?speechid=1593>

Macdonald, RStJ, 'The Nicaragua Case: New Answers to Old Questions?' (1986) Canadian YBIL 127

Martin, C, 'Challenging and Refining the "Unwilling or Unable" Doctrine' (2019) 52(2) Vand J Transnat'l L 387

Michaelsen, C, 'Maritime Exclusion Zones in Times of Armed Conflict at Sea: Legal Controversies Still Unresolved' (2003) 8(2) JC&SL 363

Milanovic, M, 'The Soleimani Strike and Self-Defence Against an Imminent Armed Attack' (*EJIL:Talk!*, 7 January 2020) <https://www.ejiltalk.org/the-soleimani-strike-and-self-defence-against-an-imminent-armed-attack/>

Milanovic, M, 'What is an Imminent Armed Attack? A Hopefully Helpful Hypo' (*EJIL:Talk!*, 12 January 2017) <https://www.ejiltalk.org/what-is-an-imminent-armed-attack-a-hopefully-helpful-hypo/>

Milanovic, M, 'Self-Defense and Non-State Actors: Indeterminacy and the *Jus ad Bellum*' (*EJIL:Talk!*, 21 February 2010) <https://www.ejiltalk.org/self-defense-and-non-state-actors-indeterminacy-and-the-jus-ad-bellum/>

Miller, E, 'Self-Defence, International Law, and the Six Day War' (1985) Israel L Rev 49

Moussa, J, 'Can *Jus ad Bellum* Override *Jus in Bello*? Reaffirming the Separation of the Two Bodies of Law' (2008) 90 International Review of the Red Cross 963

Murphy, SD, 'Protean *Jus ad Bellum*' (2009) 27 Berkeley Journal of International Law 22

Murphy, SD, 'Terrorism and the Concept of "Armed Attack" in Article 51 of the U.N. Charter' (2002) 43 Harv Int'l LJ 41

Murphy, SD (ed), 'Contemporary Practice of the United States Relating to International Law' (2002) 96 AJIL 237
Myjer, EPJ and White, ND, 'The Twin Towers Attack: An Unlimited Right to Self-Defence' (2002) 7(1) JC&SL 5
Neff, SC, *War and the Law of Nations* (CUP 2005)
Nevill, P, 'Military Sanctions Enforcement in the Absence of Express Authorization?' in Weller, M (ed), *The Oxford Handbook on the Use of Force in International Law* (OUP 2015) 272
Newton, M and May, L, *Proportionality in International Law* (OUP 2014)
Nolte, G, 'Multipurpose Self-Defence, Proportionality Disoriented: A Response to David Kretzmer' (2013) 24(1) EJIL 283
Nolte, G and Randelzhofer, A, 'Ch.VII Action with Respect to Threats to the Peace, Breaches of the Peace, and Acts of Aggression, Article 51' in Simma, B and others (eds) *The Charter of the United Nations: A Commentary, Volume II* (3rd edn, OUP 2012) 1397
O'Connell, DP, *The International Law of the Sea* (Oxford, Clarendon Press 1984)
O'Connell, DP, *The Influence of Law on Sea Power* (Naval Institute Press 1975)
O'Connell, ME, Tams, CJ and Tladi, D, *Self-Defence Against Non-State Actors* (CUP 2019)
Oeter, S, 'Methods and Means of Combat' in Fleck, D (ed), *The Handbook of International Humanitarian Law* (3rd edn, OUP 2013) 115
Office of the Legal Adviser, Department of State, 'Rights and Duties of States' (1972) 66 AJIL 836
Ohlin, JD (ed), *Theoretical Boundaries of Armed Conflict and Human Rights* (CUP 2016)
Ohlin, JD, 'The Doctrine of Legitimate Defense' (2015) 91 Int'l L Stud 119
Ohlin, JD and May, L, *Necessity in International Law* (OUP 2016)
O'Keefe, R, 'Protection of Cultural Property' in Clapham, A and Gaeta, P (eds) *The Oxford Handbook of International Law in Armed Conflict* (OUP 2014) 492
Okimoto, K, 'The Cumulative Requirements of *Jus ad Bellum* and *Jus in Bello* in the Context of Self-Defense' (2012) 11 Chinese JIL 45
Okimoto, K, *The Distinction and Relationship between Jus ad Bellum and Jus in Bello* (Hart 2011)
O'Meara, C, 'Should International Law Recognize a Right of Humanitarian Intervention?' (2017) 66(2) ICLQ 441
O'Meara, C, 'The Relationship Between National, Unit and Personal Self-Defence in International Law: Bridging the Disconnect' (2017) 4(2) JUFIL 273
Oppenheim, L, *International Law: A Treatise*, Vol. II (H. Lauterpacht (ed), 7th edn, Longmans 1948)
Paddeu, F, *Justification and Excuse in International Law* (CUP 2018)
Paddeu, F, 'Use of Force against Non-state Actors and the Circumstance Precluding Wrongfulness of Self-Defence' (2017) 30 LJIL 93
Paddeu, F, 'Self-Defence as a Circumstance Precluding Wrongfulness: Understanding Article 21 of the Articles on State Responsibility' (2015) 85 BYIL 90
Paust, J, 'Use of Armed Force against Terrorists in Afghanistan, Iraq, and Beyond' (2002) 35 Cornell Int'l LJ 533
Pobjie, E, Declercq, F and Van Steenberghe, R, 'The Israeli Raid Against the PLO Headquarters in Tunis–1985' in Corten, C and Hofer, A (eds) *The Use of Force in International Law: A Case-Based Approach* (OUP 2018) 395
Quigley, J, 'The Six Day War–1967' in Ruys, T, Corten, C and Hofer, A (eds) *The Use of Force in International Law: A Case-Based Approach* (OUP 2018) 131
Quigley, J, 'The Afghanistan War and Self-Defense' (2003) 37 Val UL Rev 541

Raby, J, 'The State of Necessity and the Use of Force to Protect Nationals' (1988) 26 Canadian YBIL 253

Reinold, T, 'South African Incursions into Lesotho–1982' in Ruys, T, Corten, C and Hofer, A (eds) *The Use of Force in International Law: A Case-Based Approach* (OUP 2018) 379

Reisman, WM, 'Self-Defense in an Age of Terrorism' (2003) 97 Am Soc Int L Proc 141

Reisman, WM, 'Criteria for the Lawful Use of Force in International Law' (1985) 10 Yale J Int'l L 279

Reisman, WM, 'International Incidents: Introduction to a New Genre in the Study of International Law' (1984) 10 Yale J Int'l L 1

Reisman, WM and Armstrong, A, 'The Past and Future of the Claim of Preemptive Self-Defense' (2006) 100 AJIL 525

Richemond-Barak, D, 'Is Money a Legitimate Target?' (*Just Security*, 10 February 2016) <https://www.justsecurity.org/29255/money-legitimate-target/>

Roberts, A, 'Environmental Destruction in the 1991 Gulf War' (1992) 291 International Review of the Red Cross 538

Rodin, D, *War and Self-Defense* (OUP 2002)

Ruys, T, 'The Indian Intervention in Goa–1961' in Ruys, T, Corten, C and Hofer, A (eds) *The Use of Force in International Law: A Case-Based Approach* (OUP 2018) 85

Ruys, T, 'Israel's Airstrike Against Iraq's Osiraq Nuclear Reactor–1981' in Ruys, T, Corten, C and Hofer, A (eds) *The Use of Force in International Law: A Case-Based Approach* (OUP 2018) 329

Ruys, T, *'Armed Attack' and Article 51 of the UN Charter: Evolutions in Customary Law and Practice* (CUP 2010)

Ruys, T, '*Quo Vadit Jus ad Bellum*?: A Legal Analysis of Turkey's Military Operations Against the PKK in Northern Iraq' (2008) 9 Melbourne Journal of International Law 334

Ruys, T, 'Crossing the Thin Blue Line: An Inquiry into Israel's Recourse to Self-Defense against Hezbollah (2007) 43 Stan J Int'l L 265

Ruys, T and Corten, O and Hofer, A, *The Use of Force in International Law: A Case-Based Approach* (OUP 2018)

Ruys, T, Corten, O and Hofer, A (eds) 'Introduction: The *Jus Contra Bellum* and the Power of Precedent' in *The Use of Force in International Law: A Case-Based Approach* (OUP 2018) 1

Ruys, T, Ferro, L and Maelen, CV (eds), 'Digest of State Practice: 1 January—30 June 2017' (2017) 4(2) JUFIL 371

Ruys, T, Maelen, CV and Van Severen, S (eds), 'Digest of State Practice: 1 January—30 June 2018' (2018) 5(2) JUFIL 324

Ruys, T and Verhoeven, S, 'Attacks by Private Actors and the Right of Self-Defence' (2005) 10(3) JC&SL 289

Ryngaert, C, 'State Responsibility, Necessity and Human Rights' (2010) 41 NYIL 79

Sands, P, *Lawless World: America and the Making and Breaking of Global Rules from FDR's Atlantic Charter to George W. Bush's Illegal War* (Viking Penguin 2005)

Sands, P, Peel, J, Fabra, A and MacKenzie, R, *Principles of International Environmental Law* (4th edn, CUP 2018)

Saul, B (ed), *Research Handbook on International Law and Terrorism* (Edward Elgar 2014)

Saul, B, 'Attempts to Define "Terrorism" in International Law' (2005) 52(1) NILR 57

Schachter, O (Chair), 'Implementing Limitations on the Use of Force: The Doctrine of Proportionality and Necessity' (1992) 86 Am Soc Int L Proc 39

Schachter, O, 'United Nations Law in the Gulf Conflict' (1991) 85 AJIL 452

Schachter, O, *International Law in Theory and Practice* (Martinus Nijhoff Publishers 1991)

Schachter, O, 'Self-Defense and the Rule of Law' (1989) 83 AJIL 259

Schachter, O, 'The Extraterritorial Use of Force against Terrorist Bases' (1988-1989) 11(2) Hous J Int'l L 309

Schachter, O, 'In Defense of International Rules on the Use of Force' (1986) 53 The University of Chicago Law Review 113

Schachter, O, 'The Lawful Resort to Unilateral Use of Force' (1985) 10 Yale J Int'l L 291

Schachter, O, 'The Right of States to Use Armed Force' (1984) 82 Mich L Rev 1620

Scharf, MP, Sterio, M and Williams, PR, *The Syrian Conflict's Impact on International Law* (CUP 2020)

Schmidt, DR and Trenta, L, 'Changes in the Law of Self-Defence? Drones, Imminence, and International Norm Dynamics' (2018) 5(2) JUFIL 201

Schmitt, M (ed), *Tallinn Manual on the International Law Applicable to Cyber Warfare* (CUP 2013)

Schmitt, M, 'Drone Attacks under the *Jus ad Bellum* and *Jus in Bello*: Clearing the "Fog of Law"' (2010) 13 YIHL 311

Schmitt, M, '"Change Direction" 2006: Israeli Operations in Lebanon and the International Law of Self-Defense' (2008) 29(2) Mich J Int'l L 127

Schmitt, M, 'Preemptive Strategies in International Law' (2003) 24(2) Mich J Int'l L 513

Schmitt, M, 'State-Sponsored Assassination in International and Domestic Law' (1992) 17 Yale J Int'l L 609

Schrijver, N and van den Herik, L, 'Leiden Policy Recommendations on Counter-Terrorism and International Law' (2010) 57(3) NILR 531

Seger, P, 'The Law of Neutrality' in Clapham, A and Gaeta, P (eds) *The Oxford Handbook of International Law in Armed Conflict* (OUP 2014) 248

Simma, B, 'NATO, the UN and the Use of Force: Legal Aspects' (1999) 10 EJIL 1

Simma, B and others (eds), *The Charter of the United Nations: A Commentary, Volume II* (3rd edn, OUP 2012)

Sivakumaran, S, 'Exclusion Zones in the Law of Armed Conflict at Sea: Evolution in Law and Practice' (2016) Int'l L Stud 153

Sofaer, AD, 'On the Necessity of Pre-emption' (2003) 14(2) EJIL 209

Spoerri, P, 'The Law of Occupation' in Clapham, A and Gaeta, P (eds) *The Oxford Handbook of International Law in Armed Conflict* (OUP 2014) 182

Starski, P, 'The US Airstrike Against the Iraqi Intelligence Headquarters–1993' in Ruys, T, Corten, C and Hofer, A (eds) *The Use of Force in International Law: A Case-Based Approach* (OUP 2018) 504

Starski, P, 'Silence Within the Process of Normative Change and Evolution of the Prohibition on the Use of Force: Normative Volatility and Legislative Responsibility' (2017) 4(1) JUFIL 14

Taft, W, 'Self-Defense and the *Oil Platforms* Decision' (2004) 29 Yale J Int'l L 295

Talmon, S, 'Determining Customary International Law: The ICJ's Methodology between Induction, Deduction and Assertion' (2015) 26(2) EJIL 417

Tams, CJ, 'Self-Defence Against Non-State Actors: Making Sense of the "Armed Attack" Requirement' in O'Connell, MR, Tams, CJ and Tladi, D (eds) *Self-Defence Against Non-State Actors* (CUP 2019) 90

Tams, CJ, 'The Necessity and Proportionality of Anti-Terrorist Self-Defence' in Van den Herik, L and Schrijver, N (eds) *Counter-Terrorism Strategies in a Fragmented International Legal Order: Meeting the Challenges* (CUP 2013) 373

Tams, CJ, 'The Use of Force against Terrorists' (2009) 20(2) EJIL 359

Tams, C and Brückner, W, 'The Israeli Intervention in Lebanon–2006' in Ruys, T, Corten, C and Hofer, A (eds) *The Use of Force in International Law: A Case-Based Approach* (OUP 2018) 673

Tams, C and Devaney, J, 'Applying Necessity and Proportionality to Anti-Terrorist Self-Defence' (2012) 45(1) Israel L Rev 91

Tams, C and Sloan, J (eds), *The Development of International Law by the International Court of Justice* (Oxford Scholarship Online 2014)

Teitel, RG, *Humanity's Law* (OUP 2011)

Trapp, KN, 'The Turkish Intervention Against the PKK in Northern Iraq–2007-08' in Ruys, T, Corten, C and Hofer, A (eds) *The Use of Force in International Law: A Case-Based Approach* (OUP 2018) 689

Trapp, KN, 'Actor-Pluralism, the "Turn to Responsibility" and the *Jus ad Bellum*: "Unwilling or Unable" in Context' (2015) 2(2) JUFIL 199

Trapp, KN, 'Can Non-State Actors Mount an Armed Attack?' in Weller, M (ed), The *Oxford Handbook on the Use of Force in International Law* (OUP 2015) 679

Trapp, KN, *State Responsibility for International Terrorism* (OUP 2011)

Trapp, KN, 'The Use of Force against Terrorists: A Reply to Christian J. Tams' (2009) 20(4) EJIL 1049

Trapp, KN, 'Back to Basics: Necessity, Proportionality and the Right of Self-Defence against non-State Terrorist Actors' (2007) 56(1) ICLQ 141

Tsagourias, N, 'The US Intervention in Panama–1989' in Ruys, T, Corten, C and Hofer, A (eds) *The Use of Force in International Law: A Case-Based Approach* (OUP 2018) 426

Tsagourias, N, 'Self-Defence Against Non-State Actors: The Interaction Between Self-Defence as a Primary Rule and Self-Defence as a Secondary Rule' (2016) 29(3) LJIL 801

Tsagourias, N, 'Necessity and the Use of Force: A Special Regime' (2010) 41 NYIL 11

Tzouvala, N, 'TWAIL and the "Unwilling or Unable" Doctrine: Continuities and Ruptures' (2015) 109 AJIL Unbound 266

UK Attorney General's Speech at the International Institute for Strategic Studies, 'The Modern Law of Self-Defence' (11 January 2017) <https://www.gov.uk/government/uploads/system/uploads/attachment_data/file/583171/170111_Imminence_Speech_.pdf>

UK Ministry of Defence, *The Manual of the Law of Armed Conflict* (OUP 2005)

Upcher, J, *Neutrality in Contemporary International Law* (OUP 2020)

Van den Herik, L and Schrijver, N (eds), *Counter-Terrorism Strategies in a Fragmented International Legal Order: Meeting the Challenges* (CUP 2013)

Van Schaack, B, 'Targeting Tankers Under the Law of War (Part 1)' (*Just Security*, 2 December 2015) <https://www.justsecurity.org/28064/targeting-tankers-law-war-part-1/>

Van Steenberghe, R, 'State Practice and the Evolution of the Law of Self-Defence: Clarifying the Methodological Debate' (2015) 2(1) JUFIL 81

Van Steenberghe, R, 'Proportionality Under *Jus ad Bellum* and *Jus in Bello*: Clarifying their Relationship' (2012) 45(1) Israel L Rev 107

Van Steenberghe, R, 'Self-Defence in Response to Attacks by Non-state Actors in the Light of Recent State Practice: A Step Forward? (2010) 23(1) LJIL 183

Vidmar, J, 'The Use of Force as a Plea of Necessity' (2017) 111 AJIL Unbound 302

Von Heinegg, WH, 'Blockades and Interdictions' in Weller, M (ed), *The Oxford Handbook on the Use of Force in International Law* (OUP 2015) 925

Waldock, CHM, 'The Regulation of the Use of Force by States in International Law' (1951) 81 Collected Courses of the Hague Academy of International Law 451

Watkin, K, 'Proportionality and 150 Iranian Lives: Do They "Count"?' (*Just Security*, 16 August 2019) <https://www.justsecurity.org/65831/proportionality-and-150-iranian-lives-do-they-count/>

Watkin, K, *Fighting at the Legal Boundaries: Controlling the Use of Force in Contemporary Conflict* (OUP 2016)

Watkin, K, 'The ICRC Updated Commentaries: Reconciling Form and Substance, Part II' (*Just Security*, 30 August 2016) <https://www.justsecurity.org/32608/icrc-updated-commentaries-reconciling-form-substance-part-ii/>

Watkin, K, 'Sustaining the War Effort: Targeting Islamic State Oil Facilities' (*Just Security*, 3 October 2014) <https://www.justsecurity.org/15890/sustaining-war-effort-targeting-islamic-state-oil-facilities/>

Waxman, MC, 'Regulating Resort to Force: Form and Substance of the UN Charter Regime' (2013) 24(1) EJIL 151

Wedgwood, R, 'The ICJ Advisory Opinion on the Israeli Security Fence and the Limits of Self-Defense' (2005) 99 AJIL 52

Wedgwood, R, 'Responding to Terrorism: The Strikes Against bin Laden' (1999) 24 Yale J Int'l L 559

Wedgwood, R, 'Proportionality and Necessity in American National Security Decision Making' (1992) 86 Am Soc Int L Proc 58

Weller, M (ed), *The Oxford Handbook on the Use of Force in International Law* (OUP 2015)

Weller, M, 'Permanent Imminence of Armed Attacks: Resolution 2249 (2015) and the Right to Self Defence Against Designated Terrorist Groups' (*EJIL:Talk!*, 25 November 2015) <https://www.ejiltalk.org/permanent-imminence-of-armed-attacks-resolution-2249-2015-and-the-right-to-self-defence-against-designated-terrorist-groups/>

Wettberg, G, *The International Legality of Self-Defense Against Non-State Actors, State Practice from the U.N. Charter to the Present* (Peter Lang 2007)

Willard, AR, 'Incidents: An Essay in Method' (1984–1985) 10 Yale J Int'l L 21

Wilmshurst, E (ed), *International Law and the Classification of Conflicts* (OUP 2012)

Wilmshurst, E, 'The Chatham House Principles of International Law on the Use of Force in Self-Defence' (2006) 55(4) ICLQ 963

Wilmshurst, E and Wood, M, 'Self-Defense Against Nonstate Actors: Reflections on the "Bethlehem Principles"' (2013) 107 AJIL 390

Wolfrum, R and Philipp, C (eds), *United Nations: Law, Policies and Practice* (Nijhoff 1995)

Wood, M, 'The Caroline Incident–1837' in Ruys, T, Corten, C and Hofer, A (eds) *The Use of Force in International Law: A Case-Based Approach* (OUP 2018) 5

Wood, M, 'The Use of Force in 2015 With Particular Reference to Syria' (2016) Hebrew University of Jerusalem Legal Studies Research Paper Series No. 16-05

Zimmermann, A, 'The Second Lebanon War: *Jus ad bellum, Jus in Bello* and the Issue of Proportionality' (2007) 11 Max Planck Yrbk UN L 99

Index

For the benefit of digital users, indexed terms that span two pages (e.g., 52–53) may, on occasion, appear on only one of those pages.